the american radical

the american radical

edited by Mari Jo Buhle, Paul Buhle
& Harvey J. Kaye
foreword by Eric Foner

Routledge ▪ New York & London

Published in 1994 by

Routledge
29 West 35 Street
New York, NY 10001

Published in Great Britain by

Routledge
11 New Fetter Lane
London EC4P 4EE

Library of Congress Cataloging-in-Publication Data

The American radical / edited by Mari Jo Buhle, Paul Buhle, and Harvey
   J. Kaye.
      p.   cm.
   Includes bibliographical references (p.).
   ISBN 0-415-90803-5 HB — ISBN 0-415-90804-3 (PB)
   1. Radicals—United States—Biography. 2. Radicalism—United
States—History. 3. United States—Politics and government.
4. United States—Social conditions. I. Buhle Mari Jo, 1943– .
II. Buhle, Paul, 1944– . III. Kaye, Harvey J.
E176.A516   1994
320.5′3′0973—dc20   93-41221
                                                           CIP

British Library Cataloguing-in-Publication Data also available.

To the memory of
E. P. Thompson,
historian and radical
(1924–1993)

CONTENTS

Foreword   xi
  Eric Foner

Introduction   xv

Acknowledgments   xix

Timeline   xxi

1 PONTIAC AND NEOLIN   1
       Gregory Evans Dowd

2 TOM PAINE   9
       Harvey J. Kaye

3 FANNY WRIGHT   17
       Lori D. Ginzberg

4 SOJOURNER TRUTH   25
       Nell Irvin Painter

5   GEORGE LIPPARD   33
     Joseph Jablonski

6   ABBY KELLEY   41
     Dorothy Sterling

7   FREDERICK DOUGLASS   49
     Waldo E. Martin, Jr.

8   WALT WHITMAN   57
     Robert K. Martin

9   ELIZABETH CADY STANTON   63
     Ellen Carol DuBois

10   EDWARD BELLAMY   69
     Daphne Patai

11   JOHN MUIR   77
     Franklin Rosemont

12   EUGENE V. DEBS   85
     Scott Molloy

13   UPTON SINCLAIR   91
     Greg Mitchell

14   EMMA GOLDMAN   97
     Alice Wexler

15   WILLIAM D. HAYWOOD   105
     Dan Georgakas

16   W. E. B. DU BOIS   113
     Thomas C. Holt

17   ISADORA DUNCAN   121
     Elizabeth Francis

18   ELIZABETH GURLEY FLYNN   129
     Rosalyn Baxandall

19   ARTURO GIOVANNITTI   135
     Robert D'Attilio

20   JOHN REED   143
     Robert A. Rosenstone

21   IDA B. WELLS   151
     Paula Giddings

22   ROBERT M. LA FOLLETTE   159
     R. David Myers

23   RICARDO FLORES MAGON   167
     Juan Gomez-Quiñones

24   MOTHER JONES   177
     Elliott J. Gorn

25   JOHN DEWEY   183
     Kenneth Teitelbaum and Michael W. Apple

26   CLARENCE DARROW   191
     Joanne Pope Melish

27   WILLIAM Z. FOSTER   197
     James R. Barrett

28   DOROTHY DAY   205
     Nancy L. Roberts

29   NORMAN THOMAS   213
     Gary Dorrien

30   LEWIS MUMFORD   221
     Paul Buhle

31   CLIFFORD ODETS   229
     Norma Jenckes

32   WOODY GUTHRIE   237
     Craig A. Lockard

33   RUTH FULTON BENEDICT   245
     Mari Jo Buhle

34   CARLOS BULOSAN   253
     E. San Juan, Jr.

35   A. J. MUSTE   261
     Staughton Lynd

36   VITO MARCANTONIO   269
     Gerald Meyer

37   PAUL ROBESON   279
     Lamont H. Yeakey

38   ELLA JOSEPHINE BAKER   287
     Barbara Ransby

39   I. F. STONE   297
        Eric Alterman

40   WILLIAM APPLEMAN WILLIAMS   305
        Edward Rice-Maximin

41   RACHEL CARSON   313
        Vera Norwood

42   MALCOLM X   321
        Michael Eric Dyson

43   MARTIN LUTHER KING, JR.   329
        James H. Cone

44   MICHAEL HARRINGTON   337
        Robert A. Gorman

45   ABBIE HOFFMAN   345
        Marty Jezer

46   AUDRE LORDE   353
        Lisa Duggan

        Afterword   361

        Additional Suggested Readings   365

        Historical Glossary   367

        Contributors   375

        Photo Section following page 166

FOREWORD

From the beginning of our history, radicalism has been a persistent feature of American society. Many of the earliest settlers viewed emigration to the New World as an opportunity to escape the deeply rooted inequities of the Old. Succeeding generations of radicals have tried to force American society to live up to its professed ideals of liberty and equality.

Through portraits of nearly four dozen individuals, *The American Radical* offers a compelling introduction to past and present radical movements, leaders, and ideologies. Taken together, these brief biographies underscore both the persistence of American radicalism and the diversity of its protagonists. The book introduces readers to radicals who worked within the political system, and those who stood resolutely outside it; to Protestants, Jews, and Catholics, immigrants and natives, leaders of mass movements and lonely crusaders. Some radicals have broken completely with the values of their contemporaries, others, demanding change in one aspect of American life, have accepted without challenge many mainstream conventions.

Thanks to the rise of the "new social history" in the past two decades, historical inquiry has expanded enormously, to include groups previously excluded from accounts of the American past. *The American Radical* reflects this broadened historical perspective. In previous generations, books on radicalism, like narratives of the American experience generally, concentrated almost exclusively on white males. Charles A. Madison's *Critics and Crusaders* (1948), and Harvey Goldberg's *American Radicals* (1957), for example, between them contained thirty-two portraits of radical leaders—all but two male and none nonwhite. *The American Radical* includes a far more diverse cast of characters, emphasizing that the protagonists of radicalism's history are as heterogeneous as the American people itself.

Although often castigated as foreign-inspired enemies of American institutions, radicals have always sprung from and spoken the language of their culture, and appealed to some of its deepest values—facts that help to explain radicalism's survival even in the face of tenacious opposition. As the portraits that follow show, many radical movements have accepted the society's prevailing emphasis on the ideal of the free individual (often linked with ownership of property as the guarantor of personal autonomy) and have sought to eliminate obstacles to its fulfillment or extend it to excluded groups such as enslaved African Americans or disenfranchised women. Other movements, based on a collectivist outlook, have rejected individualism and private property itself as obstacles to genuine freedom, but these too have derived much of their political vocabulary from the ideals of the American Revolution, with its promise of equality and personal fulfillment. Despite occasional resort to violence, most radical movements have reflected the democratic ethos of American life—they have been open rather than secretive, and have relied on education, example, or "moral suasion," rather than coercion, as the means of achieving their goals.

The American Radical appears at a time of both crisis and opportunity for American radicalism. After a decade or more of conservative hegemony in the United States and Western Europe, the labor movement is in decline and the spectrum of political debate has shifted markedly to the right. The collapse of the communist governments, first in Eastern Europe and then the Soviet Union, has produced a profound challenge to assumptions widely shared among radicals in the West. Radicals have been forced to rethink the idea that history is moving in a predetermined direction in which the inequities of capitalism would be superseded by a more cooperative organization of politics and society.

This is not the first time that radicals have faced an intellectual crisis. Nineteenth-century radicalism reflected the values of artisans, farmers, and other small producers. Its ideology saw the rise of capitalism as incompatible with customary values of personal independence and social cooperation. This tradition, reflected in movements as diverse as the labor organizations of the 1830s and the Populist upheaval sixty years later, eventually gave way before the reality of a society whose characteristic laborer was the wage earner, not the small independent producer. Today, we stand at the end of another long era of radical history, during which socialism was the characteristic radical vocabulary and the classic labor movement, resting on the industrial working class, seemed the leading agent of radical change.

To some, the events of the past few years signal the death of radicalism, or even the "end of history" itself. But others may find that the end of the Cold War creates opportunities for new kinds of radical thought and action. From Tom Paine's ideal of an America freed from the hereditary inequalities of Europe, to the vision of liberation from legal and customary bondage espoused by abolitionists and feminists, the Knights of Labor's idea of a cooperative commonwealth, socialists' call for workers to organize society in accord with their own aspirations, and the New Left's enunciation of personal liberation as a goal as worthy as material abundance, each generation of American radicals has made its distinctive contribution to an ongoing radical tradition. There is no reason to believe that new radical movements will not arise in the future, to offer their own answers to our society's problems. History cannot provide the answers to these problems, but it can offer perspective on them. By helping to introduce a new generation of Americans to the vitality and diversity of the radical tradition, *The American Radical* enables us to think creatively about our nation's future as we approach the twenty-first century.

Eric Foner
New York City
—May 1993

INTRODUCTION

The story of American radicalism seems at the present time discontinuous at best. But this is a narrow view. Rather, notions of a usable past have changed over time. Even long-neglected traditions reappear to inspire new generations while familiar figures take on dramatically different qualities in new light.

A sense of continuity among this book's cast of characters dates to the beginning of the nineteenth century. Fanny Wright, a pioneer of women's emancipation, became widely known as the "female Tom Paine," after the hero of the American Revolution she admired most. George Lippard, agitator and prolific writer of fiction, frequently drew his protagonists—including Paine, who penned the famed agitational pamphlet *Common Sense*—from the same pantheon. Woman's rights leader Elizabeth Cady Stanton similarly looked back to this early generation, opening a volume of her *History of Woman Suffrage* with a drawing of Wright as the frontispiece. Poet Walt Whitman considered Wright to be an embodiment of the idea of freedom. Whitman perfectly captured in his poetry his predecessor's dedication to individual liberty.

A new mood swept radicalism after the Civil War. The Industrial Revolution and a rapid increase in population—both developments most dramatic in the cities—focused attention on the working class. Immigrant groups with strong traditions of trade unionism prompted American-born radicals to examine economic inequalities. Author Edward Bellamy spun his best-selling utopian novel *Looking Backward* around the vision of a new order based on voluntary cooperation: there would be no rich and poor, as all citizens shared the bounty of industrial progress. *Looking Backward* inspired an elderly Elizabeth Cady Stanton to rethink her own ideas of social change, and planted the seed of socialism in the mind of a young Indiana labor leader, Eugene Victor Debs.

Artists, writers, and activists struggled for the next several generations to combine both traditions, individual liberty and collective obligation. In so doing, they returned again and again to the examples of past radicals, reinterpreting them repeatedly and sometimes drastically. The American socialist movement, which reached its apex between 1910 and 1920, expanded the legacy of Walt Whitman to encompass the collectivist vision. Eugene Debs, perennial Socialist party candidate for president, became a devotee of Whitman through the poet's literary executor and prominent socialist editor, Horace Traubel. For Debs and many other socialists, the overthrow of economic privilege made possible the realization of the Self.

Nineteenth-century radical traditions also inspired other movements in the opening decades of the new century. The rising African-American leader and socialist W. E. B. Du Bois, antilynching campaigner Ida B. Wells, and a small circle of white socialists restored the legacy of abolitionists Sojourner Truth, Frederick Douglass, Abby Foster Kelley, Elizabeth Cady Stanton, and a generation of radicals virtually forgotten since Reconstruction. A physical embodiment of women's emancipation, modern dancer Isadora Duncan claimed to carry Walt Whitman's *Leaves of Grass* with her everywhere. Italian immigrant poet and labor agitator Arturo Giovannitti likewise swore his personal allegiance to Whitman even as he led several of the most sensational strikes of the era.

World War I and the curtailment of civil liberties during the Red Scare of the early 1920s rolled back this tradition. And yet the passing giants soon became legends for the newer age. Bohemian journalist John Reed of Greenwich Village, who wrote about the Russian Revolution and died in the Soviet Union, was adopted as a saint of American communism. "Mother" Mary Jones, who at a grandmotherly age had led mineworkers' strikes, became a living legend. Emma Goldman willingly made herself the free-spirited model of anarchism. Gene Debs and 1924 Progressive party presidential candidate Robert M. LaFollette, dead within a year of each other, became icons of a third-party radical challenge to the entrenched political system.

A handful of radicals emerged larger than life in the conflict-ridden

1930s, adding new dimensions to the radical tradition. Norman Thomas, Debs's successor as the perennial presidential candidate of the Socialist party, became "Mr. Socialism"; gaining renown for his unswerving pacifism, Thomas became the "conscience of the nation" and chief moral guide to youngsters of the 1940s such as Martin Luther King, Jr., and Michael Harrington. Woody Guthrie, songster of the working poor, launched the "folk song" movement and set a still younger generation (including Bob Dylan) to playing guitar and singing topical songs. African-American actor and concert singer Paul Robeson was a great figure in American popular culture.

Like the Palmer Raids a quarter century earlier, the Cold War once again drew the radical legacy to a temporary close. By the time a full biography of Eugene V. Debs finally appeared in 1950, the bygone days of socialism seemed a thousand light-years away, the legacy almost too dangerous to discuss in print. But even then the story was passed on to another generation. The time came, and the legend grew—but in ways that no one could have anticipated.

The civil rights movement kept alive the radical tradition and brought African Americans to the forefront of this history. Frederick Douglass, Sojourner Truth, and Ida B. Wells, heroes of the abolitionist and anti-lynching causes, became forerunners of civil rights pioneers Ella Josephine Baker and Martin Luther King, Jr. W. E. B. Du Bois returned from obscurity to become the foremost scholar, an inspiration for the establishment of black studies. Martin Luther King, Jr., martyred in 1968, had become the most admired leader in the United States.

The 1960s renewed the legacy of individual liberty and erected a new pantheon of heroes through popular culture. The face of anarchist Emma Goldman, idol of the rising women's liberation movement, appeared for the first time on T-shirts. Woody Guthrie's son Arlo Guthrie restyled his father's ballads as a mass audience thrilled to the image of Woody in the cult film *Bound for Glory*. Similarly, modern dancer Isadora Duncan was plucky and glamorous in *Isadora,* the movie starring the British radical Vanessa Redgrave. Warren Beatty's hugely successful *Reds* made John Reed one of the most romantic characters of the century.

New social movements similarly rewove traditions to fresh purposes. The rising environmentalist cause recalled and reinterpreted the nature lore of earlier days, as it made Rachel Carson, author of *Silent Spring,* into a prophet. The Sierra Club, which naturalist John Muir had launched in the 1890s, grew to hundreds of thousands of members, a living monument to the importance of wilderness. Environmentalists who fought the degradation of wildlife and human health looked back to the historical studies of Lewis Mumford, who had foreseen and warned against the consequences of commercial irresponsibility. Sympathetic historians of the American Indian saga portrayed Pontiac and Neolin not as violent "savages" but as courageous protectors of their own tribal cultures.

Individual courage and creative forms of radical expression have continued to evoke adulation. Audre Lorde, the poet and political leader who died in 1993, seemed to encompass the movement for gay and lesbian rights. Abbie Hoffman, the antic radical prankster who had led antiwar demonstrations, similarly earned wide respect by the time of his death in 1992. The dramatic return of Malcolm X's memory, a quarter century after his assassination, is yet another chapter in the recurring search for a usable past, dramatized this time by Spike Lee's epic film *Malcolm X* and the burgeoning of the "X Generation." A new and renewed tradition of American radicalism brings history to life.

ACKNOWLEDGMENTS

In the making of a book such as the present one, not all of the contributions take the form of chapters. Here we need to acknowledge Robin Kelley and Steve Paulson for their interest and advice at the formative stages of the work. Additionally, we want to express our appreciation for the enthusiasm and commitment shown by Cecelia Cancellaro, our editor at Routledge, and by her assistant, Maura Burnett. Finally, for their editorial assistance and encouragement, we must thank Lorna Stewart Kaye and—those American radicals in the making—Rhiannon and Fiona Kaye.

Mari Jo Buhle, Paul Buhle, and Harvey J. Kaye
Providence, RI, and Green Bay, WI
—June 1993

TIMELINE

1763 — Pontiac's Rebellion.

1776 — Tom Paine's *Common Sense* published.

1829 — Fanny Wright lecture tours.

1837 — Anti-Slavery Convention of American Women.

1844 — George Lippard's *The Quaker City* first published.

1848 — Woman's Rights Convention, Seneca Falls, New York.

1851 — Sojourner Truth speaks at Woman's Rights Convention.

1863 — Emancipation Proclamation.

1867 — John Muir's Great Walk to the Gulf.

1877 — Uprising of 1877, Great Railroad Strike.

1886 — Haymarket Affair.

1888 — Edward Bellamy's *Looking Backward* published.

1892 — Ida B. Wells launches antilynching campaign.

1894 — Clarence Darrow defends Debs in Pullman Strike.

1901 — Socialist Party of America founded.

1903 — W. E. B. Du Bois's *Souls of Black Folk* published.

1905 — Industrial Workers of the World (IWW) founded.

1906 — *Mother Earth* begins publication.

— *Partido Liberal Mexicano* launched by Ricardo Flores Magon in St. Louis.

1909 — Spokane Free Speech fight.

1911 — *The Masses* begins publication.

1912 — Lawrence, Mass., Textile Strike.

1913 — Paterson, N.J., Strike.

1916 — Fellowship of Reconciliation formed.

1917 — Russian Revolution.

1919 — Steel Strike.

— Communist Party and Communist Labor Party formed.

1920 — Trade Union Educational League formed.

1921 — Brookwood Labor College Founded.

1926 — Passaic, N.J., textile strike.

1927 — Sacco and Vanzetti executed.

1928 — Trade Union Unity League formed.

1933 — Upton Sinclair launches EPIC plan.

— Catholic Worker movement founded.

1936 — Spanish Civil War begins.

— American Labor Party formed.

— Congress of Industrial Organizations formed.

1937 — John Dewey heads commission defending Trotsky.

1938 — Lewis Mumford's *Culture of the Cities* appears.

1941 — Woody Guthrie joins Almanac Singers.

1946 — Carlos Bulosan's *America Is in the Heart* appears.

— Cold War begins.

1948 — Henry Wallace Progressive Party campaign.

1949 — Peekskill Riot against Paul Robeson Concert.

1952 — *I. F. Stone's Weekly* begins publication.

1953 — Execution of Ethel and Julius Rosenberg.

1955 — Montgomery Bus Boycott.

1957 — Committee for Nonviolent Action formed.

1959 — *Studies on the Left* begins publication.

— William A. Williams's *The Tragedy of American Diplomacy* appears.

1960 — Student Nonviolent Coordinating Committee founded.

1962 — Rachel Carson's *Silent Spring* published.

— Students for a Democratic Society formed.

1963 — Birmingham demonstrations.

— March on Washington.

1964 — Freedom Summer.

1965 — Organization of Afro-American Unity formed.

— Malcolm X assassinated.

— Selma March.

— First mass demonstrations against Vietnam War.

1968 — Martin Luther King, Jr., assassinated.

— Youth International Party, "Yippie," formed.
1969 — Conspiracy Trial of Chicago Seven.
— Stonewall Riot.
1972 — George McGovern campaign for presidency.
1982 — Audre Lorde's *Zami: A New Spelling of My Name* appears.
1983 — March on Washington for Jobs, Peace, and Freedom.
— Democratic Socialists of America formed.
1986 — January 20, King's birthday, becomes a public holiday.

PONTIAC AND NEOLIN

Gregory Evans Dowd

In the spring of 1763, Native Americans from Wisconsin to New York stormed the garrisons and frontier villages of the British North American empire. They came from at least eight tribes, and from two dramatically different language groups. Their attacks were neither spontaneous nor coordinated by a grand strategy, but they were quick, in many cases effective, in some cases, devastating. The assaults began at Detroit, Michigan, in early May, and then spread with news and rumor of Indian victories to the eastern slopes of the Allegheny Mountains and the western reaches of the Great Lakes. British officers, taken by surprise and thrown into confusion, confronted what appeared to be a general Indian uprising. The multitribal warriors were not followers of any single leader or pair of leaders, but two men, Pontiac and Neolin, may be taken as exemplars of the warriors' militancy, a religiously spirited challenge to the world's most powerful empire. Pontiac, an Ottawa warrior, led the Indians' seige of British Fort Detroit. Neolin, a Lenape religious leader in what is now eastern Ohio and western Pennsylvania, led no warriors, but his teachings inspired Pontiac and others to defy Great Britain.

Pontiac had emerged from youth as a steadfast supporter of the Ottawas' alliance with France. The French had never conquered the Ottawas. Nor had they conquered any of the other tribes that would rise in 1763 against Britain. The French may have called their relationship with Indians an "empire," but recent historians have seen it more as an alliance, or association, in which unconquered Indians had more power than the imperial French would openly admit. Various unreliable memoirs place Pontiac among the allies of France in three major actions which brought on or escalated the French and Indian War (1754–1760): the Pickawillany raid (1752), Braddock's Defeat (1755), and the Fall of Fort William Henry (1757). Pontiac definitely stood with the French at Fort Duquesne (Pittsburgh) in 1757, where he spurned British peace offers. There, in western Pennsylvania, he must have come to know many Lenapes; perhaps he met Neolin among them.

The tide of war turned against Pontiac's French allies in 1758, as British successes on the coasts and high seas cut off French supplies. Without supplies, Fort Duquesne's Indians drifted off, and the French abandoned it in the autumn. By 1760, Britain had conquered French Canada, gaining in the surrender terms the French forts on the Great Lakes. Pontiac, born and raised practically under the walls of the French fort at Detroit, saw it placed in the hands of the British.

We do not know Pontiac's attitude toward the British occupation of Detroit, but his compatriots allowed the redcoats to garrison the fort peacefully in 1760. Having dealt successfully for well over a century with one European power, the Indians had hope that they could deal as well with another. They expected the British to act like good allies, as the French had usually done. They wished the British, like the French before them, to give the Indians goods, traditionally called "presents." In exchange, they would allow the redcoats their forts, and promise loyalty in war.

But the British Army's upper echelons, flush with their conquests of Quebec and Montreal, had not occupied Detroit to take French lessons from Ottawas. While French officers had earlier learned, through generations of Indian negotiation, to act as mediators of peace, providers of "presents," allies in war, and strong, even loving, "Fathers," the British high command demanded that its officers act as conquerors. The British attitude surfaced most clearly over the issue of "presents." The North American commander in chief, General Jeffery Amherst, considered the "presents" to be but a form of bribery for good behavior. The British treasury considered them a costly waste. Detroit's British officers therefore terminated the French practice of giving gifts either on special occasions or in great annual councils.

This was more than an insult. It did more than demonstrate British contempt for Indians: it had material and political consequences. All cloth, metal goods, spirituous liquors, and ammunition ultimately originated in either Europe or a European colony. Without gifts, Indians could obtain these goods, on which they had come to rely, only by trading—and their most valuable commodities were animal pelts. French gifts had formerly provided an essential hedge against poor hunting or market conditions. British policymakers saw nothing of this. Like the inexperienced trader Alexander Henry, they saw in the Great Lakes region a "vast new market to British adventure." The peltry trade alone, they assumed, would supply Indians with the needed goods. Theoretically, it might have: had Indian men acted only as hunters, had hunters remained well, and their hunting good. But Ottawas did not live in a theoretical marketplace. They lived in a world that knew war and disease, threats to the trading economy against which the French gifts—received in exchange for alliance—had once been a necessary buffer.

By refusing to distribute presents, the British proved themselves to be unfit as allies of the Great Lakes Indians. Pontiac sought in 1763 to prove them to be unfit as conquerors, and he had many supporters. As Pontiac called for the storming of Detroit in late April 1763, he invoked the spiritual teachings of the Lenape Indian "prophet" Neolin.

Neolin's birth, parentage, family, development, appearance, and death are all unknown. His name meant "four," a sacred number. In 1763 he lived at the Lenape village of Tuscarawas in the Tuscarawas Valley region of eastern Ohio. In 1764 he lived among Shawnees at their village of Wakatomica, lower down the valley. Later he moved back upstream to live in the most important Lenape town, Newcomer's, where he counseled the important chief Netawatwees until at least 1766.

The Lenapes had a history that differed greatly from that of the Ottawas. They had once lived near the Atlantic, in what is now New Jersey and eastern Pennsylvania. British colonization had, in the late seventeenth and early eighteenth centuries, encouraged their westward migration, many as far as eastern Ohio by the 1730s. Because they had so recently arrived in the upper Ohio River region, and because the French were even later intruders into that area, the Lenapes did not have the long experience with the French that had been shared by the Ottawas of Detroit. Lenapes had only reluctantly allied with the French during the recent imperial war, and for but three and a half years between the summer of 1755 and winter of 1758–59. As the French then abandoned the region, Lenapes reentered into an uncertain peace with the British. They remained wary of the British posts, most notably at Fort Pitt (Pittsburgh), and they grew angry at the freckling presence of British squatters and hunters west of the Alleghenies. Still, they hoped for good trade and good relations. Wariness and anger gained the upper hand over hope, however, as the

British developed Fort Pitt on an immense scale, as the British troops did little to prevent British squatting, as the prices of British goods rose, and as game, now also hunted by Britons, became harder to find. A British sergeant reported in 1761 that white hunters were infiltrating Indian lands in "crowds . . . at which the Indians seem very much disturbed and say the white people kills all their deer." By 1762, an Ohio Indian accused Britons of making "our Game scarce."

In short, though Lenapes had in 1759 hoped for good trade from the British, British officers and subjects had undermined those hopes. In both the upper Ohio and the Detroit regions, then, Indians had expressed a willingness to coexist with a limited, carefully defined British presence. They had not been hostile to British people, much less to all Europeans. But Britons failed to meet Indian expectations. "Your Conduct," an Ohio Indian had told the British the previous December, "makes all the Indian Nations round you very Jealous that you have some bad designs against them."

Turning militantly against the British, Neolin began predicting a war in 1761. By 1763, Pontiac was quoting his teachings. On the increasing shortages of game, Neolin promised that if the Indians drove out the British, the Master of life would "send back the animals for your food." On British expansion, he warned that "if you suffer the English among you, you are dead men." On the devastating effects of liquor and of European diseases, he cautioned distance from the British, else "Sickness, smallpox, and their poison [alcohol] will destroy you entirely."

Though we have such vivid renditions of Neolin's teachings and prophecies, the man himself remains obscure. Historians have not been kind to him. In 1851 Francis Parkman, employing racism as his guide, attributed his rise to "the great susceptibility of the Indians to superstitious impressions." Howard Peckham, in 1947, declared him "psychopathic." Charles Beatty, a Presbyterian missionary who actually met Neolin in 1766, was more impressed: Beatty called Neolin a "young man," which is all we know of his age. He struck Beatty as gentle, attentive, and respected. He treated Beatty well, demonstrated great hospitality, listened to sermons, and, when the village council concluded that it didn't need Presbyterian advice, he politely (no doubt gladly) ushered Beatty from the village.

Neolin had by 1763 won over Pontiac, who himself exhibited a strong concern for the sacred. Much as Neolin is known as a "prophet," Ottawas have remembered Pontiac as a religious leader, a *mide*, a high-ranking shaman in their important *Midewiwin* festival. Still, Neolin and Pontiac came from different peoples and regions, and had different experiences with European empires. There was, therefore, a tension between the local and the intertribal dimensions of the event we call "Pontiac's War."

Pontiac and Neolin both sought to drive out the British, but for reasons that differed in emphasis. Pontiac, because the British had not behaved as the European occupiers of Detroit should behave. "When I go to see the English commander and say to him that some of our comrades are dead, instead of bewailing their deaths, as our French brothers do, he laughs at me and at you. If I ask anything for our sick, he refuses with the reply that he has no use for us." Pontiac even visited the French officers who still remained in lower Illinois in 1764, asking them to "fight against this bad meat that would come and infest our lands." In the same speech, he also obliquely referred to Neolin, when he told the French that to remain at peace was to go "against the orders of the Master of Life." With sacred and profane arguments, he attempted to rally France against Britain. Pontiac could live with European allies; he would not live under European lords.

Like Pontiac, Neolin may have favored the French over the British, but he probably did not give them as much thought. One document states that, in July 1763, several of Neolin's Lenape followers demanded that Pontiac protect the French inhabitants of the Detroit region. They proclaimed to Pontiac that "thou art French as well as we." What's more, though Lenape disciples of the prophetic movement would kill and capture thousands of British traders, soldiers, and settlers during the war, they did not make deliberate targets of French traders or settlers who remained neutral.

But despite these indications, Neolin was clearly less interested in the prospects of a new French alliance than he was in getting rid of the British posts and British trade. Indeed, most renditions of his visions say nothing of the French. The Lenapes had never been as concerned as the Ottawas with the French, so this is not surprising. Many of his speeches, recorded in English, condemn all "whites," but the Lenape language has no colorless racial equivalent of the English term "white." Perhaps he meant, in these speeches, only to condemn the British. Nervous Britons, recording secondhand news, may have taken him to mean all whites. Neolin had become fervently anti-British; it is doubtful that he lumped the French and British under a single racial heading. What is clear is that he looked more to sacred powers than to old allies for aid. Pontiac looked to both.

Pontiac's call to arms, supported by Neolin's sacred visions, initiated a war that stunned the British officers. Not only had they failed to preserve the peace; not only were they unable to defend the long borderlands of Virginia, Maryland, Pennsylvania, and New York; but their own posts faced siege and collapse. While Pontiac's forces failed to take Fort Detroit, and while Neolin's Lenapes failed to drive the British from Fort Pitt, nine smaller posts fell quickly to Indian siege or had to be abandoned.

Even Fort Bedford, Pennsylvania, east of the Alleghenies, came under attack. Most astonishing was the fall in May 1763 of Fort Michilimackinac at the top of Michigan's mitten, taken by an Ottawa and Chippewa ruse that involved a game of lacrosse, a ball tossed over the ramparts, and the rush into the fort of warriors, ostensibly chasing the ball—but picking up weapons and killing Britons along the way. In June, Fort Presque Isle fell to an intertribal force of Ottawas, Chippewas, Wyandots, and Senecas. Senecas annihilated two British infantry companies just south of Fort Niagara on September 23. By the war's end, some 450 British soldiers, and probably 2,000 British subjects, had been killed or captured.

British responses were confused, ferocious, and then, conciliatory. At first, strong measures were taken and countenanced by officers from Amherst down. In the most savage of these, Fort Pitt's beleaguered garrison distributed blankets from a smallpox ward to Lenapes, a deliberate step toward germ warfare. On the strategic level, the British managed to reinforce Forts Niagara, Detroit, and Pitt. They also sent large armies into the upper Ohio country in 1764; which saw some heavy fighting and scattered Indian villagers, but which did not, by themselves, compel Indian surrender. On the popular level, in the frontier communities of Pennsylvania and Virginia, reeling from attacks and anxiety, vigilantes murdered neutral Indians of all sexes and ages—most of them local and Christian. But what brought the militant Indians to seek terms was their lack of ammunition, their realization that France was not resuming the· war, and perhaps a growing sense that they had taught Britain a lesson.

Over the course of 1764 and 1765, as the war festered and negotiators struggled, the British quietly acknowledged greater responsibilities toward the Indians. Amherst left North America shortly after the outbreak of the war, and his replacement, General Thomas Gage, was more willing to accommodate Indian demands. Historian Richard White notes that the British reformed their Indian department, resumed the practice of dispensing gifts, limited to the Crown alone the right to purchase Indian land, and attempted to regulate the trade. Neither Ottawas nor Lenapes ceded any lands at the close of the war; the outcome was largely a draw. The British maintained a reduced presence in the west, but they did so at the cost of accepting, to some degree, the Indian demand that they behave as allies, not conquerors.

In the short term, Pontiac could be content that he had taught the British how to behave, as they now began to take up some of the obligations expected of them by the Indians. His policies had been somewhat successful, but he himself became an unfortunate failure. The British, who overestimated his importance, began to treat him as the most important "chief," not just among the Ottawas, but west of Fort Pitt, a role for which there was no Indian precedent. As White argues, Pontiac "made the fatal mistake of acting the part." During negotiations at Detroit in 1766, moreover, he killed an Illinois Indian. Resentment at his growing claims to authority, based largely upon mistaken British assumptions, led to his having to leave his homeland among the Ottawas, and his power quickly deteriorated. In April, almost six years after his opening calls for war, he was killed by an Illinois Indian in Cahokia.

Neolin's failure is more clear: no cosmic upheaval dislodged the British. While he had shown some favor for the French, and while, as the war wound down, he attempted to arrange a negotiation through the mediation of Pennsylvania's Quakers, he had long given up on reforming the British. Unlike Pontiac, he could not have been at all satisfied with the results of the war. Still, he retained local influence, and oddly—though no towns or automobiles bear his name—his ideas would be more lasting than Pontiac's. The Ohio region became home to many other Lenape "prophets" in the 1760s, who battled against Christian missionaries for the soul of the region's Indians. Because Neolin's vision of prophetic resistance depended less upon a European ally than did Pontiac's, it was more suited to Indian needs in later years. After the American Revolution, the region's Indians learned that they could count very little upon European imperial powers for assistance. Like Neolin, militants would turn to sacred powers instead. It is no accident that fifty years after the end of the war we now call "Pontiac's War," a Shawnee man would collapse in a Lenape village and experience visions. These visions—strongly reminiscent of Neolin's—would set him and his followers against alcoholism and against trade with the Anglo-Americans. He too would strongly oppose any loss of Indian land to the expanding power in the East. Like Neolin, he would inspire Ottawas and others. His name was Tenskwatawa, the Shawnee Prophet. Together with his brother, Tecumseh, he would lead another intertribal effort to defend Indian lands. Between 1805 and 1813 these brothers would attempt to unite the tribes from the Great Lakes to the Gulf of Mexico in a spiritually charged struggle for independence from the United States. Very much in the tradition of 1763, they and their followers would not, in the Shawnee Prophet's words, "sit still and see the property of all the Indians usurped."

Suggested Readings

Gregory Evans Dowd, *A Spirited Resistance: The North American Indian Struggle for Unity, 1745–1815*. Baltimore, Md.: Johns Hopkins University Press, 1992.

W. J. Eccles, *Essays on New France*. Toronto: Oxford University Press, 1987.

Michael N. McConnell, *A Country Between: The Upper Ohio Valley and Its Peoples, 1724–1774*. Lincoln: University of Nebraska Press, 1992.

Howard H. Peckham, *Pontiac and the Indian Uprising*. Princeton, N.J.: Princeton University Press, 1947.

Richard White, *The Middle Ground: Indians, Empires, and Republics in the Great Lakes Region, 1650–1815*. New York: Cambridge University Press, 1991.

2

TOM PAINE

Harvey J. Kaye

Leaving England in 1774 at the age of thirty-seven, Tom Paine came to America and became a radical. Invigorated by the society he discovered and inspired by the great possibilities he recognized within it, Paine wrote a pamphlet, *Common Sense*, which succeeded in redefining American struggles against British imperial rule as a war for national independence and political revolution and, moreover, as the fundamental act of a world revolution against the tyranny and corruption of the old regimes of Europe. As Paine himself declaimed in words which fired the imagination of his fellow citizens-to-be: "We have it in our power to begin the world over again."

Born in 1737 at Thetford in Norfolk, Paine's life confirms that "only the past is predictable," for it is only with the hindsight of history that we can see in the years before his coming to America the making of a revolutionary and world-historical figure. His father, Joseph Paine, was a Quaker and staymaker, and his mother, Frances Cocke, was an Anglican and lawyer's daughter. Neither a happy nor an affluent couple, they nevertheless were extremely fond of their son and committed to his receiving a formal education. Thus, in addition to becoming well versed in the Bible at home, from the age of six to thirteen young Paine was enrolled

9

in the village school where his favorite subjects were science and poetry. At fourteen, however, he was apprenticed to his father, from whom he learned the craft of corsetmaking and also, no doubt, the dissenting and egalitarian spirit of the Quakers and the historical memory of "turning the world upside down" in the English Revolution of the 1640s and '50s. It seems an artisan's life promised too sedentary a future, for at nineteen Paine ran away to serve aboard the privateer *King of Prussia*. Yet, whatever the adventure, the rigors and oppressions of life between the devil and the deep blue sea were too great and after a year he managed to get himself released, whereupon he went to London to work as a journeyman staymaker.

The next decade and a half were filled with tragic disappointments, mistakes, and failures. In 1759 Paine set up shop as a master craftsman on the southeast coast where he met and married his first love, Mary Lambert. Sadly, within a year he lost his wife in premature childbirth and soon after was forced to give up his business. He then prepared to become and in 1764 secured appointment as an excise officer, but was expelled a year later for having stamped goods without inspecting them (a not unusual practice). During the next few years he kept alive by working as a staymaker, a teacher, and even a preacher while he petitioned for reinstatement. Finally, in early 1768 Paine was posted to Lewes in Sussex. There he boarded with a tobacconist, whose daughter, Elizabeth Ollive, he married in 1771 on the shopkeeper's death. He also became active in local affairs and a "regular" in the Whiggish political debates at the White Hart Tavern, developing a friendly reputation as a man who enjoyed a few good drinks and who had a "skill with words." David Freeman Hawke describes Paine, now in his early thirties, as possessing "a long face dominated by a large, drooping nose and blue eyes so lively and piercing that few failed to remark upon them after a first meeting."

Recognizing his talents, Paine's fellow officers chose him to lead their campaign for higher salaries and, so commissioned, he penned his first pamphlet, *The Case of the Excise Officers* (1772), and moved to London to lobby Parliament. This stay in the capital increased his knowledge and resentment of aristocratic government and politics but, also, renewed his awareness of the popular radicalism of the middling and artisan classes. Additionally, it enabled him to advance his interest in natural philosophy through attendance at scientific lectures—occasions that placed him among circles of intellectuals and freethinkers which, fortuitously, included Benjamin Franklin. Unfortunately, the campaign was defeated and in its wake Paine was discharged for ignoring his official duties, the tobacco shop failed, and he and his wife agreed to separate.

Penniless and without immediate prospects, but possessed of a seemingly indefatigable willingness to try again, Paine resolved to go to America, outfitted with a letter of introduction from the renowned Franklin. Little did either man suspect that the mix of historical and personal memories and skills which Paine carried with him would be so volatile when brought into contact with events in America. But, indeed, however British, America was another country and the Philadelphia to which Paine was headed was its "capital."

Arriving in late 1774, Paine's plans were to open a school. However, following the publication of a few short newspaper articles, Paine was recruited to be editor of the *Pennsylvania Magazine* which prospered under his direction. Paine himself wrote regularly and began to develop a public voice. Among the most pointed of his pieces were an essay on the oppression of women and another in which he called for the abolition of slavery and insisted upon Americans' responsibilities both to the liberated slaves and to the peoples of Africa. Although critical of British imperial practices, Paine originally favored reconciliation between Britain and the American colonies. Yet, following the events at Lexington and Concord in April 1775, he became an American "patriot" and published the poem "Liberty Tree," whose verses were enthusiastically received for their references to King and Parliament as "tyrannical powers."

In our all too cynical times, we should not assume Paine's commitment to the American cause to have been determined simply by his difficulties in England or, worse, mere opportunism. Whatever his grievances, we must not fail to appreciate the "America" he encountered. Life in the colonies was evidently structured by inequalities of class and status and Paine was well aware of the oppressions of slavery. Nevertheless, as an Englishman of some education and skill, he must have found America—an increasingly diverse society in the process of rapid growth and development—most attractive and, with Franklin's assistance, welcoming and accessible. Moreover, American resistance to British impositions, taxations, and restrictions had been under way for a decade already, politicizing not only the colonial elites but also the popular classes of artisans, shopkeepers, and farmers. Particularly in Philadelphia, Paine could perceive the promise of an even more egalitarian and democratic order, for here was a polity being remade from the bottom up by an increasingly well-organized class of "mechanics"—the very sort of people from whence he had himself emerged. Perhaps it even reminded him of the hopes and possibilities suppressed in England over a century before. Surely, it cannot have been opportunism which propelled Paine into the struggle, for who actually knew what the rebellious colonists were pursuing . . . the restoration of "Englishmen's rights," reforms to the imperial system, *or* separation? In any case, what chance of success was there, whatever the goals, against the world's greatest power?

By late 1775 independence was being spoken of in various quarters and even among elements of the Continental Congress. But it was still the pronounced ambition of only a minority. Persuaded to write in support of separation by his friend Dr. Benjamin Rush, a younger radical and member of Congress who was himself still hesitant to do so, Paine published *Common Sense* in January 1776. Calling upon Americans to recognize their historic responsibilities and possibilities and make a true revolution of their struggles, Paine's arguments took hold of his new compatriots' shared but as of yet unarticulated sentiments and thoughts and expressed them in language bold and clear. As one historian has written: "The work literally exploded in the American consciousness." Within a few months as many as 150,000 copies of the pamphlet were sold (for which Paine refused any royalties), and independence became the declared aspiration of the majority.

Arguably, independence would eventually have become the Americans' cause even without the appearance of *Common Sense*. But Paine's writing brought that eventuality forward. Even more important, it declared the cause of American independence to be more than a question of separation from Britain—it proclaimed it a struggle *against* the tyranny of hereditary privilege both "monarchical and aristocratical" and *for* a democratic republic. Paine appealed directly to Americans' economic interests. Yet, in addition to accounting their commercial prospects, Paine offered a vision of independence which asked them to see themselves as "*Americans*," a people no longer subject to king and noble but—as was their "natural right"—*constituting themselves free and equal before God and "the law" and governing themselves through democratically elected representatives.*

Reflecting Paine's self-education in eighteenth-century liberalism and republicanism alike, the ideas expressed in *Common Sense* may not have been "philosophically" original but, mobilizing biblical scripture, historical criticism, and the force of "reason" itself, Paine's arguments were radically original in appeal and consequence. It's not just that Paine addressed himself to Americans of all classes (of white society, that is), but that the very style and content of his words succeeded in articulating a more egalitarian and democratic conception of "the people" than hitherto prevailed. In fact, as Eric Foner has shown, Paine's language captured the imagination of mechanics and farmers in an unprecedented fashion and, rhetorically incorporating them into the "political nation," it both engaged the working classes to the cause of independence and further empowered them in their own movements to restructure the political and social order.

Admittedly, Paine failed to directly incorporate into *Common Sense* either his abolitionist views or his concerns regarding the oppression of women. Nevertheless, his vision of a democratic republic was potentially unlimited—a point understood not only by Tories but, also, by elite-minded patriots such as John Adams who grew anxious about the radical dreams which were bound to be engendered by so "popular a pamphlet." Paine himself projected the struggle into the future and well beyond American shores—"The cause of America is in a great measure the cause of all mankind"—*not* by way of an imperial America imposing its will upon the world but as a model of peaceful prosperity and democratic republicanism and, also, as a refuge:

> O ye that love mankind! Ye that dare oppose, not only the tyranny, but the tyrant, stand forth! Every spot of the world is over-run with oppression. Freedom hath been hunted round the globe. Asia, and Africa have long expelled her.—Europe regards her like a stranger, and England hath given her warning to depart. O! receive the fugitive, and prepare in time an asylum for mankind.

Declared on July 4, 1776, independence was far from being secured. Paine himself enlisted in the revolutionary army and was posted to forces near New York to serve as aide-de-camp to General Nathaniel Greene. But his major contribution was not to be as a combatant. The war had begun badly for the Americans and by late 1776 George Washington's army was in retreat across New Jersey. Was it to end so soon? Paine would not allow for such thinking. In December of the same year he wrote the first of his sixteen *Crisis* papers, once again proffering words of inspiration which were to resound through generations:

> These are the times that try men's souls. The summer soldier and the sunshine patriot will, in this crisis, shrink from the service of their country; but he that stands it *now*, deserves the love and thanks of man and woman. Tyranny, like hell, is not easily conquered; yet we have this consolation with us, that the harder the conflict, the more glorious the triumph.

In 1777 Congress honored Paine with appointment as secretary to the Committee on Foreign Affairs, in which post he played an important role in negotiating the crucial alliance with France. But, always quick to act, Paine got himself entangled, and in trouble, in the "Silas Deane affair" when he publicly accused Deane of profiteering in his dealings with the French on behalf of Congress. The problem was neither in Paine's suspicions nor his principles, but that he indiscreetly had made use of secret diplomatic correspondence embarrassing to the French government. Harried by his political enemies, Paine was forced to resign in 1779. Still, he *was* "Common Sense," and it was not long before he was engaged as clerk to the Assembly of Pennsylvania, whose new constitution, the most radical and democratic of all the former colonies, was shaped by the ideas that Paine had himself sketched out in his famous revolutionary pamphlet.

Paine's writings of the 1780s treated subjects commercial—he supported the controversial Bank of North America because he felt such institutions to be essential for the economic development of the country—*and* constitutional—he favored a strong central government because he believed it imperative to secure the nation and enable the United States to assert a powerful republican presence internationally. But his energies were increasingly directed to scientific and technical matters and, with peace in 1783, he applied himself to the design and construction of an iron bridge, a project which was to instigate his return to Europe in pursuit of additional engineering expertise and capital. At fifty years of age, Paine departed America in 1787 expecting to be gone for only a short while. Yet he was not to return for fifteen years.

If this biographical portrait were emanating from London or Paris, much of what has been said might well be treated merely as preface to Paine's revolutionary involvements back in England and France. The ensuing narrative would relate how he was irresistibly drawn into the politics of English radicalism and how, antagonized so by Edmund Burke's *Reflections on the Revolution in France* (1790), a fierce attack on the Revolution of 1789 which effectively launched modern Anglo-American conservatism, Paine was compelled to put aside his plans for the iron bridge and respond with *Rights of Man* (1791–92), once again directly and forcefully denying any legitimacy to monarchic and aristocratic government and advancing a defense not simply of French actions but of the right of all peoples, in every generation—including the Britons of his day—to remake their political orders in directions libertarian, egalitarian, and democratic.

This narrative would go on to tell of the irony of Paine's escaping arrest for revolutionary incitements in England by being in Paris—having been honored with election to the French National Convention—only later to be imprisoned for ten months in France for having aligned himself with the moderate Girondin faction and speaking out against the execution of the king. It would also note that in the shadow of the guillotine Paine wrote *The Age of Reason*, a work proclaiming his deism and rendering a sustained critique of organized religion which was to become a primer for nineteenth-century freethinkers. Finally, it would indicate how Paine's ideas developed beyond naive liberalism to the point where, in his final major work, *Agrarian Justice* (1797), he actually lays the groundwork for a social-democratic vision of the welfare state, apparently having recognized the threat posed to the progress of democratic republicanism by growing extremes of wealth and poverty.

Truly, Paine was the first "international" revolutionary. But the narrative of Paine's career as prophet of the Age of Revolution should fully account how "America" continued to inform and inspire his arguments and imaginings. He himself registered it clearly at the outset of Part II of *Rights of Man*. Posing the problem which still haunts philosophers today—"What Archimedes said of the mechanical powers, may be applied to Reason and Liberty: *'Had we,'* said he, *'a place to stand upon, we might raise the world'* "—Paine confidently answered with American experience: "The revolution of America presents in politics what was only theory in mechanics."

In 1802 he returned to the United States, spending his time between New York and his farm north of the city. Disappointingly, his appreciation of Americans' verve and audacity was no longer reciprocated. Once Paine had been celebrated as the champion of "common sense." Now, all but his truest friends, such as Thomas Jefferson, ignored him because of his denunciation of organized religion. He died in 1809 and, denied a place in the Quaker cemetery, was buried on his farm. In 1819, however, the coffin was dug up and loaded on a ship for reinterment in England. Curiously, but not inappropriately, it was lost in a storm somewhere mid-Atlantic.

Excluded from the pantheon of America's Founders for many a generation, Paine's historical memory was sustained by a variety of radical intellectuals and movements, democratic, socialist, and freethinking. In fact, my own introduction to Paine came not in school but from my grandfather, a brilliant trial lawyer who had come to this country as a Russian-Jewish boy in 1906. A socialist in his youth, he was eager to pass on to me a critical sense of history and a firm belief in the radical-democratic possibilities of America. Thus, among his gifts to me as a child, along with a volume of Old Testament Bible stories and personal recollections of growing up on the Lower East Side of New York, were the writings of Tom Paine.

Suggested Readings

Gregory Claeys, *Thomas Paine: Social and Political Thought*. London: Unwin Hyman, 1989.

Howard Fast, *Citizen Paine*. Originally published 1943. New York: Grove Weidenfeld, 1983. A historical novel.

Eric Foner, *Tom Paine and Revolutionary America*. New York: Oxford University Press, 1976.

Michael Foot and Isaac Kramnick, eds., *The Thomas Paine Reader*. New York: Viking Penguin, 1987.

David Freeman Hawke, *Paine*. New York: Harper and Row, 1974.

David Powell, *Tom Paine: The Greatest Exile*. London: Century Hutchinson, 1985.

3

FANNY WRIGHT

Lori D. Ginzberg

In early January 1829 a woman ascended a platform in the city of New York to speak to an expectant audience of fifteen hundred. Although her series of six lectures covered such arcane topics as knowledge, free inquiry, and applying the "test of reason" to religious dogma, her listeners were mesmerized. Cheers echoed in the hall, crowds grew with each lecture, and people spoke of little but Frances ("Fanny") Wright, leaving the modern reader to wonder what all the excitement was about.

Newspapers wondered too. At first the mainstream press was calm in the face of the praise heaped upon the "female Tom Paine" by her largely working-class listeners and by the freethought, or radical, press. The *Commercial Advertiser* only faulted her for "too much painful intensity of meaning" in her presentation; "her voice," the paper admitted, " . . . is both strong and sweet. We recollect no female whose recitations in this city have been celebrated, at all comparable to this lady." As the first woman to speak to large, sexually mixed audiences, Fanny Wright was a phenomenon to be noticed, if not admired.

The press's gentle bemusement quickly changed, as did the response of Wright's less articulate enemies; before her fifth lecture someone put a barrel of turpentine in front of the door and set it afire. By then the newspapers had grown vitriolic: Wright had attacked the clergy, had indeed denounced the very basis on which domestic stability lay: Christianity itself. Newspaper articles, replete with sexual innuendo, questioned the virtue not only of the speaker, but of anyone so brazen as to attend. The *Commercial Advertiser*, backpeddling frantically, cried that "truth demands us to say—and our cheeks burn while we record it—that there were females there without disguises." The following day the paper declared that "she has unsexed herself" and labeled Wright "a bold blasphemer, and a voluptuous preacher of licentiousness." Newspaper writers and ministers fretted that Wright would provoke a mob, would cause the lecture hall to be burned down, and would, most alarmingly, seduce happy wives "into the mazy meanderings of sinful pleasure, [where they] abandoned themselves to indiscriminate indulgence in libidinous practices." To them and, apparently, to the majority of the "respectable" middle class, "Wrightism" posed a particularly vicious threat, one which combined irreligion, calls for sexual transformation, and working-class consciousness.

What had happened? What had Frances Wright said to shatter the "respectable" press's willingness to tolerate her words? How did this thirty-three-year-old woman come to symbolize so dangerous a threat to American society that for decades radicals of any stripe suffered the epithet "Fanny Wrightism"? (Antoinette Brown would write to Lucy Stone as late as 1848 that, when she talked to people about her views on woman's rights, "sometimes they warn me not to be a Fanny Wright man." And into the 1840s abolitionists were accused of being "in one word infidels, and of the Fanny Wright school.") What anxieties about women and radical social change did her name trigger? And what in Wright's words portended future changes in American society?

Frances Wright was born in Scotland in 1795, one of three children of James Wright, a linen merchant and admirer of Thomas Paine, and Camilla Campbell, a child of the British aristocracy and goddaughter of the intellectual Elizabeth Robinson Montagu. Orphaned at the age of two, Frances and her younger sister Camilla were reared by relatives in London and in a village called Dawlish; by no account, especially her own, was her privileged childhood a happy one. Rebelling against her Tory relatives, Frances early developed an acute sense of social inequality and compassion for the poor. Even then, she might have become a charitable lady, a role that was increasingly acceptable for women of her class and inclination. But the teenage Fanny Wright showed a restlessness considered improper for such a lady and she demanded to be allowed to go with Camilla to Glasgow.

It was in Glasgow, living with a great-uncle, college professor James

Mylne, and his family, that Wright became exposed to the possibilities of intellectual growth. There she read widely, wrote a play called *Altorf* (staged anonymously), and explored utopian ideals in a brief book, *A Few Days in Athens* (published in 1822). And it was during her three years in Glasgow's intellectual community that she nurtured her attachment to the ideals of the American revolution and began to imagine, as so many radicals did, going to the United States. It would take several more years among the growing dissident community of London for the Wright sisters to act on this wish.

Frances Wright and her sister Camilla (the latter ever a rather vague, supportive figure in any story of Fanny's life) first sailed for America in 1818, where they oversaw the American staging of *Altorf* and visited widely among the new nation's liberal thinkers. Upon their return to Britain in May 1820, Frances collected the letters she had written to her friend Rabina Craig Millar and published *Views of Society and Manners in America*. Openly enthusiastic about what she saw as the nearly infinite possibilities of the so-called New World and quite unashamedly Republican in her political loyalties, Wright's anecdotal travel account was hugely popular in the United States and among such British liberals as Jeremy Bentham, one of Wright's models for social activism.

In addition to giving her some fame in America, *Views* introduced Wright to the Marquis de Lafayette, who was delighted with the book and whose political sympathies Wright shared. Their rather unusual relationship (Wright at one time suggested that Lafayette either marry or adopt her) further broadened Fanny Wright's horizons. Indeed, with Camilla again by her side, Frances Wright left England, where she felt stifled, in 1824, and followed Lafayette to America. There, strengthened by Fanny's reputation as a writer and Lafayette's fame, the sisters gained entrance to important politicians and intellectual leaders. There too Fanny Wright visited Robert Owen's utopian community, New Harmony, and became convinced of the benefits of his system of mutual cooperation and socialism. In the nation's capital Fanny Wright witnessed the system of slavery. It would not be long before she would connect the two systems— slavery and socialism—and develop her own unique plan for America.

In a kind of personal declaration of independence, Frances and Camilla Wright stayed on in America after Lafayette departed. Upon publishing *A Plan for the Gradual Abolition of Slavery in the United States without Danger of Loss to the Citizens of the South*, Frances determined to apply her own considerable financial and intellectual powers to an effort to ameliorate the condition of the enslaved. At the end of 1825 she purchased 640 acres of land in Tennessee and established an experimental plantation called Nashoba (she would eventually own eighteen hundred acres). There she intended to create a model community in which slaves would work the land, gain their freedom, and be colonized elsewhere. Wright purchased ten slaves and set about facing the realities of establishing a profitable enterprise at the same time as finding a solution to the evils of slavery.

In spite of Fanny Wright's upbeat reports, Nashoba failed miserably, in part because of economic difficulties and the hostility of neighboring farmers, in part because George Flower, Fanny's partner in the enterprise, departed. (It is likely that he and Wright had an affair, and that his wife insisted that they leave. In any case, Wright, her health broken, left with Robert Dale Owen for Europe in 1827, leaving Nashoba to others.) But the problems at Nashoba ran deep. For one thing, the life offered to blacks under overseer James Richardson and Camilla Wright's direction differed little from slavery, including separation of families, physical punishment, and lack of privacy and dignity; it was, as one biographer puts it, "deeply inhumane." In addition the project was plagued by "free love" scandals involving Richardson and Camilla herself. Nashoba, cried the *Genius of Universal Emancipation* (August 18, 1827), was "one great brothel." Frances Wright's reactions to these problems evince both her shortcomings and her strengths. Her inability to stick to a project once it had gotten past the realm of her imagination certainly did not bode well for its success; more disturbing, her failure to put a stop to the brutal treatment of the slaves made her complicit in it. In addition, Wright's increasingly radical beliefs underscore her own courage, but they doomed the community's reputation. In particular, her insistence that interracial mixing would end slavery and racism in America and her refusal to distance herself from the sexual experiments at Nashoba tarred her with the brush of unrespectability. Wright kept faith with Nashoba, but its major impact may have been in preparing Wright herself for a place on the fringe of American political and social life.

Wright next undertook the transformation of intellectual and political life in American cities. In 1828 she began her speaking tours, lecturing in Cincinnati against revivalism and then heading east in 1829. "I have wedded the cause of human improvement," she proclaimed, "staked [on it] my reputation, my fortune, and my life." She quickly became the most notorious speaker of her age: the first woman to address large-scale "promiscuous" audiences, a religious skeptic in an age of increasing clerical dominance, an advocate of free, universal education, an articulate defender of free thought, and an opponent of the traditional legal and sexual customs surrounding marriage. Above all Wright emphasized reason. These ideas were, in the context of the antebellum United States, explosive.

Fanny Wright challenged the most sacred tenets of American society. Reflecting British skepticism about religious institutions, she insisted that the clergy were hired hacks, out to control American minds. They raised tremendous sums of money for tracts and missionaries, she claimed, but opposed every reasonable effort to ameliorate the conditions of people in the United States. Similarly, she attacked wealth. Wage slavery, she insisted, paralleled the actual enslavement of African Americans. She charged American leaders with failing to live up to the promise of the Revolution by not having full and equal education for all, poor as well as rich, slave as well as free, women as well as men. "While the many are left in ignorance," she cried, "the few cannot be wise, for they cannot be virtuous." And she called on each city to raise the money for a Hall of Science, a place where ordinary people could come together to learn to apply rational standards to the problems of their age. (In April 1829 Wright bought the Ebenezer Baptist Church in New York City and dedicated it to the acquisition of "universal knowledge." With pictures of radical heroes in the windows and its doors open to the public, the Hall stood as a daily challenge to the Bible repository just across the street.)

In New York Wright and Robert Dale Owen also edited the *Free Enquirer*, a newspaper in which her views were more widely expressed and circulated. Having already shared with him the editorship of the *New Harmony Gazette*, Wright had determined to find a larger, more urban, and more working-class audience. Thus she lectured on behalf of the New York City Working Men's party (known disparagingly as the "Fanny Wright ticket"), which elected one of its own to the State Assembly in 1829. Although the party's major focus was on the economic needs of labor, Wright (and Owen) focused on universal education in rectifying social inequality. Wright stayed in New York long enough to see the party splinter and to experience renewed and vicious newspaper attacks. In July 1830 she and Camilla sailed for Europe.

There were personal reasons for their return. That year, after traveling with French teacher and New Harmonist William S. Phiquepal D'Arusmont on a lecture tour and trip to Haiti with the Nashoba slaves, Fanny Wright confronted her own vulnerability as a woman: she was pregnant. In spite of her opposition to marriage (and probably some ambivalence about Phiquepal himself), Wright decided to hide her pregnancy and marry her child's father. Accustomed to life in the limelight, Wright found this decision demoralizing and although she wrote to the *Free Enquirer* from Paris, Wright told no one when her daughter, Silva, was born. Camilla's death that same winter and a second baby daughter's birth in April 1832 and death soon after reinforced Fanny's withdrawal. Other than an occasional foray into politics (including a controversial

lecture trip in the United States in the mid-1830s in which she supported
Andrew Jackson and avoided the issue of slavery) and autobiographical
writing, Wright spent the remaining years of her life an isolated figure,
out of touch with the major radical movements of the time. She returned
once more to America in 1843, filed for divorce in 1850, became utterly
estranged from Silva (who would later testify against woman suffrage to
a congressional committee), and died in Cincinnati in 1852.

Only by understanding the depth of antebellum belief in all that Wright
opposed can we understand the venom with which Wright and her rational-
ist message were greeted. Wright's linkage of working-class organization,
public education, greater democratization of politics, and woman's rights
earned her enemies enough. But in openly discussing two related taboos—
religion and sexuality—Wright touched mainstream Americans' deepest
anxieties. (Indeed, many of her allies anxiously distanced themselves
from her more radical proposals.) Wright's attacks on clerical dominance
were closely connected to her critique of conventional sexual morality:
both, she believed, kept Americans, especially American women, subser-
vient and stupid. Indeed, Wright was generally impatient with the general-
ity of women, whom she considered "humbugged from their cradles."
Religious revivals, she insisted, operated on "the minds of weak and
deluded women," who were thus unfit for equality with men in a truly
rational society.

Wright's views of marriage and sexuality place her at the very forefront
of the so-called free-love movement of the nineteenth century, which
demanded that marriages last only as long as emotional attachment. Wright
believed fervently that affection could not be determined or sustained by
the mere legalities of marriage. But she went further, insisting that sexual
passion was, even in women "the strongest and . . . the noblest of the
human passions." Virtue could not be ensured by clerical dictates, she
insisted; true virtue would be exhibited "in proportion as [people] are
happy, and happy in proportion as they are free." Decades before feminists
would insist upon women's right to physical and sexual autonomy, Wright
wrote:

> Ignorant laws, ignorant prejudices, ignorant codes of morals . . .
> condemn one portion of the female sex to vicious excess, another to
> as vicious restraint, and all to defenceless helplessness and slavery,
> and generally the whole of the male sex to debasing licentiousness,
> if not to loathsome brutality.

While Wright's was not a feminism that appealed to many women of her
generation (she generally disregarded the realities of women's dependence

on men and was contemptuous of women's efforts to assert authority in a religious context), her vision of a rational society that was not based on gender differences remains a challenge to our own age.

Like many American radicals, Frances Wright built no lasting institutions, wrought no long-term structural transformation of American political or economic life; she herself was more inclined to come up with a vision than to institute a plan. Yet she was unsurpassed as a spokesperson for public education, an advocate of women's civil, intellectual, and social equality with men, and a pioneer in challenging marriage and divorce laws that, she believed, sustained the sexual oppression of women. She stood almost alone among women in urging Americans to reject religious superstition and to live by reason alone. Her appeals to reason—her criticism of clerical control over American thought—her absolutely consistent demand for a separation of church and state should remind us of the elasticity of those boundaries in our own time. Indeed, almost all of Wright's ideas—miscegenation being the major exception—gained growing acceptance over the course of the nineteenth century. Finally, Fanny Wright's willingness to live on the outer fringe of American life—to be an "infidel"—marks her as a person of unusual courage for any era.

Suggested Readings

Paul S. Boyer, "Frances Wright," in E. James and J. T. James, eds., *Notable American Women*. Cambridge: Harvard University Press, 1971.

Frances Wright d'Arusmont, *Life, Letters, and Lectures, 1834–1844*. New York: Arno Press, 1972.

Celia Morris Eckhardt, *Fanny Wright: Rebel in America*. Cambridge: Harvard University Press, 1984.

Albert Post, *Popular Freethought in America, 1825–1850*. New York: Columbia University Press, 1943.

William Randall Waterman, *Frances Wright*. Originally published 1924. New York: AMS Press, 1967.

4

SOJOURNER TRUTH

Nell Irvin Painter

Sojourner Truth (ca. 1797–1883), the symbol of the heroic black woman in American history, is remembered as a former slave who made herself into an outspoken antislavery feminist. As a symbol of race and gender in a world where all the women are white and all the blacks are men, "Sojourner Truth" is often summed up in a few public speech acts, which have varied over time as the fashion in black women has shifted. She also deserves to be remembered as a woman who defied the nineteenth-century prohibition against women's preaching in public.

In the nineteenth century, when religious conviction was unambiguously admirable, Truth was known, perhaps apocryphally, for challenging the faith of a doubting Frederick Douglass with the question, "Frederick, is God dead?" Today piety has fallen away from her persona, and her more famous phrase is "And ar'n't *I* a woman?" allegedly uttered at a woman's rights convention in Akron, Ohio, in 1851. (This phrase is sometimes reworked to sound more authentically Negro as "And *ain't I* a woman?") Truth is also remembered for having publicly bared her breast in 1858 after a clergyman accused her of being a man—a charge leveled repeatedly in the early nineteenth century at powerful women speakers. Refusing to step behind a curtain, she opened her dress and showed, she said, the breast that had suckled white babies who had grown into better men than her accusers. Recently these two gestures have sometimes run together to depict an angry Sojourner Truth who snarls her question then rips open her dress in defiance.

As a figure of strength and integrity despite the relative obscurity of her origins and activities, Truth appears on lists of valiant Americans, where she balances a preponderance of men and white women. Because she functions in discourse primarily as a signifier, an analysis of the figure known as Sojourner Truth must take account of symbolism as well as lived experience.

Sojourner Truth's life begins twice: first, with the birth in the late 1790s of an Ulster County, New York, slave named Isabella, and, second, on the first of June 1843 in New York City, when Isabella rechristened herself as Sojourner Truth. As a lecturer, Sojourner Truth played upon the indeterminate but decided Southernness associated with slavery in the antebellum period, for instance, when she bared her breast in 1858. She appropriated the mothering practices of the plantation, professing, like a Southern slave, to have wet-nursed her master's family. Then as now, the metaphorical geography of slavery distanced Sojourner Truth's from Isabella's own early life.

Isabella was born in Ulster County, New York, where blacks were slaves, but which was not Southern. She was one of tens of thousands of enslaved New Yorkers. She spent her youth primarily on Dutch-speaking farms, where she was usually one of five or fewer slaves performing a variety of agricultural and household chores. As a young girl, she lived with her parents, James and Elizabeth Bomefree. One of Isabella's indelible childhood memories—mentioned five times in the early pages of her *Narrative*—is of her parents' grieving over the children they had lost to the slave trade. Burdened by her parents' loss, Isabella knew she was a survivor. She met her own disaster when she was sold away from her parents at the age of nine. As a slave she was beaten to make her work, obey, and show submission; as a parent she beat her own children for similar reasons.

Like many who have been abused as children, Isabella responded differently to the man and the woman who beat her. She hated the mistress but identified with the master, whom she elevated to Godlike status. She curried his favor and proved her loyalty through overwork, to the disgust of older slaves. Given this personal history of abuse and debasement, Sojourner Truth's later self-empowerment through religious faith ranks as an enormous achievement, one that she gained through means that have served black women well for more than a century.

Isabella became a Christian at about the same time that she gained her freedom through New York state law in 1827 and moved away from the farm on which her husband, Thomas, had chosen to remain. She joined a Methodist church in Ulster County and attended white then black Methodist churches when she moved to New York City in the late 1820s. Even before she left Ulster County, the Methodist societies she preferred tended toward Perfectionism or holiness beliefs. In the early 1830s she joined a nondenominational religious commune under the leadership of the Scots American Robert Matthews, who called himself the Prophet Matthias. After the dissolution of Matthias's Ossining "kingdom" in 1835, Isabella returned to household work in New York City until she followed her inner voice in 1843, changed her name to Sojourner Truth, and commenced an itinerant ministry.

Truth took to the roads to preach at the apogee of Millerism, a mass movement of Second Adventists who expected the world to end in mid-1843. She found a ready-made audience receptive to women's preaching at Millerite camp meetings on Long Island and along the Connecticut River Valley. When she was ready to put up for the winter, Truth followed the advice of New England Millerites, who steered her to the utopian Northampton (Massachusetts) Industrial Association, where she spent several years. In the Northampton Association, Sojourner Truth lived with well-off, well-educated people of a political turn of mind. She encountered Garrisonian reform and learned it practically at the source, for George Benson, one of the Northampton Association's leaders, was William Lloyd Garrison's brother-in-law. Garrison and other abolitionists and feminists, including Frederick Douglass, visited frequently.

Douglass and Truth did not agree on strategies of self-representation, for while he educated himself from books and remade himself into a gentleman, she did not try to become a lady. Nonetheless the Northampton experience influenced the direction of Truth's career. The success of Douglass's 1845 autobiography, *Narrative of the Life of Frederick Douglass, An American Slave* probably inspired Truth to dictate a narrative of her own, *The Narrative of Sojourner Truth* (1850), which she sold on the antislavery and women's rights lecture circuit for 25¢ per copy.

Although Truth's ways of knowing, believing, and expressing herself place her among scores of black and white women itinerant preachers who were her contemporaries—such as Jarena Lee, Sally Thompson, Molancy Wade Parker, Zilpha Elaw, Harriet Livermore, and Rebecca Cox Jackson—this evangelical tradition has not been as historically salient as that of antislavery feminists. While feminists in the late nineteenth century self-consciously published their documents and constructed their history, the memory of antebellum itinerant women preachers was lost, from the histories of both American Christians and independent women.

Had Sojourner Truth not attracted the attention of antislavery feminist women writers, her name, alongside those of Rebecca Jackson and Harriet Livermore, would also have disappeared long ago.

The process of preserving the persona of Sojourner Truth in American history began in Northampton, where Olive Gilbert, Truth's fellow utopian, wrote down the text that Sojourner Truth had printed in 1850 as *The Narrative of Sojourner Truth*. In 1853, Truth approached Harriet Beecher Stowe, author of the antislavery best-seller *Uncle Tom's Cabin*, for a promotional statement to use in the second printing of her *Narrative*, which she received. Ten years after Sojourner Truth had asked Stowe for a blurb, Stowe published a profile of Truth in the *Atlantic Monthly*, entitled "Sojourner Truth, the Libyan Sibyl."

Mining the vein that had produced her black characters in *Uncle Tom's Cabin*, Stowe made Truth into a quaint and innocent exotic who disdained feminism. Stowe also made careless mistakes: She wrote, for instance, that Truth was dead. One of Stowe's readers was a far more radical antislavery feminist named Frances Dana Gage, who had chaired the women's rights convention that met in Akron, Ohio, in 1851, where Truth had come to sell her newly published *Narrative*. Less than a month after the appearance of Stowe's "Libyan Sibyl," Gage published the account of Truth that is so familiar today:

> Well, chillen, whar dar's so much racket dar must be som'ting out o' kilter. I tink dat, 'twixt the niggers of de South and de women at de Norf, all a-talking 'bout rights, de white men will be in a fix pretty soon. But what's all this here talking 'bout? Dat man over dar say dat woman needs to be helped into carriages, and lifted over ditches, and to have de best place eberywhar. Nobody eber helps me into carriages, or ober mud-puddles, or gives me any best place; [and, raising herself to her full height, and her voice to a pitch like rolling thunder, she asked,] And ar'n't I a woman? Look at me. Look at my arm, [and she bared her right arm to the shoulder, showing its tremendous muscular power.] I have plowed and planted and gathered into barns, and no man could head me—and ar'n't I a woman? I could work as much and eat as much as a man, (when I could get it,) and bear de lash as well—and ar'n't I a woman? I have borne thirteen chillen, and seen 'em mos' all sold off into slavery, and when I cried out with a mother's grief, none but Jesus heard—and ar'n't I a woman?

Rendering Truth's speech in dialect, Gage made Sojourner Truth into a feminist emblem by stressing Truth's strength and the clash of conventions of race and gender. Gage also invented the refrain "and ar'n't I a woman?"

with which Truth is now so closely identified. Gage's rendition conveys the gist of Truth's 1851 statement, but the unforgettable, metonymic tag line around which the report revolves is Gage's, not Truth's. By transforming the power of Sojourner Truth the itinerant preacher into the eloquence of Sojourner Truth the antislavery feminist Gage made Truth into a hero who would be attractive to secular-minded reformers well over a century later, long after Harriet Beecher Stowe's naive figure of Sojourner Truth had become anachronistic.

If not in her persona, Truth in her life belonged to a marginal religious tradition that has been more hospitable than mainstream denominations to the abilities of poor black women: the holiness or sanctified movement, as embodied, notably, in the Shakers, the Christian Connection, the Freewill Baptists, and, in the twentieth century, the Church of God in Christ. Late nineteenth- and twentieth-century holiness beliefs have much in common with the early nineteenth-century Perfectionism of Sojourner Truth, James Latourette, her mentor in New York City in the early 1830s, and John Humphrey Noyes, Latourette's self-declared competitor and founder of the Oneida commune. Until they became institutionalized and began to seek respectability, these unconventional Christian groups welcomed women as preachers and leaders, if not as ordained clergy.

By valuing the knowledge that speaks through the inner voice rather than formal instruction and by prizing inspired preaching and singing, unorthodox sects have nourished people who were the poorest and most vulnerable in the nation. The conviction that Jesus was on her side emboldened Sojourner Truth to take to the roads and preach her message, which came to her directly from the Spirit. Religious faith healed Sojourner Truth's childhood wounds and made her radicalism possible, for virtually no other means could empower a poor black woman who had been a slave. Sojourner Truth's religious faith gave her a public voice, first as a preacher, then, as resistance to women preachers stiffened in the 1850s, as an abolitionist and feminist.

Truth and her daughters moved to the antislavery and reform center of Battle Creek, Michigan, in the mid-1850s. For several years she lived in her third intentional community, the commune of Progressive Friends called Harmonia. Coincidentally Battle Creek also welcomed a remnant of the Millerite movement, which after the Civil War organized as Seventh Day Adventist Church, under the leadership of another inspired woman, the prophetess Ellen White.

After the Civil War, Truth's uncompromising feminism estranged her from her black abolitionist colleagues. Although Truth had not been controversial before the war, she belonged to a small minority of African-

American abolitionists who in 1867 opposed the ratification of the Fourteenth Amendment until the deletion of the word "male." Most agreed with Frederick Douglass that it was the hour of the Negro, and that black men should vote even if women could not. Truth disagreed, maintaining that if women were not enfranchised, black men would continue to tyrannize black women. As with most utterances regarding intraracial gender politics—which tend to aggravate blacks and puzzle whites—this statement is not widely quoted.

In the 1860s Truth was in Washington, D.C., where she met President Abraham Lincoln and worked with other abolitionist women in freedpeople's relief at Freedmen's Hospital and the Freedmen's Village at Arlington Heights, Virginia. Truth was active in public life for many more years, during which she advocated the cause of ex-slave refugees, but this part of her history has not captured African-American or feminist imaginations. After she had become discouraged about the future of unemployed and impoverished freedpeople in the District of Columbia, she and colleagues in Battle Creek, Michigan, and Rochester, New York, helped several freedpeople relocate where they could find employment.

As this piecemeal undertaking could not solve the overwhelming social and economic problems of the black poor in the Washington area, Truth conceived of a plan by which freedpeople would be allocated government lands in the West. In 1870 she had a petition drafted to submit to Congress and solicited hundreds of signatures. In the following year she accepted an invitation from a supportive Kansan and visited the state that eight years later would become the goal of migrants from the Deep South fearing reenslavement after the end of Reconstruction. Truth was never able to persuade Congress to take action on her petition.

By the time of the Exodus to Kansas of 1879, however, Truth's health had deteriorated badly. The grandson who had accompanied her and written letters for her over the years had died in Battle Creek in 1875. She remained a tourist attraction in Battle Creek, even during her physical decline. After several years of painful suffering, Truth died in Battle Creek in 1883 of ulcerated sores on her legs, perhaps from diabetes or gangrene. Her longtime friend Frances Titus, who had compiled the 1875/78 edition of *The Narrative of Sojourner Truth and Book of Life*, which has been the most frequently reprinted edition of the *Narrative*, prepared a final, memorial edition of 1884 that included Truth's obituary. Although Truth has one of the largest markers in the Battle Creek cemetery in which Ellen White is also interred, few Americans recognize either the kindred nature of their gifts to American public life or the existence of a spirited antebellum cohort of itinerant women preachers who overturned the dictum that God speaks only to men.

Suggested Readings

Jacqueline Bernard, *Journey toward Freedom: The Story of Sojourner Truth*. 1967. New York: Feminist Press, 1990.

[Olive Gilbert and Frances Titus,] *The Narrative of Sojourner Truth*. Boston, New York, and Battle Creek: Sojourner Truth, 1850, 1853, 1875, 1884.

Nell Irvin Painter, "Sojourner Truth," in *The Oxford Companion to Women's Writing in the United States*. New York: Oxford University Press, 1993.

———, "Sojourner Truth," in Jessie Carney Smith, ed., *Notable Black American Women*. Detroit, Mich.: Gale Research, 1992.

———, "Sojourner Truth in Feminist Abolitionism: Difference, Slavery, and Memory," in Jean Fagan Yellin and John C. Van Horne, eds., *An Untrodden Path: Antislavery and Women's Political Culture*. Ithaca, N.Y.: Cornell University Press, 1993.

5

GEORGE LIPPARD

Joseph Jablonski

George Lippard was the most phenomenal author-activist of nineteenth-century America. He rose from the streets of Philadelphia in the 1840s with scant formal education to become a popular and controversial radical celebrity. At the age of twenty-seven he founded a nationwide industrial union to campaign for reform. Amidst uninterrupted writing, editing, and publishing activities, he toured and lectured with tireless energy and mesmerizing appeal. A harbinger of lefts before there was any self-conscious left, he was a friend and admirer of the individualistic Edgar Allen Poe, on one occasion going from door to door to collect money for the relief of that poet of icy solitude. Yet an early death dealt him and his works an undeserved eclipse.

The future author was born on April 10, 1822, on his father Daniel's farm west of Philadelphia. His colonial ancestors were English and German, but it was his father's side (the Pennsylvania German) that he romanticized in his books. In 1824, loss of the farm and an accident that crippled his father sent George and his sisters to another Lippard household in Germantown near Philadelphia. There, under the care of a German-speaking grandfather and two maiden aunts, he began an initiation into the lore of the nearby battlegrounds of the Pennsylvania phase of the American Revolution.

His mother, Jemima, died in Philadelphia in 1831. His grandfather's death and the continued loss of family property forced him to follow his sisters and aunts to Philadelphia in 1832. Fortunately, he still had with him his elder aunt, Mary, who had lived through the Revolution and provided a personal link with the history of that era. Also with him still was the ancient, winding Wissahickon Creek that flowed past Germantown to the outskirts of Philadelphia. This stream, which Lippard always loved, was steeped in a romantic lore that became linked in his mind with the epic of the Revolution. The most intriguing settlers of its environs in colonial days were millenarian mystics, the Radical Pietist community of Johannes Kelpius and fellow pilgrims from Germanic Europe. Associated with this group was another community founded by Conrad Beissel at Ephrata, which he selected for special praise during his activist years, an enthusiasm which was shared from afar by Friedrich Engels.

Legends of rebellion and millenarian quests were not the whole of young George's education. He attended the old Concord School in Germantown between 1829 and 1832. In 1837 he entered Catherine Livingston Garretson's Classical School in Rhinebeck, New York, in preparation for the Methodist ministry. However, he abandoned his conventional religious studies in disgust the same year they began, returning to Philadelphia to witness his father's death that fall. Henceforth his education, which had always been primarily a self-education, was to continue in the professional offices, public houses, streets and alleys of the Quaker City.

Lippard worked as a legal assistant between 1838 and 1841, first in a private attorney's office and then for Pennsylvania attorney general Ovid F. Johnson. Ill-paid and appalled by the hypocrisy and injustices that legal staff face daily, he left that employment and accepted work with a Philadelphia newspaper, the *Spirit of the Times*. Journalism was more in keeping with his independent and outspoken character, as well as with his impoverished, semihomeless way of life, which saw him living in the streets, sharing the garrets of friends, and frequenting the sequestered banks of the Wissahickon where he could think and freely exercise his imagination.

At nineteen, Lippard was already a natural writer and journalist. He blended critical satire, reformist zeal, and intense idealism, delivered with colorful detail, wild imagination, and black humor. He was also a natural rebel who had instinctively melded the experiences of his boyhood (the steady loss of his family's property, health, and lives) with the experience of surviving in the laissez-faire ethos of postcolonial Philadelphia. Many of his first pieces targeted the corruption and follies of the wealthy and powerful from all the "respectable" professions.

Lippard inclined toward imaginative fiction, often telling the news in the words of invented personages, such as "Flib," the invisible public "nose," and "Billy Brier," the persona he assumed in his role of police reporter—always avid to prick the hypocrisies of men of the cloth or the fat wallet. After a few months of topical writing and reporting, Lippard quit the *Spirit of the Times* to try full-time fiction writing. The *Saturday Evening Post*, which later became his severest critic, published his first story, "Philippe de Agramont," in July 1842. Several typical Lippard themes were present in this gothic tale of the Wat Tyler peasant revolt of 1381, including a cry against royal taxation that resonated in the memories of his readers. His next story appeared three months later in serialized form, achieving national success in the form of reprints of the *Post* episodes. Called *Herbert Tracy; or, The Legend of the Black Rangers*, this tale was set by the Wissahickon. It dealt directly with the era of the Revolution—Patriot vying with Tory in a romantic love triangle. Published in book form in 1844, it proved Lippard's broad appeal to a mass audience that still identified with revolt against oppression.

Despite his success as a freelance fiction writer, Lippard soon (1843) took another job with a publication, the *Citizen Soldier: A Weekly Newspaper Devoted to the Interests of the Volunteers and Militia of the United States*. Contributing gothic tales, revolutionary legends, and literary criticism, he quickly became the paper's main writer and editor. One of these legends, "Jesus the Democrat," reflected an essentially socialist understanding of Christianity.

Then came 1844 and Lippard rocketed to controversial fame in Philadelphia and the nation. He published in the fall the first of ten installments of his most famous work, *The Quaker City; or, The Monks of Monk Hall: A Romance of Philadelphia Life, Mystery, and Crime*. Into this book the young author finally poured his rebellious feelings about his community and its inhabitants, both high and low. It was written with a wildly ironic abandon, verging on irrationality, that was characteristic of Lippard in his most heated expression, leading a modern-day scholar, David Reynolds, to hail him as an early American presurrealist. The paper-covered installments were aimed at a working-class readership that bought up every copy and clamored for more. In this hallucinatory tapestry of social and individual corruption, the city masses could see grotesque caricatures of leading fellow citizens. The plot was actually borrowed from the recent news, principally a trial of 1843 in which a Philadelphian was acquitted of killing a wealthy bachelor who had dishonored his sister.

The serial's instant success led a theater owner to contract with Lippard for a dramatic version. But ironically, Singleton Mercer, the acquitted man, was resentful of Lippard's usage of his story and bought up tickets with the intention of packing the play's opening with rioters. When the theater owner canceled the play in panic, Lippard's own working-class followers caused a disturbance outside the theater that brought in the entire Philadelphia police department and was quelled only through the author's personal appeal. Now that danger of vendetta had followed upon the scandal surrounding *The Quaker City*, Lippard added a sword cane to his customary Byronic cloak and attire. He let it be known that he was likely to be further armed if any other victims of his unsparing imagination cared to object. The affair also contributed to his reputation as an immoral writer in some quarters, including the *Saturday Evening Post*, but by then he had a huge following among the masses, as well as increasing support in the literary world.

Following the publication of an expanded book version of *The Quaker City*, Lippard turned again to penning legends of the American Revolution. Some of them elaborated mystical themes in keeping with Lippard's beliefs concerning the influence of German Communal Pietism on the founding and destiny of America. The Radical Pietist variant of the Wandering Jew, the Gray Wanderer, can be found in works such as *Washington and His Generals* (1847), *Paul Ardenheim, The Monk of Wissahickon* (1848), and *Adonai: The Pilgrim of Eternity* (1851). Even his exaggerated patriotism expressed a mystical exaltation derived from Lippard's belief that his country was founded on a self-sacrificial struggle for freedom and justice. Before the legends were published in books, many of them had already been related by him in extraordinarily popular lectures delivered throughout the United States. Lippard had become a conscious advocate of the doctrines he attributed to the heroes of his legends. In fact when he formed his own "revolutionary" order, the Brotherhood of the Union, in 1849, he adapted the names of the country's founders as official titles. In addition, he based the symbolism of the organization on what he knew of the mystical brotherhoods of the past: the Rosicrucians, Freemasons, and the Pietist fraternity of "The Woman in the Wilderness."

The Brotherhood's goals, however, were truly activist: to restore justice to the working classes, and to all oppressed groups and individuals. Lippard had already lent support to those causes by launching a new reform-oriented weekly, the *Quaker City* (1848). Five serial novels from his pen began to appear in this paper, covering a range of social justice themes including antislavery, women's issues, and the rights of labor.

The weekly quickly attained a circulation of 10,000 and in July, 1849, Lippard used its pages to announce the formation of the Brotherhood. Radical-minded readers nationwide responded by writing to request charters. The rapid growth of the Brotherhood, which had over 140 chapters in nineteen states before the end of 1850, paralleled Lippard's success as an author. It was a positive refutation of those critics who claimed that George Lippard was nothing more than a writer of "dirty," sensational books.

Lippard supported and helped to organize other reform currents of the time, such as the cooperative movement, Fourierism, and Wilhelm Weitling's *Arbeitersbund*, which brought to America the working-class utopian communism of a former associate of Karl Marx. He was also involved with the Philadelphia-based Daughters and Sons of Toil. This group took a number of advanced positions, including antislavery, votes for women, extension of rights to minorities (including Native Americans), and support for a drastic reform of capitalism.

Lippard organized a cooperative store for Philadelphia seamstresses in 1850, and in the same year devoted a laudatory essay in the *Quaker City* weekly to early feminist Lucretia Mott. His increasingly evident concern for the fate of women in the society of his day may have been influenced by his marriage in 1847 to Rose Newman, for whom he named a historical romance, *The Rose of Wissahickon*, alluding to the moonlit scene of their unusual wedding ceremony. However, a feminist concern was implicit in the themes of earlier books, such as *The Quaker City*, where it was mistaken by hostile critics for "prurient" interest. In fact, Lippard moved from a focus on sexual exploitation to attacking the social and economic oppression of women. He had already addressed the conditions of the Philadelphia seamstresses in his 1848 story "Jesus the Democrat." His attitude is all the more outstanding in light of critic Leslie Fiedler's analysis of Lippard as a specialist in male-oriented fiction.

Another key to Lippard's radicalization in the late 1840s was the revolutionary wave in Europe which culminated in 1848, and for which the young American had great hopes. In the novel *Paul Ardenheim* he imagined human progress toward liberation inspired by an international movement, at once popular and esoteric. As in his attempt to allegorize the spiritual essence of the American Revolution, he was here attempting to elaborate a mythos appropriate to some great future revolution uniting all races but climaxing in America. The formal ritual of his Brotherhood, which derived from the European secret societies, was more than just the reflection of an interest in alchemy and mysticism. It was intended to arm with a universal, poetic weapon the working class whose mission he had elsewhere described as "war in any and all forms," war directed "against the tyrants of the social system—against Corrupt Bankers, against Land Monopolists and against all Monied Oppressors."

Lippard the man experienced a tragic downturn in his fortunes in 1851. His wife died on May 21 following the March death of their infant son Paul. A young daughter, Mima, had died in 1849. Tuberculosis began a rapid attack on his own health. It resulted in his death on February 9, 1854, just short of his thirty-second birthday. Earlier that year he had written his last story, titled "Eleanor; or, Slave Catching in Philadelphia." Lippard's funeral on February 13, 1854, brought together thousands of those who now regarded him as a guiding spirit. Led in the procession by the great fraternal orders, who honored him for his humanitarian ideals, the throng of readers and admirers accompanied him to his resting place in the Odd Fellows Cemetery, where the first of many periodic ceremonies in his honor was held.

At the time of his death Lippard was serving as the "Supreme Washington" of the Brotherhood of the Union. His acceptance by the reform and labor movements was attested by his participation in the National Reform Congress (1848) and the Eighth National Industrial Congress (1853). The Brotherhood had gained the approval of such notables as land reformer George Henry Evans and Fourierist Arthur Brisbane, many of whose followers joined the organization. While surviving on its own in various forms for well over a century, the order (later called the Brotherhood of America) also served as a model and inspiration for newer labor organizations, such as the Noble and Holy Order of the Knights of Labor, which was founded by another Philadelphian who was influenced by Lippard, Uriah S. Stephens. Thus the tradition of popular industrial unionism in America owes a seldom acknowledged debt to Lippard's group.

Ironically, after an era of pseudosocialisms, we again find ourselves in the conditions of Lippard's "Quaker City." Greed, hypocrisy, and miserabilism are the universal order of the day. All the more reason for investigating the works of Lippard, for he knew this terrain and its human landmarks, and his oppositional spirit is badly needed. In his last full-length book, *New York: Its Upper Ten and Lower Million* (1853), Lippard returned to the urban themes of *The Quaker City*. He had already predicted his own death within a year's time; it was as if he wanted to give his readers one last shocking view of a capitalism rotting from within both morally and socially. Clearly, he wanted to encourage them to do something about it. Perennially the youngest of America's radicals, George Lippard still manages to keep us aware that when the struggle cannot continue exactly as before, it can still begin again on a common foundation, uniting the aspirations of all who suffer from *the infamy* and want to see it ended.

Suggested Readings

Emilio DeGrazia, "The Life and Works of George Lippard." Ph.D. dissertation, Ohio State University, 1969.

Leslie A. Fiedler, introduction to *The Monks of Monk Hall* by George Lippard. New York: Odyssey Press, 1970.

Joseph Jackson, "George Lippard: Misunderstood Man of Letters." *Pennsylvania Magazine of History and Biography*, no. 54, October 1930.

Ellis P. Oberholtzer, *The Literary History of Philadelphia*. Philadelphia: G. W. Jacobs, 1906.

David S. Reynolds, *George Lippard*. Boston: Twayne, 1982.

———, ed., *George Lippard, Prophet of Protest: Writings of an American Radical, 1822–1854*. New York: Peter Lang, 1986.

6

ABBY KELLEY

Dorothy Sterling

"Nigger bitch! Where's the damned nigger bitch that's going to lecture here tonight?" A red-faced man lurched down the aisle of the schoolroom swinging a club and sending candles flying in every direction. When he smashed the oil lamp on the front desk, friends helped the lecturer to escape by a side door.

"Nigger bitch" was only one of many epithets leveled at white Abby Kelley when in 1838 she left her teaching job to speak against slavery. At a time when women were expected to remain at home, silent and submissive, she traveled from New England to upstate New York, to Pennsylvania and the old Northwest, "in the holy cause of human rights." Denounced as "Jezebel," "infidel," and "man woman," ducking showers of stones and rotten eggs, she brought the facts about slavery to millworkers, farmers, and housewives.

Born in Pelham, Massachusetts, on January 15, 1811, Abigail Kelley spent her childhood in Worcester where her father scratched out a bare living on a hundred-acre farm and her Quaker mother struggled to clothe and feed a family of ten. Abby—she soon dropped the "gail"—learned the thousand and one skills a countrywoman needed; she was also schooled in the plain ways of Friends. While other girls wore buttons on their frocks and bows in their hair, she dressed in unadorned Quaker gray and pinned her chestnut hair back over her ears, a severe style which nevertheless managed to call attention to her high coloring and pretty face.

More important than outward appearance was Friends' belief in an "inner light," which placed responsibility for correct behavior squarely on each individual's shoulders. Anyone, female as well as male, who felt "a call to speak" could rise at meeting and do so. Quaker ways were further impressed on Abby when she attended the New England Friends Yearly Meeting Boarding School, now the Moses Brown School, in Providence, Rhode Island. The school and its counterparts in New York and Pennsylvania were designed to train a generation of Quaker boys to enter their fathers' countinghouses. Because Friends believed in coeducation, Abby too was drilled in arithmetic, spelling, grammar, penmanship. She memorized long passages from the Bible and eighteenth-century didactic poetry, reciting them with expression before her classmates. She learned of the Quakers' proud history of bearing witness against unjust laws and of their opposition to war and slavery. Superior though her school was to that of most American girls of her day, it had limitations: no music or fine arts, no novels, romantic poetry, or plays. A boarding school boy was punished for reciting Shakespeare, a girl for singing "Auld Lang Syne," "a very dubious song." If Quaker youngsters were matter-of-fact and unromantic, so much the better was their chance of success in life.

After teaching in Worcester for several years, Abby went to Lynn in 1836 to take charge of its Friends' school. Less than an hour from the metropolis of Boston, Lynn was buzzing with new ideas. Abby attended lectures on physiology and phrenology, heard debates on pacifism (if all killing was wrong, had the American Revolution been justified?), joined the temperance society, and became a lifelong convert to Sylvester Graham's health regime which proscribed red meat, tea, and coffee and prescribed daily cold baths.

However, the most absorbing topic was antislavery. Had a public opinion poll been taken, a majority of Northerners would certainly have said that slavery was wrong. But how and when to bring it to an end was another matter. Even devout believers in the brotherhood of man doubted the humanity of black people and the possibility of black and white living side by side in the United States. People of goodwill favored gradual emancipation (property rights, after all, had to be respected) and the deportation of ex-slaves to Africa. Abby had not thought deeply about the question until she heard William Lloyd Garrison, editor of *The Liberator* and a founder of the American Anti-Slavery Society. Garrison declared

that the slaves must be freed *immediately* and accorded the same rights
as whites. Rejecting "carnal weapons," he and his followers proposed to
overturn slavery by appealing to people's consciences through "moral
suasion." Once Northerners were convinced of the sin of slavery they
would bring pressure on the South to set free its human property.

By the time Abby arrived in Lynn the American Anti-Slavery Society
had spawned a thousand state and local societies. She joined the Lynn
Female Anti-Slavery Society and was promptly elected corresponding
secretary. The women sewed "fancy articles" to be sold at fairs and
collected signatures on antislavery petitions. Deprived of the vote themselves, they ventured into politics by petitioning Congress and state legislators to end slavery in the District of Columbia and to repeal laws limiting
the rights of blacks and Indians. As corresponding secretary, Abby was
in touch with female antislavery societies in Boston, Philadelphia, and
New York. When the big-city women called a convention to meet in
New York in May 1837, she was one of Lynn's delegates.

The Anti-Slavery Convention of American Women, held eleven years
before the famous woman's rights convention in Seneca Falls, was the
first public political meeting of women in the United States. The delegates
conducted the three-day conference with assurance and dignity, setting
an example for male abolitionists by attacking racism and urging white
women to associate with their black sisters. Abby met the older women
who emerged as spokespersons—Lucretia Mott, L. Maria Child, Angelina
and Sarah Grimké—and mingled on an equal basis with black delegates
from Pennsylvania and New York. She spoke only briefly at this initial
convention, but the following year when the women convened in Philadelphia and a proslavery mob threw rocks and brickbats through the windows
of the hall, she made her first speech. At its conclusion, Theodore Weld,
a leading abolitionist orator, urged her to become an antislavery lecturer.
"If you don't, God will smite you," he declared.

Back in Lynn, Abby tried to ignore the message of her inner light but
was finally convinced that she had a call to speak against slavery. Resigning from her school, she went home to prepare herself. Following
Weld's advice, she studied antislavery publications, memorizing facts,
analyzing arguments, training herself to think on her feet. Most Quaker
preachers spoke in a singsong voice. Abby studied rhetoric and practiced
speaking simply and with feeling. Although still doubtful of her ability,
she set out alone in the summer of 1838, traveling to villages and towns
in Connecticut where a favorite sister lived. She held meetings in churches
if ministers permitted, otherwise in schoolrooms and town halls. A handful
of local abolitionists assisted her, but a far greater number of good citizens
rallied in opposition. Some, like the club-swinging workingman who

smashed her oil lamp, supported slavery or feared to endanger economic ties with the South; others opposed "a public-speaking woman." Had not Paul ordered women to remain silent? Did not the cult of True Womanhood require them to remain in their sphere, the home? Minister after minister proclaimed Abby a Jezebel who used her beguiling voice and manner to lead men to evil.

The clerical attacks on Abby came to a climax at the 1840 meeting of the American Anti-Slavery Society when leading conservatives, largely Presbyterian and Congregational ministers, determined to wrest control from Garrison and his followers. The Garrisonians had recently formed a Non-Resistant Society (a predecessor of the twentieth-century nonviolent movement) and were refusing to participate in government or electoral politics. Bad enough that they were "no-government men," their opponents said. But when they nominated a woman, Abby Kelley, to the convention's business committee, the conservative delegates walked out, taking all of the society's assets with them. Abby was "the bombshell that exploded the convention," wrote poet John Greenleaf Whittier, as he compared her to such women as Eve, Delilah, and Helen of Troy.

Schooling herself to ignore personal attacks, Abby carried on her crusade with increasing confidence. Over the next fifteen years, she traveled across the North from New England to New York and Pennsylvania and, in 1845, to Ohio and the western states and territories. "New England's eloquent daughter" as one editor called her, won over audiences by her sincerity and deep feeling. Copying the tactics of the temperance crusaders, she spoke day after day in a country district until she had an army of converts. Starting by reminding her audiences that the Declaration of Independence had pronounced all men equal, she detailed "heart-sickening and astounding facts" of slave life. She then appealed to her listeners to come forward and sign a "Tee Total Pledge" binding them to withdraw from all organizations, including churches, which failed to demand immediate abolition. After arousing antislavery sentiment in the rural meetings where she spoke alone or with such companions as young Frederick Douglass, she then organized a convention in a nearby city and called on Garrison and other notables to attend.

Wherever she went she left antislavery societies and sewing circles in her wake. Not satisfied to have women only in auxiliary organizations, she kept a sharp eye out for potential female leaders, beckoning them to join her on the platform. Although many were too timid to address "promiscuous audiences" of men as well as women, Abby recruited Susan B. Anthony, Lucy Stone, and a core of lesser-known figures who became active in the antislavery struggle and, later, in the woman's rights movement.

Almost from her first day as a public speaker, she encountered opposition from orthodox members of the Society of Friends. Friends had "made themselves honest" by freeing their own slaves, but disapproved of joining "the world's people" in public protests. Many Friends' meetings barred abolitionist speakers and maintained separate "Negro pews." After sorrowful deliberation, Abby resigned from the society in 1841, and they in turn disowned her. Although the break meant some broadening of her interests—she read her first novel that year—her belief in the inner light remained unchanged and she never put aside Quaker ways of thinking and behaving.

While Garrison and his associates organized in New England, Abby became their eyes and ears in the rest of the North. She told them what pamphlets were needed to explain a new position, where and when teams of lecturers should be sent. Conscious of the importance of antislavery newspapers as organizing tools, she helped establish the *National Anti-Slavery Standard* in New York and, on her first trip to Ohio, sparked the publication of the *Anti-Slavery Bugle*, the voice of the Garrisonians west of the Alleghenies. She found editors to write the papers, scolding them when she thought they strayed from the correct line, raised money for salaries and printing, and sold subscriptions at every opportunity. Accepting no pay for her own labors, she became the society's prize money raiser. No meeting adjourned before she called for contributions and gave generously from her own slender means.

Among the speakers sent from New England to join Abby was Stephen Symonds Foster, a New Hampshire "fanatic" whose fiery language and aggressive tactics disturbed even fellow abolitionists. On Sunday mornings he would enter a church, interrupting the services with a lecture against slavery. When strong hands ejected him, as they invariably did, he went limp, obliging his opponents to carry him out. His career as a "steeple-house troubler" resulted in broken ribs, torn waistcoats, and sometimes jail. Abby admired his courage and plain speaking and soon came to love him. However, she postponed marriage for four years, fearful that the tie would curtail her usefulness. They married during a tour of Ohio in 1845 and continued to lecture together until she became pregnant a year later. Returning to the East, they purchased a rundown farm in Worcester in time for the birth of their daughter.

While Stephen performed backbreaking labors on the farm, Abby spent a brief period as a housewife and mother. She dearly loved her daughter, Alla, but felt guilty about neglecting the struggle. Weaning the baby early, she left her with Stephen's sister so that she could resume lecturing. It felt like death to leave Alla, she confided to Lucy Stone, but she did it "for the sake of the mothers whose babies are sold away from them."

After years in the field, the rigors of travel—riding in jolting farm wagons, sleeping in flea-bitten chambers, eating fried, greasy food—took their toll. By her mid-forties, Abby had a chronic hoarse throat (endemic to public speakers in those premicrophone days), dyspepsia, and, perhaps most troubling, false teeth. In the West, where barbers functioned as dentists, the only remedy for a toothache was extraction. Abby was only forty-six years old when she acquired a full set of dentures, but, Lucretia Mott reported, "she is fine looking yet."

After her appointment as general agent of the Anti-Slavery Society in 1857, Abby was able to lead a more sedentary life. In charge of organizing teams of speakers in New England and the West, she left home only to raise money for their expenses. Midway through her first "tour of finances," she found that the biggest contributors were turning her away. Not only were their incomes curtailed by the depression of 1857, but many were giving generously to the new Republican party, which opposed slavery in the territories but said nothing about the South. For two decades, the Garrisonians had criticized politicians as compromisers and had refused to vote or hold office. Now even Garrison was overlooking the Republicans' failure to demand immediate emancipation and was giving them tacit support. In 1860 while Abraham Lincoln stumped the North, his supporters singing "Ain't You Glad You Joined the Republicans?" Abby toured Ohio seeking support for the *Anti-Slavery Bugle*, "the only paper in all the western country that is [for] freedom." Although she pledged to make up the paper's deficit out of her own pocket, the Western Anti-Slavery Society suspended publication when the Confederates attacked Fort Sumter.

The Fosters remained on the sidelines throughout the Civil War, refraining from applauding the Emancipation Proclamation because it only freed the slaves in the Confederacy where it could not be enforced, and did not affect slavery in the loyal border states. After the war, when it became clear that amendments to the Constitution were necessary to abolish slavery forever and to protect the rights of the freedpeople, Abby came out of retirement. For the only time in her life, she entered mainstream politics, working with the Radical Republicans in Congress to secure the passage of the Fifteenth Amendment, which would guarantee suffrage to freedmen. Convinced that the vote was necessary for their very survival, she organized a campaign for ratification in the state legislatures. When the amendment became part of the Constitution in 1870, the American Anti-Slavery Society held its final meeting—and Abby Kelley broke all precedent by appearing in a new dress.

During the next decade, her main preoccupation was woman's rights. On the outs with Susan B. Anthony and Elizabeth Cady Stanton, who had opposed the Fifteenth Amendment because they believed that black men should not have the vote before women, Abby joined with Lucy Stone in the American Woman Suffrage Association and its Massachusetts affiliate. The Fosters, "those indefatigable stirrers-up of public feelings," found the suffrage meetings dull and overly polite. To prod the women into action, they initiated a dramatic new tactic, refusing to pay taxes on their farm until Abby was permitted to vote. While the sheriff seized their cows and the tax collector auctioned their farm, they kept up the protest for six years. Thirty-four thousand women owned property in Massachusetts. If even a thousand had copied Abby's example, the legislature might have authorized a limited franchise. But only one other woman refused to pay her taxes and the Fosters gave up when Stephen suffered a paralytic stroke.

After Stephen's death in 1881, Abby sold the farm and boarded with her youngest sister in Worcester. She read the newspapers avidly, corresponded with those few abolitionists who were still alive, and attempted, unsuccessfully, to write her memoirs. She died on January 14, 1887, the day before her seventy-sixth birthday. "Mrs. Foster stood in the thick of the fight for the slaves, and at the same time she hewed out the path over which women are now walking toward their equal rights," Lucy Stone said. "She had no peer and she leaves no successor."

Suggested Readings

Margaret Bacon, *I Speak for My Slave Sister*. New York: T. Y. Crowell, 1974. For young readers.

Milton Meltzer and Patricia Holland, eds., *Lydia Maria Child: Selected Letters, 1817–1880*. Amherst: University of Massachusetts Press, 1982.

Walter Merrill and Louis Ruchames, eds., *The Letters of William Lloyd Garrison*. 5 vols. Cambridge: Harvard University Press, 1971–79.

Dorothy Sterling, *Ahead of Her Time: Abby Kelley and the Politics of Antislavery*. New York: W. W. Norton, 1991.

7

FREDERICK DOUGLASS

Waldo E. Martin, Jr.

Early in his life as a young slave on Maryland's eastern shore, Frederick Douglass (born Frederick Augustus Washington Bailey, 1818–1895) came to detest slavery and thus dedicated himself to becoming free. This lifelong freedom quest likewise early on revealed its inextricable tie to full liberty for all blacks, free and slave. Douglass's deep-seated involvement in the African-American liberation struggle constituted the essential basis for his insurgent politics and his progressive vision of the United States. Out of the fire of his experiences in a white-dominated nation as a fearless black leader, he emerged as the quintessential African American of the nineteenth century. As a result, his life struggle has come to personify not merely his individual story, but even more significantly, his people's continuing liberation struggle. Douglass's primacy as a radical American leader derives from his complex and interrelated roles as African-American insurgent, exemplar, and symbol.

Douglass's radicalism transgressed many boundaries, not just those marked by race. His profound belief in universalist notions of freedom, equality, and justice fueled a varied and rich activist career. That activism in part grew out of the nurturing and knowledge he imbibed from his environment, notably the African-American societies and cultures, slave and free, wherein he matured. That the bulk of his formative experiences transpired in black communities, situated within larger white-dominated plantation and urban worlds, broadened him immeasurably. He learned early to negotiate to his own advantage within and across both the white and black worlds. At the same time, he began to question the boundaries circumscribing those worlds.

Douglass's insurgent spirit also grew out of his fundamental commitment to America's democratic promise as codified in the Declaration of Independence and the Constitution. Like innumerable oppressed individuals and groups before, during, and after his time, Douglass located much of the inspiration for his activism in the revolutionary legacy of America's founding generation. He saw himself and his life's work as building upon that tradition. Once free, he never tired of drawing upon the natural and necessary links between his people's freedom quest and that of other oppressed groups. Still, for him, the black liberation struggle, given the centrality of blacks to the national experience, epitomized the continuing struggle to realize the ideals of the Revolution. Indeed, the optimism and belief in progress which guided his life flowed from his own remarkable story of upward mobility and middle-class success as well as the inextricably bound histories of African Americans and the young American nation.

Douglass's radicalism operated on several fundamental and interrelated levels: he was a black freedom fighter and American nationalist, on one hand, and an egalitarian, democrat, and humanist, on the other. That these beliefs and some of his actions led to errors, inconsistencies, and irresolvable problems reveals imperfections in addition to both the depth of his insurgent commitment and the enormity of the challenges he confronted. Still, these explanatory categories do not capture the range and intensity of his radicalism. To do so, it is imperative to see that Douglass played various, often subversive, roles, including: rebellious and runaway slave, orator, abolitionist, feminist, autobiographer, world citizen, journalist, and politician. Ultimately, Douglass's progressive agenda demands an expansive view of American radicalism.

Douglass's radicalism can be subdivided into three overlapping phases. In 1838, at age twenty, he escaped to freedom with the help of his future wife, Anna Murray—a free black. By 1865, with both the destruction of slavery and the end of the Civil War, he had become the major spokesman for his people, a tireless social reformer, and an inveterate American nationalist. Between Reconstruction and his death in 1895, he developed into a stalwart Republican: continued to demand that the nation live up to its democratic and egalitarian rhetoric, and thus do right by his people; and increasingly called for a more inclusive view of America. The two pre-1865 phases of Douglass's career saw the activist at the height of his aggressive militancy and public notoriety. The latter phase increasingly witnessed him as a major keeper of the pre–1865 radical flame and as elder statesman.

Douglass's subversive personality dawned early. He discovered the revolutionary power of the written and spoken word well before he was ten years old. His mistress, Sophia Auld, at one point had begun to read to him and to teach him his letters, but the stern opposition of Hugh Auld, her husband, made her desist. Hugh's fulminations about the dangers of slave literacy—he argued that it would unfit them to be slaves—further convinced Frederick of literacy's power and forced him to redouble his efforts to achieve it. Consequently, he took it upon himself not only to teach himself how to read and write, but also how to do basic arithmetic, employing a variety of tricks and strategies to achieve these goals.

Frederick continually developed and employed the liberating power of the "word," spoken and written, throughout his life. At twelve, he spent fifty cents for a copy of *The Columbian Orator*, a rhetorical handbook aimed at cultivating young citizens. Frederick proved a quick and lifelong study. This guide to persuasive public speaking and the illustrative examples, notably the "Dialogue between Master and Slave," in which the latter convinced the former to free him, touched Douglass deeply. In concert with his earlier discovery of the Bible, especially its interrelated spiritual and emancipatory thrusts, he now possessed a basic intellectual framework for mounting his personal assault against slavery. Fortuitously, Father Lawson, a black lay preacher, not only furthered Frederick's biblical instruction, but also convinced him that he was foreordained to achieve greatness.

Douglass's evolving radicalism thus had religious as well as secular roots. Increasingly appalled by a proslavery and antiblack Christian theology and practice, his inveterate skepticism in time pushed him toward religious liberalism. This critical religious stance nonetheless built upon his black Christian upbringing, its ethical imperatives, and its fundamental adherence to a liberation theology. Even while more religiously liberal than the bulk of his people, he understood and related to the spiritual dimension of insurgency, especially the black liberation struggle.

Nurtured during his earliest years largely by his grandparents, Betsy and Isaac Bailey, he rarely saw his mother, Harriet, who worked on a separate plantation. His father, most likely his master Aaron Anthony, never acknowledged him. Nevertheless, he learned a great deal about familial connection, on one hand, and modes of "day-to-day" resistance, on the other, within the extended family of the slave community. He also learned of physical resistance and runaways as well as the extraordinary white violence and intimidation arrayed against his people. The resistance culture which sustained black slaves clearly sustained Douglass. That culture was proactive and inventive; it encompassed concerted physical and rhetorical effort. As an adolescent, Douglass led several Sabbath schools and informal efforts to spread the subversive seeds of religion, literacy, and knowledge. At eighteen, he led an unsuccessful runaway attempt featuring his closest male companions.

The fight between the sixteen-year-old Douglass and the infamous Covey, "the Negro breaker," vividly captured his rebelliousness. Having been sent by his master to Covey because he refused to buckle under, Frederick not only fought the much older Covey to a draw, but also he was never whipped again. From that point on, he argued, he was a man, his own man. Once free, he continued to personify the contention that progress demanded ceaseless struggle and agitation.

The principal political challenges he confronted were the black liberation struggle and the larger movement to reform America in the direction of democracy and equality. Both challenges encompassed his interrelated roles as race advocate, integrationist, antiracist, abolitionist, feminist, and Republican. Throughout his life, African-American community life fostered his political education in addition to his social and cultural development. Consequently, he continually grappled with the complexities of white power and privilege as against relative black powerlessness and subordination. That lifelong task called upon his exceptional skills as a mediator and bridge between white and black. Much of his influence and effectiveness as a national leader derived from his ability to speak to both groups at once in a shared language of democratic hope. Stressing a common humanity and an egalitarian outlook, he dwelled upon ways to empower his people, alleviate the racial divide, and ultimately strengthen all of America.

Douglass's ability to speak with the moral authority of his people's freedom quest as well as that of the contemporary social-democratic reform movement immeasurably enhanced his impact. Besides reflecting his acculturation within African-American community life, his uncommon abilities as an interracial communicator and leader reflected also his substantial, albeit imperfect, acculturation over time into the largely white world of middle-class success and respectability. From his early days as a slave, he learned how to operate within the world of white cultural expectations and to manipulate that world to his advantage. He learned how to identify well-meaning whites with whom he could work to advance their mutual interests.

Shortly after his escape to freedom, he emerged as a powerful and representative black abolitionist voice: an extraordinary orator in an age of great oratory. For most of the next ten years (1841–1851), he honed his rhetorical and organizing skills as a member of that small yet influential band of militant and mostly white abolitionists headed by the uncompromising William Lloyd Garrison. Committed to a moral suasionist strategy and opposed to struggling within a proslavery political system, Garrisonians like Douglass promoted disunionism and mounted all-out attacks on the structural supports for slavery. At the same time, having come out of the black abolitionist component of the black liberation insurgency, he brought the experiential and philosophical dimensions of his status as a black "insider" to bear on his evolving abolitionism.

The uneasy alliance between black and white abolitionists represented a significant effort in interracial coalition politics and did much to advance the abolitionist cause. That black and white abolitionists had to struggle with issues of antiblack prejudice and discrimination within their own ranks cannot be denied. Nevertheless, working separately and together, they forged a compelling critique of racial slavery in a democratic republic. Offering at best a mixed legacy about the prospects for overcoming white racism—even within a progressive social movement—white abolitionists, with the insistent prodding of their black colleagues, nonetheless pioneered white efforts to come to grips with the dilemma of race.

Douglass and his Garrisonian colleagues spoke to white, black, and interracial audiences throughout the North trying to convert them to the cause and deepen their commitment to it. Increasingly, Douglass himself spoke eloquently about issues of prejudice, discrimination, and reform concerns branching beyond race, like temperance and woman's rights, in addition to the need to overcome the monstrous evil of slavery. Strongly influenced by prevailing notions of perfectionism and progress, he offered optimism as well as invective, a sermon of hope as well as a jeremiad.

Douglass increasingly understood the need for greater independence of thought and action. Growing criticism that so eloquent a voice could never have been a slave exacerbated an intensifying need to verify his own history. A step toward self-authentication and greater independence, his classic autobiography, *Narrative of the Life of Frederick Douglass, An American Slave, Written by Himself*, appeared in 1845. In concert with a successful abolitionist speaking tour of Great Britain on the heels of its publication, he became the most celebrated and influential African American in the transatlantic crusade against slavery. Revealing an uncanny comprehension of the importance of the public persona, especially to political effectiveness, he penned two subsequent autobiographies: *My Bondage and My Freedom* (1855), and *Life and Times of Frederick Douglass* (1881; rev. ed., 1892).

In the late 1840s and early 1850s, this added self-confidence helped him to reject the antipolitical thrust of Garrisonianism in favor of political abolitionism, a movement willing to agitate against slavery working within and outside of traditional political channels. Marrying moral suasion with political action, Douglass's pragmatic abolitionism mirrored an increasingly powerful perspective within the movement. Also during this time, Douglass invigorated his ties to the black abolitionist community and began to speak more forcefully of the need for enhanced black self-reliance. More avowedly nationalistic and militant black colleagues like Henry Highland Garnet and Martin Robison Delany forced Douglass to reassess and reconfigure his leadership. For instance, the debate caused by Garnet's 1843 call for a collective slave insurrection (which Douglass opposed at the time) and Douglass's discussions with revolutionary white abolitionist John Brown aided Douglass's escalating belief that slavery would inevitably end in apocalyptic violence.

Douglass enhanced his influence and fame through his prominent career as a journalist. *The North Star* (1847–1851), *Frederick Douglass' Paper* (1851–1860), *Douglass' Monthly* (1859–1863), and the *New National Era* (1870–1874) were vital to the development and dissemination of his thinking, notably his political maturation. During the war, he was a compelling spokesman urging that the conflict be made into an abolitionist war and, in turn, urging the recruitment and fair treatment of black soldiers. The role of the Republicans in emancipation and Union victory solidified Douglass's ties to the party and made him a major postbellum advocate for sustaining its emancipationist vision. Likewise, the 1870 passage of the Republican-sponsored Fifteenth Amendment certifying the right of black men to vote further tied Douglass to the party. Even as the Republicans veered away from their exceedingly fragile commitment to blacks, Douglass did not, and he valiantly, yet unsuccessfully, fought to shift the party in a problack and progressive direction.

Douglass's service as a stalwart Republican earned him positions as U.S. marshall for the District of Columbia (1877–1881), recorder of deeds for the District of Columbia (1881–1886), chargé d'affaires for Santo Domingo, and minister to Haiti (1889–1891). Unfortunately, his continued personal ascent paralleled an increasingly vicious late nineteenth-century white assault against black advancement that severely tested his belief in America. The ubiquitous racism infecting movements like woman suffrage and labor made him considerably critical of both, especially the latter. Having been a public supporter of women's rights since the 1840s, his postbellum support for a suffrage amendment which did not include women clearly revealed that for him the racial (and male) struggles took precedence. For that, he met stern criticism from those who favored universal suffrage: a position Douglass favored but in the late 1860s thought premature.

The centerpiece of Douglass's radicalism remained his democratic and egalitarian humanism. With the help of a new generation of race leaders like Ida Wells Barnett, in his last years he launched a blistering offensive against the rising tide of white racism, especially the appalling rise in the numbers of lynchings of black men. For him, the soul and the future of America were at stake. It was not a matter of white Americans accepting "outsiders," principally blacks, into their country. Rather, he envisioned a radically different concept of America: a vastly more open and inclusive composite nationality truly belonging to all and transcending divisive categories like race, religion, gender, class, and national origin. The multifaceted and enduring ramifications of this radical vision provide an illuminating window onto the American experience and resonate profoundly in our own troubled "multicultural" times.

Suggested Readings

John W. Blassingame et al., eds., *The Frederick Douglass Papers*. 5 vols. New Haven: Yale University Press, 1979.

David Blight, *Frederick Douglass' Civil War: Keeping Faith in Jubilee*. Baton Rouge: Louisiana State University Press, 1989.

Nathan Irvin Huggins, *Slave and Citizen: The Life of Frederick Douglass*. Boston: Little, Brown, and Co., 1980.

William S. McFeely, *Frederick Douglass*. New York: W. W. Norton and Co., 1991.

Waldo E. Martin, Jr., *The Mind of Frederick Douglass*. Chapel Hill: University of North Carolina Press, 1984.

8

WALT WHITMAN

Robert K. Martin

"I am as radical now as ever," Whitman told Horace Traubel at the end of his life. A few months later he remarked to Traubel that "there wouldn't be much wealth left in private hands—that is, if my say was final." But Whitman's radicalism was individualistic; as he put it, he didn't "belong to any school." In Whitman's earlier life he had been more willing to affirm party affiliations. In 1848 he had been a Brooklyn delegate to the Free Soil convention, calling for unconditional backing for Martin Van Buren, and editing the new Free Soil paper, the *Freeman*. He gave up the venture after the office burnt, and after he had come to recognize the role of compromise in politics.

Whitman's radicalism had much in common with his age and his American roots. Radicals in America seem generally to have preferred the individual and the anarchistic to the collective and the socialist. Whitman might reject the idea of private property, but he cared too much about his self to be able to adapt to any political program. Whitman's radical origins included the utopian movements that flourished in the American 1840s. He was a great admirer of Frances Wright, the British reformer who had founded the Nashoba Community and collaborated with Robert Dale Owen on New Harmony. Wright's talks on education, birth control, and the distribution of wealth and her attacks on the church lie behind much of Whitman's poetry. Another important formative influence on the young Whitman were the views of Quaker reformer Elias Hicks. Hicks's transformation of American Quakerism brought it into line with a growing evangelism, replacing a strict code of unworldliness with an emphasis on the personal voice or "inner light." The appeal of Quakerism for Whitman was, as Newton Arvin put it, the Quakers' "spiritual independence and self-trust."

The American 1848 was not a program for political revolution, although it included a justification for resistance by individuals. It was instead a reaffirmation of American ideals of selfhood and individualism. Whitman imbibed these ideas above all from Emerson, in essays such as "Self-Reliance." It was that joining of the celebration of the individual consciousness with the celebration of the young nation that appealed to Whitman, who saw himself as the national poet Emerson called for. However much Whitman was a spiritual descendant of Emerson's, there were significant differences. Just as Whitman knew and admired the actual radicals and utopians of his day, and had himself participated in some of the moral/social crusades, such as the temperance movement, while Emerson remained aloof, so too Whitman saw himself as providing a place for the body that was strikingly absent, or derided, in Emerson's Platonism.

Whitman's vision was not merely a product of the Concord philosophers of his time, but even more of an American radical tradition, an antinomianism perhaps derived from the early Puritans and their dissenters, and from the revolutionary voice of Thomas Paine. For Whitman America's "radical human rights" were in large part the work of Paine. They were also the product of his own childhood and young adulthood. Whitman was the first major American writer to come from a working-class background that was far from the privileged elites of Boston, Philadelphia, or Virginia. Whitman was born in West Hills, Long Island, into a family of English and Dutch farmers. His father was part of the first Revolutionary generation, and subscribed to the hopes of a democratic future. A few years after young Walt's birth in 1819, the family moved to Brooklyn, where they occupied a series of houses, as Walt's father built frame houses he hoped to sell at a profit. In an age of speculation, he failed. By the time he was twelve, Walt Whitman had begun work as a printer's apprentice. After completing his apprenticeship at sixteen, he was unable to find work as a printer, and turned to rural teaching (for which he had no training and scarcely any formal education) for several terms until returning to New York to work as a printer. Whitman had lived in democratic America, and not merely its theory, and knew firsthand the dangers of a free economy as well as the possibilities of self-creation. He was also a remarkable autodidact, absorbing his reading and incorporating it into an eclectic, undisciplined body of heterogeneous knowledge. His poetry reflects his enormous storehouse of obscure information, as well as his disdain for "official" knowledges: as he would write in his greatest poem, "Song of Myself," "I have no chair, no church, no philosophy."

Whitman applied Emerson's theoretical democracy of the nation to the body, claiming a radical equality of body parts and functions. He expressed this not only as a statement of principle, "Welcome is every organ and attribute of me, and of any man hearty and clean, / Not an inch nor a particle of an inch is vile, and none shall be less familiar than the rest," but in shockingly concrete terms, "The scent of these arm-pits aroma finer than prayer." The Concord philosophers sought to escape experience by a withdrawal into a world of pure idea; nature was the site of a disembodied experience (Emerson's "transparent eyeball") of an eternal world of forms. Whitman's celebration of the radically new self was based on a recuperation of the body, and a breaking down of a body/soul hierarchy or binarism. A crucial arm in the struggle against Western philosophical idealism was the recuperation of "lower" forms. In this struggle the resistance to Western philosophy ran parallel to a struggle against Victorian prudery. In the famous section 11 of "Song of Myself," Whitman allied himself with the lonely woman observer who seeks to join in the erotic celebration of the young men bathing. The gender boundaries that normally enforce the image of the "lady" in nineteenth-century culture break down in a vision of the men touched by "an unseen hand" until they give in to the anonymous sexual encounter and "souse with spray."

That final image of an undirected seminality is crucial to Whitman's program of resistance to the antimasturbation campaign of his day. In a social context where masturbation was seen as an economic crime ("spending") as well as a moral transgression, Whitman celebrated the autoerotic, as well as the homo- and heterosexual. Well aware that the status of women was connected to the cultural silence around sexuality, he argued that "only when sex is properly treated, talked, avowed, accepted, will the woman be equal with the man, and pass where the man passes, and meet his words with her words, and his rights with her rights." A fervent believer in the equality of women, Whitman began the practice of inclusive language, insisting on "the man or the woman" rather than the generic masculine. His adoption of such language also served to mask his own homosexual desires.

Honest about his sexual attraction to other men, Whitman found himself lacking a community. Sexual encounters were probably not difficult (his notebooks include many names of young men who spent the night with him), and "bohemian" bars like Pfaff's may have provided some sort of place for homosexual desire, but Whitman found himself largely alone in his desire to understand his sexuality in a democratic culture. Nineteenth-century homosexuality was fundamentally classical, from Byron at the beginning of the century to Symonds at the end. Whitman learned about classical models of pederasty, since they were just about the only models available, but he also sought to displace them. It was in his sequence of "Calamus" poems that he sought to give expression to his desires and to theorize their nature and possible social place.

The sequence begins with that most famous of classical homosexual allusions, Virgil's second eclogue, but even here Whitman is making the landscape American and constructing a role for himself as the originator of "athletic love" and the celebrator of "the need of comrades." Although "athletic love" carries with it echoes of the Greek *gymnasium*, it is also being offered in opposition to a cultural assumption, both already existing and being constructed, of the homosexual as effete, decidedly unathletic dandy. Although's Whitman presentation of himself as the poet of homo-sexual love has made him a figure of enormous importance for later gay writers and readers, his position on desire between men has little in common with the "minoritarian" view taken by many sexual radicals in the 1960s. For Whitman homosexuals do not constitute a small group that requires equal rights; instead homosexuality is seen as the fundamental condition of a democratic society.

Whitman's influence has been enormous, and has always included a recognition of his part in the redefinition of sexual desire. Homosexual writers including García Lorca, Pessoa, Hart Crane, Jack Spicer, Allen Ginsberg, and many others have felt themselves enabled by Whitman's example. Women writers, too, although sometimes troubled by the almost exclusively male world of Whitman's imagination, have often responded enthusiastically to his affirmation of female desire and his insistence upon sexual equality. Kate Chopin's *The Awakening*, in particular, derives its heroine's sexual awakening from Whitman's model. And black writers have found Whitman's democratic poetics a source of inspiration. In the 1930s Whitman's influence on Richard Wright and Langston Hughes was considerable. Such writers saw beyond the sentimental adaptations of Whitman that had been offered by American liberals such as Carl Sandburg or Sherwood Anderson, and tried to enlist Whitman in a radically engaged struggle against racism and economic privilege.

In matters of poetic form Whitman was even more of a radical, although his transformations have turned out to be so lasting that it may now be difficult to recognize the magnitude of his accomplishment. As Ezra

Pound put it, Whitman "broke the back" of conventional meter, thus putting into practice Emerson's famous dictum that "it is not metre but a metre-making argument" that defines poetry. There were other radical attempts at redefining English meter in this period, including notably Hopkins's "sprung rhythm," but they failed to take. Whitman invented the long unmetrical line that allows him to expand, to dilate. Avoiding prose by paratactic structures and parallelism, Whitman is able to shift the spine of the poem to its left-hand margin. Only such an open form could give voice to Whitman's inclusiveness, his refusal of principles of order and subordination. His famous "catalogue" technique, or enumerative style, allows him to celebrate the thing itself, without a surrounding fabric of hierarchies of value. At the same time the very act of inclusion, in the genteel world of verse, amounts to a confrontation of the reader with the reality and diversity of experience, unfiltered by "art." His poetry is, as he put it in "Song of Myself," "the meal equally set, . . . the meat for natural hunger, / It is for the wicked just the same as the righteous, I make appointments with all, / I will not have a single person slighted or left away."

Whitman's self-presentation, as in the famous frontispiece to the first edition of *Leaves of Grass*, the book coterminous with the life that Whitman constantly rewrote and revised, was that of a worker in open-necked shirt, with arm jauntily on the hip. The poems, too, try to break away from the power of the salon, offering instead the outdoors of adventure and freedom. "Song of Myself" proclaims the natural man of Romantic origins, now physically present in an American landscape. To go outdoors was also to liberate the self, to "come out": "I will go to the bank by the wood and become undisguised and naked." Conventional life, like conventional sexuality, was a disguise: nakedness was the condition of truth. "Song of the Open Road" brought together Whitman's love for the natural world with his sense of political mission, as he adapted the French Revolutionary call, "Allons," into a call for a "greater struggle" of the self for freedom from the fixed paths. Whitman's "open road" created American space and possibility, later to be claimed by the Beats, and it associated it with what Whitman called "adhesiveness," adopting a phrenological term and making it into a name for a love of men that was casual, spontaneous, and omnipresent, "the talk of those turning eyeballs."

Although Whitman's indifference to the proprieties alarmed many of his literary colleagues, he found a warm response among many readers. His work as a nurse in the Civil War brought out his qualities as friend and caregiver. The letters between him and the wounded soldiers are an extraordinary testimony to the power of his sympathy to cross lines of class, and in an age before the sharp demarcation of kinds of desire, to offer loving affection to the men in his care. These men, often barely literate, were moved by Whitman's care and kept in touch with the poet even after they returned to civilian life and, in most cases, marriage. The war tested Whitman's faith in the power of the American democratic vision, but he emerged from it convinced that liberty cannot be obtained by legal documents, but only with "manly affection" that can tie the states with "the love of lovers."

Whitman's dream of national unity and his vision of friendships across class lines made him a powerful attraction for English socialists of the late nineteenth century. Edward Carpenter did more than anyone to apply Whitman's ideas and poetic practice, and tried to develop a community of lovers devoted to social and sexual equality. In his Whitmanlike poem *Towards Democracy* and in essays such as *Love's Coming of Age* and *The Intermediate Sex*, Carpenter developed a social critique based on the adaptation of feminist and socialist theory. The views of Carpenter and his colleagues in Sheffield, joining as they did multiple reform movements and utopian strains, looked back to the same kind of radical impulse that had given rise to Whitman, but they were increasingly removed from a socialist movement now linked to trade unionism and uninterested in sexual reform. The last gasp of this line of influence, at least during this period, came in E. M. Forster, whose final novel, *A Passage to India*, records the impact of Carpenter on the young Forster and the novelist's attempt to imagine the power of an interracial, intercultural male friendship to overcome imperialism and racism. But Whitman's India, apparently untouched by the colonial experience, seemed unattainable. So too the poets of the 1950s could only look back to Whitman with a sense of loss. Allen Ginsberg could find the older man only in "a supermarket in California," the American dream gone sour. It would take a still later generation of poets, such as Marlon Riggs, to recapture something of Whitman's original sense of possibility. In his "Tongues Untied" the ability to find a voice, to speak for the speechless and silenced, which Whitman had taken as his task, becomes real again. Whitman's lasting power has remained one of enablement, of allowing the excluded to speak: "I act as the tongue of you, / Tied in your mouth, in mine it begins to be loosen'd."

Suggested Readings

Newton Arvin, *Whitman*. New York: Macmillan, 1938.

Justin Kaplan, *Walt Whitman: A Life*. New York: Simon and Schuster, 1980.

Paul Zweig, *Walt Whitman: The Making of the Poet*. New York: Basic Books, 1984.

9

ELIZABETH CADY STANTON

Ellen Carol DuBois

Elizabeth Cady was born in Johnstown, New York, on November 15, 1815, to Daniel Cady, an influential legal reformer, and Margaret Livingston Cady, a member of one of the state's wealthiest families. Elizabeth's only brother died young, and she strove, futilely, to replace him in her father's estimation. She received the best education available to young women at the time, at Emma Willard's Troy Academy, but resented the fact that only men could attend college. Like other young women of leisure, she spent the years between school and marriage in visiting and socializing, but with a difference: she did so in the home of her maternal cousin, the influential abolitionist and reformer Gerrit Smith. There she fell in love with the life of the reformer and with one reformer in particular, Henry Brewster Stanton. An older, romantic figure, Henry was a great orator and bold organizer, Theodore Weld's second in command in the campaign to "abolitionize" the North. Despite her family's opposition, Elizabeth married Henry in 1840. They had seven children and what Elizabeth judged to be a relatively satisfactory marriage, but over the years their relative positions shifted dramatically; within two decades, it was Elizabeth, not Henry, who was becoming widely known as a visionary and reformer.

In 1840, on the occasion of her honeymoon trip with Henry, Elizabeth met Lucretia Mott, the leading woman abolitionist in the United States. Mott had come to London, as had Henry Stanton and his bride, to attend the World's Anti-Slavery Convention. There, American women abolitionists, led by Mott, tried and failed to be admitted as delegates to the convention, which British abolitionists and their conservative American allies were determined to keep exclusively male. This experience helped to crystallize Elizabeth's rage at women's subordination, even as it served to introduce her to the woman under whose guidance she would enter into the Anglo-American tradition of women's rights.

Eight years later, in the international revolutionary year of 1848, Stanton and Mott called the world's first women's rights convention. It was a small affair, involving a hundred participants, all Quaker (except Stanton, whose own faith was somewhere between Episcopalianism and free thought) and was held in the small manufacturing town of Seneca Falls, New York. The Stanton family had moved from Boston to Seneca Falls in 1843 and Elizabeth, now with four sons and a husband who was frequently away in Albany or Washington engaged in the exciting world of politics and reform, had grown intensely restive under her domestic confinement. Her response was to turn her discontent outward, to identify the social, economic, and political structures that maintained women's inferiority. She drafted a Declaration of Sentiments, modeled on the Declaration of Independence, which condemned the history of men's tyranny over women. At the Seneca Falls convention, Cady Stanton insisted on highlighting a demand that even her mentor, Mott, resisted: women's "sacred right to the political franchise," which eventually became the linchpin of the American women's rights movement.

Three years after the Seneca Falls convention, Elizabeth Stanton met Susan B. Anthony, a younger Quaker abolitionist and teacher from nearby Rochester, who quickly became devoted to her and to the women's rights enterprise. Their first joint effort was within the women's wing of the New York temperance movement, but they soon learned that they would have to undertake a far more ambitious task, to form their own political movement to advance their radical ideas about women's equality. Stanton schooled Anthony in politics and reform, while Anthony helped Stanton through the birth and rearing of the last of her seven children (including two daughters, long awaited.) Their collaboration, which remained more or less firm throughout the rest of their long lives, was crucial to the growth of women's rights sentiment in the nineteenth century. To simplify their complex interaction, Anthony brought a great faith in women's capacity to cooperate and change while Cady Stanton offered a uniquely clear vision of radical alterations in women's place in the world and their relationship, both public and private, with men. In the pre–Civil War years, their focus was on securing equal economic and legal rights for married women. In 1854, Cady Stanton addressed the New York Legislature on an omnibus women's rights bill, backed up by petitions that Anthony had gathered from women all over the state. In 1860, these efforts were rewarded with the passage of a comprehensive Married Women's Property Act in New York, which secured to wives their rights, not only to property, but to wages and to the custody of their children on divorce.

The Civil War and Reconstruction drastically altered the political world in which Stanton and Anthony operated. The abolition of slavery highlighted issues of citizenship, questions of enfranchisement became paramount, reformers' attention shifted from the state to the federal level, and the links between women's rights and abolitionism were strained to the breaking point. Stanton in particular threw herself into the drama of the Civil War. With Anthony, she formed a Women's National Loyal League to pressure Congress to make abolition, not union, the focus of the war. They worked closely with the Radical Republicans to collect a half-million signatures calling for the constitutional abolition of slavery and expected, when further amendments were drawn up to secure national citizenship and enfranchisement, that the rights of women along with those of the freedmen would be constitutionally recognized. As it turned out, the Reconstruction amendments not only ignored women's demands for political equality, but, in the case of the Fourteenth Amendment, explicitly defined the basis of congressional representation as men. To protest this situation, Stanton and Anthony formed the National Woman Suffrage Association, while other woman suffragists, eager to avoid an outright break with supporters of the freedmen, formed a rival organization. Stanton was fierce to the point of racism, in challenging the acceptability of enfranchising ex-slave men before free-born white women. By the late 1860s, the long-standing alliance between abolition and women's rights, out of which her own radicalism had been born, was shattered.

Stanton's focus for the next decade was to complete the process of national reconstruction by securing the constitutional recognition of women's political equality. Along with Anthony, her first approach, called the "New Departure," rested on the conviction that the Constitution as amended and reinforced by the dictates of equal rights and natural law, already secured the full rights of national citizenship to women, certainly including the right to vote. They pursued this claim through direct action and constitutional challenge, until, in its 1874 *Minor v. Happersett* decision, the Supreme Court ruled that, while women were citizens, enfranchisement was a privilege not a right. In many ways, Stanton never gave up important elements of this approach, continuing to identify women's right to vote with the supremacy of national citizenship even after the Reconstruction era came to its end. However, from the mid-1870s on, the only course left to secure national enfranchisement was to press for the passage of another constitutional amendment, parallel to the Fifteenth, which prohibited disfranchisement by sex. Stanton authored and introduced this amendment, originally intended to be the Sixteenth, in 1878, and it was eventually passed, almost two decades after she died, as the Nineteenth Amendment.

As early as her 1850s temperance activism, Stanton advocated liberalization of divorce laws as part of her women's rights faith. In 1860, she precipitated a major debate within the women's rights movement over whether women would benefit more from loosening or tightening the bonds of marriage, during which it became clear that her own position, of liberalization, was a minority one even among other women's rights advocates. In the heady years of Reconstruction, she moved even further in this direction, insisting on women's right to sexual self-determination (which she called "self sovereignty") and encouraging women to take deliberate measures to avoid becoming pregnant. During this period, she became associated with the free love radical Victoria Woodhull, whose notoriety reached its pinnacle in 1872 when she made public the adulterous triangle known as the "Beecher Tilton scandal." These events, which resulted in the triumph of a newly repressive public attitude to sexuality, tainted Cady Stanton's leadership and added to her marginalization among the growing number of woman suffragists, many of whom were far more concerned than she to maintain their reputation for respectability.

Through the 1870s and 1880s, Stanton traveled throughout the United States as a popular lyceum lecturer (she used her earnings to send her children through college). Her vision of women's emancipation was crowned by enfranchisement but not limited to it. She was intensely interested in women's higher education and one of her most popular lectures was entitled "Our Girls." She also spoke and wrote about enlightened motherhood, which she regarded as an avenue for women's authority and self-development. Both concerns came together in the pride she took in her own children, especially her two daughters, both of whom were college graduates. She became particularly close to Harriot, her sixth child, who was preparing to follow in her mother's footsteps and to become, after Cady Stanton's death, a leader in the movement for women's emancipation and enfranchisement. After 1883 Harriot lived in England, and Elizabeth spent long periods there, raising her grandchildren and extending her women's rights sights beyond national horizons. In 1888, she and Anthony organized an International Council of Women, in 1890 formalized into a permanent organization, ironically one in which the demands for woman suffrage were subordinated.

The reform passion of Stanton's final years was free thought, which alienated her even further from the mainstream women's movement. Her deep dislike of organized religion, especially evangelical Protestantism, grew out of her traumatic experience with conversion when she was young. In the 1880s, while in England, her hostility to organized Christianity was reawakened by the influence of British freethinkers, positivists, and biblical critics. Trying to understand the stubborn hold that ideas about women's inferiority continued to have, despite decades of women's rights agitation, she decided that the answer lay in the patriarchal character of Christianity, its centuries of teaching about women's subordination, and especially its suspicion of women's sexuality. Back in the United States she found that the Christian reform movement was attempting to close public institutions on the Sabbath, roll back divorce liberalization, and even establish Christianity as the State religion; determined to oppose its efforts, she found herself on a collision course with the Women's Christian Temperance Union, a new generation of woman suffrage leaders, and even her own comrade Susan B. Anthony. In 1898, she published *The Woman's Bible*, an irreverent but scholarly critical commentary on the Bible from a feminist perspective, for which the suffrage organization that she had formed thirty years before voted to censure her. Embittered, she nonetheless continued to write, speak, and agitate for women's emancipation until her death in 1902.

Suggested Readings

Ellen Carol DuBois, *Feminism and Suffrage: The Emergence of an Independent Women's Movement, 1848–1869*. Ithaca, N.Y.: Cornell University Press, 1978.

Ellen Carol DuBois, ed., *Elizabeth Cady Stanton, Susan B. Anthony: A Reader*. Boston: Northeastern University Press, 1992.

Eleanor Flexner, *Century of Struggle: The Women's Rights Movement in the United States*. Boston: Athenaeum, 1968.

Elizabeth Griffith, *In Her Own Right: The Life of Elizabeth Cady Stanton*. New York: Oxford University Press, 1984.

Elizabeth Cady Stanton, *Eighty Years and More: Reminiscences, 1815–1897*. Boston: Northeastern University Press, 1992.

10

EDWARD BELLAMY

Daphne Patai

"The title of every man, woman, and child to the means of existence rests on no basis less plain, broad, and simple than the fact that they are fellows of one race—members of one human family." This sentiment, expressed in Edward Bellamy's utopian novel *Looking Backward* (1888), one of the great best-sellers of the nineteenth century and a book that disseminated Bellamy's vision worldwide, synopsizes the philosophical and social grounds of the radical economic egalitarianism to which Bellamy devoted the last ten years of his life.

Looking Backward: 2000–1887 tells the story of a wealthy Bostonian, Julian West, who wakes up in the year 2000 to a new world in which a nonviolent revolution has done way with both the wage and the dole, class conflict and exploitation, war, crime, sexual exploitation, environmental pollution, and all the other ills that plagued Bellamy's day. Instead, society has been reorganized by the principle of absolute economic equality, and government merely coordinates industrial production and distribution. Political democracy, which Bellamy contended is a sham without economic democracy, has become a reality. From this fundamental transformation of society flow many additional benefits: production for use instead of for profit; a redefinition of work so that it takes up but a small part of each individual's life; respect for nature and, especially, wilderness; assurance of conditions that foster the health and well-being of all; education aimed at the "highest possible physical, as well as mental, development for everyone."

Attempting to name this homegrown form of socialism untainted by the violence and class warfare of the European revolutionary tradition, Bellamy opted for the term "Nationalism." Though his vision was in fact international (and found resonance throughout the world), its essence was the idea of the nation taken to its logical conclusion. The call to national solidarity already underlay the political, judicial, and military systems of all modern states, he argued. It only remained to extend this appeal to the citizen's right to economic security. "The demand of the nation upon all is equal," Bellamy wrote in one of his "Talks on Nationalism," published in the *New Nation,*

> but where there is inability, either partial or complete to fulfill the demand, the nation does not, therefore, diminish its service of protection toward the citizen. The army fights for him though he cannot fight, and the taxes are spent for him though he can pay none. It is not possible that any other law should prevail under a national organization of industry.

Behind this extension of the idea of the nation to the guarantee of economic rights lay Bellamy's fundamental challenge to America's self-image as a country of individualists. No one is self-made, Bellamy asserted; we are all equally heirs to the past and equally deserving of all that our society can provide. Bellamy's belief that a shift of focus from the individual to the group did not require recourse to revolutionary politics was an important part of his public appeal in the years immediately after the Haymarket Riot of 1886 and the nation's first Red Scare. Always nonviolent, Bellamy offered a solution couched in essentially historical terms. The late nineteenth-century consolidation of capital, manifest in the economic power of trusts, contained within itself, he said, the seeds of a better future; now the entire nation could be organized into one great trust of which each person—man, woman, child—would hold an equal share in the form of a credit card, to be issued at birth and replenished yearly. Public ownership and control of the means of production was the linchpin of Bellamy's vision. On the model of the "national" organization that already governed the structure of military life, he imagined an "industrial army"—a concept perhaps borrowed from the *Communist Manifesto*—as the fundamental organizing principle of his future United States.

This, in turn, led critics to see Bellamy as an authoritarian technocrat, a view that a careful reading of his works, particularly those of the 1890s, should dispel.

Like other utopian visionaries as distant as Thomas More, Bellamy found the possibility of change not in human "nature" but in social institutions. As expressed in his famous simile of the rosebud, unable to grow in a marsh but capable of blooming when transplanted to healthy soil, Bellamy's belief was that human beings respond rationally to their environment. It was social institutions, therefore, that needed to be altered if the anxiety that drives rapacious accumulation and the ensuing indifference to one's fellow beings were to cease to be common, indeed reasonable, forms of behavior.

Bellamy's scathing attack on the capitalist excesses of his time came from his deep-rooted conviction that ordinary human beings, condemned to a life of labor in conditions of the utmost insecurity, threatened by unemployment and ill health, could not fulfill their true potential. Never one.to cast personal blame, he saw the roots of the problem as inherent in social and economic structures that pitted capital against labor for the sake of private profit. But in the industrial forces that were rapidly changing American life, Bellamy glimpsed the possibility of a massive and unprecedented transformation. The absolute economic equality projected by this great change was never an end in itself to Bellamy, however. It was to be a precondition for setting free those creative and spiritual energies that give true significance to life.

Who was this man whose vision sparked a worldwide social movement? Born on March 26, 1850, in Chicopee Falls, Massachusetts, Bellamy was the son of a liberal Baptist minister and his devout and austere wife. Maria Bellamy, well educated and high-minded, committed to studying and constant religious observance, was the strongest influence on Bellamy. Reserved and reticent like his mother, he grew up with a desire to escape the limitations of human selfishness by serving humanity. He also found in his native place the roots of his later critique of exploitative capitalism. During his youth, Chicopee Falls was developing into an industrial town, and the Bellamy house (in which he was to live his entire life) was not far from the cotton mills and tenements of the factory workers, and from the elegant homes of the owners, whose power he described as "feudal." It was this power that was transforming Chicopee Falls into a factory city characterized by ugliness and ever sharper class divisions. While his writings in some respects express nostalgia for a small-town America already fading as he was growing up, Bellamy knew that, although one could look backward, one could not go backward. One must imagine something different: the only way out of the competitive nightmare, he came to believe, was to reject private capitalism and the "inferno of poverty beneath civilization" it produced.

By 1873, the religious intensity of his adolescence having waned and after experimenting with a number of philosophies and creeds, Bellamy had developed his "religion of solidarity," which held that all men are brothers because all contain in them a spark of the divine. Drawing on his wide readings—of Plotinus, Epictetus, Marcus Aurelius, Emerson, Whitman, Swedenborg, Comte, and many others—Bellamy contrasted the impersonal self or divine essence, which impelled men to self-sacrifice and service to humanity, with man's selfish appetite and individuality. In this way he combined the ideals imbibed from his mother with the fruits of his introspection and his growing habit of social criticism. Lifelong consistency of ideals and purpose was a characteristic of Bellamy. In his maturity, in 1887, he reaffirmed ideas he had advanced in his 1873 essay on the religion of solidarity, and they are evident as well in his utopian novels.

Unable to serve his country by following a military career (he did not pass the physical examination required for entry into West Point), Bellamy entered Union College in Schenectady, New York, for a brief time. After a year spent in Europe, he returned to Massachusetts and began to study law, passing his bar examinations in 1871. But he found lawyering an uncongenial profession, one he was later to criticize as a mainstay of the plutocracy. He had been writing since his early adolescence, and his first known published article, "Woman Suffrage," appeared in the March 1871 issue of a radical weekly, the *Golden Age*. In 1872, he went to work as an editorial writer and literary editor for the *Springfield Union*. Ill health ended this activity in 1877, but by then Bellamy was already seriously embarked on his career as a writer. From 1875 to 1889 he published twenty three short stories in some of the major magazines of his day, *Scribner's, Atlantic Monthly, Harper's Monthly,* among others. For the most part these were speculative and supernatural tales, and they made his name known even before the publication of *Looking Backward*. Between 1878 and 1884 he published four novels, bringing him further attention. *Dr. Heidenhoff's Process* (1878–79), an engrossing psychological fantasy that turns on the tragedy of social stigma and its persistence in memory, elicited lavish praise from William Dean Howells, who judged Bellamy to be the literary successor to Hawthorne. In the historical novel, *The Duke of Stockbridge* (1879), Bellamy gave the first accurate portrayal of the causes of Shays's Rebellion, located in the frustrations of debt-ridden farmers who, having fought in the Revolution, found themselves in the late 1780s at the mercy of plutocrats. Following this came his period of greatest productivity, which lasted but a short time. Always frail in health, Bellamy died of tuberculosis on May 22, 1898.

Bellamy's fame was without doubt due to his political vision, but this should not cause his commitment to the life of the imagination to be overlooked. In tales of science fiction and fantasy he explored the workings of memory, imagination, the psyche, altered physical senses and states of consciousness, always adopting the odd angle of vision that brought new aspects of reality into focus. These continued to be important aspects of Bellamy's major novels (as *Looking Backward*'s secondary theme, the transformation of Julian West, reveals). But once he had turned his attention more intensely toward the need for broad social change, larger plans for his literary work emerged. Bellamy commented on his decision not to continue as a successful writer of short fiction in a letter to Horace Scudder, editor of the *Atlantic Monthly,* in 1890, two years after the publication of *Looking Backward*: "My eyes have been opened to the evils and faults of our social state and I have begun to cherish a clear hope of better things." In other words, Bellamy was radicalized by his own novel. Though revived by conservatives, his message clearly struck a chord of public sympathy.

And that sympathy was, it turned out, deep. The publishing history of *Looking Backward* is extraordinary: by 1897, the novel had sold over 400,000 copies in the United States alone, and it had been translated into more than two dozen languages. It also spawned Nationalist Clubs all over the world, including 165 chapters in the United States—the first in Boston in late 1888. Dedicated to educating the public in the reforms advocated by the book, these clubs initially enjoyed a largely middle-class membership of lawyers, journalists, artists, doctors, and business-men. Their moderate reformist agenda was promoted in a didactic journal, the *Nationalist,* which presented Nationalism as a movement not *of* but *for* the proletariat. The membership of well-bred reformers such as Edward Everett Hale, Thomas Wentworth Higginson, and Mrs. Frances E. Russell testified to the appeal Nationalism had in the late 1880s to intellectuals disillusioned with their previous reformist affiliations. This first, mild phase of Nationalism was said to have merely put "the silk hat on socialism."

A second phase—no longer aimed at education but at political action—was inaugurated by Bellamy himself with the launching of the weekly *New Nation* in January 1891. *Looking Backward* had attracted large numbers of working-class readers. In turn, the increasing presence of workers in Nationalist activism caused the movement to change. Instead of the edifying dullness of the monthly *Nationalist,* for which Bellamy himself had little respect, the *New Nation,* in which he saw a propaganda organ capable of more directly advancing Nationalism's political aims, was a lively and practice-oriented journal. It soon became active in agitating on behalf of the People's party or Populists, formed in 1891, whose platform owed much to Bellamy's ideas. Writing in the first issue, Bellamy announced that the purpose of the weekly was to "criticize the existing industrial system as radically wrong in morals and preposterous economically," and to "advocate the substitution, therefore, as rapidly as practicable, of the plan of national industrial cooperation, aiming to bring about the economic equality of citizens, which is known as nationalism."

Throughout the 1890s, Bellamy moved steadily leftward in his writings. A cultural critic in the broadest sense of the word, he touched on a vast range of concerns; virtually no aspect of late nineteenth-century life went unrecognized in his utopian novels and his extensive journalism. As his commitment to a transformative politics deepened, he abandoned his earlier disparagement of labor parties and his criticism of socialism; Nationalism, he now wrote, was "the only really practical labor party in the world" and "the most radical form of socialism." Having absorbed the criticisms of *Looking Backward* made by feminists, Marxists, anarchists, and workers (conservative attacks on the book and on Nationalism were ignored), Bellamy expressed his renewed radicalism in his final novel, the long and didactic *Equality* (1897). Although the sequel was not nearly as successful as the earlier novel, its one-word title perfectly expressed Bellamy's passionately sought goal. *Equality* shows the progression in Bellamy's social thought, particularly in his recognition of the gender issue. Throughout the 1890s Bellamy had been arguing that Nationalism promoted, in particular, the cause of women. He did not mince words: in the new society women are "absolutely free agents in the disposition of themselves," and enjoy "absolute sexual autonomy." *Equality* also demonstrated Bellamy's sensitivity to criticisms of his "industrial army" and its political organization, which now disappear. Instead, new themes are taken up, including animal rights and what we today call environmentalism.

Bellamy's impact was extensive and his ideas pervaded virtually every current of American radicalism, from the People's party to advocates of temperance and Theosophy. Innumerable radicals and social critics credited Bellamy for having been a major influence on their thinking. These included Oscar Ameringer, Heywood Broun, Eugene Debs, Daniel De Leon, John Dewey, Elizabeth Gurley Flynn, Charlotte Perkins Gilman, Charles H. Herr, Austin Lewis, Jack London, Scott Nearing, Upton Sinclair, Elizabeth Cady Stanton, Mark Twain, and Thorstein Veblen. But as Bellamy's ideas penetrated into the 1930s, they underwent a transformation. The economic egalitarianism at the core of his vision was stripped away while individual reformist measures were adopted by different political groups, including the New Deal. Today, his true radicalism has been all but forgotten, so far ahead was he not only of his own time but also of late twentieth-century America's prevailing sense of economic justice.

Suggested Readings

Sylvia E. Bowman, *The Year 2000: A Critical Biography of Edward Bellamy*. New York: Bookman Associates, 1958.

Sylvia E. Bowman et al., *Edward Bellamy Abroad: An American Prophet's Influence*. New York: Twayne, 1962.

Arthur Lipow, *Authoritarian Socialism in America: Edward Bellamy and the Nationalist Movement*. Berkeley: University of California Press, 1982.

Daphne Patai, ed., *Looking Backward, 1988–1888: Essays on Edward Bellamy*. Amherst: University of Massachusetts Press, 1988.

John L. Thomas, *Alternative America: Henry George, Edward Bellamy, Henry Demarest Lloyd, and the Adversary Tradition*. Cambridge: Harvard University Press, 1983.

11

JOHN MUIR

Franklin Rosemont

Few of America's public figures diverged so radically from the nation's prevailing values and institutions as John Muir; even fewer had anything close to his impact on American society. His influence, moreover, has not only endured but increased—immeasurably so in our own time. To a degree he himself would find astonishing, he has received official consecration by the very mainstream he rejected. Major publishers reprint his books in ever larger editions. Six biographies are currently in print. His home in Martinez, California, is a national shrine visited annually by many thousands of tourists. His image has even graced a U.S. commemorative postage stamp.

Muir's posthumous celebrity status was achieved partly through the efforts of less militant followers who played down the subversive outlook that guided his life. The transformation of revolutionary fighters into innocuous saints is an old story. In Muir's case, however, he himself helped set the stage for the ambiguity of his legacy. Aware that his basic ideas conflicted with long-established norms, he confined much of his sharpest criticism to his personal journals. In his published writings, even when he boldly affirmed values that he knew were incompatible with predominant social, political, and economic opinion, he rarely challenged that opinion head-on; his opposition to the existing order appeared mostly in undertones. From the 1890s on he was celebrated as an inspired "nature writer." Muir the "radical environmentalist" emerged years later, long after his death, as the problems he addressed grew more severe, and as his unpublished writings found their way into print.

John Muir was born April 21, 1838, in Dunbar, Scotland, thirty miles east of Edinburgh. His parents were descended from Highlanders. In 1849 the family emigrated to Wisconsin and took up farming.

Muir's childhood was dominated by the brutality of his father, a fanatical Christian who tolerated no book beside the Bible. Although his mother loved the raucous Highland ballads, singing them was forbidden by paternal decree. For years the lad's only respite from his father's bigotry was the joy he found in "wild nature."

Love of nature stimulated his intellectual curiosity. His clandestine reading as a child included bits of natural history by Wilson and Audubon. In his mid-teens, at a neighbor's house, he discovered poetry and found it "inspiring, exhilarating, uplifting." At once "anxious to know all the poets," he saved his pennies to buy books. Not surprisingly for a Scotsman, the works of Robert Burns were an early and lasting inspiration.

The teenaged Muir enjoyed a local reputation as an inventor. His dozens of novel devices included timepieces, waterwheels, hygrometers, a lamplighter and a self-feeding lathe. In the summer of 1860, a neighbor suggested that he exhibit some of his gadgets at the state fair in Madison, where he met a student who urged him to enter the university. His studies there in geology and botany gave him a firm grounding in science. He also enjoyed his first experience of philosophical discussion, for the University of Wisconsin in those years was a frontier hotbed of New England Transcendentalism. Jeanne Carr, feminist wife of one of his teachers and the first to recognize Muir's genius, was a particularly important intellectual guide for the young farmboy; it was at her instigation that he later became a writer.

Muir was not long at the University of Wisconsin, however, for he soon enrolled in what he called the "University of the Wilderness." A thoroughgoing pacifist—it is hard to imagine a man less suited to military life—he fled to Canada to avoid the draft during the Civil War, and wandered around the northern Great Lakes "botanizing" at leisure. Returning to the United States after the war, he found a job at a steam-powered wagon factory in Indianapolis. In March 1867 an accident at work left him agonizing and blind for weeks, suddenly aware of the precariousness of human existence. It was a decisive turning point in his life. As soon as his eyesight returned he settled his affairs and started on the famous journey chronicled in his book *A Thousand-Mile Walk to the Gulf*. When people asked him where he was going he replied, "I don't know—just anywhere in the wilderness."

Early on his walk Muir liberated himself for good from his religious upbringing, not only from the "miserable hymns" inflicted on him as a child, but from the central beliefs that define the Christian tradition. He recognized Christian theology as an intrinsically nature-despising system. The biblical notion that the world was "made for man" he found to be "a presumption . . . totally unsupported by facts." Opposition to all forms of anthropocentrism became central to his worldview. "No dogma taught by the present civilization seems to me to form so insuperable an obstacle in the way of a right understanding of the relations which culture sustains to wilderness."

For Muir, "a palm tree preached far grander things than was ever uttered by human priest." An animal rights pioneer, he carried no gun on his wanderings, and urged his friends to harm no living creature. In his journal he went so far as to say that if war should ever break out "between the wild beasts and Lord Man, I would be tempted to sympathize with the bears."

Muir abhorred what he regarded as Christianism's (and therefore Western civilization's) fundamental error—the separation of humankind from nature. Increasingly he pointed to this dichotomy as the cause of society's many woes. It was precisely the self-serving arrogance and greediness of such dogmas, he argued, that left the world's wild places, and the wild creatures who live in them, vulnerable to the horror of human exploitation. In degrading nature, moreover, humankind also degraded itself. Muir recognized, in this regard, that Christian teaching, as Karl Marx was arguing around the same time, was ideally suited to capitalism, the most ruinously exploitative of all social systems.

In Muir's vocabulary, "capitalist" and its synonyms were pejorative terms. Again and again he railed against the "devotees of ravaging commercialism," the "gobble-gobble school of economics," the system of "legal theft," and those "robbers of every degree, from Satan to Senators" who try "to make everything dollarable." His anticapitalism did not derive from books, but from his antianthropocentrism, which in turn sprang from his abiding love of wild nature. No evidence suggests that Muir ever read Marx or any Marxist. In a period when socialist agitation was much in the air, he does not appear to have commented on it. This is not too unusual, in view of most Marxists' indifference to nature, and their glorification of "productivity" and "progress" that spelled devastation to wildlife.

He was not, however, altogether unacquainted with radical thought.

He had not missed the blasts at industrialism in the works of Emerson and Thoreau, and clearly he absorbed much of the latter's anarchism. He had at least a smattering of knowledge of Henry George's land-reform theories, and for a time attended meetings of the Grange, the radical farmers' movement. He was particularly interested in John Ruskin, whose radicalism, like Muir's, had deep roots in poetry. Ruskin excoriated the degradation of natural beauty by a machine-mad social order that put profits before all else. Hostile to a technology out of control and to what he regarded as the inherent misery of modern cities, Ruskin was sensitive—as few then were—to the problems of air and water pollution as well as human overpopulation. Muir's program took up these themes.

None of the social critics who influenced him, however, were wild enough for Muir. His single-minded devotion to wilderness, and his certainty that the *direct experience of wilderness* provided the fundamental solution to all social problems, were the alpha and omega of his radicalism. As his biographer Stephen Fox put it, Muir "hoped both to save humans *for* the wilderness and the wilderness *from* humans." Nothing less than profound communion with wild nature, he argued, could restore people's consciousness of their own true nature, so ruthlessly ravaged by industrial society. According to Muir, such words as "pollution, defilement [and] squalor . . . never would have been created had man lived conformably to Nature." Humankind's disastrous efforts to "conquer" nature he regarded as the greatest mistake of all time. In the reintegration of humankind and the natural world he believed he had found the answer to drudgery, poverty, war, disease, and the entire self-defeating routine of the daily "struggle for existence." The "hope of the world," he insisted, lies in "the great, fresh, unblighted, unredeemed wilderness [where] the galling harness of civilization drops off, and the wounds heal ere we are aware."

The key to Muir's revolutionary worldview was the concept of *ecology*. The word, invented in the 1860s by German biologist Ernst Haeckel to designate the science of the interrelations of the various components of the natural world, was used only by specialists until the 1920s when Robert E. Park and the "Chicago School" of sociology applied it, in a specifically sociological sense, to their popular studies of urban life. Not until the publication of Rachel Carson's best-selling *Silent Spring* in 1962 did ecology enter everyday speech. Although Muir did not use the term, his writings are among the clearest expressions of ecological consciousness in American literature. "Are not all plants beautiful?" he asked, challenging the conventional wisdom of his time. "Would not the world suffer by the banishment of a single weed?" In the late 1960s, when ecology became a cause and a battle cry, Muir was recognized as its outstanding prophet.

Indeed, the visionary mountaineer who signed himself "John Muir, Earth-planet, Universe" lives today in the hearts of millions as ecology's exemplary figure, the ideal "eco-warrior" whose life prefigured the radical environmentalist slogan of the 1980s: "Think globally, act locally."

By the end of the 1860s Muir had settled in the Yosemite Valley in California which remained, symbolically at least, his base of operations for the rest of his life. His ecological, antianthropocentric worldview was already well developed. From the standpoint of traditional politics—even revolutionary politics—his holistic vision had all the qualities commonly called utopian, but it has proved not only tenacious but also capable of remarkable development.

Muir considered himself a scientist; his new theory of glacial formation was laughed at by the scientific establishment for years, but eventually won acceptance. His influence on scientists, however, has been slight. What has been called the "Muir tradition" in environmentalism has consisted overwhelmingly of small bands of determined amateurs whose passionate love of the wild—and direct-action tactics in defense of the wild—has tended to put them in opposition to the conservative professionals who like to control the movement.

Well before Muir's death in 1914 the professionals had arrived, led by Gifford Pinchot, founder of the U.S. Forest Service. In glaring contrast to Muir's adoration of forests as sacred places of freedom, Pinchot defined them as "manufacturing plants for the production of wood." He was not interested in wilderness or wildlife for their own sakes, but only as *commodities* for future generations to exploit.

That Muir had nothing in common with such dismally utilitarian views is plain in every line he wrote, as well as in his wilderness-centered approach to building a movement. To advance the cause of nature's liberation he characteristically organized neither a political party nor a propaganda group, but a mountaineering club that combined public agitation and education with the actual experience of the wild. The original Sierra Club, which he founded in 1892, serving as president until his death, embodied a unity of theory and practice wholly foreign to the government-oriented, business-as-usual environmentalist organizations that dominate the field today.

Second to none as a defender of wilderness, Muir proved an effective mobilizer of public opinion in several hard struggles against nature-destroying special-interest groups—lumber barons, mining corporations, the meat industry, and so forth, all of whom received then, as they receive now, huge government subsidies to further their profitable devastation. Thanks to Muir, Yosemite Valley was saved from rampaging "developers," and there are still giant redwoods in California.

His basic plan was to save all surviving wilderness by fostering an immense system of "forest reserves" (later renamed national parks), that would be guaranteed protection forever against all commercial exploitation. His principal aim was never to elect new officials, or even to enact new laws, but rather to change people's antinatural attitudes and ways of life. He had nothing of the politician about him—his friends said he "hated politics"—and he chafed even at his administrative chores in the Sierra Club. "This formal, legal, unwild work is out of my line," he complained, revealing his preference for the informal, extralegal, and wild. Offered prestigious, well-paying positions on university faculties in Massachusetts and California, he turned them down. The foremost pioneer of the "preservation" movement, as he called it, had no desire to be a leader. Indeed, he proclaimed himself "a tramp and vagabond, without worldly ambition." Muir's radicalism basked in the pleasure principle, uncontaminated by self-sacrifice and deferred gratification. When he started on his thousand-mile walk to the Gulf in 1867 he left the work ethic behind, and lived the rest of his life free of its tyranny. Even in old age he enjoyed climbing mountains in "dancing rhythm, so that in leaping from boulder to boulder one's feet keep time to music."

His greatest contributions to the cause of wilderness preservation were the articles and books he wrote in between long sojourns in wild places. Not until the age of thirty-seven did he decide to become a writer, but from then on he was a frequent contributor to newspapers and magazines. His first book, *The Mountains of California,* appeared in 1894, when he was fifty-six. Like many of his later works—*My First Summer in the Sierra, Travels in Alaska,* and *The Story of My Boyhood and Youth*—it was hailed as a near classic in his own day, and its stature has not diminished. He wrote with the simplicity and freshness of one who has stumbled on great truths and is eager to share them.

Happily, many readers made his cause their own. From the 1930s Wilderness Society, founded by socialists Benton MacKaye, Robert Marshall, and Aldo Leopold, to the 1980s Earth First! with its motto "No Compromise in Defense of Mother Earth" Muir's defiant spirit has animated the most militant currents in the movement to save our planet from destruction.

In his questioning of industrial society's basic beliefs, and his emphasis on living a new way, Muir was a harbinger of the new radicalism that emerged after World War II and started blossoming in the sixties. At its heart was a yearning for *life* and a revulsion against repressive (unnatural) institutions. The revolution Muir dreamed of owed less to politics than to poetry, and it is no accident that poets have done so much to fan its flames. Muir is touchingly invoked, along with anarchism and the Industrial Workers of the World (IWW), in Jack Kerouac's mountain-climbing novel *The Dharma Bums*. Poets Gary Snyder and Philip Lamantia, and novelist Edward Abbey (*The Monkeywrench Gang*), are prominent among those who have heeded the call of the Yosemite Prophet in recent years.

For Muir, as for today's "deep ecologists," the cause of nature's emancipation goes hand in hand with human emancipation; they are indeed but one cause, and indivisible. Those who are out to "subvert the dominant paradigm" and live wild and free will always recognize him as a marvelous inspirer, provoker, and guide.

Suggested Readings

Robert Engberg and Donald Westling, eds., *John Muir: To Yosemite and Beyond: Writings from the Years 1863 to 1875*. Madison: University of Wisconsin Press, 1980.

Dave Foreman and Bill Haywood, *Ecodefense: A Field Guide to Monkeywrenching*. Tucson, Ariz.: Ned Ludd Books, 1987.

Stephen Fox, *The American Conservative Movement: John Muir and His Legacy*. Madison: University of Wisconsin Press, 1985.

John Muir, *The Writings of John Muir*. 10 vols. Boston: Houghton Mifflin, 1916–1924.

Roderick Nash, *Wilderness and the American Mind*. 3d ed. New Haven: Yale University Press, 1982.

Linnie Marsh Wolfe, ed., *John of the Mountains: The Unpublished Journals of John Muir*. Madison: University of Wisconsin Press, 1979.

12

EUGENE V. DEBS

Scott Molloy

Eugene Debs stands alone at the acme of the American socialist pyramid, a symbol of courage and dedication even to those not associated with the cause. Although other tiers contain the names of numerous victims of capitalist oppression, Debs's visage outshines all others. It is not surprising then that a fractured, minority political movement has sought to protect its one icon from vilification. Socialists, communists, and countless independent radicals have all lionized him in anecdotes, pamphlets, and full-scale biography.

Debs's lifespan encompassed three important periods in American social history: the Gilded Age, the Progressive Era, and the Red Scare. That timeline was punctuated by innumerable labor battles and societal conflicts, and Debs constantly crisscrossed the front lines of those insurgencies. His legendary altruism and dedication earned him a Christlike reputation that camouflaged any and all shortcomings. Debs both nurtured and fed from the ensuing mythology and, in the process, rewrote his own personal history. He became a radical, transformed almost overnight by the reading of Marx's *Das Kapital* while in Woodstock Jail in 1894. Contrary to this almost mystical conversion to socialism, Debs waged a lifelong individual struggle to break with a capitalist mindset inculcated during his formative years. His earlier antagonism to the 1877 railroad strike and the Haymarket Martyrs was spuriously altered to convey unstinting support later in his career. In reality, the Good Samaritan frequented bars and brothels and, not surprisingly, suffered from psychological problems associated with being a social pioneer.

Eugene Victor Debs was born in Terre Haute, Indiana, on November 5, 1855. His parents, recent émigrés from France, operated a small grocery store in his birthplace. The child was named after Eugène Sue and Victor Hugo, two inspirational French novelists. Throughout his long career, Debs often reflected this literary heritage by sprinkling his talks with references to the classics rather than Marxist canons.

Perhaps because of his parents' emphasis on education, Debs displayed a penchant for scholarship. However, after a year of high school, he opted for the "pluck and luck" of his generation and went to work as a locomotive paint scraper, more for adventure than remuneration. Although Debs eagerly joined and participated in the local lodge of the Brotherhood of Locomotive Firemen, he was also active in other fraternal, civic, and political organizations, including the Democratic party in Terre Haute. He continued his education at night school and embarked on a strenuous regimen of self-improvement. By the end of his teenage years, Debs already displayed a flair for oratory, a skill he tenaciously practiced and honed. In 1879 he was elected city clerk and in 1884 went to the state capital as a representative.

There was no hint of radicalism as of yet in the young Debs as he won elections with the solid backing of workers and businessmen. The schoolboy who regaled in tales of the American Revolution would eventually find a future seedbed in the labor movement but germination was a slow process. The fledgling Railroad Brotherhoods offered more in the way of sick and relief assistance than opposition to corporate ownership. The unions were preoccupied with developing an educated and responsible workforce acceptable to the railroad managers. Labor meetings resembled upper-class lyceums but with proletarian trappings. Debs assumed the editorship of the *Locomotive Firemen's Journal* in 1880 and was elected national secretary-treasurer in 1885 as his labor and political careers intertwined harmoniously.

Debs had no quarrel with these arrangements in a Midwestern milieu that offered the opportunity for rapid class advancement. He believed there was a social contract in America between employer and employee and that both parties had mutual responsibilities to one another and to society in general. Debs certainly did everything in his power to uphold his end of the bargain. On the other hand, Gilded Age captains of industry transformed themselves into robber barons and abandoned their earlier noblesse oblige to rail workers. At first, Debs chose to ignore the entrepreneurial retreat from mutuality and blamed the changing temper of the times on the misdeeds of a few renegade industrialists. The reality of the situation would slam Debs against his childhood idealism. Once experience reset his political compass, Debs would turn with fury against the industrial world order. But even long after he broke with the American two-party system, listeners could sense in Debs the yearnings for a bygone world once safe and structured with hope.

Debs turned thirty the year he became second in command of the union in 1885. A year later he railed against the unbridled militance of the Chicago anarchists as he had bristled for almost a decade against strikes, boycotts, and other forms of class mutiny in America. Outwardly Debs endorsed the status quo but inwardly he agonized over the increasing and alien power of pools, cartels, court injunctions, and a steady diet of Gilded Age wage reductions. The straw that broke the camel's back was the firemen's strike against the Burlington Railroad in 1888 when labor disunity and corporate political power torpedoed the walkout. Once Debs understood that revolutionary capitalism had overthrown the old conservative order and the social contract, his political metamorphosis had begun.

Understanding the problem was one thing, doing something about it was quite another. Although Debs reluctantly searched for an antidote, he did so with customary vigor. The perennial backbiting between the Railroad Brotherhoods, the Knights of Labor, the nascent American Federation of Labor, and the emerging socialist movement always needled Debs's sense of solidarity. He understood that union bickering was a way of life, so he sought an organizational approach that might mitigate such conflict. The concept of industrial unionism had rattled around Europe for a long time but a practical application in America was quite novel. Debs envisioned a payroll stub from a railroad—whether in actual service, mining, or some other enterprise owned by the train magnates—as a ticket into a new federated union embracing both skilled and unskilled.

Debs launched this blue-collar venture, after resigning from his beloved Locomotive Firemen, the same year as the financial panic of 1893. As railroads and financial institutions slipped into bankruptcy, he readied the American Railway Union with a cadre of rail veterans who were just as likely to hold a union card in another labor organization as the ARU. Even the eternally optimistic Debs could not have forseen the magnitude and reach of the ARU's initial victory over management. Debs employed a top-down, ironclad discipline in a nonviolent battle with the powerful head of the Great Northern Railroad, James Hill. By isolating Hill from his important transportation clients, Debs cleavered capitalist unity and pressured Hill into a court of arbitration. The judge amazingly restored the wage cuts that had precipitated the strike in the first place.

Such a victory, and a peaceful one at that, was unprecedented. There was little time to savor the outcome, however. Within months the ARU sported a greater membership than all the Brotherhoods combined as the rail grapevine buzzed with excitement over the union's brash triumph. Debs and the ARU leadership as well as the rank and file sensed a worker's nirvana, the dawning of a new era in labor-management relations.

It was not to be. The corporate iron heel that President Grover Cleveland admitted ran the U.S. government was quickly re-heeled. The industrial and idealistic juggernaut unleashed by the vanquishing of Hill, led to the affiliation with the union of striking factory workers at the Pullman car works in Chicago in 1894. Although Debs cringed at an impending show-down so quickly in the organization's history, he bowed to democratic rank-and-file sentiment. The American Railway Union voted to boycott all trains carrying Pullman sleeper cars, which were rented, not sold, to individual carriers. Railroad managers, using the fear of the upstart ARU as an organizing tool within their own jealous ranks, seized the opportunity to rid themselves of the new labor pest. Injunctions, federal troops, and the arrest of Debs prematurely smashed the experiment in industrial organizing.

Debs spent six months in jail for contempt of court charges arising from the walkout. He emerged in mid-1895 as America's first national working-class hero and, as legend would have it, a committed socialist after reading radical literature while imprisoned. Still, Debs couched his idealism and anger in the spirit of the Founding Fathers: "To the unified hosts of American workingmen Fate has committed the charge of rescuing American Liberties," he wrote after his release, "from the grasp of the vandal horde that have placed them in peril."

Although the ARU was broken, Debs gravitated to the emerging American Socialist party. His popularity and oratorical skills made him the party's standardbearer in 1900 for the first of five presidential campaigns, more agitational than electoral in nature. In a mere dozen years, and against great odds, Debs went from 100,000 votes in his initial run to almost a million by 1912.

Debs was more than just a figurehead despite staying out of the prickly philosophical battles that punctuated the left in those halcyon years. He never held office in the Socialist party hierarchy. If he remained aloof from the bureaucracy that even leftists could create, he did not shirk from the rank-and-file association that kept him close to the workers' pulse. He was at the founding of the Industrial Workers of the World, although he would shy away from leadership struggles there as well; he was an invited counsel at most of the period's major strikes; and he maintained an overwrought schedule of writing and speaking. He was a virtual free agent in the political field, operating out of his Terre Haute office with the help of his brother, Theodore, and his wife, Kate Metzel, although the marriage had been romantically estranged for years.

The Socialist party had reaped its greatest rewards during the Progressive Era when membership soared to 100,000 and hundreds of local candidates were elected to various offices. The advent of World War I demoralized the international socialist movement as national parties splintered over the combat issues. In the United States the Socialist party remained firm in its opposition to the war. The Wilson administration hectored and suppressed the party for its stand. Debs, sensing the denouement of his career and a crossroads for the party, waged a dynamic personal crusade against the European conflagration and in defense of imprisoned war critics. "I am not a capitalist soldier; I am a proletarian revolutionist," he declared in one of his most famous quotations, "I am opposed to every war but one; I am for that war with heart and soul, and that is the world wide war of the social revolution."

The government vacillated in arresting Debs for sedition fearing a backlash among the American public. Once the Allied victory was assured, federal authorities detained Debs for a standardized antiwar speech in Canton, Ohio, in June 1918. He was sentenced to ten years in prison, months after the war had ended. From Atlanta Penitentiary in 1920 "Prisoner 9653" ran for president one last time and, as in 1912, garnered another million votes. He was pardoned by President-elect Harding on Christmas in 1921. Defiantly, he lived until 1926 in the shadow of the Red Scare. By the time the left was pieced together again the Great Depression was on and the Communist party had relaced Debs's pragmatic brand of socialism.

At his trial in 1919 Debs ended his futile appeal to the judge and jury in words that serve as a fitting memorial to his own career and still provide inspiration to activists today:

> When the mariner, sailing over tropic seas, looks for relief from his weary watch, he turns his eyes toward the Southern Cross, burning luridly above the tempest-vexed ocean. As the midnight approaches the Southern Cross begins to bend, and the whirling worlds change their places, and with starry finger-points the Almighty marks the passage of Time upon the dial of the universe; and though no bell may beat the glad tidings, the look-out knows that the midnight is passing—that relief and rest are close at hand. Let the people take

heart and hope everywhere, for the cross is bending, the midnight is passing, and joy cometh with the morning.

Suggested Reading

Bernard Brommel, *Eugene V. Debs: Spokesman for Labor and Socialism*. Chicago: Charles H. Kerr, 1978.

J. Robert Constantine, *The Letters of Eugene V. Debs*. 3 vols. Urbana: University of Illinois Press, 1991.

Ray Ginger, *The Bending Cross: A Biography of Eugene Victor Debs*. New Brunswick, N.J.: Rutgers University Press, 1949.

Nick Salvatore, *Eugene V. Debs: Citizen and Socialist*. Urbana: University of Illinois Press, 1982.

13

UPTON SINCLAIR

Greg Mitchell

Upton Sinclair, muckraking author and hero of workers around the world, had notable and wealthy ancestors, including a great-grandfather who commanded American naval forces in Lake Huron during the War of 1812. His immediate family, however, was not so distinguished. Sinclair was born in a boardinghouse in Baltimore in 1878. When Upton was nine, the family moved to New York. The Sinclairs lived in one wretched apartment after another, and young Upton spent hours smashing bedbugs. One day he discovered his alcoholic father, an itinerant salesman, in a gutter down in the Bowery.

His mother periodically sent Upton to stay with rich relations in Maryland, but he despised their snobbery. Returning to the New York slums, he would ask his mother, "Why are some children poor and others rich? How can that be fair?" She had no answer.

Years later, Upton Sinclair's muckraking novels would obsessively probe the clash between social classes. Asked to explain how a world-famous Socialist emerged from such a conservative family, Sinclair described his "psychology" as that of the "poor relation." His books and political crusades would plague "the ruling class apologists of the world," as Sinclair put it—and still he received no answer to the question he had asked his mother.

"All my life," Upton Sinclair once observed, "I have had fun in controversy." He was one of the original turn-of-the-century muckrakers, that group of journalist-novelists (including Lincoln Steffens and Ida Tarbell) who exposed wretched social conditions and corporate crime. Sinclair is known today for just a single book, *The Jungle,* the classic exposé of Chicago meatpacking. *The Jungle* closed with a passionate plea for socialism as the cure for all that ailed America. "I aimed at the public's heart," Sinclair later confessed, "and by accident I hit it in the stomach."

More often than not Upton Sinclair is confused with a more literary writer, Sinclair Lewis, often to comical effect. But *The Jungle* was published in 1906 when "Uppie," as he was known to his friends, was still in his twenties, and he wrote dozens of popular and influential books for another half century. Some were so controversial he had to publish them himself. Among the institutions Sinclair muckraked: the press (*The Brass Check*), the church (*The Profits of Religion*), and the educational system (*The Goslings*). He also wrote a best-selling novel depicting the Sacco-Venzetti case, *Boston.* When it was banned from bookstores in Boston, the author sold it on the streets.

Sinclair was among the best-selling American authors abroad (particularly in Russia). "When people ask me what has happened in my lifetime," George Bernard Shaw told Sinclair in 1941, "I do not refer them to the newspaper files or to the authorities, but to your novels."

Yet Sinclair's fame and influence went far beyond his books, which didn't always sell well in this country and were often attacked by critics. Sinclair may not be well remembered today, but in his day he was a prominent figure on the American left. For most of his career, he was one of the country's foremost members of the Socialist party. John Reed declared that Sinclair's 1915 anthology of left-wing writing, *Cry for Justice,* "made more radicals than anything I ever heard of." No writer converted more young people to socialism. "Upton Sinclair first got to me when I was fourteen or so," Kurt Vonnegut, Jr., has confessed, in explaining how he became a lifelong socialist.

Few public figures jumped so nimbly from so many frying pans into so many fires. Like Normal Mailer, circa 1969, Upton Sinclair was often in the news for reasons that had little to do with writing: getting arrested (on several occasions), running for office (numerous times), or financing films (just one, but it was Sergei Eisenstein's only movie in the West, *Que Viva Mexico*). He was a vegetarian before it became fashionable. With the profits from *The Jungle* in 1906 he founded a controversial utopian community in Englewood, New Jersey, called Helicon Hall, and later lived in a single-tax colony in Delaware. He cofounded the League for Industrial Democracy with his friend Jack London, and the Southern California branch of the American Civil Liberties Union. Charlie Chaplin considered Sinclair his political "mentor." His engine was forever racing. Accused of having a Jesus complex, Sinclair cheerfully pointed out that the world needed a Jesus more than it needed anything else. His slight stature and sweet nature belied a fierce militancy.

Practically alone among the American writers of his generation, Upton Sinclair "put to the American public the fundamental questions raised by capitalism in such a way that they could not escape them," Edmund Wilson observed. In this regard, Sinclair's career reached its climax with his EPIC crusade in 1934, and left-wing activists in California—and the American political campaign—would never be the same.

Fifty-six years after his birth and twenty-five hundred miles from the hovels and mansions of his youth, Upton Sinclair stopped waiting for the answer to his question about why some people were rich and others poor. "You have written enough," he told himself. "What the world needs is a deed."

The year was 1934. More than a year into the New Deal, ten million Americans were still without work, and even Shirley Temple could not lift their spirits for long. Out in California, a general strike shut down San Francisco, vigilantes attacked union organizers in the Central Valley, and the Red Squad hunted suspected Communists in Los Angeles.

From his Santa Monica ranch, Will Rogers observed that a celebrated author, a Socialist no less, was running for governor of California—"a darn nice fellow, and just plum smart, and if he could deliver even some of the things he promises, [he] should not only be governor of one state, but president of all of 'em." Six weeks later, on August 28, 1934, the Socialist writer, Upton Sinclair, swept the Democratic primary for governor of California, and all hell broke loose from San Diego to Sacramento. The *Los Angeles Times* denounced Sinclair's "maggot-like horde" of supporters. Former president Herbert Hoover called the coming campaign the most crucial election in California history. Earl Warren, the Alameda County district attorney, warned that the state was about to be overcome by Communism, and the movie studios threatened to move back East if Sinclair took office.

Upton Sinclair had created a crisis not for just his home state, but the entire nation. No politician since William Jennings Bryan had so offended the Vested Interests, *Time* magazine declared. "Upton Sinclair has been swallowing quack cures for all the sorrows of mankind since the turn of the century," H. L. Mencken explained, and he "is at it again in California,

and on such a scale that the whole country is attracted by the spectacle."
Political pundits, financial columnists, and White House aides, for once,
agreed: Sinclair's victory represented the high tide of radicalism in the
United States. The country stood at a crossroads, and some predicted that
a Sinclair win in November would set America squarely on the path to
destruction.

Win or lose, Sinclair's End Poverty in California—or, EPIC—movement was, in the words of Theodore Dreiser, "the most impressive political
phenomenon that America has yet produced." The *New York Times* called
it "the first serious movement against the profit system in the United
States." Almost overnight, nearly two thousand EPIC clubs had popped
up like mushrooms all over the state, embracing Sinclair's precept of
"production-for-use, not profit" (borrowed largely from Edward Bellamy)
and a system of state-run cooperatives. The Communist party denounced
Sinclair as a "social fascist" and the Socialist party expelled their longtime
hero from its ranks. Still, many Communists and Socialists joined his
campaign and EPIC radicalized a new generation of activists in California.
Franklin Roosevelt may have revived the Democratic party in California
in 1932, but it was EPIC which established it as a progressive force.

The prospect of a Socialist governing the nation's most volatile state
sparked nothing less than a revolution in American politics. With a crucial
assist from Hollywood, Sinclair's opponents virtually invented the modern
media campaign. It marked a stunning advance in the art of public relations, "in which advertising men now believed they could sell or destroy
political candidates as they sold one brand of soap and defamed its competitor," Arthur M. Schlesinger, Jr., had observed. Media experts, making
unprecedented use of film, radio, direct mail, opinion polls, and national
fund-raising, devised the most astonishing smear campaign ever directed
against a candidate.

Today, political consultants package candidates for the media and advertising has an overwhelming impact on public opinion. For most voters,
an election campaign has no reality apart from television. It was the riotous
1934 race for governor of California that pointed political campaigns down
this path. This was not exactly the "answer" Upton Sinclair, the last of
the romantic socialists, was looking for when he launched his people's
campaign.

Sinclair described his amazing California political experience in a memoir, *I, Candidate for Governor, and How I Got Licked* (1935) and a
novel, *Co-Op* (1936). Ironically, by this time the Communists who had
so bitterly opposed EPIC had accepted Sinclair as a major intellectual for
the Popular Front milieu. A noted speaker at the Western Writers Congress
in 1936, he emerged a much celebrated figure of the League of American

Writers. His *No Pasaran!* (1937), a Spanish Civil War novel, featured Loyalist heroes and heroines. The Hitler-Stalin Pact of 1939 closed off this period and set Sinclair against communism for the rest of his life.

From 1939, he composed a popular series of eleven "Lanny Budd" novels, a saga of twentieth-century American history through the life of the leading character. The third in the series, *Dragon's Teeth,* won the Pulitzer Prize in 1943. In some others of the series, Franklin Roosevelt took on heroic status, suggesting Sinclair's shift of political perspective. The final Lanny Budd novel, *The Return of Lanny Budd* (1953), highlighted the author's vision of democracy against communism, and further established his respectability as a distinguished liberal author. Praised in the mainstream media, translated into forty languages, Sinclair remained in his own eyes a socialist and visionary perpetually ahead of his time.

Suggested Readings

Leon Harris, *Upton Sinclair: American Rebel.* New York: Crowell, 1975.

Eric Homberger, *American Writers and Radical Politics, 1900–39: Equivocal Commitments.* London: Macmillan, 1986.

Greg Mitchell, *The Campaign of the Century: Upton Sinclair's Race for Governor of California and the Birth of Media Politics.* New York: Random House, 1992.

14

EMMA GOLDMAN

Alice Wexler

Years later, Margaret Anderson, editor of the avant-garde *Little Review,* recalled the demonic legend of the anarchist Emma Goldman, whose presence in town had once caused riots. "Her name was enough in those days to produce a shudder," wrote Anderson in her memoirs. "She was considered a monster, an exponent of free love and bombs." Yet if police often rushed to arrest her, thousands of people flocked to her lectures on subjects ranging from trade unionism, anarcho-syndicalism, antimilitarism, and atheism to birth control, women's emancipation, sexual freedom, and homosexual rights. Equally at home leading labor demonstrations in the streets or lecturing to intellectuals on Dostoyevsky and Tolstoy, Goldman combined charisma with courage in a life-long struggle against injustice. Almost from the moment she entered the anarchist movement in New York City in 1889 until her deportation to Soviet Russia in December of 1919, she remained one of the most controversial women in American public life. Her monumental autobiography *Living My Life,* published to acclaim in 1931, remains a compelling account of a radical life outside the conventions of marriage and motherhood, written by a woman "woven of many skeins, conflicting in shade and texture."

Emma Goldman was born June 27, 1881, in Kovno, Lithuania, into a petit bourgeois, Russian-Jewish family of declining fortunes. Her father, Abraham Goldman, an angry patriarch, struggled to make ends meet by managing an inn, and later a series of shops, with his wife, Taube Zodikoff, who had been widowed as a young woman. The young Emma grew up feeling lonely and unloved, nurtured mainly by her beloved older half sister Helena, and also by a gifted female teacher who encouraged her intellectual aspirations. On completing the *Realschule* in Königsberg, East Prussia, Emma aspired to study medicine. But the family moved to St. Petersburg in 1881, shortly after the assassination of Czar Alexander II. The family's precarious financial status compelled Emma to withdraw from her Russian high school after only a year, in order to go to work. In the charged atmosphere shaped by czarist anti-Semitism, the beginnings of Russian feminism, and stories of the heroic young revolutionists of the People's Will, forced underground following the assassination of the czar, Emma developed a rudimentary political awareness and sense of identification with the Russian revolutionary tradition, particularly the women, who remained her inspiration and "guiding stars."

Goldman carried this identification with her to Rochester, New York, where she emigrated in the winter of 1885 with Helena. Working in a Rochester sweatshop, she met and married a fellow immigrant, Jacob Kersner. But she found herself increasingly absorbed by the trial of a group of anarchist labor organizers in Chicago, convicted and eventually executed for allegedly inspiring a bomb explosion in Haymarket Square in 1886. After hearing a compelling anarchist speaker, Johanna Greie, defend their cause, Emma became convinced of their innocence and persuaded by their politics. These events, along with her disappointing marriage and her experience of exploitation as a garment worker, inspired her decision to leave Rochester for New York City. Here she immediately became part of the group around the flamboyant German immigrant agitator Johann Most, editor of the paper *Die Freiheit*. Within a few years, Emma Goldman became one of the most admired and controversial figures in the anarchist movement and in American public life.

In the 1890s, Goldman gradually pieced together the iconoclastic anarchist vision to which she adhered for the rest of her life. Blending both European and American influences, she attempted to combine the anarchist communism of the Russian theorist Peter Kropotkin with the individualism of her intellectual heroes Max Stirner, Friedrich Nietzsche, and Henrik Ibsen. Like most anarchists, Goldman believed that people were naturally social beings. Freed from domination by exploitative institutions, men and women would freely cooperate. Following Kropotkin, she offered a vision of a stateless, decentralized, communist society in which coercion would be replaced by cooperation and mutual aid. Organized around small face-to-face communities, the anarchist society envisioned by Goldman would also respect the rights of minorities and individuals. Her definition of the emancipation of women applied to men as well. "Emancipation should make it possible for woman to be human in the truest sense," she wrote. "Everything within her that craves assertion and activity should reach its fullest expression; all artificial barriers should be broken, and the road towards greater freedom cleared of every trace of centuries of submission and slavery."

Like most anarchists, Goldman vehemently opposed all participation in electoral politics, such as voting, holding office, or campaigning for candidates. Instead of political action, she urged "direct action," such as strikes, boycotts, demonstrations, and acts of civil disobedience. But unlike many anarchists, Goldman placed particular emphasis on the transformation of consciousness as a prerequisite to economic and social change. She urged women especially to start with their "inner regeneration, to cut loose from the weight of prejudices, traditions and customs." In Goldman's view, "the right to vote, or equal civil rights, may be good demands, but true emancipation begins neither at the polls nor in courts. It begins in woman's soul." Goldman believed that education and the arts, particularly the theater, were important means to such an awakening. As she wrote in her 1914 book, *The Social Significance of the Modern Drama,* "any mode of creative work, which with true perception portrays social wrongs earnestly and boldly, may be a greater menace to our social fabric and a more powerful inspiration than the wildest harangue of the soapbox orator."

Lecturing hesitantly at first, in German and in English, Goldman gradually grew more confident, traveling to East Coast cities to speak before small groups of comrades. When her lover and comrade Alexander Berkman decided to commit an act of "propaganda of the deed" to inspire the masses to revolt, she willingly aided him. Yet his failed attempt to assassinate Henry Clay Frick during the Homestead Steel Strike of 1892 merely landed him in prison for fourteen years without noticeably aiding the strike. Goldman subsequently repudiated such acts of individual violence, though not her admiration for those whom she saw as willing to sacrifice their lives for an ideal. She herself spent a year in prison, in 1893–94, for telling starving people to "take food" during a hunger demonstration in New York City.

After her release from prison, Emma Goldman addressed a broad array of topics that sometimes shocked her more conventional comrades. She defended the rights of homosexuals and spoke of sex as a "creative force." She angered feminists with her talks on "Woman's Inhumanity to Man," and "The Tragedy of Woman's Emancipation," criticizing the suffrage movement for its hostility to sexuality and what she considered its genteel, middle-class propriety. But she remained staunchly anti-capitalist and anti-militarist. She vehemently criticized the patriarchal family and conventional marriage, monogamy, and motherhood. She called for women's right to control their own bodies, and publicly explained methods of birth control. She also offered short lecture courses on Russian literature and on European dramatists such as Ibsen, Shaw, Strindberg, Wedekind, Hauptmann, and Gorki, using literary and dramatic criticism as vehicles for social critique. Placing gender at the center of her analysis, Goldman pointed out that even within the anarchist movement, women were subordinate to men; the anarchist emphasis on the individual often neglected to consider the individual as a woman. For Goldman, demands for formal equality failed to address the economic, social, and also psychological subordination of women. In particular, women had internalized a psychology of subordination, what Goldman called the "internal tyrants—economic and social conventions"—which she believed were harder to overcome than legal inequality. Criticizing the limited vision of Progressive Era feminists, Goldman suggested wryly that "women will have to emancipate themselves from emancipation if they really desire to be free."

Goldman's lectures touched a responsive chord in thousands of people, and she often turned persecution into public relations triumphs. Still, she faced great danger. Arrested on charges of inspiring the McKinley assassination in 1901, Goldman narrowly escaped a trial in which she almost certainly would have been convicted. The anarchist movement was forced underground for several years in the wake of antianarchist hysteria. Goldman herself temporarily returned to private life, practicing nursing, midwifery, and massage, which she had learned during a year's sojourn in Vienna in 1895–96.

With the release of Alexander Berkman from prison in 1906, the two comrades began publication of a successful monthly anarchist magazine, *Mother Earth,* combining cultural criticism with social and political analysis. The decade prior to World War I represented one of the high points of American radicalism, and Goldman found herself sought out by young intellectuals and feminists, as well as radicals of many stripes. She worked often with the Industrial Workers of the World, or Wobblies, in many of their strikes and free-speech fights. Still controversial, she nonetheless won the admiration of many who disagreed with her ideas, yet mobilized around her right to express them in public without interference. She was almost a walking free-speech case, pushing against the borders of the permissible and the proper, extending the realms of free speech for everyone.

World War I ended the Progressive Era, with a massive assault on civil liberties and on radicals and trade unionists generally. Goldman and Berkman spent two years in prison for opposing the draft. On their release in the winter of 1919, they were deported to the newly established Soviet Republic, then in the midst of a devastating civil war. Although Goldman had defended the Bolshevik fight against czarism, the Leninist vision of a highly centralized, socialist state conflicted sharply with the anarchist vision of a libertarian, decentralized socialism. Within a few months, Goldman had grown bitterly disillusioned, angered particularly by the Bolshevik persecution of other left-wing revolutionists, including many anarchists. She and Berkman left Russia at the end of 1921, recounting their experiences in two autobiographical narratives offering an anarchist critique of the Soviet state.

During the ensuing years Emma Goldman suffered the devastating loneliness of her double exile from both Russia and the United States. In Stockholm, in Berlin, in England, and in Toronto, she struggled to reestablish herself as a lecturer, focusing the bulk of her energies now around her anti-Soviet campaigns. Although the Soviet Union remained a pariah nation throughout most of the 1920s, Goldman's vehement opposition to Marxism as well as her anticommunism alienated her from much of the left, including the anti-Soviet socialists and the cultural avantgarde. Feeling deeply isolated, she spent two years in St. Tropez writing her autobiography, which later enabled her to secure a three-month lecturing visa to the United States. She had hoped to remain, but refused to cooperate with the right-wing Congressional Dies Committee which was evidently the price of reentry. Once again a political exile, she found herself nowhere at home, "cast out and a stranger everywhere."

Living My Life told how Goldman's commitment to anarchism opened up vast new worlds of politics and love, centering her life around the quest for an ideal, and offering access to a public stage. Though representing herself as a self-made revolutionist, the autobiography also suggested how networks of strong women offered Goldman both models and support—from her outspoken and capable mother, Taube, to the female revolutionists of the People's Will to her supportive sister Helena and the speaker Johanna Greie, who predicted her future vocation. Despite her competitive relationships with women, Goldman drew on female friendships all her life for nurturing and affection, in turn offering younger women an inspiring, if sometimes rivalrous, model and ally in their struggles. Unlike many radicals of her generation, Goldman insisted in her memoir on the vicissitudes of her private as well as public life, frankly admitting her hunger for love and her complicated erotic experience. Emphasizing the intensity of female sexuality, she sketched the outlines of her "great Grand Passion" for a flamboyant Chicago physician, Ben

L. Reitman, who for a time satisfied her needs for both companionship
and love. Shocking to her more conventional comrades, *Living My Life*
remains a classic anarchist text, as well as the story of a lifelong resistance.

In her sixties, Goldman lived to see her anarchist dreams briefly realized. In July of 1936, as civil war erupted in Spain, the powerful Spanish
anarcho-syndicalist movement began a social revolution along anarchist
lines in the provinces of Catalonia and Aragon. Grief-stricken over the
death of her beloved Berkman just weeks before the outbreak of war,
Goldman was drawn into the excitement of revolution by an invitation
from her comrades to join them in Barcelona. Seeing anarchism in action,
Goldman felt her dreams vindicated. She agreed to act as agent in London
for the Confederacion Nacional del Trabajo-Federacion Anarquista Iber-
ica, the combined anarchist and syndicalist organization in Spain. From
1936 to 1939, she struggled against enormous odds to secure British aid
for her beleaguered Spanish comrades. With their defeat and later that
of the Republic, Goldman traveled with a heavy heart to Toronto to raise
money and secure aid for all refugees from European fascism. Only after
her death, in May 1940, did she receive permission to reenter the United
States. Her body was buried in Haymarket cemetery, in Chicago, in the
country she always considered her home.

Emma Goldman left a lecacy of controversy, inside and outside the
anarchist movement. Widely admired for her courage and tenacity in the
face of persecution, she was also criticized as a prima donna who created
a cult of personality around herself. Though she sought to bring anarchism
out of its immigrant enclaves into the mainstream of American life, she
never succeeded in creating an English-speaking movement. Yet she
helped introduce anarchist ideas to the IWW (Industrial Workers of the
World), and to many pre–World War I intellectuals and artists. Goldman
brought keen theatrical skills to the performance of protest, using her
demonic popular persona to open up new space for women in public,
and using the controversy she created to educate and mobilize people
around progressive issues. Attempting to bring together many disparate
strands of anarchism, socialism, feminism, and free love, Goldman concocted an iconoclastic radicalism that rejected the economism of most
leftists of her generation and brought gender squarely to the center of her
critique. Her physical presence as a woman in public embodied anarchism
as a feminist ideal and anticipated the emergence of anarcha-feminism
in the 1960s. Moreover her anarchist critique of the women's movement
helped create a libertarian strand of feminism and brought many young
1960s feminists to an appreciation of anarchist ideas. Perhaps no other
figure so powerfully dramatized the rebellious social and cultural currents
of Gilded Age and Progressive America, making the anarchist revolt

against injustice visible in people's everyday lives. "Anarchism to me was not a theory for a distant future," she wrote in her autobiography; "it was a living influence to free us from inhibitions, internal no less than external, and from the destructive barriers that separate man from man."

Suggested Readings

Richard Drinnon and Anna Maria Drinnon, *Nowhere at Home: Letters from Exile of Emma Goldman and Alexander Berkman*. New York: Schocken, 1975.

Emma Goldman, *Anarchism and Other Essays*. New York: Mother Earth Publishers, 1910.

———, *Living My Life*. New York: Knopf, 1931.

Alice Wexler, *Emma Goldman in America*. Boston: Beacon Press, 1984.

———, *Emma Goldman in Exile*. Boston: Beacon Press, 1989.

15

WILLIAM D. HAYWOOD

Dan Georgakas

William Dudley Haywood begins his autobiography by stating that his father came from American stock that went back to either Puritan bigots or the Cavalier pirates. Neither possible ancestral line was judged a source of pride. Such blunt language and harsh evaluation of the American mainstream was characteristic of the two-hundred-pound-plus sixfooter who came to be known to friend and foe alike as Big Bill. From the turn of the century through the 1920s, Big Bill Haywood would personify Western radicalism and industrial unionism as he served as a leader of the Western Federation of Miners (WFM), the Socialist party (SP), and the Industrial Workers of the World (IWW).

The future labor radical was born February 4, 1869, in Salt Lake City. His father, a former Pony Express rider, was a miner; his mother, a recent South African immigrant, was the daughter of his father's landlady. A whittling accident at age nine cost the young Haywood his right eye. The adult Haywood, when confronting photographers, offered a left profile, while mythmakers would attribute the lost eye to a mining accident or strike action. At age twelve, Haywood left school to find work and three years later he left home to become a miner in northwest Nevada.

The bunkhouses of that era were de facto symposia where radical views predominated. Haywood listened avidly and got his first lessons in socialist and trade union thought from a miner who belonged to the Knights of Labor. During this time, he also met and wed Nevada Jane Minor, the daughter of a local rancher. The couple attempted to homestead some federal land, but their enterprise failed when the army repossessed the land for Indian resettlement. After various temporary jobs, including some work as a cowhand, Haywood found permanent employment as a miner in Silver City, Idaho.

The volatile Haywood was soon attracted to the recently formed WFM. Unlike the craft-based American Federation of Labor (AFL) locals, the WFM was an industrial union that represented all workers on a given site whatever their skills. In 1896 Haywood became a charter member of Silver City's new Local 66 (WFM). His considerable administrative talents soon brought him to the leadership of the local and election to the union's national board. Haywood peacefully negotiated such good contracts that Local 66 virtually governed Silver City. His performance so impressed the national WFM leaders that in 1891 he was brought to Denver to become the national secretary-treasurer, the WFM's number-two post. Haywood's new responsibilities included editing the union's influential *Miner's Magazine*.

During Haywood's tenure as secretary-treasurer, the WFM became involved in a series of often violent strikes, including historic battles at the Telluride, Cripple Creek, and Silver City mines. Haywood emerged as the WFM's most charismatic and effective leader. Armed with a revolver and wearing his trademark Stetson hat, the one-eyed secretary-treasurer was not one to avoid physical blows or verbal insults if circumstances demanded them. The WFM grew substantially stronger and was often cited as a model by those calling for a new national labor union. Haywood's creative flair also generated a growing jealousy among some of the other WFM leaders, most notably Charles P. Moyer, the relatively conservative WFM president.

Haywood's family life suffered from the frequent absences from home that his work required, a problem substantially compounded by his hard drinking and womanizing. Nevada Jane, who suffered from a severe arthritic condition, had to raise their two daughters, Vernie (b. 1890) and Henrietta (b. 1897), with little assistance from her famous husband. As her disease began to immobilize her, Nevada Jane was drawn to the healing promises of Christian Science. The couple became estranged and lived most of the rest of their lives apart.

The growth of the WFM was unusual as the surplus of workers was so great that millions of men were itinerant laborers who drifted from one job to another, certain only of chronic unemployment. Massive components of the labor surplus were millions of child laborers and the huge influx of immigrants. These circumstances shaped a working environment in which safety was a marginal concern and pay cuts were more common than pay raises. Employers were so secure in their power that they did not recognize the right of their employees to bargain collectively, much less to strike or picket.

The quarter-century-old AFL with a million and a half members felt the unskilled were unorganizable. Some of its locals further stratified the working class by prohibiting membership to any woman, nonwhite, or immigrant. Frustrated by unsuccessful attempts to reform the AFL from within, many trade unionists concluded that the only viable option left was to create a new, industrially based national union. A convention to launch such a union took place in Chicago in June 1905. The delegates were called to order by Chairman William D. Haywood who suggested a second American Revolution was at hand by stating, "Fellow workers, this is the Continental Congress of the working class."

The convention eventually declared that "the working class and employing class have nothing in common." The ultimate goal of the "One Big Union" (OBU) was to replace the capitalist system with a worker-controlled economy administered by trade unions. Strikes and other conventional actions were seen as means of strengthening working-class power and solidarity until the OBU was strong enough to call a general strike. This ultimate strike would bring the economy to a standstill until the agencies of commerce and governance were assumed by trade unions. This peaceful syndicalist revolution would be paralleled in other lands giving a literal meaning to the new organization's name, the Industrial Workers of the World.

A key issue in this revolutionary vision was whether or not the IWW should affiliate with a political party. Although Haywood was a strong advocate of nonaffiliation, the position which prevailed, his thinking had considerable nuance. He was also a member of the Socialist party and believed the SP had a ballot-box appeal that could rally middle-class professionals and alleviate political injustice. The SP's potential, however, was severely limited as all women, all workers under twenty one, all unnaturalized immigrants, and most blacks could not vote. Other large blocks of itinerant workers were unable to maintain a fixed polling address. Only the IWW could mobilize this vast majority of Americans. By placing emphasis on the point of production, the IWW could maximize working-class power where it was most decisive.

Haywood declined an offer of formal leadership of the IWW due to his WFM obligations. Any IWW work was soon put on hold by events in the West. On December 30, 1905, Frank Steunenberg, the former governor of Idaho, was killed by an assassin's bomb. With some Pinkerton Agency encouragement, Harry Orchard, an ex–WFM member, "confessed" to the crime. He said he had acted under orders of the WFM leadership who wanted to punish Steunenberg for breaking a miner's strike with troops after having been elected with labor backing. Moyer, Haywood, and George Pettibone, another ex–WFM member, were indicted for the crime. With more Pinkerton help, Idaho and Colorado officials managed to abduct the trio across state lines to stand trial.

The kidnapping set off a national storm. Eugene V. Debs wrote in a special issue of *Appeal to Reason* that if the Idaho authorities prevailed, "a million revolutionists will meet them with guns." Clarence Darrow, the preeminent civil libertarian of the day, agreed to head the legal defense of Haywood, the first of the three to stand trial. As a gesture of solidarity, Colorado's SP put Haywood on the 1906 state ballot as its candidate for governor. Such support was characteristic during the fifteen months Haywood sat in jail awaiting trial. By the time he was exonerated on July 28, 1907, Haywood had become a national celebrity. Vaudeville operators offered him thousands of dollars a week to lecture on their circuits. Haywood declined commercial contracts in order to advance his political agenda. At one meeting sponsored by the SP in Chicago's Riverside Park he spoke to an audience of 60,000. A similar meeting in Milwaukee drew 25,000. This kind of national attention proved too much for Moyer's ego. In alliance with WFM officials who feared their union was getting too radical an image, he arranged for Haywood to be removed from his official duties. Less than a year later, the WFM withdrew from the IWW.

Having been deprived of his trade union base, Haywood devoted his energies to the SP. Sensitive to charges that it was dominated by the foreign born, the SP was delighted to have a homegrown radical as a drawing card. For the next four years, Haywood toured the nation as a speaker at SP functions, a major fundraiser, and a member of the national executive board. In 1910 he traveled to Copenhagen as a delegate to the convention of the Second International. In that capacity Haywood met many prominent revolutionaries and reformers. Among them were George Bernard Shaw, V. I. Lenin, Rosa Luxemburg, Ramsey MacDonald, Jean Jaurès, and Clara Zetkin. Haywood addressed gatherings in Scandinavia and Great Britain, displaying an uncanny ability to strike the right tone wherever he went and whatever the class composition of his audience.

Upon his return to the United States, Haywood found himself caught up in the growing friction between the IWW and SP. A major sore point was the IWW's use of the term *sabotage* to indicate a wide range of direct action that did not exclude violence. Many Socialists felt it essential to disassociate their party from any suggestion that it advocated or tolerated violence. A new bylaw, partly drafted with Haywood in mind, denied SP membership to anyone who condemned political action or supported sabotage. Haywood refused to alter his views and was ejected from the national executive board by a controversial 1913 vote by mail.

Before his expulsion from the SP became formalized, Haywood had become an organizer-at-large for the IWW. His most important service came in the successful 1912 Lawrence textile strike. Asked to comment on child labor in the mills, Haywood observed, "The worst thief is the one who steals the playtime of children." Pressed to define sabotage, he said it meant "to push back, pull out, or break off the fangs of capitalism." The Lawrence strike came to exemplify hallmark IWW tactics such as mass picketing, communal singing, and multilingual strike committees. It set off a series of other strikes and concessions in the East that brought 438,000 textile workers better working conditions and fifteen million dollars in wage hikes.

The IWW hoped to repeat the Lawrence formula in a series of actions in the East and Midwest. The indefatigable Haywood moved from one state to another, raising money, buoying local leadership, and addressing the press. One day he might speak to crowds that barely understood English and the next he might appear in the Manhattan salon of a culture maven like Mabel Dodge. Despite propaganda high points like the Paterson Pageant held in Madison Square Garden, most of the battles of 1913 were lost.

Although the organizational momentum set off by Lawrence had been broken, Haywood's aura remained untarnished. The 1914 IWW convention elected him secretary-treasurer, the union's highest office. He quickly brought order to IWW finances and began to rationalize its chaotic structure. Not least of Haywood's virtues was accessibility. Visitors to national headquarters might find him playing checkers with rank-and-file members or discussing someone's personal problems. Rather than paternalism, this sensibility was integral to Haywood's own working-class culture.

A new roving delegate system devised in 1915 to organize harvest workers proved to be an organizational breakthrough. Dues-paying membership tripled to 100,000 with the highest concentrations among maritime, lumber, agricultural, and mine workers. Support for the IWW could also be found in the left wing of the SP, in most ethnic federations, and many WFM and AFL locals, particularly in the West. More than a dozen newspapers in as many languages were being published daily. The establishment of a strong industrial union with an anticapitalist perspective seemed within reach. This potential dissipated when the United States entered World War I on April 16, 1917, some three years after the war had begun in Europe.

The IWW judged World War I to be a conflict between capitalists fought by their workers. Haywood expressed the IWW view when he opined, "It is better to be a traitor to one's country than to one's class." Nonetheless, Haywood and the IWW understood it would be organizational suicide to formally oppose a declared war. The organization took no official position on the war and left war resistance as a matter of individual choice. Despite this stance, in September of 1917 federal agents raided IWW halls with warrants for the arrest of all present and past IWW leaders on the charge they had conspired to obstruct the war effort.

Rather than go into hiding or use delaying legal tactics, Haywood opted to meet the federal assault head-on. He convinced the IWW to agree to a mass trial to be held in Chicago. This win-all-or-lose-all strategy was based on his certainty that the government's case was baseless and his sense that many government officials were upset by the persecution of a trade union. Recalling the public response to his 1907 legal triumph, Haywood felt a victory in federal court would provide the IWW with incalculable impact and prestige.

The case of the *United States v. William D. Haywood et al.* concluded on August 17, 1918. All defendants in the four-month trial were found guilty and sentenced to ten to twenty years in prison and fines of $10,000 to $20,000 each. The fifty-year-old Haywood, now suffering from diabetes, got a twenty-year, $20,000 sentence. After raising bail in 1919, he was rearrested in 1920 on new charges of criminal syndicalism. An appeal of the second charges led to a second release on additional bail.

Haywood found that the organization that had been so vibrant in the spring of 1917 was being shattered by an onslaught of state and federal prosecutions. He also found enormous ideological turmoil. The Russian Revolution had generated five communist factions in the United States, most with roots in the old SP or ethnic federations. Many IWWs, judging their former anarcho-syndicalism inadequate to deal with American capitalism, were attracted to the new movement. Haywood was among those approached by American communists and Soviet representatives to fuse the failing IWW with the new party being formed. The 1920 IWW convention rejected this option.

In March of 1921, Haywood made a de facto break with the IWW by joining a small group that jumped bail and sought sanctuary in the USSR. He had lost hope of getting a fair hearing in the Supreme Court and felt his illness would bring a useless death in prison. Although IWWs could sympathize with his plight, many were bitter that Big Bill had deserted them, particularly as he had devised the showcase trial strategy. Haywood later offered to return to the United States if the $50,000 seized bail money was returned, but the government would not agree. Federal authorities preferred a tarnished exile in Moscow to a steadfast hero in Leavenworth Prison.

Failing health and the usual problematics of exile severely constrained Haywood's activities in the USSR. Up through 1923, however, he worked to develop the Kuzbas mine basin with volunteers from the United States. Thereafter, he spent most of his time in Moscow where he met with radical visitors, journalists like William Duranty of the *New York Times'* Moscow Bureau, and Americans studying at the Lenin School. James Cannon has written that while in Moscow in 1925, Haywood proposed to him the formation of the International Labor Defense, an organization that subsequently played a major role in defending political prisoners in the United States.

While living in Moscow, Haywood married a Russian who spoke little English. He also began to write his autobiography, a work that seems to have been completed by other persons. The concluding chapter does not discuss any post-1921 events and has an uncharacteristic triumphal meeting with Lenin on its final pages. Haywood's writing pace and physical ills were not well served by continued heavy drinking. He suffered a series of strokes early in 1928 and died on May 18. Half of his ashes were buried in the Kremlin Wall, an ironic final resting place for this most indigenous of American radicals.

Suggested Readings

James P. Cannon, *The First Ten Years of American Communism*. New York: Pathfinder Press, 1962.

Peter Carlson, *Roughneck: The Life and Times of Big Bill Haywood*. New York: Norton, 1983.

Joseph B. Conlin, *Big Bill Haywood and the Radical Labor Movement*. Syracuse, N.Y.: Syracuse University Press, 1969.

Melvyn Dubofsky, *"Big Bill" Haywood*. New York: St. Martin's Press, 1987.

William D. Haywood, *Bill Haywood's Book*. New York: International Publishers, 1929.

16

W. E. B. DU BOIS

Thomas C. Holt

W. E. B. Du Bois was a Renaissance man in a modern epoch. Teacher, scholar, activist, novelist, poet, sociologist, and historian, he managed in his ninety-five-year lifespan to author seventeen books, to found and edit four different journals, and to pursue two full-time careers—scholar and political organizer. But more than that, he reshaped how the very experience of America and African America could be thought; he made us know both the complexity of who we have been and are, and why it matters; he left us—black and white—a legacy of intellectual tools, a language with which we might analyze our present and imagine a future. And, yet, writing his last autobiographical statement in his waning years, he was to lament that his very existence might well be effaced for a whole generation: "The colored children," he wrote, "ceased to hear my name."

Being one of that generation, growing up in a segregated South, learning of the world in "a wee wooden schoolhouse" not entirely unlike one Du Bois himself had once taught in, I can confirm how thoroughly Du Bois's memory was effaced in that era of McCarthyism and Southern "massive resistance." There were schools named for his great rival and antagonist Booker T. Washington, whose life and work my high school principal often conjured up as a model for me and my classmates, gathered in restless assemblies. The tiny school library possessed copies of Washington's autobiography, *Up from Slavery,* and even boasted J. Edgar Hoover's *The Masters of Deceit,* a treatise on the Communist menace—which pleased my principal because it absolved Negroes of any significant complicity in such un-American activities. (The latter text I recall being encouraged to use for a civics report in my sophomore year.) I don't remember finding there copies of *The Souls of Black Folk,* or *Dusk or Dawn,* or *The Crisis,* or any other work by Du Bois, who was, I later learned, a notable exception to Hoover's patronizing absolution of the race. It is probable, of course, that I actually did hear Du Bois's name at some point thereafter, but I certainly never realized his significance before I and others of that generation had taken up the very struggle he had done so much to pioneer. Thus I remember standing before the podium near the Washington Monument, waiting to begin the historic march down Constitution Avenue toward the Lincoln Memorial, hearing the announcement that Du Bois had died. And though I then knew little of the man's life, I sensed, even then, something of its significance, and something of the poetry (which he himself would have appreciated) that his death should have come on that day.

Born William Edward Burghardt Du Bois in Great Barrington, Massachusetts, on February 23, 1868, he was the son of Mary Burghardt, a thirty-six-year-old domestic worker, and Alfred Du Bois, a somewhat peripatetic laborer. But Alfred and Mary had married in defiance of her family's wishes, and their union did not survive more than one year after William's birth. Consequently, Will—as he was known—was raised by his mother, whose relative working-class impoverishment was probably relieved in some measure by aid from the extended Burghardt clan. Du Bois remembers being poor, but not deprived. One can imagine that that same ethos of extended kinship also softened any stigma the son might have felt at being abandoned by his father. Certainly, the mature Du Bois would make a close study of his family origins, returning to those origins rhetorically and conceptually again and again in almost everything he wrote in later years. He was to discover that his mother hailed from a family long resident in New England and descended from a freedman of Dutch slave origin who had fought in the American Revolution. His father, born in Haiti and descended from Bahamian mulatto slaves, was himself a private in the Union Army during the Civil War.

Despite the obvious material disadvantages of his youth, Du Bois received a typical college preparatory education in the public schools of Great Barrington, a small town that included perhaps twenty five African-American families in its population. In 1884, he would become the first black graduate of his high school, but young Will does not appear to have experienced much by way of overt racial prejudice. Although he records one memorable incident of racial snubbing in his autobiographical reflections, generally, he played with, led in games, and proudly took his measure against white classmates who were themselves from diverse backgrounds. After briefly editing his high school newspaper, the adolescent Will became what we would now call a stringer, at various times, for the *Springfield Republican,* and for two African-American weeklies, the *Globe* and the *New York Age.*

In the autumn following his mother's death in March 1885, Du Bois went off to Fisk, a black college in Nashville, Tennessee, supported by funds raised by white well-wishers, including his former high school principal. There he not only studied the classical college curriculum of that era but learned of the pains and pleasures, the limitations and abundant variety of black life in America. Some sense of that traumatic experience can be gleaned from his later poignant descriptions of teaching summer school in the hills of eastern Tennessee during the summers of 1886 and 1887. Some sense of his still naive take on the world might be guessed from his 1888 Fisk commencement address—an appreciation of Bismarck, the late nineteenth-century leader of German reunification.

Du Bois continued his education at Harvard, where he enrolled as a junior and from which he received his M.A. in 1891 and the Ph.D. in 1895. In the interim Du Bois studied and traveled in Germany from 1892 to 1894, after which he returned to the United States and taught for two years at Wilberforce. After receiving his doctorate from Harvard, Du Bois was associated with two other universities: the University of Pennsylvania in 1896–97, where he did not teach, and Atlanta University, where he would spend a total of almost a quarter century (1897–1910 and 1933–44). During this period he also managed to write four books (*The Suppression of the Atlantic Slave-Trade* [1896], *The Philadelphia Negro* [1899], *The Souls of Black Folk* [1903], and *John Brown* [1909]) and edit two short-lived magazines (*Moon,* 1905–6; and *Horizon,* 1907–10).

No conventional résumé quite captures Du Bois's life and work, however. He came of age in an era that historian Rayford Logan dubbed "the nadir" of black life in America following the Civil War. Brief efforts at interracial cooperation in politics and labor during and after Reconstruction having failed, African Americans were beset, between 1890 and 1920, by an onslaught of violence, race-baiting, and racist stigmatization unequaled before or since. Throughout this period Du Bois remained active in organizing and directing black intellectual life and political agitation. He was a leading spirit within an organization of black intellectuals, the American Negro Academy, having delivered its inaugural paper ("The Conservation of the Races") in 1897. From Atlanta he attempted to reorient discussions of the race problem by organizing collaborative historical-sociological investigations into Southern black life. As a member of the Afro-American Council, one of the precursors to the NAACP, he examined the national prospects for black business enterprise. From the initial conference held in London in 1900, Du Bois was a leading spokesman for the cause of pan-Africanism, playing a prominent role in four subsequent international conferences held between 1919 and 1945. And after publishing *The Souls of Black Folk*, he became the most prominent spokesman for the opposition to Booker T. Washington's policy of political conservatism and racial accommodation. At age forty-two, he embarked on a new career as an officer in the newly formed NAACP, editing its monthly magazine, *The Crisis*.

Editorship of *The Crisis* enabled Du Bois to join many of the diverse but interrelated strands of his life's work. The NAACP represented a dramatic challenge to Washington's philosophy of accommodation and political quietism. Through legal suits, legislative lobbying, and propaganda, the organization uncompromisingly attacked lynching, Jim Crow, and disfranchisement. As, initially and for many years, its lone black director, Du Bois used *The Crisis* to rally black support and excoriate white opposition to the cause. But the journal was all this and much more. By writing and opening its pages to discussion of all species of subjects and to diverse modes of expression, Du Bois literally crafted a vital public sphere for African Americans nationally. Although there were, or soon came to be, other black media with national circulations—the *Chicago Defender,* the *Pittsburgh Courier, Opportunity,* the *Negro World,* and so forth—none rivaled Du Bois's magazine in presenting a forum for the coherent representation and enactment of black intellectual and cultural life. Gracing its pages were discussions and emblems of black religious, cultural, and social life; poetry and song; together with visual images of the richness and diversity of the black presence in America. Thus the magazine embodied all the strands that were Du Bois himself; and as if holding a mirror he showed black people themselves. Equally important—perhaps even as a consequence—he helped give birth, as an appreciative NAACP would note years later, to a politically engaged black intelligentsia.

Du Bois would leave the NAACP twenty-four years later, following a celebrated dispute at the onset of the Great Depression over its future direction and policies. He returned to Atlanta University to teach sociology, found and edit a new scholarly journal (*Phylon*), and add three more books (*Black Reconstruction, Black Folk Then and Now,* and *Dusk of Dawn*) to his already impressive oeuvre. (He had published three novels and two other books of social commentary while with the NAACP.)

During this period Du Bois continued to be an active lecturer and an interlocutor with young scholars and activists; he also deepened his studies of Marxism and traveled abroad.

In 1944 he was invited to return to the NAACP by its executive secretary and his former antagonist, Walter White. The NAACP had undertaken some modifications in its programs and tactics during, and partly in response to, the depression, such as addressing the problems of labor; possibly it anticipated that other shifts in its approach would be necessary in the coming postwar era. Clearly it was Du Bois's understanding that the invitation to return presaged study and agitation around the implications of the coming postwar settlement as it might affect black peoples in Africa and the diaspora. Representing the NAACP, he was a consultant to the U.S. delegation at the founding of the United Nations, and in 1947 he prepared and presented its antiracist appeal, *An Appeal to the World,* to the U.N. Secretary-general. He also attended the Fifth Pan-African Congress in Manchester, England, and wrote two books devoted to issues of Africa, colonialism, and achieving world peace. His outspoken radicalism and refusal to be confined to a safe domestic agenda, however, led to renewed tensions with Walter White and in 1948 his forced departure from the NAACP for a second time.

Du Bois's continuing agitation for radical causes, and specifically his involvement with the Peace Information Center, led to his federal indictment along with four others on February 9, 1951, as an "unregistered foreign agent." Although acquitted, he was subjected to continued harassment for much of the decade, being denied a passport between 1952 and 1958. Once his passport was restored he undertook a world tour, including on his itinerary China and the Soviet Union (where he received the Lenin Prize). Meanwhile, he wrote an account of his ordeal with McCarthyism (*In Battle for Peace*), a trilogy (*Black Flame*), and his final autobiography, which would be published posthumously by his friend Herbert Aptheker.

In 1960 Du Bois received an invitation from Kwame Nkrumah, the first president of newly independent Ghana, to come there to direct preparation of an *Encyclopedia Africana,* a project that had figured in Du Bois's ambitions since the early twentieth century. Du Bois accepted the invitation and eventually removed to Accra. Just days before his departure in late 1961, he officially joined the U.S. Communist party. Later he became a citizen of Ghana, where, upon his death of August 27, 1963, he was buried.

To state that Du Bois was the most important intellectual in modern African-American letters is unlikely to risk contradiction by even his most determined detractors. Arguably, he literally invented modern African-

American letters. Much more controversial is an assessment of his leadership, both in the sense of its significance for his own time and for his posterity. Du Bois has been categorized as a "racial integrationist," a "black nationalist," "a radical democrat," and "a socialist." He was in many ways all of these and none. Certainly no political label captures the full range of his ideas and convictions. His life encompassed the beginnings of the first Reconstruction and the eve of triumph of the so-called second reconstruction, the civil rights movement. Born in a world lit by candlelight, he passed from a world cringing before the nuclear fire. He witnessed the formal détente among European powers by which the African continent was colonized in the late nineteenth century; he lived to taste the fruits of the struggle to decolonize it in the late twentieth century. In truth, then, his value to us may be that, having lived through almost a century of such amazing transformations, he tested, discarded, resynthesized all the possible political strands and analyses available to him. His value to us may lie precisely in that diligent, impassioned, and uncompromising quest.

At its core that quest was an attempt to comprehend modern life (perhaps modernity itself) and the possible role that the peoples of the African diaspora might play in evading its horrors and in the realization of its potential. That quest was first a task of historical retrieval, with his own biography framing the template for a whole people. As *The Souls of Black Folk* demonstrates, perhaps like no other text in African-American letters, Du Bois was not only fascinated by, but intensely proud of the culture, ideals, and courage black peoples had managed to fashion under the most forbidding circumstances. But here as elsewhere in his work he also recognized what many of us have only recently come to see: that race—for whites as well as blacks—is not a reality of human biology but a social construction (see esp. "The Souls of White Folk," in *Darkwater* [1915]). And, yet, the making of a race—or of the culture that becomes conflated with "race"—is not simply imposed from without; it is the product of that very process of struggle, of survival, and of the surplus beyond mere survival that living under oppression and repression sometimes brings forth.

Confronted, then, at the turn of the century with a Booker T. Washington who appeared ready to renounce this cultural and spiritual patrimony in the name of a pragmatic present and future material "progress," Du Bois joined vehemently in opposition, despite sharing many of Washington's ideas about the necessity for establishing a material base for political struggle. Thus he would return to this theme in the 1930s and be ridiculed for his apparent apostasy at then embracing the Washingtonian philosophy against which he had himself led the struggle.

Similarly, Du Bois had long recognized not simply a cultural kinship with Africa but that the destiny of its diaspora was inevitably linked to the fate of the continent. His work for pan-African goals and his eventual adoption of citizenship in an African nation were practical counterparts of his lifelong intellectual effort to "reinvent" Africa. Confronted in the 1920s, however, with a Marcus Garvey who appeared ready not only to abandon African-American claims to America—claims won with the sweat of slaves and sharecroppers, the blood of martyrs, and the tears of many thousands gone—but to treat with his most vicious enemy, the Ku Klux Klan, he again spoke in emphatic opposition. The issue—as with Washington—was never simply a choice between integration and national-ism. The reality of the lived experience of black peoples in America had always encompassed both intimate participation in and brusque exclusions from the life and culture of the nation. What was important now was how to marshall the unique knowledge, special insights, and prophetic visions to which that African-American historical experience might lend itself for the common struggle to create a world we all could democratically inhabit. Whence came his powerful struggle to transform the mission of the NAACP in the early 1930s. That organization's traditional program of attacking legal segregation was commendable, but inadequate to the problems blacks would confront in the new political-industrial regime that was modern America. Blacks must organize themselves economi-cally—but along socialist rather than petit capitalist lines—in order to gain a stronger bargaining position for the coming struggles with big labor as well as big capital.

As always Du Bois realized that these struggles were international in scope, and in time he came to believe that the most promising models for what could be achieved were the Soviet Union and Communist China. In this view, of course, he was not alone among thoughtful progressives, white and black, in the early postwar period. And despite the subsequent disappointments those regimes proved to be, nothing known then about a racially segregated, antirevolutionary, nuclear-armed America suggested that it offered any better hope of being a beacon of human freedom and social progress. The most likely allies for both African and for African-American freedom struggles appeared to be rising in the East. So after a decade of political persecution, and ironically at the very moment that a new generation of black freedom fighters were launching a decade of militant protests in the American South, Du Bois joined the U.S. Commu-nist party he had once vehemently criticized as largely irrelevant to that struggle and departed for Africa.

Arguably, this act helped deprive him of the influence and recognition his life and work so richly deserved. Arguably, about this and much else, he was wrong. Arguably, but not certainly. Both the African-American freedom struggle and African independence took turns—enjoyed both successes and defeats—he could scarcely have predicted or imagined. But conceivably the precedents for the fundamental tasks of these movements (and of all progressives since), possibly the ways of thinking about those tasks, but most certainly the courage and impassioned commitment required to pursue them are to be found in Du Bois's life and work. The problem of the twentieth century, it turned out, *was* the problem of the color line (broadly defined), "in Asia and Africa, in America and the islands of the sea." The problem of consciousness in the modern era *is* that we all inhabit multiple identities ("a double-consciousness" *at the least*) and that our personal and collective struggles are marked by an effort to recognize in them (if not to "merge" them into) "a better and truer self." Certainly the problem of "work, culture, liberty" in the contemporary age is that our academic scholarship is too fragmented and self-servingly professional to be adequate to the problem of human liberation and self-realization. And, finally, there can be no justice or peace for any until the most deprived among us have justice and peace. All this he stood for; all this he spoke, "in the name of an historic race, in the name of this the land of their fathers' fathers, and in the name of human opportunity."

Suggested Readings

W. E. B. Du Bois, *The Autobiography of W. E. B. Du Bois: A Soliloquy on Viewing My Life from the Last Decade of Its First Century*, ed. Herbert Aptheker. New York: International Publishers, 1968.

Thomas C. Holt, "The Political Uses of Alienation: W. E. B. Du Bois on Politics, Race, and Culture, 1903–1940." *American Quarterly*, vol. 42, 1990.

Gerald Horne, *Black and Red: W. E. B. Du Bois and the Afro-American Response to the Cold War, 1944–1963*. Albany: SUNY Press, 1986.

Manning Marable, *W. E. B. Du Bois: Black Radical Democrat*. Boston: Twayne, 1986.

Arnold Rampersad, *The Art and Imagination of W. E. B. Du Bois*. Cambridge: Harvard University Press, 1976.

17

ISADORA DUNCAN

Elizabeth Francis

Isadora Duncan sought to emancipate the female body and thus change the world. When Duncan began her career as a modern dancer at the turn of the century, she dedicated herself to stripping away the limits on women's expression as artists like so much nineteenth-century clothing. We now see Duncan through the veil of the socially constructed body, on which political and cultural ideologies are both displayed and challenged. Performers like Madonna express the changing and unstable masquerade of femininity, posing a subversive challenge to "woman's place" by slipping into roles and donning images that convey the diversity of conceptions of womanhood. In contrast to manipulating fashion and appearance, however, Duncan sought to reveal an essential body beneath the surface of culture. "She ripped off all the corsets. She let herself go," as one of her admirers put it. Seeking to unify the mind and body, Duncan reinterpreted the ancient Greek balance between ecstasy and harmony to project a universal image for modern womanhood. Duncan's idea was that the free body unlocks all of the doors of freedom as well. With the body at the center of her theory of modernity, Duncan believed hierarchies and social divisions would disappear.

Duncan is thus important to study not only for her impact on the history of modern dance, but for her role in the history of cultural radicalism in the United States. Duncan engendered a vision of a liberatory modernity for many who attended her performances on her U.S. tours, which began in 1908. Her audiences believed that they discovered a new relation to the world through the figure of Duncan dancing on a stage. In this sense, Duncan's concerts were key to the development of modernism in America; her performances of unfettered freedom were connected to revolutions in literature and art. More broadly, Duncan's ideas circulated widely among cultural radicals who were rethinking the relationship between art and politics and the boundaries of the public and the private. In turn, her focus on the liberated body was immensely generative for Duncan. It led her to take up a range of political and cultural positions that included dress reform, women's emancipation, and education. Duncan also sought to redefine who art was for: Duncan wanted her performances to reach everyone, not just the rich or the bourgeoisie. Just as many artists and radical thinkers proclaimed that they were dismantling any separation between art and life, Duncan reached toward a unity between dance and life.

Duncan defined her aesthetic practice against the artifices of dance at the turn of the century: she attacked the ballet and popular revues for their rigid and trite commonplaces and their vulgar displays. At a Duncan performance, the stage was simple and uncluttered, with no decoration except a backdrop of long, blue-gray curtains, a carpet, and simple, diffuse lighting. Duncan dressed in a sheer, short tunic, secured only at the breast and hips. Significantly, she did not wear stockings, shoes, or a corset, all signifiers of the layers of culture that constrained the body and its expressive potential. In conceptualizing herself as both an artist and a revolutionist, Duncan distanced herself from the commonplaces of dance and in so doing from the conventions of Victorian culture. Those conventions were deeply linked to conceptions of womanhood, and Duncan disrupted many viewers' associations of dance, sexuality, and the female form. Duncan also chose music far beyond the boundaries of what was considered proper dance music: Wagner and Gluck operas, Tchaikovsky and Beethoven symphonies, Chopin concertos.

Duncan used dance to restore wholeness in a fragmented world, in itself a radical response to a capitalist modernity that stressed an increasing division of labor and turned bodies into machines. "We are always in paroxysms," she told her audiences, and her plastic poses and rhythms were intended to slow down the acceleration of life in the twentieth century and reveal the connections between the body, space, and time. Duncan broke from a formal choreography and danced using movements rooted in everyday life—runs, walks, and skips—that she saw as expressing a natural, unmechanical relation to the world. Her gestures, though they encompassed the lyrical, the mimetic, and the majestic, emphasized an upward movement. Duncan sought to bind feeling into movement and to connect the one to the many, the solitary individual to a collective whole.

Many philosophers and radical thinkers had argued in the nineteenth century that civilization crippled individuals rather than enabled them to develop, but Duncan began with the body at the center of her vision and social critique. Duncan tells us in her autobiography that early in her career, she stood for hours in front of a mirror and finally discovered the origin of movement in her body, at the solar plexus. From this central place, movement radiated outward, toward connection and a unity of self and world. Like Walt Whitman, whose *Leaves of Grass* she carried with her everywhere, Duncan wanted her dancing body to "contain multitudes." She wrote, "I have never once danced a solo." Freedom, for Duncan, began with an embodied relation to the world: the individual becomes aware of the world through sense—through nerves, muscles, and perception. If one is trained to make the most of this encounter, then one also has the means to resist the moral and social prohibitions that dominate the body. In theorizing dance as a primary and uncorrupted relation to the world, Duncan posed her interpretation of Greek civilization against the censorship and constraint she associated with Victorianism. Duncan thus overturned a central tenet of the Victorian worldview: the body must not *be* civilized, rather the body *was* the source of civilization. The body was at the center of Duncan's theories, but she extended it beyond the individual and beyond a moral domain. For her, the liberated body was a civilizing force, but it was revolutionary as well because it was expressive, not repressive.

This revolutionary sensibility had special meaning for women, who in Duncan's view had the most to gain from eradicating the prohibition of Victorian culture. Duncan's uncorseted, tunic-draped figure became a symbol of the reform of the image of women before World War I, and Duncan called for "the highest intelligence in the freest body!" In a famous essay in which she figured herself as the muse for her new civilization, Duncan wrote, "She will dance, the body emerging again from centuries of civilized forgetfulness, emerging not in the nudity of primitive man, but in a new nakedness, no longer at war with spirituality and intelligence, but joining itself forever with this intelligence in a glorious harmony." Duncan enraged bourgeois sensibilities when she attempted to make this point about an evolved, integrated nakedness by baring one of her breasts in her performances. But she succeeded in revealing her body as a source of progress, when before, women's bodies had to be covered up to be understood.

In a related way, Duncan believed that sexuality must be separated from performance itself, arguing that society repressed its desires by projecting them onto women performers. Despite that separation, Duncan was famous for her open expressions of sexual desire and her many affairs. Duncan oriented her ideas about women's freedom toward sexuality, marriage, and child rearing, not gaining the vote and other reforms. Duncan opposed marriage, claiming that women would only be able to develop "the freest body" outside an institution that tied women to home and childbearing. As a property relation between women and men, marriage also enforced a division of public and private spheres that Duncan deplored because it went against the grain of her philosophy of unity and wholeness. At the same time, Duncan supported women's right to bear children outside of marriage with partners of their own choosing, and she proudly ignored anyone who opposed her decision to have two children without being married.

Many of Duncan's beliefs about the body, civilization, and women's emancipation were rooted in her experience growing up in genteel poverty in the San Francisco Bay area. Duncan's father, Joseph, abandoned her mother, Mary Dora Gray, soon after Duncan's birth on May 26, 1877, when his banking business failed. Duncan claimed she had become a revolutionary at age five after experiencing the poverty that followed. She expressed very little nostalgia for her childhood, recounting bitter episodes of fleeing landlords when her family could not pay the rent and hating the rigid rules and boredom of school. But Duncan's radicalism was rooted in more than hardship; it was nourished by her mother's love of music and utopian socialist beliefs. Duncan remembered that her mother encouraged her four children's talents in theater and dance, and read to them nightly from the essays of progressive thinkers. Duncan and her siblings, Augustin, Raymond, and Elizabeth, developed their ideas about the expressive body within the physical culture movement that flourished in Oakland and San Francisco in the 1880s. Duncan's education was informal, but she grounded her practice in the ideas of thinkers she considered fundamental to her vision of modernity: the educational philosophy of Rousseau, Nietzsche's dancing philosopher, and the ideal of a mystical and erotic American democracy expressed by Whitman.

Duncan appealed to American radicals, who saw themselves battling dominant culture through a critique of the conventions of middle-class American life. In the bohemian rhetoric of the 1910s in America, Duncan was a "pagan" fighting the "Philistines." Rather than rehearsing the choreography of an outworn culture, Duncan's dances seemed to vividly bring to life a modernist critical vocabulary. Bohemian Mabel Dodge Luhan wrote, "Power rose in her from her Center and flowed vividly along her limbs before our eyes in living beauty and delight. We saw a miracle happen before us when Isadora stood there, passive, and Pure Being incarnated itself in her." Duncan's passion for wholeness and unity led her, indeed, to attempt to get outside the aesthetic category of dancing itself. She wrote, "I hate dancing. I am an expressioniste of beauty. I use my body as my medium, just as the writer uses his words. Do not call me a dancer."

Duncan's understanding of her body as an aesthetic medium appealed to other artists. Painter and sketch artist John Sloan was one of many American artists breaking away from the techniques and subjects of academic, genteel art and moving toward representing life as they found it— on the streets and from the rooftops of immigrant neighborhoods—with a style to depict both the beauty in everyday life and the injustice they saw all around them. Duncan became a special subject for Sloan's painting because she enabled him to see in aesthetic terms a new iconography of the body different from both mannered portraits of society women and academic conceptions of the nude. Duncan's iconography was connected to a new conception of womanhood, an equally important step for Sloan. He wrote, "Isadora as she appears on that big simple stage seems like *all* womanhood—she looms big as the mother of the race. A heavy solid figure, large columnar legs, a solid high belly, breasts not too full and her head seems to be no more important than it should to give the body the chief place." Sloan's 1911 painting of Duncan performing on a darkened stage indicates the quality she projected for radicals. Duncan is painted in broad strokes, caught in bold, yet lyrical, natural movement. Her transparent body is figured with head back and an arm flung wide with the fluttering tunic draped lightly over her body. Reds, pinks, and browns give the painting both a revolutionary and an earthly hue, and a bunch of roses—emblematic of both modernist manifestos and working-class calls for a good life as well as fair labor—are flung onto the stage. Duncan's performances helped many cultural radicals to see a relation between art and theories of revolution.

Duncan made it possible for many cultural radicals to forge links between the body, socialism, and liberation. Bohemian socialist Floyd Dell wrote, "I remember the revelation it was of the full glory of the human body, when I first saw her dance. . . . It is not enough to throw God from his pedestal, and dream of superman and the co-operative commonwealth: one must have *seen* Isadora Duncan to die happy." Duncan seemed to make the wildest dreams of a socialist body politic come true. But Dell's revelation along with those of many others presents a problem for how Duncan and those that responded so deeply to her used an idealized notion of womanhood to locate and visualize their desires for a world remade through equality and self-expression.

Duncan's success in the early 1900s was remarkable: students enthralled by her concerts in Berlin and Munich, for example, carried her out of the theater and into the streets chanting their adoration. Duncan's relation with America was more embattled, and she angrily denounced both the prudish rejection that sometimes greeted her performances and the tendency of the press to comment on her unconventional lifestyle to the exclusion of her ideas. This combative stance, however, sharpened her perception of herself as a radical American, especially after the war, when political conservatism enveloped the country and the fluid association between art and radical ideas broke apart. Duncan continued to search for a political, artistic space where she could express her idea of dance on a large scale, and to work for the school that would enable her to educate the "whole" child. This search took her to revolutionary Russia in 1921, where she spent several years developing the school and free theater she had tried to establish both in Europe and in the United States.

Toward the end of her career, Duncan's quest for a revolutionary body and a unified culture foundered as both modernist and popular culture changed. As she became more influenced by nationalism, Duncan began to tell stories in her dances, to narrate a revolutionary tale of struggling out from under oppression and into freedom. She began to wear a short, red tunic and sometimes draped herself in flags. Modernists and cultural radicals who were critical of nationalism rejected this change because Duncan appeared to move away from presenting inner unity of the body when she told what they saw as sentimental stories in her dances. Not only did Duncan lose favor with modernists in the 1920s, but she herself was unable to find value in popular culture either. Young women and men, she said, had forsaken her desire for a communion of self, the natural world, and social collectivity in their jazz-age revelry. While Duncan used a rhetoric of universality in her earlier essays, the disturbing implications of her division between primitive nudity and civilized nakedness came into full force in her later manifestoes, which deplored popular culture. Duncan used a devisive racial rhetoric to criticize the "primitivism" of popular dances and music influenced by African Americans.

Duncan's cultural practice did not match the mood of disillusionment in the twenties, and radicals saw a gap between her performances and her social agitation, rather than a whole, revolutionary idea of the body. As Duncan danced less, modernists and radicals began to reify the ideas she had represented and to describe Duncan as if she were a monument, associating her with that other symbol of freedom—the Statue of Liberty. Casting Duncan as either a parody or a legend has left little room for a critical appreciation of her place in cultural history, because those responses immobilize her philosophy of the emancipated body. However, Duncan continues to be radical in her resistance to categorization.

Studying Duncan's life, ideas, and performances enables us to see the connections between modern culture, radicalism, and feminism. Duncan redefined the terms for women's consciousness of their own subjectivity on the basis of the body and sexuality. But in dancing to free the female body, Duncan pointed not toward a stable, essential ideal for women, but rather established one of the bases for women to change their lives. In 1929, two years after Duncan died in a car accident in southern France, Marxist editor Michael Gold wrote a review of Duncan's autobiography, *My Life*. She was, he wrote,

> the genius of the transition period between two worlds, a forerunner, like Walt Whitman. She prophesied the future, when in a free society there will be neither money nor classes, and men will seem like gods, when the body and mind will form a radiant unity. Her own mind and body approached that unity. But she was the product of an environment, and never shook it off. She sensed the future, but she would have been unhappy if forced to live in that future.

Gold's description of Duncan as a transitional figure is apt. In a prose that alternates between ebullience and pathos, Duncan's autobiography vividly describes her adventures as a forerunner, an artist, and a freethinker, and the liberatory principles that guided her.

Suggested Readings

Isadora Duncan, *My Life*. New York: Liveright, 1927.

———, *The Art of the Dance*, ed. Sheldon Cheney. Originally published 1928. New York: Routledge, 1969.

Deborah Jowitt, "Images of Isadora: The Search for Motion," in *Time and the Dancing Image*. New York: William Morrow and Co., 1988.

The Loves of Isadora, film directed by Karel Reisz, with Vanessa Redgrave, 1969.

Franklin Rosemont, ed., *Isadora Speaks*. San Francisco: City Lights Books, 1981.

18

ELIZABETH GURLEY FLYNN

Rosalyn Baxandall

Elizabeth Gurley Flynn led a long, illustrious and stormy life. She was brought up in the Bronx by educated, militant Irish-American working-class parents. Her father, Thomas Flynn, was a quarry worker and civil engineer who disliked working, rationalizing that his labor would only make some capitalist richer. A member successively of the Knights of Labor, the Anti-Imperialist League, the Socialist Labor and Socialist parties, he loved political debate, arguing in the pub, in the park, and in political groups. Her mother, Anne Gurley, was by contrast extremely diligent, supporting the household by taking in sewing. She read aloud to the family from Irish history and poetry volumes, joined an Irish club of women suffrage supporters, and went out of her way to hear Susan B. Anthony and other suffrage speakers. Rich in culture, the family remained economically impoverished. Bills went unpaid, the gas was turned off repeatedly, and during some winters all four children slept in a single bed with their coats on.

Young Elizabeth, born in 1890, was the apple of her father's eye, a child prodigy. While the other children quickly lost interest in their father's diatribes, Elizabeth listened to and argued with him, inspired to read even the Marxist classics then available. In return, he took her to political meetings of various kinds, where the feisty, intelligent, and lovely girl impressed visiting dignitaries like Irish heroes James Connolly and James Larkin.

Elizabeth eagerly joined forensic activities in high school, winning several debating prizes. A fellow club member and anarchist, her first boyfriend, took her to meet Alexander Berkman and Emma Goldman, who remembered Flynn as a "fascinating picture" and could hardly take her eyes off the dynamic girl. (Elizabeth, for her part, was rather disappointed to find Goldman short and squat, not the amazon that she had imagined.)

As Elizabeth's reputation as a debater spread, the Harlem Socialist Club asked her to give a speech. Hoping to avoid a conflict with her father, who resented not being asked himself, she chose a topic that seemed of little importance to him: "What Socialism Will Do for Women." Basing her ideas on Mary Wollstonecraft's *Vindication of the Rights of Women* and on August Bebel's *Women and Socialism,* she argued that capitalism denied women freedom and that government support of children would free women from financial reliance upon men. Then as so often later, she spoke boldly for women's independence and suggested their sexual as well as economic emancipation.

Overnight, Elizabeth became a media star. A daily press headline read, "Mere Child Talks Bitterly of Life." Famed radical novelist Theodore Dreiser called her the East Side Joan of Arc. David Belasco, a major theater producer of the day, proposed that she play the lead in a labor drama he was producing. She "preferred," she said, to "speak my own piece." That year, 1906, she dropped out of high school and joined the Industrial Workers of the World, launching her spectacular labor career. Over the next decade, she led several of the major Wobbly strikes and participated in many more.

Gurley, as she was frequently called by that time, quickly became the IWW's female ideal. Celebrated in song—Joe Hill wrote *The Rebel Girl* for her—she inspired crowd enthusiasm by her mere appearance at an event, and met the expectation with some of the finest oratory of the day. Much of her prominence came from her ability to touch and move a crowd, first on street corners and then in mass strike meetings. Even unions bitterly hostile toward the IWW, like the United Mine Workers, enlisted her for crucial strike campaigns. During this period, Flynn also wrote some of her most fiery and original appeals for the IWW and Socialist party press, usually on class themes with little feminist content.

But she found other ways to stress women's place in the struggle. Her speeches often took up female topics that other Wobblies neglected, such as birth control, labor legislation for women, divorce, prostitution, and the desire for love. Lacking the vote in politics, women strikers could vote in IWW strike decisions and did so with her encouragement. Flynn thus served as a role model and guide, while making herself into one of the best reporters on the activities of women and children in strike situations. Indeed, the chapter on the famed "Bread and Roses" Lawrence textile strike of 1912 in her autobiography, *The Rebel Girl,* remains one of the fullest, most dramatic and detailed accounts of the heroic acts of female strikers and reporters.

Most of all, she was an organizer. Bringing together women and girls on strike at the Coombe Garment Company of Minersville, Pennsylvania, in 1911, rallying Lawrence textile workers in 1912, she battled police with the Paterson, New Jersey, silk weavers and ribbon weavers who endured months of police brutality and near starvation before defeat in 1913. She also marched with New York City hotel and restaurant workers and with the unemployed in 1914, and helped guide the bitter Mesabi Range miners' strike of 1916. Years after her IWW days, she played a key role in the Passaic, New Jersey, textile strike of 1926 as workers withstood for thirteen months gassings and clubs, ice-cold drenchings, injunctions, and jailings.

Unlike what happened in Lawrence, many or perhaps most of these strikes ended finally in defeat. Even when the IWW could successfully win the immediate aim of workers to halt a decline in wages, it could not build local units able to withstand the combined pressures of employers, hostile press, and AFL unions. These defeats were particularly hard on Flynn because of her difficult homelife. Male agitators might find rest and resuscitation with their families, amidst the hardship and poverty of their calling. Flynn left her son to be cared for by her sister and mother. He complained understandably that she rarely seemed on hand, and that she led a tumultuous romantic life when she managed to come home. Indeed, Carlo Tresca, a colorful anarchist, courageous Italian-American journalist, fellow Wobbly agitator, and the love of her life, was also a trial to her: while living in the Flynn household he fathered a child by her sister, Bina, and had countless other female companions.

Flynn's labor defense work also wore her down. A pioneer in this area, Flynn had rightly insisted that strike defense did not drain needed energies and funds, but broadened the strike's potential appeal and created a base for further organizing. She participated in the first "free-speech fight," challenging the authorities' casual arrest of labor agitators in Missoula, Montana, in 1908 and the dramatic, prolonged free-speech battle in Spokane, Washington, in 1909–10. Together with the IWW, the Socialist party, and several independent-minded AFL unions, Flynn put together in 1914 the pathbreaking Workers Defense Union. She also organized defense committees and directed strategy for Joe Ettor and Arturo Giovannitti, the Lawrence strike leaders; Joe Hill, the IWW bard; Tom Mooney and Warren Billings, two socialists accused of throwing a bomb during a Preparedness Day parade in San Francisco in 1916; and Nicola Sacco and Bartolomeo Vanzetti, being the first non-Italian to bring their case before the English-language public. All this work involved long hours under dreary conditions, visiting jails, raising money for prisoners' families, writing publicity, lining up lawyers and speakers in several languages, and gaining union and liberal support.

Flynn also conducted a vigorous defense in her own behalf. In 1917, she was the lone woman among 166 Wobblies indicted for antiwar propaganda. Charged with violating the Espionage Act, she faced a probable forty-year sentence and $4000 fine. Lacking money for a lawyer or defense, she refused to turn herself in as most Wobblies did; instead, she moved for severance and advised others to do likewise. She also wrote directly to President Wilson, denying that she was still an IWW member and avowing that she had engaged in no antiwar activities. Her strategy worked, although it meant lying and pulling strings with liberal friends; she remained free to mount defense campaigns for her jailed comrades.

But a yet more difficult period in her life followed. Left groups grew smaller, and liberal or bohemian support for radical causes dwindled. The IWW had been crushed, and Flynn felt alienated from the Communist party, which spent the decade in factional wrangling. Physically and mentally exhausted, she experienced family and romance problems which precipitated a total collapse in 1926. She spent the better part of the next ten years recuperating in Portland, Oregon. There Dr. Marie Equi, an abortionist and Wobbly sympathizer who had herself been jailed for progressive activity, cared for Flynn. There is also evidence that Flynn and the openly lesbian Equi were lovers.

After a decade convalescing, Flynn returned to New York and joined the Communist party, no doubt to ease her way back into political activity. Party leaders had long wooed her, but in private looked down on her as unsophisticated and untheoretical, with little feeling for abstraction. For her part, she detested the CP's discipline and constant political intrigue, but kept silent about policies of which she disapproved. Once more a dynamic, popular speaker, she became typecast as the medium for ideological messages to party members and the public. She was elevated to the National Committee in 1938, and the same year ran for representative at large on the CP ticket.

Flynn had barely settled into CP life when she was ousted from the American Civil Liberties Union (ACLU), which she had helped found and on whose National Board of governors she served. Asked to resign (along with other CP members), she alone refused, and defended her position in the *Daily Worker* column she wrote two to three times per week. Refused a hearing and expelled, she fought bravely for reinstatement although personally devastated, at the time, by the sudden death of her son Fred with whom she had recently reconciled. In 1976, the ACLU repudiated the ouster.

The Second World War period was one of the most productive in Flynn's Communist career. She felt at home in the now-respectable, expanding party and was greatly in demand as a speaker and writer. Unlike most *Daily Worker* columnists, Flynn often spoke and wrote about her family, childhood, and friends, and this added to her popularity. She even wittily praised the army for teaching men to clean and to cook. However, she remained unsympathetic to women complaining about being forced into overtime on their jobs and coerced morally by the party into further extra work. Usually on the hedonistic or sensual side of debates on party responsibilities, she was uncharacteristically stoic or stodgy in wartime. The fight against fascism came first, before family and love. She even condemned women for moving near army bases to be close to loved ones.

Worse, she reversed a courageous stand she had taken on reproductive rights. During her World War I days she had fought and lectured on birth control. She wrote only one column in her CP days on abortion, opposing it and citing Stalin who outlawed abortion and rewarded women for raising large families. Flynn did fight for day-care centers during the war, but did not join others who fought to keep them open when the war ended.

More generally, she continued to follow the twists and turns of the party line in her speaking and writing, despite the reservations she described in private diaries. In turn, she held many honorific party and progressive-group positions, such as chair of the party's Women's Commission, chair of the Women's International Democratic Federation, vice-chair of the Congress of American Women, and in 1961 the first female Communist party chair.

McCarthyism reduced the Communist party to a political sect, but Flynn tried to make the best of the situation. She openly disagreed—one of the rare times—with the decision of party leaders to go "underground" in order to escape arrest. Flynn inevitably became chair of the defense committee for the victims of the Smith Act (passed in the war years with the support of the Communist party, and used against the Minneapolis Trotskyists), which made it illegal to teach or advocate the overthrow of the government by force or violence. She toured widely, raising money and raising consciousness for the victims of anticommunist hysteria. In 1951, Flynn was arrested. Representing herself in court, she testified over two months, using her wit and passion to defend her lifetime of radical activities. While awaiting prison, she wrote *The Rebel Girl,* an autobiography of the first half of her life.

At sixty-five, she entered the Federal Reformatory at Alderson, West Virginia, where she remained for twenty eight months. She used her time in prison to read the classics, social science, and generally to catch up on the world outside the party. She was out of circulation just as the Hungarian Revolution and the revelations of Stalin's anti-Semitism stimulated contentious party debates, followed by a mass exodus from the party. She had planned on settling down and writing the second half of her autobiography; she did manage to write a prison memoir, *Alderson Story: My Life as a Political Prisoner.* But the party needed her now more than ever, and she continued speaking and traveling as soon as she was released. Denied a passport under the McCarren Act, she fought for the right to travel and won her case in the Supreme Court.

Free to travel to the Soviet Union, she went there to rest and to write. Instead, Flynn lived the final chapter of her life; she died after only a month there, in 1964. Elizabeth Gurley Flynn received a full-scale funeral in Red Square, and some of her ashes were sent to Waldheim Cemetery in Chicago to lie with those of America's great radicals, Eugene Debs, Big Bill Haywood, Emma Goldman, and the Haymarket martyrs.

Suggested Readings

Rosalyn Baxandall, *Words on Fire: The Life and Writing of Elizabeth Gurley Flynn.* New Brunswick, N.J.: Rutgers University Press, 1987.

Elizabeth Gurley Flynn, *Alderson Story.* New York: International Publishers, 1955.

————, *The Rebel Girl: An Autobiography, My First Life, 1906–26.* Originally published as *I Speak My Own Piece,* 1955. New York: International Publishers, 1973.

Mary Heaton Vorse, *Footnote to Folly.* New York: Farrar Rhinehart, 1935.

Vera Buch Weisbord, *A Radical Life.* Bloomington: Indiana University Press, 1977.

19

ARTURO GIOVANNITTI

Robert D'Attilio

Two vivid phrases were introduced into the American language by events that took place in the first decades of the twentieth century. Though they were both inspired by the American left, they sprang from very different circumstances. "Bread and Roses" came from the grim mill town of Lawrence, Massachusetts, words written on a placard carried by young striking immigrant women workers during the bitter Lawrence textile strike of 1912. "Lyrical Left" came out of the mighty metropolis of the modern world, New York City. It described the buoyant bohemia that had been created in Greenwich Village, by artists, radicals, and intellectuals trying to resist the grasp of American Puritanism and to flee from the cultural restrictions of small-town America. The phrases expressed a common desire for a social transformation in America that would fulfill both economic and spiritual needs. The figure of Arturo Giovannitti—poet, immigrant, socialist, editor, lover, Wobbly, labor organizer, womanizer, anarchist, orator/agitator—bridged these two different worlds in a unique and compelling fashion.

It began with his physical presence. A tall, handsome, red-bearded figure, flamboyantly dressed, costumed one might say, with a black broad-brimmed hat, a soft white linen shirt, dark jacket, and a large black

butterfly tie—in that period the defiant challenge of a rebel against bourgeois convention. This operatic figure would stride before his audience—
a crowd of immigrant garment workers, a judge and jury, a gathering of
artists and writers, a convocation of Italian antifascists—and would preach
revolution, resistance, and social justice either in his native Italian or in
his flawless English. His sonorous, schooled words, replete with many
an allusion to the heroic past, never failed to capture his listeners whether
on the picket line, in a union hall, a Greenwich Village salon, or in
Carnegie Hall. It was a time when "springtime and love and revolution"
marched together and Giovannitti was their poet.

Giovannitti had come to America from a very inauspicious beginning,
Ripabottoni, a small, isolated hill town of several thousand inhabitants,
in Molise, one of Italy's poorest and most backward regions. He was
born on January 7, 1884, the eldest of three sons, to modest but compara-
tively well-off parents: his father was a pharmacist/doctor for the area.
As a result, Giovannitti was one of the fortunate few in his little *paese*
able to attend *liceo* (preparatory high school) in the nearby provincial
capital of Campobasso.

The school was a decent one and Giovannitti excelled in his studies.
It was there that his poetic gifts were first noticed and it is probable that
in his school he picked up the usual mild anticlericalism of the educated
Italian. There was, however, no trace of any particularly strong interest
in politics. With a reasonably promising future in front of him (both of
his younger brothers did have professional careers—one was a military
doctor, the other a lawyer), Giovannitti suddenly left for America. The
reason remains uncertain, but he did not emigrate out of economic despera-
tion, as most Italians did, nor for political motives. At the turn of the
century, young Arturo Giovannitti left Italy never to return.

Giovannitti first went to Montreal, where some of his townspeople had
earlier emigrated. There he continued his studies, evidently through one
of the Protestant seminaries connected with McGill University. Since he
had been raised a Catholic, how or why he became interested in Protestantism remains a puzzle. Near the end of his life, he did tell his son that
he had attended seminary not because of religious feelings, but only as
a means of getting free schooling. Such a calculated motive is belied to
a certain extent by his writings, for they always exhibited a deeply felt
religious imagery throughout his life. All in all, little remains known about
Giovannitti's Canadian years, except that by 1904, when he emigrated to
the United States, he had become fluent in both French and English.

Giovannitti went directly to New York City, the great "Cosmopolis,"
as he would call it. It was a city which cast Giovannitti so completely
under its spell that he would call it home for the rest of his life. He

seemed well on his way to becoming an evangelical minister, albeit "with a queer and peculiar conception of Christianity," when, as Giovannitti himself recounted, life changed with a dazzling suddenness. Consorting with a mixed lot of intellectual misfits and would-be artists, he frequented a favorite restaurant, where, in a scene worthy of *La Bohème,* he quickly became close friends with the owner's son. The two had, as the young often have, intense discussions about the meaning of life: by their end Giovannitti had been convinced by his new friend to become an atheist and a militant socialist; his friend in turn was convinced by Giovannitti to leave his father's restaurant, study voice, and become a singer. Giovannitti's experience once again was opposite to that of most of his fellow immigrants: he became a radical not because of economic hardship or social injustice, but from romantic and moral motives, much like many of his later American comrades, many of whom had turned to radicalism as a surrogate for religion.

By 1908 Giovannitti had in fact acquired definite political ideas and had joined the Federazione Socialista Italiana. In that year his name first appeared in print in the special May Day edition of the party's journal, *Il Proletario,* as the author of a poem. Within a year's time, because of an uneasiness with *Il Proletario's* too gradualist policies, Giovannitti attempted in 1909 to start a more radical journal of his own, the Italian-language *La Rivista Rossa.* He was convinced, instead, to remain and to become a member of *Il Proletario's* editorial committee. In 1911 Giovannitti was appointed sole editor of *Il Proletario.* As Giovannitti was an ardent supporter of revolutionary syndicalism and the IWW, political articles, polemics, plays, appeals, poems, rolled off his pen at an astonishing rate. In the May Day issue of that year two long poems, the translation of the first act of a revolutionary drama, and a short novel appeared under his own name; two other poems appeared under an assumed name, Nino Gavitti. He alone accounted for one-half of the writing in this issue. He also began to publish in English; his first article, a polemic against Italy's imperialistic designs in Libya, appeared in the *International Socialist Review.* His role as editor had also placed him in a close and fateful collaboration with Joseph Ettor, the Organizer-General of the IWW.

When the great Lawrence textile strike exploded in January of 1912, the workers, practically all immigrants, called on Joe Ettor to help them fight. Upon his arrival he saw the immensity of the task and summoned Giovannitti to join him in the struggle. They had stepped upon the stage of a great social drama. It would be the turning point of their lives.

The astounding effectiveness of Ettor and Giovannitti in organizing thousands of workers of many different nationalities made them marked men in the eyes of Massachusetts authorities. During a confrontation with the state militia, a young girl among the striking demonstrators was killed. Although Ettor and Giovannitti were not present at the shooting incident, as strike leaders they were arrested and charged for inciting to murder. This blatant effort to break the strike by framing its leaders on false charges was not an unusual occurrence in that period (evidence actually indicated that a police officer's bullet had inadvertently killed the young girl). This time it catapulted the case into national attention and turned their names into a rallying cry for the IWW and American labor.

To save Ettor and Giovannitti the IWW sent their leading figures to Lawrence—Bill Haywood, Carlo Tresca, Elizabeth Gurley Flynn. They initiated a tremendous agitation which captured the imagination of America and the world. Many international figures spoke out on their behalf. (Among them appeared a fiery revolutionary socialist from Italy, Benito Mussolini, who wrote editorials supporting them in his ferocious-sounding journal *Lotta di Classe*.) This worldwide attention focused upon Lawrence helped the strikers to win one of the most memorable victories in American labor history and played an important role in frustrating the attempt of the authorities to frame the two men. After almost a year of imprisonment, Ettor and Giovannitti were found innocent by a jury and set free. Their names were known throughout the radical world. Labor and the left were exultant. They did not realize that Lawrence was their high tide. The captains of American industry had been aroused, and harder times would follow.

Upon his release from prison Giovannitti continued to write for *Il Proletario*, though he did not reassume his position as editor. He became involved in another fierce strike, the Paterson Silk Strike of 1913, again with the IWW and his earlier comrades-in-arms, Tresca, Gurley Flynn, Ettor, Haywood. It was here that revolutionary labor and the radical intelligentsia of America met in an unforgettable fashion. To help raise badly needed funds for the continuation of the strike, John Reed, inspired by Mabel Dodge, promoted the idea of a Paterson Strike Pageant in Madison Square Garden, using the actual strikers to portray themselves. The dramatic effect of the pageant and the red letters IWW pulsating on the Garden's tower for all New York to see have entered into the mythology of American cultural history: few seem to remember that the pageant failed its purpose (it barely broke even in raising funds) and helped to crush the spirit of the strikers, who finally lost the strike.

Giovannitti, through his roles in the Lawrence and Paterson strikes, had become associated with many American radicals, writers, and artists, such as Max Eastman, John Reed, Floyd Dell, Helen Keller, Art Young, Mike Gold. He began to frequent the American radical and cultural circles that were then flourishing in Greenwich Village and he became one of the few Italian-born radicals of his generation who moved easily through the wider world of American culture.

Giovannitti started to write regularly in English; he wrote poetry and articles for *The Masses,* whose editor, Max Eastman, remembered that Arturo had "a larger English vocabulary than any of us and wielded it with compelling force." Despite the frankly radical nature of his subjects, he had become the first of the newly arrived Italian immigrants to write in English for any significantly sized American audience.

During this extraordinarily fecund period he would publish an English translation of Emile Pouget's *Sabotage* for the IWW, translate Leopold Kampf's drama *On the Eve* into Italian (from the German), and come out with his first book of poems (in English), *Arrows in the Gale,* in 1914. The poems, with a spirited introduction by Helen Keller, were enthusiastically received by critics and public. Joseph Freeman, from a later generation of American radicals, would remember in his remarkable memoir *American Testament* how, Giovannitti's poems, a Whitmanesque mix of lyricism and class struggle came "nearer to the people in thought and speech; it was using the language not of the few but of the majority." They inspired many a young radical.

The outbreak of the Great War in Europe now complicated the labor struggles and social upheavals in the United States. The question of what role Italy should play (it had not been among the initial belligerents) was to divide all segments of Italian life, politically and personally. Giovannitti's own response mirrored the ambiguity within the Italian-American community and himself. While Italy was still a noncombatant, he started a short-lived journal, *Il Fuoco* (in New York City, 1914–15), which tried to be "not of any movement, Italian but not patriotic, nationalist but not warlike." Aimed at the young and the irreverent, it had curiously futuristic overtones within a somewhat equivocal antiwar message.

The entrance of Italy into the war ended Giovannitti's indecisiveness; he became militantly antiwar; in Italy, however, his two brothers chose to serve their country. The title of his next journal, *Vita* (also published in New York City, 1915) would turn into a tragic irony for him. In its last issue he would write a poem for his mother; it dealt with the death of his brother Aristide, who had died a hero while serving in the war. Neither of his brothers would survive the war.

During this period of personal and social tragedy Giovannitti continued to respond with extraordinary energy. Now fighting to prevent America's entry into World War I, he undertook an intense schedule of antiwar agitation. Since the Federazione Socialista Italiana had broken apart over the issue of war, much as his own family had, Giovannitti had gone over to the anarchist press—Carlo Tresca and *Il Martello*—where there could be no doubt about his antiwar position.

When President Woodrow Wilson betrayed his pledge and took America into the war, the American left came under furious and often illegal attack by the federal government for its antiwar position. During these difficult days, Giovannitti's hopes for the future, like those of many radicals, were revitalized by the Russian Revolution of 1917. His imagistic poem that celebrated the Red Army entering Moscow so moved Eastman that he placed its four lines right in the center of a single page of *The Masses*. (Giovannitti would also name his only son (Len) after Lenin, who would always remain a personal hero.) It was only by good fortune that Giovannitti, one of the prominent targets of the authorities, managed to escape the arrest and imprisonment that was the fate of most of the IWW leadership.

At this time the political activity of Giovannitti changed direction. With the IWW essentially destroyed as a major force within the ranks of labor by governmental repression and internal dissension, he began to move from his almost total involvement with revolutionary syndicalism into a closer association with the trade labor union movement. He played an important role in establishing Local 89, the Italian Dress Makers' Union, of the International Ladies Garment Workers Union. At the same time he continued his close association with the American left. He became a contributing editor to *The Liberator,* a member of the Workers Drama League, and a contributor to the *New Masses,* all of which were coming under the influence of the new emerging force on the American left, the Communist party.

A new enemy appeared on the horizon. In Italy, Fascism, headed by the renegade socialist Benito Mussolini, took power in 1922. To fight his formal ally Giovannitti quickly helped to organize the Anti-Fascist Association of North America and became its secretary-general in 1923. Too honest a broker among the warring factions of the Italian left, he was eased out from that position within several years due in part to Communist maneuvering. In 1924–25 he undertook, with the sponsorship of the union-backed Camera Del Lavoro (the Italian Chamber of Labor, New York City), his last major editorial effort, the Italian-language cultural/antifascist journal *Il Veltro*. Its name meant "greyhound," the animal, according to Dante, that would hunt down and kill the wolf of Rome.

During 1925 Ettor and Giovannitti reunited and fought together for a radical cause one last time. They made public appearances on behalf of two other Italian-born radicals, Sacco and Vanzetti, whose murder trial would have a more tragic outcome than their own.

By this time, the active radical phase of Giovannitti's life was over. He no longer wrote much for the American press, radical or cultural;

his activities were almost completely circumscribed by Italian-American enclaves and the Bronx, where he lived. Fire and direction had disappeared from his life; he drank too heavily and he womanized compulsively. He had become more of a romantic symbol of the past than an energetic actor in the politics of the present. He grumbled about the gray routine that political life had become; it was not his way.

> Shall I be forever immobile in the Bronx singing to the tailors
>   and the dressmakers
> the glory of man is on the picket line downtown
> and the end of life is two hundred dollars a week?

After World War II age and sickness brought whatever remained of his political activities to a total halt. He would be bedridden for the last ten years of his life, cared for by a companion from the old days of Greenwich Village. When he died in 1960, his obituary in the *New York Times* ignored the militancy of his youth, simply noting his participation in the 1912 Lawrence strike; it ignored the wide scope of his literary work, describing only in a prosaic manner his association with the American labor establishment.

The revolutionary culture that Giovannitti tried to create with his writings, his speeches, his organizing, did not win its necessary battles. The old dualisms of society did not break down as he wanted them to and he ended in the cracks between too many opposite worlds—rich and poor, native and immigrant, Italian and American, socialist and anarchist, revolutionary-syndicalist and trade-unionist, bohemian and worker, poetic and political, work and thought, love and lust. In a eulogy to his dear murdered comrade-in-arms Carlo Tresca, Giovannitti's words, meant as praise, beyond any irony, fit his own life all too well: "He liked to call himself an Anarchist, and if that term connotes a man who is absolutely free, then he was an anarchist; but from the point of view of pure doctrine, he was all things to all men, and in his endless intellectual vagabondage he never really sought any definite anchorage or moorings." He was left with "words without song."

And yet, whatever missteps he may have taken, whatever work he may have left undone, amid his impossible victories and his inevitable defeats, he had those very special moments when "he unfurled the banner of his heart among the musketry of his words."

142   ROBERT D'ATTILIO

Suggested Readings

Dorothy Gallagher, *All the Right Enemies: The Life and Murder of Carlo Tresca*. New Brunswick, N.J.: Rutgers University Press, 1988.

Arturo Giovannitti, *The Collected Poems: Part I: Words before Dawn, and Part II: Arrows in the Gale*. Chicago: E. Clemente and Sons Publishers, 1962.

————, *Quando Canta Il Gallo*. Chicago: E. Clemente and Sons Publishers, 1957.

Len Giovannitti, *The Nature of the Beast*. New York: Random House, 1977. A confessional novel by the son of Arturo Giovannitti.

20

JOHN REED

Robert A. Rosenstone

Even to contemporaries, John Reed seemed larger than life. Good-looking and dashing, he was a romantic figure whose lengthy American pedigree showed that radicalism was not a foreign import but could be the product of conditions within the United States. None of his friends, many of them among the nation's cultural elite, would have been surprised that Reed's thirty-three hectic years would, more than half a century after his death, become the source for three motion pictures, produced in three different countries—the American multiple Academy Award winner *Reds* (1982); the six-hour Soviet epic *Red Bells* (1981); and the Mexican drama *Reed—Insurgent Mexico* (1970).

Reed's period of fame was the second decade of the century. Between 1910 and 1917, he was one of the heroes of the youthful bohemia that centered in Greenwich Village, a man equally renowned as poet and tough-minded short story writer; as foreign correspondent, contributing editor of *The Masses,* and cofounder of the Provincetown Players; as lover of attractive women like the famed salon hostess Mabel Dodge and the writer Louise Bryant (whom he married in 1917); as friend of the notorious such as Bill Haywood, Emma Goldman, Margaret Sanger, and Pancho Villa. When the repression attendant upon United States participation in World War I destroyed bohemia and devastated the ranks of American political radicals, Reed moved onto a global stage. He became a chronicler of the Russian Revolution, an associate of Trotsky and Lenin, and a member of the Executive Committee of the Communist International, before dying of typhus in Moscow in 1920.

The man who took this road to a grave before the Kremlin Wall was a product of an upper-middle-class family in which radicalism was not so much despised as simply unknown. Reed's heritage and upbringing were genteel; his family politics, those of reform; and his personal ambitions, enormous. He may best be understood as a leader in what was America's first real bohemia, a broad, inchoate movement in which children of the liberal middle classes were—in the name of freedom and self-expression—testing and finding inadequate the behavior patterns and core beliefs of their parents: that competitive economic individualism is the engine of personal and social progress; that the ideas and morals of WASP Americans are superior to those of the working class, immigrants, and all foreign cultures; that the practical and instrumental constitute the best possible approach to social and political life. By contrast, young bohemians exhibited a disdain for economic competition and a desire for some form of extended family or community; a belief that the lower classes at home and abroad are morally equal, if not superior, to those who lord it over them; and a tendency to make aesthetic judgments take precedence over practical ones. In Reed, these themes would be played out upon a world stage.

Reed's life began, quite literally, at the top. Born in 1877, Reed spent his early years in a mansion on a five-acre estate overlooking Portland, Oregon, that had been built by his maternal grandfather, a pioneer capitalist. A sickly child who was indulged by his parents, Reed attended a private academy before going East to a prep school and then on to Harvard. His mother, herself the product of a finishing school, hoped such an education would make her son acceptable in the "best circles" anywhere in the United States.

A lack of political concerns in Reed's classical education was offset by his father's involvements. Businessman Charles Jerome Reed entered the world of political reform in 1905 when, under the Teddy Roosevelt administration, he accepted the job of U.S. marshall to help in a special investigation of fraud in Northwest timberlands. Reed did his job so well that a goodly number of the leading political and social figures in Oregon were either prosecuted, convicted, or implicated in the illegal dealings. This activity made C.J. something of a pariah among his associates, and led him to run, unsuccessfully, for Congress as a Progressive in 1910.

The politics that were central to the last years of C.J.'s life—he died suddenly in 1912—touched his son deeply but did little to affect his behavior. At college between 1906 and 1910, John exhibited minimal concern for social, political, or international affairs. The focus of his college days was on school activities—clubs, sports, and, most important, campus literary reviews. Work on such publications reaffirmed a decision he had made in his early teens, a decision that would shape the rest of his life: after graduation he was determined to become a writer.

In 1910 Reed gravitated to Manhattan, the cultural as well as financial capital of the nation. Supporting himself by writing for popular magazines, he was dismayed to find his most serious literary work—poems, stories, essays—unacceptable in the world of commercial publishing. Soon these same efforts were welcomed into the pages of *The Masses*, a small-circulation, experimental monthly that served as one of the chief mouthpieces of Greenwich Village, the capital of bohemia, a place where the worlds of avant-grade art and political radicalism intersected.

From 1910 until the World War, Reed was a major figure in bohemia without ever losing his position in the high-paying realm of commercial journalism. So enormous were his drive and energy that the range of his activities can only be suggested: he was an editor of and frequent contributor to *The Masses;* a highly paid correspondent for the mass-circulation *Metropolitan Magazine;* an author of poems, plays, humorous sketches, book reviews, and short stories both commercial and serious; a crucial force in the creation of the Provincetown Players; a member of the Liberal Club; a supporter of feminism and birth control; and a lover of more than a few young women anxious to shed the restrictive bonds of Victorian morality.

During those years, artistic issues merged into social and economic ones, as Reed was slowly pulled toward radical politics. In *The Masses* he read about the doctrines of Marxism, socialism, anarchism, and syndicalism, but on the whole, words affected him less than the glaring contrast between rich and poor, the sharp evidence of exploitation he could see each day on Manhattan streets. His first political involvement began in April 1913. In response to the impassioned words of "Big Bill" Haywood, chief of the Industrial Workers of the World (IWW), Reed nipped over to Paterson, New Jersey, to report on the 25,000 strikers who had shut down the town's silk mills. An argument with a quick-tempered cop landed Reed in jail, and he emerged four days later with blood in his eye and vitriol on his pen. In hard-hitting articles, he exposed the complicitous efforts of industrialists, the police, and Paterson city government to break the strike. His commitment to the "Wobblies" went beyond the written word. It was Reed's prodigious efforts which were instrumental in bringing to life a stunning piece of worker's theater, the Paterson Pageant—a money-raising venture for the IWW—which played to a packed house in Madison Square Garden.

Paterson made Reed notorious; his next radical involvement made him famous. Late in 1913, he accepted assignments from the *Metropolitan* and the *New York World* to cover the little-understood events of a revolution in Mexico. Unlike reporters who concocted their stories from rumors circulating in El Paso, Texas, Jack journeyed far south of the border, became friends with Pancho Villa in Chihuahua, rode with a detachment of horseback troops, and joined footsoldiers when they stormed toward the important victory at Torreón in March 1914. So vivid were his articles from the front that Walter Lippmann would say they were "Undoubtedly the finest reporting that's ever been done. . . . I say that with Jack Reed reporting begins."

Much of the strength of Reed's work derived from his identification with the revolutionaries, whose joy in daily life, beliefs in equality, and bravery under fire helped to solidify his commitment to radical politics. This identification clearly showed later in 1914, when, as a highly paid correspondent on the Western Front in the opening months of the World War, Jack could not fill his reports with the color and excitement that editors craved. Reed could not write because the war seemed wholly meaningless, no more than a squalid struggle over markets that was detrimental to artistic, social, and personal progress. To see the war as a logical outgrowth of capitalism was to endanger his livelihood. As the United States drifted toward involvement, Reed became active in the antiwar movement, and, unlike many radicals, he remained in opposition even after America's entry into the conflict in April 1917. One by one, periodicals that had welcomed his articles dropped him as a traitor to his country.

The Russian Revolution saved him from despair. A combination of savvy intuition and financial support from friends landed him in Petrograd in September 1917. Even before the ten days that he would make famous, Reed became a Bolshevik partisan, convinced that only that party was serious about ending Russia's involvement in the war. The fulfillment of that promise, and the subsequent feverish plans for social reconstruction, wedded him to the Revolution. Briefly he served as a propagandist in the Soviet Foreign Ministry, then he returned to the United States, where his papers were seized by the government. Along with the other *Masses* editors, he was forced to stand trial twice (he was acquitted) for antiwar writings that dated from 1917.

Influence from his more famous days helped win the release of his

papers, and Reed swiftly wrote the acknowledged masterpiece of twentieth-century revolutionary reportage, *Ten Days That Shook the World*
(since translated into more than thirty languages), then hurled himself
into the task of bringing revolution to America. His path led from the
left wing of the Socialist party to the founding convention of the Communist Labor party (CLP) and then back to Russia in 1919 to lobby for
recognition of the CLP by the Communist International. Shortly after the
Second Congress of the Comintern, he contracted typhus and died. Like
millions of Russians, he was a victim of insufficient medical supplies
caused by the Allied blockade of the new Russian regime.

John Reed may have ended his life as a martyr to the Revolution, but
his most natural tendency was to deal with the world—even in journalistic
reports—as a poet, a person ready to intensify certain aspects of reality
with the power of art. That it was hardly a practical way of handling life
never bothered him, for he lived in a subculture of like-minded people
for whom play, drama, and experience took precedence over the practical.
Reed and his friends happily experimented with new forms of lifestyles
and social and sexual behavior, happily flouting the middle-class tradition
in which the control of impulses was identified as the basis of civilization
itself. Such self-control was seen by older Americans as the measure of
Anglo-Saxon superiority; it was a notion they hoped to spread to immigrants and the lower classes through education, legislation, and propaganda. The aim was to control not just sexual behavior, but drinking,
singing, gambling, and all other frivolous or licentious amusements.
Reed found such attitudes ridiculous. Many decades before the word
was coined, he was a believer in multiculturalism. Experiences in immigrant ghettos and in lower-class districts of Manhattan, Paterson, and
Lawrence; among Mexican, Italian, and Serbian peasants; and at the
homes of French and Russian intellectuals reinforced his own beliefs that
different behavior patterns, including sensual pleasure, were part of the
splendid diversity of humankind. To him, the level of a civilization
was not marked by its industrial progress, but by its quota of cultural
expressiveness and human happiness.
As part of his American birthright, Reed believed in the pursuit of
happiness. But in his case this quest was not simply a personal demand;
it had a social and a public dimension as well. The plight of the working
classes in Manhattan, Paterson, Mexico, and Russia taught Reed that he
could not be happy and free unless human beings everywhere could share
the happiness and freedom. For Reed, personally, part of that happiness
was the ability to find, in the social arena, the same color and excitement

that he sought in private life. Which is to say that, for Reed, radical movements were at once important, enjoyable, and fulfilling, an area of action and a kind of theater spread across a broad social canvas.

Reed liked to depict strikes and revolutions as morality plays, with bloated capitalists and their minions—the police, the national guard, or the army—on one side and the oppressed workers and their leaders on the other. The Paterson strike he depicted as "drama, change, democracy on the march . . . a war of the people." Mexico was even more colorful: in his prose, Villa appeared as a kind of Robin Hood; peons delivered lines full of uncanny folk wisdom; and ragtag armies moved through startling landscapes of desert and mountain beneath theatrically lit skies. At the time of the Bolshevik takeover, a Greek-tragedy feeling of fate pervaded Reed's words: the Revolution was a force of nature "endowed with the patient inevitability of mounting sap in spring," one that arrived like the turning of a season, with "tempest and wind, and then . . . a rush of red blossoming."

A vision of social and artistic revolution as companions was common enough among radicals. Certainly for Reed, creation and social conscience were inextricably linked. His best stories and one-act plays are critical views of city life. Full of immigrants, derelicts, corrupt cops, shopgirls, hustlers, hookers, and ward-heel politicians, they portray an urban landscape where joy is a fleeting emotion in a realm of exploitation and loneliness. Paterson provided another opportunity for transmuting radicalism into art. The pageant Reed wrote and directed, in which Wobblies reenacted their own roles in the strike, stirred some critics to envision a new form of popular, revolutionary theater with the power to move the masses toward action.

Four years later, in the days after the Bolshevik Revolution, Reed had similar notions in mind. Half jokingly, he nominated himself Commissar of Art and Amusement for the Ukraine. His aim was to "get up great pageants" and to sponsor festivals "with fireworks, orchestras, and plays in the squares and everybody participating." In the winter of 1919–20, when Russia was suffering civil war, famine, and epidemics, he took time to seek out the haunts of Moscow's avant-garde, where he enjoyed the company of the explosive Vladimir Mayakovsky and the Cubo-Futurists, as well as the worker artists of the Prolet Kult movement.

In 1910, when Reed arrived in Manhattan, his father wrote to journalist Lincoln Steffens, "He is a poet, I think; keep him singing." The young man needed no encouragement. Not for Reed was life a somber moral pilgrimage, a burden of weighty duties and obligations. His was always a poet's vision, a demand that experience continually burst through the confines of mundane reality. Serious folk, including radicals, are sometimes inclined to judge such a demand as juvenile. Yet it is also possible to see this refusal to accept life as gray, drab, and routine, and the attempt to make it more venturesome, aesthetic, colorful, and passionate as a kind of experiment in a new form of maturity. The bohemian view that Reed embraced looks two ways: back to preindustrial times, before what Max Weber called the "iron cage" of industrialism and bureaucracy was fastened upon the bourgeois world; and forward to postindustrial society, when the cage may be open once again. It is no exaggeration to say that, more than seventy years after his death, the critique of American society implicit in John Reed's life is still applicable to the social order in which we live.

Suggested Readings

Leslie Fishbein, *Rebels in Bohemia: The Radicals of the Masses, 1910–1917*. Chapel Hill: University of North Carolina Press, 1982.

John Reed, *Adventures of a Young Man*. San Francisco: City Lights Books, 1975.

————, *Insurgent Mexico*. Originally published 1914. New York: International Publishers, 1968.

————, *Ten Days That Shook the World*. Originally published 1919. New York: Bantam Books, 1992.

Robert A. Rosenstone, *Romantic Revolutionary: A Biography of John Reed*. New York: Knopf, 1975.

————, John Stuart, ed., *The Education of John Reed: Selected Writings*. New York: International Publishers, 1955.

21

IDA B. WELLS

Paula Giddings

Ida B. Wells, who launched the nation's first antilynching campaign from Memphis, Tennessee, in 1892, was one of the most militant black leaders in American history. Throughout her activist life, she not only fought to regain the civil rights of African Americans, but also challenged the sociosexual order that oppressed disenfranchised groups in the late nineteenth and twentieth centuries. It was the latter that seemed to especially radicalize her vision, moving her toward a more militant outlook than virtually all of her peers.

Ida Wells's activist career began in earnest on September 15, 1883, the day she refused to leave the first-class "ladies car" on the Chesapeake, Ohio, and Southwestern Railway. At the time she was twenty-one years old and a schoolteacher who regularly traveled in the first-class coach for the ten miles between Memphis, where she had been living for the past three years, and Woodstock, where she taught school. Although the state legislature had passed a Jim Crow law calling for separate but equal accommodations in 1882, there had been no uniform enforcement of it in Memphis, where black and Republican legislators held office longer than in many of her sister Southern cities. Nevertheless by 1884, Republican strength was on the wane. Even more demoralizing, in 1883, the

U.S. Supreme Court ruled that the 1875 Civil Rights bills that prohibited discrimination in public accommodations were unconstitutional, provoking a firestorm of criticism by leading black journalists like T. Thomas Fortune, then publisher of the *New York Freeman,* who counseled African Americans to resist segregation, even if meant getting beaten or killed for it.

Fortune's advice, so boldly offered from his New York offices in the North, would be taken quite literally by Wells in the city that stood on a bluff of the Mississippi River. Wells's seat-gripping refusal resulted in her being physically extricated from the car by three conductors (not before she got a bite out of the hand of one of them, however).

Although she did not realize it at the time, when Wells subsequently sued—and successfully, it turned out, as her case was heard by a former Union officer from Minnesota who awarded her $500 in damages for not being provided first-class accommodations for the price of her first-class ticket—she became, she wrote, the first African American to challenge the recent Supreme Court ruling in a state court. In any case, not even the Christmas-day headline "Darky Damsel Obtains a Verdict for Damages" could dampen her sense of triumph. When asked to write about the experience for a Baptist weekly called *The Living Way,* she would mark the beginning of a journalistic career that found her, by 1889, a co-owner of a militant weekly, *The Free Speech,* and dubbed Princess of the Press by her colleagues of the Afro-American Press Association.

What would shape such vivid political sensibilities in a twenty-two-year-old born in Holly Springs, Mississippi? Her father, James Wells, a carpenter and son of his master and a slave woman named Peggy had no doubt influenced his oldest daughter's political and racial consciousness. As she recalled in her autobiography, James, who worked for the leading contractor in Holly Springs, had refused to be intimidated by his employer to vote for Democrats in the election of 1867—the first in which he would have a chance to vote as a freedman—to determine delegates to Mississippi's constitutional convention. Consequently, he returned from the polls to find that he was locked out of his carpentry shop. Without saying anything to anyone, Ida Wells recalled in her autobiography, her father, simply went back to town, bought a new set of tools, and, in an act of defiant independence, rented a house across the street for himself and his family.

Ida Wells also wrote that among her most indelible memories were hearing the words "Ku Klux Klan," even before she knew what they meant, and the nervous pacing of her mother, Elizabeth, when her father was out to late-night political meetings. James Wells was probably a member of the Republican-led Loyal Leagues—organized across the

South to educate freedmen about the franchise—and participated in its mile-long torchlight processions through the main square of Holly Springs. And although his candidates lost the 1867 election, there were important lessons of political possibility in the Mississippi electorate where in the 1870s, blacks held the posts of U.S. senator (Hiram Revels and Blanche K. Bruce), Speaker of the House (John R. Lynch), and secretary of state (James Hill), among other posts. Hill, a friend of Wells's father, and Revels both resided for a time in Holly Springs.

The other set of memories that shaped her sensibilities involved the struggles of women and men around a broad range of gender and sexuality issues. She may or may not have been aware of the well-publicized incident in 1866 where blacks formed a posse to avenge the murder of a freedwoman by a white man in Holly Springs, but she clearly remembered a stunning conversation between her father and his mother. In angry tones, James Wells told his mother that he would never forget how his former mistress had had her "stripped then whipped" the day after the master had died. As Ida Wells wrote over a half century later: "I have never forgotten those words. Since I have grown old enough to understand I cannot help but feel what an insight to slavery they give."

In Wells's family, a meaning of freedom, in the phrase of Eric Foner, was the right to insulate themselves from such violation through the conventions of Victorian propriety and morality. James and Elizabeth Wells, who were married as slaves, were one of the few black couples in Holly Springs whose remarriage under the auspices of the Freedmen's Bureau was registered. Wells was also subjected to a strict and Christian discipline. Her mother, she reported proudly, once won a church prize for the Sunday school attendance of Ida and her six brothers and sisters.

Nevertheless, among her most bitter lessons was that even in freedom "respectability" was both gendered and racialized. After the tragic death of her parents in the yellow fever epidemic of 1878, when Wells was only sixteen years old, the determination to take care of her siblings herself—rather than "parcel" them out to friends of the family—was misconstrued by town gossips. When a white doctor, who had attended and befriended the dying James Wells, was overheard telling one of Ida's sisters that he would give her the money that evening—referring to money James had left for the children—it was deduced that Ida was involved in sexually illicit activity with white men. "I am quite sure," Wells noted in her autobiography "that never in all my life have I suffered such a shock as I did when I heard this misconstruction."

This would perhaps provide the legal suit against the Chesapeake and Ohio Railroad in 1884 with an additional sense of urgency. For not only were the rights of race in contention but also the latter's relationship to gender, as the term "ladies coach" with its first-class status and prohibition of smoke and lewd language implied. As the case file noted, there were "six passengers in the front [smoker's] car, one of them a *woman*. The rear [first-class] car was set apart for white *ladies* and their gentlemen attendants" (emphasis mine).

Wells lost the case on appeal in 1887. Her sensitivity to the fact that black women were being set outside any realm of protection was no doubt responsible, in part, for Well's exposé on sexual relations—made illicit by the state's miscegenation laws passed in 1870—between white male Memphis board members and black female teachers—contributing to the suicide of one of the latter. The editorial she wrote lost her her job, and also subjected Wells to speculation about her own character. When she heard that a black minister had raised a question about her morality and that of Southern black women in general, Wells forced him—explaining how black women had fought for their sexual integrity in slavery and that she herself had no protection save her good name—to recant his words in front of his entire congregation.

And so, when Wells initiated the antilynching campaign in 1892, a year when lynching reached a new height of 241 incidents, as she reported, her sensitivity to gender and its relationship to race, class, and sexuality was reflected in her two-pronged strategy to combat lynching.

The first aspect of the campaign—begun soon after March 9, 1892, when a friend of Wells's, Tom Moss, and two of his co-owners of the People's Grocery were lynched in Memphis because they had successfully competed with a white proprietor—was a direct-action strategy aimed at economic subversion. In a city where blacks represented forty-four percent of the population—and which was still recovering from the yellow fever epidemic that killed more than 17,000 citizens; seeking foreign investment; and trying to sustain its growth as the fifth largest wholesale grocery market, the largest hardwood market, and a major cotton market—the rationale for Wells's protest became clear. "To Northern capital and Afro-American labor, the South owes its rehabilitation," Wells wrote. "If labor is withdrawn, capital will not remain. . . . A thorough knowledge and judicious exercise of this power in lynching localities, could many times effect a bloodless revolution." That perspective was reflected in her subsequent (and successful) entreaties to the black community to emigrate from Memphis for the Oklahoma territories—leaving business practically at a "standstill" as she wrote—and to boycott the Northern-financed trolley car system.

That Moss and his partners were killed because of economic competition, rather than the prevailing rationale that black men were being murdered for raping white women, spurred Wells to investigate the circumstances of some 728 lynchings over the preceding decade. Concluding that only a fourth of the victims were accused of rape, much less guilty of it, Wells would begin to expose ways that not only race but gender was used as a means of oppression in order to reestablish the uncontested dominance of white males. Now that Memphis, like much of the South, had effectively disenfranchised blacks (by 1889, the year the Bluff City's registration and poll tax laws were passed), proclamations of racialized gender dominance began to be reflected in the press. "The Negro as a political factor can be controlled," announced the *Memphis Daily Commercial,* "but neither laws nor lynchings can subdue his lusts."

At the root of the emergent rape-lynch syndrome was the reestablishment of not only white, but white male supremacy. For white men, the traditional measures of manhood: economic autonomy, dominance over women, and restraint, including sexual self-restraint, had been eroded. Late nineteenth-century Memphis, for example, saw an influx of poor white farmers giving up their agrarian independence in a promising but tenuous and increasingly urbanized economy. In the same period, the Bourbon class experienced a new and disturbing dependence on cotton factors and brokers who controlled credit markets, mortgages, and access to goods.

In addition, newspaper articles of the period warned of the new independence of both working women, due to their having to work and earn wages, as well as the elite, who by 1889, had formed the first woman suffrage league in the state, devoted to "the promotion of the equal rights movement." Finally, new opportunities to have sex outside the family, new sex/gender/race possibilities arising with the separation of sexual intercourse and reproduction, and the growth of sexual commerce, including a lively array of brothels in the port city, challenged the principle of restraint, a masculine necessity to prevent enervation—according to the medical ideas of the day—and to distinguish oneself from the lower, immoral, classes. And, the well-publicized story, in 1892, of a woman who committed suicide on Beale Street because of the infidelity of her female lover could not have made things any easier.

What did reestablish the old hegemony was the rape-lynch syndrome. As a number of historians have contended, the syndrome simultaneously terrorized blacks, especially economically competitive ones; made white women submissive in order to benefit from patriarchal vengeance and protection; and subverted sexual tension by defining whiteness in binary opposition to notions of black lasciviousness. Thus, "the best," that is, chivalrous, men were white as compared to unmanly, uncontrollably lustful black men. Black men, in turn, had been corrupted by black women so lascivious and degenerate, as articles and studies of the period noted, that they welcomed predation. Their very contrast to pure, feminine white womanhood is what made the latter so "alluring" to black men. In this Darwinistic age, oppression of blacks and repression of white women maintained a sociosexual order that was, in the racist mind, synonymous with the very meaning of "civilization."

In her articles, Wells sought to undermine these constructs. Often citing the number of black women who were lynched she laid the rationale of revenge for the crime of rape open to question. More dramatically, her evocation of the continuing "rape of helpless Negro girls and women, which began in slavery days" divested white men, especially those of the class that would have had slaves, of a chivalry that made them manly and worthy of governing. Of course, her most explosive words, ones that would ultimately exile her from the South on the threat of her life, were those that challenged the passionless purity of white women by evoking her findings that a number were involved in interracial liasons with black men. As she stated in her famous May 21 editorial and challenge to the rape-lynch syndrome: "Nobody in this section of the country believes the threadbare lie that Negro men rape white women. If Southern white men are not careful . . . a conclusion will be reached which will be very damaging to the moral reputation of their women." According to Wells's sociosexual order, white men not black men were the rapists; black women didn't do "what nature prompted," as one observer put it, white women did, and with black men, no less.

In 1893 and 1894, Ida Wells would take the discourse to another level when she went to the British Isles to garner support for her campaign. Stating that "America cannot and will not ignore the voice of a nation that is her superior in civilization," she went on to challenge Southern white supremacist exigencies of oppression where "human beings are burned alive in a Christian (?) country and by civilized (?) Anglo-Saxon communities." Her insistence that blacks were not the cause but the victims of uncivilized violence and violation convinced many of the English, such as the editors of the *Birmingham Daily Gazette,* that "the American citizen in the South is at heart more a barbarian than the negro whom he regards as savage." In the process, Wells specifically reclaimed the protective Victorian mantle of ladyhood for herself and black women when she rebutted such characteristics as "dirty-minded mulatress" in the American press by stating, "so hardened is the Southern public mind (white) that it does not object to the coarsest language and most obscene vulgarity in its leading journals so long as it is directed against a negro."

As remarkable as Ida Wells's campaign was in and of itself, it becomes more so when seen in the context of black thought in the 1890s. For under the withering blows of terrorism and disenfranchisement, most black leaders were, in the words of August Meier, "veering away" from political activity toward accommodation, economic advancement, and self-help with its inherent tendency to blame blacks for their own condition. Ida Wells's deconstruction of gender roles, embedded in racial ideology, undermined the logic of accommodation, self-blame, and progress through the accumulation of wealth—an endeavor that got Southern black men killed. Instead she called for a feminist assertion, and "manly resistance" (including armed self-defense), when both seemed to be anachronistic after the demise of the black Convention movement and the Afro-American League, three years before Booker T. Washington's Atlanta Exposition address, and a full thirteen years before the Niagara movement.

Ida Wells's deconstruction was also an important catalyst to the organization of the National Association of Colored Women in 1896, which as historian Darlene Hine notes, "quickly became the largest and most enduring protest organization in the history of Afro-Americans," and which distinctly aimed to combat negative sexual stereotypes, and to protect black women from sexual exploitation.

Subsequently, from her home base in Chicago where she married a like-minded lawyer and publisher (in 1895) and reared four children, Wells would partake in activities common to the Progressive Era. She organized a settlement house for blacks, organized the first black woman's suffrage club in Illinois, and in 1930, a year before her death of uremia, ran for a state senate seat as an independent. But she also continued throughout her life the militant fight against lynching, even as accommodationism and the gradualist liberalism of the NAACP became ascendant. By the World War I years, Wells's activities included exposés of the racist origins of the East St. Louis and Chicago riots in 1917 and 1919 respectively, and her election as the representative of the United Negro Improvement Association's (UNIA) Paris Peace delegation. In this period, Wells was closely watched by military intelligence agencies who characterized her as "a known race agitator," one "considered far more dangerous than Marcus Garvey." The assessment would have made her proud.

Suggested Readings

Gail Bederman, "Civilization, the Decline of Middle-Class Manliness, and the Ida B. Wells Anti-lynching Campaign (1892–94)," *Radical History Review,* no. 52, Winter 1992.

Jacquelyn Dowd Hall, " 'The Mind that Burned in Each Body': Women, Rape and Racial Violence," in Ann Snitow, Christine Stansell, and Sharon Thompson, eds., *Powers of Desire: The Politics of Sexuality.* New York: Monthly Review Press, 1983.

Trudier Harris, ed., *The Selected Works of Ida B. Wells-Barnett.* New York: Oxford University Press, 1991.

Darlene Clark Hine, "Rape and the Inner Lives of Black Women in the Middle West: Preliminary Thoughts on the Culture of Dissemblance," in Ellen Carol Dubois and Vicki Ruiz, eds., *Unequal Sisters: A Multicultural Reader in U.S. Women's History.* New York: Routledge, 1990.

Ida B. Wells, *Crusade for Justice: The Autobiography of Ida B. Wells,* ed. Alfreda Duster. Chicago: University of Chicago Press, 1970.

22

ROBERT M. LA FOLLETTE

R. David Myers

A constant struggle for post–Civil War American radicals was the quest to overcome the inequities caused by the growth of large-scale corporate capitalism. For several decades, Robert M. La Follette was arguably the most important and recognized leader of the opposition to the growing dominance of corporations over the government of the United States. First as governor of Wisconsin and later as a United States senator, La Follette waged a constant battle against corporate domination. He was very much part of a tradition that emphasized popular control of the government and the economy.

The future progressive leader was born June 14, 1855. The death of his father in 1856 and an unhappy relationship with his stepfather led to a difficult early life, but he attended school and developed an active social life. After his stepfather's death, his mother sold the farm and moved to Madison. La Follette taught school to earn tuition for the University of Wisconsin. He was a very mediocre student who enjoyed social activities, especially debate. University president John Bascom deeply influenced La Follette's lifelong commitment to morality, ethics, and social justice. He also developed a love for oratory and won a major Midwestern competition during his senior year. As a student, he met Belle Case whom he

married in 1880. Already a leading feminist and outspoken advocate of
women's suffrage, she was always a crucial element in the development
of La Follette's ideas.

After graduation, La Follette began a public career that lasted from
1880 to 1925. After attending law school briefly and passing the bar in
1880, he immediately sought and won the Republican nomination and
general election for Dane County district attorney. Following two successful terms, he was elected to the House of Representatives and served
three undistinguished terms, although he did become a champion for
Native and African-American rights.

Defeated for a fourth term, La Follette returned to Madison to build a
private law practice, but he was completely committed to politics. So,
even with a busy practice and four children, he spoke frequently on
politics at social gatherings. During the early 1890s, La Follette realized
that the Republican party was abandoning its antislavery roots and becoming dominated by corporate interests. In Wisconsin this meant the railroad
and timber industries. Deeply troubled, La Follette built an independent
organization within the party that emphasized voter control.

An 1891 incident played a particular role in developing La Follette's
outlook. Philetus Sawyer, then a United States senator and party leader,
allegedly tried to bribe La Follette to fix a case. This incident, combined
with his growing fear of corporate domination, made the need for a new
direction clear. Party dissidents became known as Insurgents, and the
party regulars were called Stalwarts. La Follette Insurgents argued for
more direct voter control and consumer rights. This message was given
a new impetus when the Panic of 1893 shattered many of the class,
ethnic, and economic assumptions that had limited previous reform efforts.
Beginning in 1894, the Insurgents openly challenged the Stalwarts for
the party's leadership. First, Nils Haugen campaigned for the gubernatorial
nomination, and La Follette ran in 1896 and 1898. La Follette's message
against the control of big business, particularly the railroads, and for
more direct democracy drew ever larger and more sympathetic crowds.

Finally in 1900 La Follette's diligence paid off. He put together a
coalition that temporarily broke the Stalwarts' hold on the nomination
process. His dedication was clearly evidenced by his indefatigable campaigning. He traveled to sixty-one counties, gave 216 speeches and spoke
to 200,000 people. Many of his speeches were delivered from the back
of a buckboard wagon and frequently lasted three hours. He won the
election by 100,000 votes.

La Follette's legislative program for his first term was modest. He
proposed to set up a powerful railroad commission, impose an ad valorem
tax on the railroads, and establish a direct primary. When Stalwarts

blocked his program, he refused to compromise. This conflict took its toll. In a pattern that would be repeated throughout his career, as soon as the legislature adjourned in May, he collapsed with severe stomach pains. For the next year, he failed to improve and several times was close to death.

For the 1902 election, Stalwarts formed an organization to oppose La Follette's nomination, while he tried to unite insurgent Democrats in a broad coalition. Again, conservative forces blocked reform legislation. La Follette forced through the primary bill and won some revision of the railroad tax structure.

Following adjournment, La Follette went on the road immediately. He placed a greater emphasis on the role of the consumer. He attacked business interests mercilessly and devised a new strategy to embarrass anticonsumer legislators. In every district where he campaigned against his enemies, La Follette used the "roll call." He discussed bills that affected consumers and then related the legislator's vote. He implied that the community's legislator was a tool of the railroads or the timber industry. In this fashion, he developed a public image as the only true spokesman for the people and earned the nickname "Fighting Bob."

As he campaigned, La Follette attracted national attention. Muckraking journalists like Lincoln Steffens came to Wisconsin to learn about this crusading governor. The reasons for this interest resulted just as much from La Follette's administration style as from his personality. La Follette was responsible for developing the Wisconsin Idea. He realized that a key ingredient in developing successful legislation was the need for thorough research and expert involvement. He worked closely with leading University of Wisconsin faculty like Richard T. Ely, John R. Commons, and E. A. Ross. In this fashion, Wisconsin became the laboratory for democracy.

During La Follette's administration and subsequent ones, Wisconsin was the most important state for the development of progressive legislation. The direct primary, railroad regulation, public utility regulation, child labor, corrupt practices, income tax, and workers compensation were only a few of the programs first developed by Wisconsin. In each area, university faculty were heavily involved. La Follette also signed legislation that created the Wisconsin Legislative Reference Library (now Bureau) to ensure there would be a research agency for the development of legislation.

These developments and La Follette's reelection made him a national figure. His message that denounced "vast corporate combinations" and the accumulation of individual wealth attracted journalists and other progressives. Realizing that the problem of corporate domination was much greater at the national level, he set his sights on the United States Senate. The first order of business for the 1905 legislature was to elect La Follette to the Senate. He remained in Madison until 1906 to redeem his 1904 platform.

When La Follette arrived in Washington in 1906 the challenges facing reformers and radicals were formidable. The American economy had undergone significant change during the previous decade. A large number of mergers had consolidated more power into fewer hands. Led by Nelson Aldrich and John C. Spooner, the Senate reflected this growing domination. In a series of damning articles, David Graham Phillips exposed the "Treason of the Senate" by charging widespread corruption and subservience to corporate interests.

As the conservative leader, Aldrich limited the effectiveness of Insurgents by placing them on insignificant committees. But in his usual fashion, La Follette quickly established himself as the consumer's champion by raising issue after issue. When, for example, the Senate debated the Hepburn Bill, La Follette argued that it discriminated against consumers and offered a series of amendments to put conservatives on record as opposing consumer interests.

As a national leader of the Insurgents, he left on a speaking tour when Congress adjourned. He did so for two reasons. First, he needed to earn money. The La Follettes were never wealthy, so he frequently supplemented family income by accepting money to give speeches. Second, La Follette saw himself as the emerging leader of progressive forces and traveled extensively to read the roll about the anticonsumer senators. In this fashion, he built a national following.

When he returned to Washington, La Follette became the progressives' leader. La Follette, Jonathan Dolliver, Albert Cummins, and others established a fairly formal circle. Frequently, they were joined by others like Steffens, Phillips, and Louis Brandeis, to discuss issues and develop strategies to limit conservative power in Congress and the judiciary. La Follette created a forum for his fellow progressives (and especially himself) when he began *La Follette's Weekly* in 1909.

La Follette's beliefs and fears about the direction of America were confirmed during the Bankers' Panic of 1907. Aldrich proposed to solve the problem by issuing $500 million in emergency currency backed in part by railroad bonds. La Follette saw Aldrich and others working closely with such financiers as J. P. Morgan to establish economic centralization and destroy American free institutions. The situation worsened as Theodore Roosevelt gave way to the much more conservative William Howard Taft in 1909.

To counteract the Republicans' growing conservatism, La Follette organized the National Progressive Republican League. He saw the League as a foundation for a 1912 presidential bid. The time certainly seemed opportune. The period before the 1912 election was one of those rare opportunities in American history when reformers and radicals had a real opportunity to build a lasting coalition to redirect fundamentally the course of American affairs. The events prior to the election and La Follette's role were symbolic of this opportunity, and the developments provide some insight into his major failings.

La Follette's tours of the country took a heavy toll on conservatives. He appealed to farmers by drawing heavily on the issues articulated by the Populists, to workers by being one of labor's most consistent supporters, and to the broader range of classes as the foremost spokesperson for consumer rights. He was a leading figure in calling attention to discrimination against women and minority groups. He also argued for a much greater degree of direct democracy by calling for the states to adopt initiative, referendum, and recall procedures, and for the direct election of senators. Politicians, farmers, workers, consumer advocates, and others seemed to be on the verge of leading the United States in a radically different direction.

The final issue that sparked a progressive revolt was the Pinchot-Ballinger controversy. Taft appeared to be selling out conservation interests to the corporations. Progressives now openly encouraged La Follette to challenge Taft. But Taft's bungling also caused Roosevelt to consider a presidential bid for himself. Attempts to reconcile differences between the two leaders failed. Roosevelt believed that La Follette like progressives were too radical because they had too much faith in direct democracy and too great a sense of moral outrage toward corporate capitalism. La Follette always questioned Roosevelt's commitment to fundamental reform.

La Follette's campaign was constantly limited by the specter of Roosevelt. Many of La Follette's supporters, like Gifford Pinchot, maintained close relations with the former president and viewed La Follette as a stalking horse. La Follette complicated matters by making a series of crucial mistakes. In the fall of 1911, he spent an inordinate amount of time writing his autobiography. He relied heavily on Wisconsin lieutenants with little national experience to run his campaign. He made a disastrous speech to an important meeting of newspaper editors, after which many supporters called upon him to withdraw. The struggle between La Follette and Roosevelt gave Taft the Republican nomination, and when Roosevelt supporters bolted to form the Progressive party, La Follette refused to support the ticket.

The struggle between La Follette and Roosevelt essentially destroyed any hope for a major leftist coalition. La Follette's bitter attacks on his erstwhile supporters who endorsed Roosevelt destroyed the Insurgent organization. In part, this failure resulted from La Follette's limitations. He tended to view issues and people in black and white terms. He saw himself as an infallible judge of right and wrong and demanded absolute obedience from his lieutenants. When they failed to follow his lead, he attacked them and thereby frequently limited his effectiveness by alienating important supporters.

Following the 1912 debacle, La Follette became a lone wolf in the Senate. At first he supported President Wilson and voted for some of his major programs. This support soon ebbed as he believed Wilson was too concerned with not offending business leaders to create effective reform legislation. He was especially appalled when Wilson introduced segregation into the federal service. La Follette remained an outspoken supporter of consumers, farmers, and workers. In 1915 he authored the only law to bear his name, the La Follette Seamen's Act, which corrected the horrible treatment of American sailors and benefited consumers. The same year he cosponsored legislation to establish what is now the Congressional Research Service. By 1917, La Follette's attention turned from domestic issues to international ones. The war in Europe was three years old, and he believed that Wilson was steering America toward intervention. La Follette was always deeply skeptical of the way big business influenced the State Department. He understood that financial imperialism inspired America's interventions in the Caribbean and Mexico. Within this framework, La Follette resisted every step toward American intervention.

The war years were La Follette's most difficult and most courageous. He assumed leadership of a small but important group of antiwar legislators. He voted against the war and battled constantly in the Senate to impose heavy taxes on war profits. In the public sphere, he was an outspoken critic of the way in which employers and journalists sought to suppress critics of the war. Vigilante groups called for his ouster, and the Senate ordered an investigation to consider his expulsion. He was deeply hurt by a petition signed by 421 University of Wisconsin faculty members who deplored his failure to support the prosecution of the war.

After the war, he continued to fight major battles for the rights of Americans and people in other countries. He criticized the administration's intervention in Russia after the Bolshevik Revolution. At home, he attacked the "Red Scare" which abrogated the rights of domestic radicals. By 1919, he was again a leader of the progressives struggling to protect the rights of individuals and against the ever-growing domination of large corporations.

Corporate domination became even a larger issue in the 1920s. La

Follette watched the new president, Warren G. Harding, openly collaborate with business leaders. The conservation program was destroyed to allow corporations to exploit mineral resources on public lands. More galling was the restoration of the railroads to private ownership. He openly called for government ownership of railroads and public utilities. The Esch-Cummins Act not only returned the railroads to private ownership but also compensated the owners with $550 million.

The years before the 1924 election were bittersweet ones for La Follette. He viewed his 1922 reelection as a vindication of his opposition to the war. On the other hand, formerly progressive colleagues like Cummins became more conservative, and Republicans were less willing to tolerate his challenges. Yet widespread corruption in the Harding administration, especially the Teapot Dome scandal, gave progressives a new lease on life.

These development encouraged La Follette to consider a presidential run. Using the Conference for Progressive Political Action (CPPA), La Follette gathered petitions. Socialists, farm groups, and labor unions all turned to the CPPA for third-party activity. Morris Hillquit, Fiorello La Guardia, and Burton K. Wheeler (the vice-presidential candidate) joined together to nominate La Follette. The Socialist party, the railroad brotherhoods, and the American Federation of Labor (its only third-party endorsement) also joined the fold. W. E. B. Du Bois, Margaret Sanger, and others worked for his election.

Again, the potential for a significant social-democratic coalition seemed eminently realizable. But again, problems outweighed progress. The campaign started slowly, and money remained a problem. La Follette alienated potential leaders like La Guardia by again relying almost exclusively on Wisconsin lieutenants. The campaign began as a contest between La Follette and Republican Calvin Coolidge. In fear of a La Follette victory, corporate leaders began pressuring employees to support Coolidge. In the end, La Follette garnered five million votes but carried only Wisconsin.

The campaign took its toll on La Follette's health. Shortly after his seventieth birthday he suffered a heart attack and died on June 18, 1925. His casket was loaded on a train in Washington and sent to Wisconsin. In every rail center, workers removed their caps and stood in silence as the train moved through. In Madison, some 50,000 people viewed the open casket. Burton Wheeler paid him the greatest homage by comparing him to Abraham Lincoln and giving him credit for being the greatest champion of industrial emancipation.

Wheeler was right. La Follette spent his public career trying to make the American government stay true to its republican ideals. In a country where fundamental reform is very difficult at any time, La Follette, unlike many of his contemporaries, never wavered from the struggle to keep control of the government at any level in the hands of the voters. True, his success was limited by some major faults, but his legacies still affect the course of government today. In Wisconsin, the role of intellectuals in government made it the model for other states and the federal government. Two of his creations, the Legislative Reference Bureau and the Congressional Research Service, still provide substantive research for legislative development. His two sons, Robert, Jr., and Philip, continued their father's work; one as a senator and the other as governor. Most important, La Follette's relentless warnings about corruptive influences on government are needed just as much today as they were ninety years ago.

Suggested Readings

Alan Dawley, *Struggles for Justice: Social Responsibility and the Liberal State*. Cambridge: Harvard University Press, 1991.

Belle and Fola La Follette, *Robert M. La Follette*. 2 vols. New York: Macmillan, 1953.

Robert M. La Follette, *La Follette's Autobiography: A Personal Narrative of Political Experiences*. Originally published 1913. Madison: University of Wisconsin Press, 1968.

Robert S. Maxwell, *Robert M. La Follette and the Rise of Progressivism in Wisconsin*. Madison: State Historical Society of Wisconsin, 1956.

David P. Thelen, *Robert M. La Follette and the Insurgent Spirit*. Originally published 1976. Madison: University of Wisconsin Press, 1985.

Thomas Paine

Painting by A. Milliére after G. Romney.
Courtesy of National Portrait Galley, London.

Sojourner Truth
Courtesy of Battle Creek Historical Society, Michigan.

Abby Kelley
Courtesy of Dorothy Sterling.

Frederick Douglass

Photo by George Warren.
Courtesy of National Portrait Gallery, Smithsonian Institution.

Upton Sinclair
Courtesy of Greg Mitchell.

John Reed

Painting by Robert Hallowell.
Courtesy of The Harvard University Portrait Collections.

Robert M. LaFollette
On steps of the Wisconsin State Capitol.
Courtesy of the State Historical Society of Wisconsin.

Mother Jones
Courtesy of the Library of Congress.

Dorothy Day
Milwaukee Journal Photo.
Courtesy of Marquette University Memorial Library.

Clifford Odets
Courtesy of Walt Odets.

Paul Robeson, W. E. B. Du Bois, and Vito Marcantonio
Courtesy of Moorland-Spingarn Research Center,
Howard University.

Martin Luther King, Jr. and Malcolm X
Courtesy of the Library of Congress.

23

RICARDO FLORES MAGON

Juan Gomez-Quiñones

Ricardo Flores Magon (1873–1922) was ideologically a reflection of his age and certainly among Mexicans a major contributor to the intellectual climate and political process of the time; his voice was the most radical of the time, at its height during the years between 1901 and 1912. Flores Magon lived in the United States from 1904 to 1922, among Mexican Americans and Mexican immigrants.

Ricardo Flores Magon came of age in the late nineteenth century influenced by his family and by the education then in vogue, and reflecting the idealistic anxieties of his social surroundings. To be sure, nativist communal ideals permeated his early upbringing. He was also the bearer of the Mexican liberal inheritance of the nineteenth century. He was closer to the radical rather than the moderate variety of liberals. As his thought evolved over time, there were certain constants as well as changes in his ideas.

The education which Flores Magon received in his youth was to strongly mark his writings and political tactics. Apart from what he learned in his Zapotec indio-mestizo home, first in Oaxaca then in Mexico City, Flores Magon received a college-preparatory and positivist education that stressed rational analysis, evidence, and objectivity. This educational framework upheld the primacy of the material world which, according to positivism, followed "laws." Accordingly, the world was evolving, all spheres of life interacted, progress was possible. Life, as struggle, was an integral premise in this worldview. Society had the potential for improvement through effort and education. Utilitarian tenets upheld the greatest good for the greatest number, and the idealist content urged the efficacy of personal volition, and the ideal of individual liberty.

Flores Magon, as he received these particular analytical tools and premises for approaching and dealing with the world, also turned to other influences that provided a political and social complement. Conversant in English, he also knew some French and Italian. Throughout his life he read literature, such as Shakespeare and the naturalist writers, and read political literature from several countries. From childhood, because of his family, he was inclined to democratic liberalism as a political creed; his writings evidence a thorough knowledge of the mid-nineteenth century generation of liberals. Up to his conversion to anarchism, he too upheld the democratic republican axioms as sufficient civic objectives.

Flores Magon amended and rejected some of these formative influences during his lifetime. He maintained throughout, however, a critical view of life, remained a materialist, and firmly pegged his political ideas to conform to a world of natural laws. Life was worth living for him and what disorder there was, through rational reasoning, individuals could bring to harmony. Yet in his thought there were always theoretical and humanist preoccupations. He held as goals for political activity solidarity, generosity, selflessness, harmony, and social well-being. These to him summed up ages-old indigenist communalism to which he repeatedly referred. He later questioned progress through evolution; the solution was revolution to reestablish progress. He became convinced that the problems of Mexico were integrally associated with worldwide conditions. This realization affected his focus of concern. To change Mexico, the world had to be changed—thus he became an internationalist. Flores Magon emerged an organizer as a student activist and member of several radical newspapers, invariably working as a member of a group. His family, particularly his mother, wholeheartedly supported his public advocations. He crossed into the United States on January 4, 1904.

The PLM

In contrast to, but concurrent with, the participation of Mexicans in United States electoral political parties, civil rights advocacy groups, and cultural social service activities, stand the radical actions of Mexicans during the first two decades of the century. The rise of the Partido Liberal Mexicano (PLM), led by Ricardo Flores Magon, represents a benchmark in the political history of the Mexican people in the United States and Mexico. Its origins stem from the more radical tendency among reformist liberals in Mexico and along the border. As an organized effort the PLM formed in St. Louis, Missouri, September 25, 1906. The PLM saw itself as an international, revolutionary-ideological, semiclandestine party. PLM propagated the destruction of the state and capitalism in Mexico and capitalism in general. The PLM evolved from a radical liberalism to an anarcho-communist position and to a consideration of anarcho-syndicalism.

PLM had a base of operations and support in the U.S. Southwest. Several thousand in the Mexican community in the United States participated in and supported the PLM in all its activities. The widespread and diverse areas of radical activity included forming local PLM chapters, agitating unionization, organizing newspapers, conducting propaganda and legal defense work, raising funds, and securing supplies for revolutionary participation in direct action against both Mexican and United States authorities. These activities attested to the solidarity and relatively extensive support of the PLM in the Mexican community in the United States. The PLM, however, suffered from the limitations created by an inability to stabilize its membership base, factionalism, and of course, intense persecution. The PLM in particular had a definite socioeconomic base of aggrieved members of different strata among workers but it was only one of several groups reflecting discontent. PLM organizing influence in Mexico and in the United States was visible through the 1930s, though the organization had ceased to exist by 1920. However, PLM material and the writings of Flores Magon have continually been reprinted and widely distributed through the 1990s.

Activities

Under the leadership of Ricardo Flores Magon, the PLM was the ideological vanguard of the Mexican revolutionary process, one eventually constrained by more conservative elements in the political organizational spheres. Flores Magon and PLM received severe censure and persecution. While upholding an uncompromising anarchist-communist ideology whose clear goal was the overthrow of capitalism and the capitalist state in Mexico, the PLM acknowledged the need to struggle for democratic demands and to develop a broad democratic movement among the laboring people, not as ends in themselves but as a basis to organize and move toward an ultimate revolutionary confrontation.

PLM strategy for organization involved the creation of a widespread propaganda network to reach its supporters and the laboring people. Central to this strategy was the reestablishment of *Regeneracion,* previously at Mexico City, in the United States, initially at San Antonio, then St. Louis, and ultimately at Los Angeles. Integral to the effectiveness of the publication was the organization of a clandestine network to disseminate *Regeneracion,* pamphlets, and other propaganda throughout Mexico and the Mexican population in the United States.

Within a year, distribution exceeded twenty thousand copies. Despite police vigilance, the newspapers were smuggled to many regions of both republics. PLM militants and sympathizers among the railroad workers were able to distribute the paper to the major centers of population along the rail lines, where copies could be redistributed to other nuclei. Also key to this strategy was the establishment of a network of local publications in Mexican communities throughout the United States, as well as clandestine publication of materials in Mexico. Some materials were in English, and *Regeneracion* on occasion had English and Italian articles. Within two years a network of several local PLM and allied publications more or less functioned, including four by women, which disseminated information through the United States and Mexico. These efforts often became local organizing vehicles for the PLM, reporting the progress of the struggle in Mexico and championing the struggle of the Mexican laborers against ethnic and labor oppression in the United States.

Organizing and Constituency

The party organized under the central leadership of a junta and operated through local chapters in both the United States and Mexico. Financially the party depended on contributions, membership dues, and the sale of *Regeneracion.* Organizational activity centered around the ongoing struggle against the regimes in Mexico, support for revolutions abroad, and local struggles in both the United States and Mexico. The central focus of party activity was on propaganda to workers and support of labor organizing waged on both sides of the border, and preparations for armed struggle. Major general organizing drives were conducted in 1906, 1908, and 1910, when the PLM message was reaching thousands of Mexicans throughout Mexico and the United States. After 1914, PLM emphasized propaganda and working through specific unionization activity both in the United States and Mexico. Pockets of labor influence remained among farm, mine, track, and cargo workers in the United States and in Mexico among electrical, oil, and rail workers. Although the PLM focused generally on the industrial worker, its influence was also felt among sectors of the rural work force, the rural petty bourgeoisie, and among some progressive intellectuals.

The PLM's constituency and partisans among the Mexican people fell into two groups: 1) a broad audience of sympathizers composed primarily of artisans, industrial workers, and laborers in both Mexico and the United States. This sector between 1906 and 1910 rapidly expanded with the increasing dissemination of *Regeneracion* and the press efforts, forming the basis for recruitment and the organization of new branches of the party and sympathizing affiliated groups; and 2) the local leadership core of district organizers, chapter officers, and journalists, operating in conditions of semilegality, under constant threat of suppression, within the United States and in Mexico.

The PLM's major constituencies among Mexicans in the United States were strongest in three major areas: 1) along the Texas border involving renters and agricultural and town workers; 2) among the miners of Nuevo Mexico, Arizona, and El Paso; and 3) among the large, expanding, Mexican semiurban and urban-laborer population of Los Angeles and among some California farm workers. The specific emphasis and character of PLM organizing in these and other areas reflected the specific local social and economic conditions existing in those areas.

Programs

Significant to the influence of PLM in particular was the issuing of several major statements. The PLM "Program of 1906" in the February 20, 1906, issue of *Regeneracion* was the most widely received. Months in advance, PLM's reading public had been asked to contribute suggestions for the formulation of the program. This drive stimulated the interest and contributions of thousands of Mexican workers and progressive intellectuals, on *both* sides of the border. The program stressed the appeal to the broad masses of the working people and in particular the progressive opposition. The program incorporated many democratic demands. Among the more salient points were those which called for an eight-hour workday, minimum wages, prohibition of child labor, compensation for work-related injuries, the abolition of fines and deductions from salaries, the confiscation of uncultivated lands to be distributed to the landless, education for all children to the age of fourteen, protection of the Indian communities, suppression of the death penalty, and abolishment of compulsory military service as well as the establishment of prodemocracy unity with groups in Latin American countries. Moreover, the program's general democratic, labor, and social aspirations were translatable into a United States context for Mexicans. The program was to become a vehicle for organization and for ideological debate among the public up to 1910.

The Manifesto del Partido Liberal Mexicano issued on September 23, 1911, stated the current position of the party and was published to correct and supplant the one of 1906. Thousands of copies were distributed. The anarchist ideology was explicit. The call advocated the total destruction of capital, government, and the church. Workers were not to lay down their arms until poverty and authority were abolished. Local communities of women and men in assembly would determine procedures and actions. Only thus would economic, social, and political equality and freedom be brought about. The influence of Kropotkin was strong in this document as well as in other writings of the period.

After 1914, what remained of the PLM now considered the alternate name of Union Obrera Revolucionaria, Workers' Revolutionary Union. Whatever radical spirit there had been in the United States was chilled by the winds of World War I. By 1916, the time for PLM's revolution had come and gone. In Mexico, Flores Magon did not have much of an audience left or even a stable forum for developing an audience. The last numbers of *Regeneracion* were two pages, and it had lost its mailing privileges. Even the post office box had been withdrawn. However, Flores Magon still persisted to project radical concepts in his time and to propagandize a utopian vision.

Though critical of trade unionism, he now emphasized site and occupations in his organizational efforts. He saw radical potential in urban alienated populations as confrontational forces; however, he believed in urban agricultural unity and he looked to economic crisis as catalyst. Flores Magon, like Lenin, was among the international militants not to be confused by the surface patriotic rhetoric of World War I. Rather than an interregnum in revolutionary activity, he saw the war as the most propitious of times for revolt against the bourgeoisie. He pointed out that the workers had class interests, not state ones, in a war among imperialists and he analyzed for whom and for what World War I was being fought, for capitalists and capitalist states. Flores Magon viewed World War I as signaling the breakup of the old order and ushering in a period of instability. PLM welcomed the revolution in Russia as a sign of world crisis. In 1917, Flores Magon emphasized a redefined internationalist and syndicalist direction; the consequences, however, would be the same as in the past; persecution and imprisonment.

The last manifesto was published on March 16, 1918. This call addressed the "Workers of the World." It was an exhortation to be firm in revolutionary faith, a call to revolutionary idealism. The manifesto stated that civilization was in crisis quickly passing from one historical stage to another. Rather than the direct, immediate violence that had been part of the tone of previous statements, this manifesto emphasized the creative humanitarian task of the revolutionary to forge a new world. A primary task was to prepare, to seed, to educate for the coming worldwide revolution.

Final Arrest

The manifesto was a farewell for *Regeneracion* and the PLM group: the last two issues were those of February 9 and March 16, 1918, the latter featuring the manifesto. PLM junta members Ricardo Flores Magon and Librado Rivera were charged under the Espionage Act; the allegation argues they were hindering the war effort with their ideas. Both were arrested in Los Angeles on March 18, 1918. Bail was set at $50,000 and $15,000 respectively. Moreover, PLM veteran Maria Talavera was arrested and held for five months without trial, then released. These arrests were part of a large-scale effort by the federal government directed against radicals and dissenters. The Mexican radical suffered at the same time the same fate that many other dissenters in the United States faced. Flores Magon and Rivera were sentenced to twenty and fifteen years respectively and fined $5,000 each. Clearly these were political charges and a violation of basic rights guaranteed by the Constitution; no overt act was involved. Years later, Congressman George Huddleston was to say as much on the floor of Congress. Ricardo Flores Magon died at Leavenworth Federal Prison on November 21, 1922.

Precedents

Within its major revolutionary goals and according to language and means available at the time, five major trends were championed by the PLM:

1) There was a uniquely strong emphasis on the role of the woman in the revolutionary drive and on women's rights. This was reflected in the key roles played by many women in the party and affiliated organizations and the many outstanding PLM women activists.

2) The party worked with the progressive sectors of the socialist and syndicalist movements of the United States. Several European-immigrant and Anglo militants from the Socialist party, and IWW in particular, played roles in support of the PLM struggles. PLM was in contact at one time or another with nearly all the left groups and figures of the time. The PLM consistently supported the struggle of the United States workers in general, and maintained an active support for revolutionary movements.

3) Supportive selective interrelations with labor and trade unionists were practiced. PLM believed the unity in action of agricultural and industrial workers crucial. PLM worked with members of the Western Federation of Miners, the Industrial Workers of the World, and some of the more politicized federal union locals affiliated with the AFL.

4) PLM argued for ethically combining the personal and political, and practiced a cultural program concurrent with a political one which PLM developed rudimentarily, focused on schooling, literature, drama, songs, and visual art.

5) PLM clearly stated the need for a worldwide revolution, including the United States as well as Mexico.

Ethical and humanist emphases were visible in their activities. As stated, the major focus of PLM was mobilizing the agricultural and industrial worker, and the PLM militants were among the organizers of several trade union efforts in the United States and Mexico. Flores Magon and other PLM members faced charges and imprisonment on several occasions. PLM turned trials and imprisonment into political causes. Significantly, the last trial in federal court and the conviction of Flores Magon were based on charges pertinent to the United States for actions directed at the United States government in behalf of the antiwar effort.

The PLM represented a continuing tradition of ideological, political, and organizational interrelations of Mexicans on both sides of the border. In many respects the broad influence of the party as well as its leadership of radical efforts throughout the U.S. Southwest and Mexico, its base of sympathizers and network of branches throughout the Southwest can be said at the time to represent a high tide of radical organizational success. The PLM, despite its ultimate failure to prevent the reformist direction of the mass movement during the insurgency in Mexico, or to consolidate the advance sector of the Mexican-American community into coalition with anarchist and socialist groups in the United States, reflected the vitality of radical organization among the Mexican people across the border. To some activists in the post-60s years the PLM's experience, its successes and failures, represented an instructive guide, symbol, and challenge.

During the times of the PLM, many radical Mexicans carried out activities with other organizations such as the Socialist party and the Industrial Workers of the World (IWW). Much of the activity centered on organizing workers in the cities and on farms, sharecroppers and tenant farmers in the rural areas. There was Mexican participation in the Socialist party and the IWW in areas where Mexicans lived and worked from the Canadian to the Mexican borders. This solidarity was the greater to the extent local organizations of these groups were empathetic and effective. Whatever differences existed ideologically among them, through specific solidarity actions the Mexicans in the Socialist party, the IWW, and the PLM expressed their class consciousness and left ideological preferences.

Suggested Readings

Ward S. Albro, *Always a Rebel: Ricardo Flores Magon and the Mexican Revolution*. Fort Worth: Texas Christian University Press, 1992.

Ricardo Flores Magon, *Prison Letters of Ricardo Flores Magon to Lilly Sarnoff*. Amsterdam: International Review of Social History, 1977.

Juan Gomez-Quiñones, *Sembradores, Ricardo Flores Magon y el Partido Liberal Mexicano: A Eulogy and Critique*. Los Angeles: Chicano Studies Center, UCLA, 1973.

John Mason Hart, *Revolutionary Mexico*. Berkeley: University of California Press, 1987.

Salvador Hernandez, *El magonismo: Historia de una pasión libertaria*. Mexico, D.F.: Era, 1984.

24

MOTHER JONES

Elliott J. Gorn

In one of the most quoted passages in American literature, Tom Joad declared in John Steinbeck's 1939 novel *The Grapes of Wrath,* "I'll be everywhere—wherever you look. Wherever they's a fight so hungry people can eat, I'll be there. Wherever they's a cop beatin' up a guy, I'll be there. . . ." Thirty years before Steinbeck created Tom Joad, Mother Jones, when asked to state her residence in testimony before the House Rules Committee, declared, "I live in the United States, but I do not know exactly in what place, because I am always in the fight against oppression, and wherever a fight is going on I have to jump there . . . so that really I have no particular residence." Millions of Americans have read Tom Joad's words; hundreds of scholars have written about John Steinbeck. Yet the story of a woman who *lived* those words, whose name was legendary a few generations ago, is now largely unknown.

Mary Harris "Mother" Jones was one of the most prominent figures in the history of American radicalism, yet her legacy is unclear. In terms of organizations built, strikes won, or industries unionized, she was not notably successful. Measured by the depth or cogency of her intellectual contribution, the history of the American left would scarcely be altered had she never lived. But for roughly a quarter century, Mother Jones could be said to have embodied the conscience of the American left.

"She is a wonder," Carl Sandburg wrote of Mother Jones during World War I; "close to 88 years old and her voice a singing voice; nobody else could give me a thrill just by saying in that slow solemn orotund way, 'The kaisers of this country are next, I tell ye.' " It was with America's working class, however, that she exercised her greatest influence. Eugene Debs, Socialist party candidate for president, said of her in 1907, "She has won her way into the hearts of the nation's toilers, and her name is revered at the altars of their humble firesides and will be lovingly remembered by their children and their children's children forever."

Yet Debs was wrong. Mother Jones fell victim to what the English historian E. P. Thompson calls "the enormous condescension of posterity." The now elderly twentieth century seems embarrassed by its adolescence and determined to forget its youthful indiscretions. But the early decades of this century in fact were filled with dissent and conflict; radicalism helped foster a creative dialogue within American society. During the years of her greatest fame, Mother Jones's voice was one of the most powerful in that dialogue. As a tireless organizer and fearless agitator, she was unique.

The first half of her life is shadowy, and a full account remains to be written. In her autobiography (coauthored with Mary Field Parton in 1925 and published by Charles Kerr and Company) she claimed to have been born on May Day, 1830. But Jones was never very precise in her recollections, and some scholars believe that she was at least a decade younger than she claimed. We do know that she was born Mary Harris in Cork, Ireland, but that when she was a young girl, her father, Richard, moved his family to Toronto, Canada, where he worked on railroad construction. Before migrating, however, her people had been active in the Irish resistance against England; indeed, she claimed that her grandfather had been hanged by the hated British for sedition. So we know that hard physical labor, exploitation, class consciousness, and political dissent were part of Mary Harris's heritage.

Mary attained a basic education, attended normal school, acquired some skills as a seamstress, then taught in a convent school in Michigan. Just before the Civil War she moved to Memphis, where she met and married an iron moulder, a union man named George Jones. They had four children, according to her autobiography, but in 1867, a yellow fever epidemic took her entire family, including her husband. Mary Jones moved to Chicago, and opened a small seamstress shop with a partner, but was burned out in the Chicago fire of 1871. We do not know a great deal about the next quarter century of her life, but these years—spent mostly in Chicago, with its unprecedented industrial growth, union organizing, and radical ferment—were the crucible of her ideology. "Often while sewing for the lords and barons who lived in magnificent houses on the Lake Shore Drive," she remembered of her seamstress days, "I would look out of the plate glass windows and see the poor, shivering wretches, jobless and hungry, walking along the frozen lake front. The contrast of their condition with that of the tropical comfort of the people for whom I sewed was painful to me."

Until just before the turn of the century, Mary Jones was a bit player in the labor movement. The sources give us fleeting glimpses of her in Pittsburgh amidst the great railroad strike of 1877, in San Francisco during the anti-Chinese agitation, in Chicago for the Haymarket riot of 1886, and in Washington with Coxey's Army in 1894. Sometime in the early 1880s she joined the Knights of Labor, and began a lifelong friendship with Master Workman Terrance Powderly. By the 1890s, she was helping to organize miners in Virginia and Pennsylvania. Her work with textile operatives in Cottondale and Birmingham, Alabama, impassioned her against child labor. In the 1890s, she had made the acquaintance of Eugene V. Debs, worked to help organize the Socialist party, and tirelessly distributed Julius Wayland's new socialist newspaper the *Appeal to Reason*.

And then she burst on the American scene. By 1900, Mary Jones was probably about sixty years old, white-haired, grandmotherly in her black dress with bits of lace. Just when many people begin to slow down their labors, hers intensified. The tragedies of her youth and relative obscurity of her middle age only served to heighten the legendary quality of her next thirty years. An immigrant, a woman, a fiercely proletarian political radical, she imposed her presence on the national consciousness.

The signal change was her invention of "Mother" Jones. Just after the turn of the century she published articles in the *International Socialist Review* under this new moniker. She also signed herself "Mother" in personal correspondence to men like Eugene Debs, Secretary of Labor William Wilson, and United Mine Workers president John Mitchell, and they, in turn, addressed her with that title. Workers too called her "Mother," and she called them her boys. The image she cultivated, however, did not represent motherhood as victimized and docile. Rather, the persona Mary Jones lived was one of motherhood aroused, of a woman who faced down old age and gun-toting thugs for the family of labor. Her imagery implicitly countered the self-celebratory ideology of triumphant capitalism—not for her the rhetoric of every man for himself, but of brotherhood, or more precisely, of labor as a family. Mother Jones did not invent the symbolism of brotherhood and family, but she dramatized these staples of worker consciousness.

It is impossible to summarize her career, but some of the highlights may be noted. Before the turn of the century she had become a paid organizer for the United Mine Workers, an on-again, off-again relationship that lasted thirty years. Soon she was organizing anthracite miners in Pennsylvania, but she attracted especial attention by organizing the miners' wives into broom and mop pickets who routed strikebreakers (she opposed President Theodore Roosevelt's intervention in settling the strike because it precluded union recognition). She traveled from town to town in the bituminous regions of West Virginia and Colorado, talking to the miners, giving speeches, and always organizing despite the threat of company guards and court injunctions. Meanwhile, she found time to help support striking machinists on the Southern Pacific Railroad, and to aid the Western Federation of Miners (a militant organization always dear to her heart) in shutting down the copper pits of Arizona. And in 1903, she organized a children's crusade of underage textile workers in a march on President Roosevelt's home in Oyster Bay, New York.

Perhaps the most dramatic episodes in her life occurred in the years before World War I, again in the coal fields. Organizing efforts in West Virginia culminated in an intense strike in 1912–13. In the midst of her organizing efforts, violence broke out between miners and the private detectives hired by the owners. Seeing her as a rabble-rouser, a military court charged Mother Jones with conspiracy to commit murder, and sentenced her to twenty years in prison. A newly elected governor commuted her sentence, but not before a tremendous nationwide outcry against her incarceration in the "military bastille." She no sooner was freed than she headed to Colorado, where miners had struck Rockefeller's Colorado Fuel and Iron Company. Three times she was locked up then deported from the state, and three times she snuck back in and continued organizing. Her charges of brutality against private detective agencies—the "Baldwin-Felts thugs"—were borne out when they machine-gunned and torched the miners' tent colony at Ludlow on April 20, 1914, resulting in the deaths of twenty women and children. She moved audiences to tears with her accounts of the massacre, she testified before Congress, and for years thereafter Ludlow became a byword for the oppression of the miners, the greed of the operators, and the courage of Mother Jones.

Even as she entered her ninth decade, her efforts did not slacken. She helped organize New York City streetcar and garment workers just before World War I, and rallied steel workers after it ended. The 1920s found her in Mexico for the Pan-American Federation of Labor meeting (her third trip to Mexico, where previously she had supported the Revolution and the rights of Mexican nationals held in American prisons). She even continued organizing West Virginia miners. But while the old revolutionary fervor still showed itself, Mother Jones's loyalties grew increasingly erratic. Never overly consistent about her ideological commitments, she now veered from calling herself a Bolshevist to supporting Calvin Coolidge. Poor health slowed her down, and she also took time to work on her autobiography. A grand hundredth birthday party was given for her on May 1, 1930, but half a year later Mother Jones was dead. She insisted on being buried with "her boys," the victims of the Virden Massacre, in the Union Miners Cemetery in Mount Olive, Illinois.

While her commitment to organizing workers and to the ideals of socialism was unwavering, Mother Jones frequently became entangled in sectarian struggles and personality disputes, and these could bring out in her a streak of pettiness. More fundamentally, her gift for on-site agitation seemed to preclude the patience for long-term organization building. She was a founding member of the Industrial Workers of the World, for example, but abandoned that organization after its opening days. And her relationship with middle class women and feminism was particularly disturbing. She organized women in various industries, and brought the wives of workingmen into the labor movement. But she repudiated the suffrage movement as a bourgeois diversion from the real issue, from class struggle. Women, Mother Jones believed in good Victorian fashion, must educate, support, and elevate their men. Her goal, however, was not middle-class respectability, but rebellion.

Despite Mother Jones's long and varied career, we can identify some consistent themes. She articulated for the labor movement a sense of passion, unity, and sacrifice as powerful as the Catholic Mass she knew so well. While her relationship with the church was at best conflicted, she tended to see the role of labor through Christian imagery. Writing in her autobiography of her early years in the movement, she recalled those times as ones of selfless sacrifice, before highly paid labor leaders had grown chummy with businessmen: "Those were the days of the martyrs and the saints," she concluded. Indeed, it was the metaphor of Christian martyrdom—of crucifixion—that she took as the essence of labor's plight in a capitalist society: "I learned in the early part of my career that labor must bear the cross for others' sins, must be the vicarious sufferer for the wrongs that others do."

Yet suffering was never to be borne meekly. Suffering for Mother Jones was a source of rage, and rage the engine of collective power. The emotional and ideological weight of her family imagery comes through in the words of workingpeople. In a 1913 letter to the secretary of labor protesting her arrest in West Virginia, an aged worker from Missouri declared that he had carried a gun in previous industrial wars, and that "by the Eternal, if any harm comes to the old Mother, I'm not too old nor . . . to cowardly, to carry it again." During the same episode, another woman warned that if any injury befell "our brothers and sisters" the government would face an aroused working class "more dreadful than any this country has ever seen."

Such loyalty was born of workingpeople's sense that Mother Jones was *with* them. A key element of the persona she created was being always amongst workers and their families, or on the road to wherever she was needed to organize, agitate, and educate. She exaggerated her age and wore very old-fashioned Victorian dresses because doing so underscored her claims to motherhood. Her speeches often invoked past triumphs, where, elderly and frail, she nonetheless made hired thugs back down. Her supporters and enemies constantly remarked on her fearlessness and fighting spirit.

It was this image of the willful old woman—telling miners to "pray for the dead, and fight like hell for the living," organizing sites where no one else would venture, articulating a vision of justice not just for workers but for working-class families—that helped energize a powerful critique of the social order. Mother Jones gave voice to the belief that men and women might transform their world. She helped them believe that they could step outside their present circumstances to imagine, and then to create, a just society. The feeling she gave workers of belonging to a cause larger than themselves was captured in the much repeated story of her leaving a tip for an attentive waiter, and his refusing the money: "Oh no, Mother, not in the family."

Suggested Readings.

Dale Fetherling, *Mother Jones: The Miners' Angel*. Carbondale: Southern Illinois University Press, 1974.

Philip S. Foner, *Mother Jones Speaks*. New York: Monad, 1983.

Mother Jones, *The Autobiography of Mother Jones*, ed. Mary Field Parton. Originally published 1925. Chicago: Charles H. Kerr, 1972.

Edward Steel, ed., *The Correspondence of Mother Jones*. Pittsburgh: University of Pittsburgh Press, 1985.

———, *The Speeches and Writings of Mother Jones*. Pittsburgh: University of Pittsburgh Press, 1988.

25

JOHN DEWEY

Kenneth Teitelbaum and Michael W. Apple

Education is not a neutral instrumentality. Rather, it is inherently political in a variety of ways. From the vast universe of possible knowledge, only some groups' knowledge is declared legitimate to teach. From the many different forms of pedagogy that could be used, the ones that dominate tend to silence the voices and experiences of students. Schools themselves are linked as well to the reproduction—and subversion—of existing race, gender, and class relations. While today we have a much clearer understanding of the complex relationship between education and differential power, these concerns have a long history. It is almost impossible to think about these issues—at the level of theory or practice—without dealing with John Dewey's legacy. This legacy is contradictory, but extremely important as a foundation for a vision of education that is rooted in the expansion of democracy to all spheres of social life.

John Dewey (1859–1952) is generally recognized as the most renowned American educator of the twentieth century. In a prolific career that spanned seven decades (his collected works comprise thirty-seven volumes), Dewey focused on a wide range of concerns, most notably within the fields of philosophy, education, psychology, sociology, and politics. As much after his life as during it, Dewey's writings and other public statements have been the subject of interpretation and reinterpretation by countless scholars. A voluminous literature exists as much about him as by him, with vastly different assessments made of the nature and impact of his work.

He has been referred to literally as a saint and as a sinner, honored for his commitment to progressive education and democratic politics and villified for his presumed role in the "softening" of American schooling and the destruction of age-old traditions. He has been hailed for aligning with the cause of industrial democracy and denounced for his lack of a truly radical vision. Currently, more than forty years after his death, he is again the subject of debate, portrayed either as an important forerunner of poststructural cultural criticism or as the preeminent philosopher of American pragmatism. Ironically, and contrary to the assumptions made by some commentators on his work, Dewey's own ideas never really permeated the American education system, despite his central place in academic discourse throughout this century. As he himself wrote shortly before his death in 1952: "There is far more talk about it [progressive education] than the doing of it."

Dewey was born in 1859 in Burlington, Vermont. Burlington itself during Dewey's youth was in the midst of changing from an intimate, rather homogeneous small-town community into a bustling, socially diverse city that would be the commercial and cultural center of the state. Indeed, the United States generally during the late nineteenth and early twentieth centuries was rapidly evolving from a relatively simple frontier-agricultural society to a much more complex urban-industrial nation. Ways in which a genuine and cohesive democratic community could be maintained amidst the wrenching economic and cultural changes of the new industrial order were Dewey's paramount concern throughout his life.

After graduating from the University of Vermont in 1879, he taught Latin, algebra, and science for two years at a high school in Oil City, Pennsylvania, and then for a short time was the sole teacher in a rural school near Burlington. During these years, with the encouragement of one of his Vermont professors, he also wrote three philosophical essays which were accepted for publication in the *Journal of Speculative Philosophy*. His success in this area whetted his interest to continue his studies and he subsequently enrolled in the graduate program in philosophy at Johns Hopkins University. Among the faculty with whom he worked closely were George Sylvester Morris, known for his embrace of German idealism and antipathy toward British empiricism; Charles Sanders Peirce, who, with William James of Harvard, laid the basis for pragmatic philosophy; and G. Stanley Hall, a psychologist who advocated intensive study of children and adolescents to determine teaching methods that were developmentally appropriate.

After completing his doctoral dissertation in 1884 on the psychology of Immanuel Kant, Dewey secured a position as instructor in philosophy and psychology at the University of Michigan. In 1888 he left for the position of chair in philosophy at the University of Minnesota, but he returned to Michigan after only one year to take a similar position. In 1894, the University of Chicago offered Dewey the chairmanship of the combined department of philosophy, psychology, and pedagogy. Upon his arrival in Chicago, Dewey witnessed for himself the turbulence of life in a large city at the turn of the century, and in particular the Pullman Strike and the results of President Grover Cleveland's decision to send in federal troops to support corporate interests. The events of the strike, as well as his association with social activists like Jane Addams and educators like Ella Flagg Young, served to enhance his commitment to wide-ranging progressive reforms.

While at the University of Chicago, Dewey established an elementary-level Laboratory School to help assess, modify, and develop his educational and psychological ideas. However, a dispute with the president of the university, William Rainey Harper, in part over the use of the Laboratory School as a teacher-training institution, resulted in Dewey's resignation from Chicago in 1904. Columbia University immediately offered him a position as professor of philosophy, with arrangements made to also occasionally offer lectures at the university's well-known Teachers College. In 1930, he was appointed professor emeritus of philosophy in residence at Columbia, a position he held until his eightieth birthday in 1939.

Dewey was actively involved in a diverse array of educational, social, and political causes throughout his life. For example, he was a fellow of the National Academy of Sciences; helped to found the American Association of University Professors, the New School for Social Research, and the American Civil Liberties Union; was a charter member of the first teachers union in New York City; was a regular contributor to and an editorial board member of the *New Republic;* and during the early 1930s served as president of two groups that attempted to organize a radical third party based on a coalition of labor, farmers, and the middle class (the League for Independent Political Action and the People's Lobby). In addition, as a further indication of his lifelong commitment to progressive causes, in 1937 (at the age of seventy-eight) he traveled to Mexico to head a commission that investigated the charges of treason and murder leveled against the exiled Leon Trotsky during the infamous Moscow purge trials.

Perhaps Dewey's greatest legacy, however, is the many articles and books that he authored, including *The School and Society* (1899), *The Child and the Curriculum* (1902), *How We Think* (1910), *Democracy and Education* (1916), *The Public and Its Problems* (1927), and *Experience and Education* (1938). Dewey conceived of the philospher's role as engaging intimately with social criticism, rather than participating in abstract exercises of contemplation that remained aloof from practical morality. He was particularly concerned with the enhancement of democratic community in a nation that seemed to be in danger of losing its moral and spiritual compass. For Dewey, genuine democracy did not refer simply to governmental agencies and rituals, but rather to a dynamic process of daily active and equitable participation that included not simply the formal political apparatus but culture and economics, indeed *all* spheres of life. It was, he wrote, "primarily a mode of associated living, of conjoint communicated experience."

Intertwined with Dewey's concern for democratic community was the pragmatism that undergirded all of his work. Dewey believed that every idea, value, and social institution originated in the practical circumstances of human life. They were neither divine creation nor did they reflect some type of ideal. Truth did not represent an idea waiting to be discovered; it could only be realized in practice. Every institution and every belief, viewed within its specific context, should be subject to the test of establishing its contribution in the broadest sense to the public and personal good.

Dewey viewed change and growth as in fact the nature of things. Thus, social experimentation, rather than absolute principles, was needed to assess the worth of an idea or practice. This experimentation was to be guided not by random trial and error, however, but rather by scientific habits of mind. For Dewey, "an articulate public" that had developed methods of intelligence, not narrowly defined but broadly with regard to the capacity for rigorous reflective (scientific) inquiry, was the foundation of democratic community. He attacked absolute principles and imposition strategies because, while some good may be accomplished from them, they would not help to establish a genuine form of democracy in a constantly evolving society. Only rational criticism and experimentation, linked to concern for the creation of a humane and just society, could do so.

For Dewey, the key to intellectual development, and consequently to social progress, was schooling, especially at a time when the educational influences of other institutions (the home, the church, etc.) had decreased so drastically. Dewey stressed the social and moral nature of the school and believed that it should serve as a "miniature community, an embryonic society," specifically one that actively fostered the growth of democracy which was being undermined by urban industrial society. This view was in stark contrast to "the factory system" model being adopted by school planners (and "efficiency experts") across the country, which emphasized students as relatively passive raw materials to be molded by teachers, repetitious methods of teaching, and subject matter divorced from social content. Not only, then, was universal schooling crucial in a rapidly changing society, but a "new education" was vital as well, one that was guided by the perspective that school is life, rather than a preparation for it. Thus, the best preparation for democracy was to provide opportunities for students (and teachers) to be actively engaged in democratic life.

The most effective curriculum for such a school would attend seriously to the present interests of children, not as a motivational "gimmick" but as a way to teach the essential relationship between human knowledge and social experience. Dewey severely criticized public schools for silencing or ignoring student interests and experiences, using artificial language (perhaps about some vague future) that only served to alienate students, overrelying on testing to assess student learning, differentiating students according to their presumed ability to partake in mental or manual learning instead of offering both to all, and isolating subjects from one another instead of uniting them around students' lived experience with knowledge. Rather than blaming students for their passivity, Dewey focused attention directly on the *pedagogy* of schools. However, it is important to emphasize as well that Dewey strongly disagreed with the more extreme proponents of child-centered progressivism. He made it clear that a crucial role was to be played by teachers in helping to link children's interests to sustained intellectual development and to educative (rather than what he thought were noneducative or miseducative) experiences. To emphasize this point, he defined education as "that reconstruction or reorganization of experiences which adds to the meaning of experience, and which increases ability to direct the course of subsequent experience." Freedom, for example, for the child in the classroom, was not to be an end in itself.

This dispute with some child-centered educators in part illustrates Dewey's long-held antipathy toward dichotomous thinking and absolute principles. He attacked such common dualisms as theory and practice, individual and group, public and private, method and subject matter, mind and behavior, means and ends, and culture and vocation. His attempt was not to find a compromise but rather, for example in the case of starting with the child or the subject matter in curriculum planning, to reconstruct the debate so that they were no longer viewed as opposites. Thus, it was not a question of a choice between validating the interests of the child or the subject matter in constructing the curriculum, but rather of understanding and developing the continuum of experiences that links them.

Dewey remained steadfastly in support of an "intentionally progressive" society throughout his lifetime. He condemned the traditional view of culture as blatantly aristocratic in its exclusivity and inequity and chose instead to root culture and aesthetics in common experience. Similarly, rather than the school remaining isolated from social life, he advocated it taking on the role of helping in the transformation to a better social order. He recognized the nature of class barriers and distinctions and advocated that schools should help in their elimination. Indeed, his strong opposition to separate trade schools was based in part on his awareness of the class inequities of such vocational education schemes. However, it did not follow, according to Dewey, that the school's role in the amelioration of social life in general and the evils of capitalism in particular should include the teaching of any kind of economic or social "ism." Instead, through the study of and active engagement in basic social activities (what he referred to as "occupations"), such as growing food, cooking, building a shelter, making clothing, creating stories and artwork, and so forth, children could best be initiated into moral social membership. They would be provided with opportunities to learn "the instruments of effective self-direction," as well as a sensitivity toward social issues and the ability (including reading, writing, and problem-solving skills) to act on them. In effect, the classroom was to embrace the kind of democratic community life, concern for human dignity, and scientific intelligence that was sought outside the school. The "means" were in fact the "ends."

Dewey's place in the American radical movement has always been somewhat problematic. For example, he wavered in his identification with socialism (e.g., he supported United States entrance into World War I) and referred to Marxism as "unscientific utopianism." Moreover, in his efforts to retain flexibility and oppose dogmatism, and in particular his disavowal of explicit ends decided ahead of time, he appeared too "neutral" to some of those actively engaged in the struggle for radical social change. His antipathy toward the teaching of fixed social beliefs was in contrast to the approach of many social-reconstructionist educators who believed that such political advocacy was an unavoidable aspect of education. Unlike Dewey, they sought to have students identify and examine specific problems of capitalist America in order to encourage an understanding of and allegiance to more cooperative economic and social relations. Socialist educators had even less hesitation in teaching the values of collectivism and class struggle to children, justifying this as necessary to counteract the pernicious influence of capitalist culture on (working-class) children's lives. The application of creative and scientific inquiry to social problems was as far as Dewey would go. Indeed, his present-oriented and experimentalist perspective tended to result in rather vague depictions of alternatives to strive for, as he sought to avoid all "blueprints," class-based or otherwise. Furthermore, it is questionable whether the kind of common social purpose and active citizenry that Dewey advocated is possible in a capitalist society of such striking inequities of power and wealth and the dominance of consumerism. Some have also argued that Dewey's faith in science was misplaced. As C. Wright Mills pointed out, scientific intelligence could be used just as easily to serve bureaucratic purposes or foster domination.

Despite these criticisms, Dewey still looms as one of the major figures of American education, philosophy, and politics, a towering presence whose work deserves to be read closely for its intensive examination of many of the pressing social issues that continue to be of such vital concern today. His articulation of and commitment to participatory democracy, in our schools and elsewhere, represents a major contribution to American radicalism. Indeed, although his optimism about progress, freedom, community, science, and so forth may seem at times to have been out of proportion to the realities of hegemonic culture, it serves during these rather cynical and pessimistic times to remind us of many of the paths to progressive social change. We may argue with some of the answers that he provided, but John Dewey was truly a radical in his attempt to get at the very root of the social world, to not only understand it but also to change it.

Suggested Readings

Reginald D. Archambault, *John Dewey on Education: Selected Writings*. Chicago: University of Chicago Press, 1964.

Richard J. Bernstein, *John Dewey*. New York: Washington Square Press, 1966.

Herbert M. Kliebard, *The Struggle for the American Curriculum*. New York: Routledge and Kegan Paul, 1986.

Katherine Camp Mayhew and Anna Camp Edwards, *The Dewey School: The Laboratory School of the University of Chicago, 1896–1903*. New York: D. Appleton-Century, 1936.

Robert B. Westbrook, *John Dewey and American Democracy*. Ithaca, N.Y.: Cornell University Press, 1991.

26

CLARENCE DARROW

Joanne Pope Melish

Clarence Darrow may be the most famous trial lawyer in American history. The principal source of his enduring fame is his role as defense attorney in two of the most sensational legal events of the twentieth century, Meyer Levin's best-selling *Compulsion,* inspired by the 1924 Leopold and Loeb trial, and *Inherit the Wind,* the popular dramatization of the 1925 Scopes "monkey" trial, have shaped the popular conception of Clarence Darrow as attorney and orator. But his narrow popular image obscures the breadth of his contribution to the political debates and struggles of his time.

Darrow's greatest importance may lie in his contribution to the popular formulation and persistent articulation of the ideology of the labor movement at the turn of the century. Throughout his life, Darrow offered trenchant critiques of corporate monopoly and the concentration of wealth produced by industrial capitalism. He defended workers, the oppressed, and the unpopular, litigating approximately two thousand cases, which often involved controversial social issues. During his lifetime, Darrow was extremely influential as a public lecturer and debater, prolific essayist, and fiction writer who supported a broad range of reformist and radical causes.

A convinced materialist, Darrow opposed what he saw as the tyranny of religious orthodoxy, seeking to substitute rational scientific inquiry for what he viewed as an enslaving superstition. A self-proclaimed agnostic, Darrow devoted a lifetime to pondering the nature of religious belief and aggressively attacking its validity, all the while searching for a rational framework for moral behavior that might be its effective substitute. While Darrow did not begin actively supporting radical social reform until he was nearly forty, the roots of his intellectual commitment to skepticism and his rebellion against many of the dominant social values of corporate capitalist society lay in his childhood in a household of freethinkers.

Clarence Seward Darrow was born in Kinsman, Ohio, on April 18, 1857, the fifth of eight children of a man he characterized as "the village infidel." Amirus Darrow had made the intellectual journey from devout Methodism to skeptic early in his life, attending a Methodist College and a Unitarian Seminary in Meadville, Pennsylvania, before abandoning his call to the ministry and becoming a religious freethinker who supported his family as a woodworker and casketmaker. He was a committed abolitionist and admirer of John Brown who drew his philosophical convictions from Jefferson, Paine, and Voltaire. Clarence's mother, Emily, was also a freethinker and a women's rights advocate. Yet the Darrow children were encouraged to attend church school and Sunday services in order to make an informed choice with respect to religious orthodoxy. Like his parents, Clarence chose to reject it.

Darrow attended the local district school and academy, after which he went for one year to Allegheny College at Meadville. Although an avid reader, he was an indifferent student and especially disliked the required study of classical languages. Nonetheless, he intended to return for a second year, but the Panic of 1873 intervened. For three winters he taught in a district school, boarding around during the week, and returning home on weekends. In the other seasons he worked in his father's woodworking shop and store.

It was during his teaching career that Darrow began reading law. After receiving formal legal training for a year at the University of Michigan and a year's preparation in the office of a lawyer in Youngstown, Ohio, he was admitted to the bar in 1878. In that year he opened a legal office in Andover, Ohio, and then moved it to Ashtabula. In Ashtabula he married Jessie Ohl and they soon had a son, Paul.

During his ten years of small-town legal practice, Darrow's activities generated no wider public attention, but they did establish certain patterns he would follow during his entire public life. In Ashtabula, Darrow often took cases for principle rather than payment because, as he later explained, fees were secondary to feelings. He continued to take pro bono cases throughout his career; more significantly, he also continued to buttress his rational philosophical positions with emotional arguments. Darrow consistently displayed a deep emotional attachment to the poor and oppressed, and he once remarked that "sympathy" gives one power to put oneself in another's place." The comment provides insight into Darrow's rhetorical strategy throughout his trial and debate career.

It was also in Ashtabula that Darrow read Henry George's *Progress and Poverty* and John Altgeld's *Our Penal Code and Its Victims*. George's scheme for a single, confiscatory rent tax to alleviate extremes of wealth and poverty awakened Darrow's disgust at the concentration of wealth under monopoly capitalism; Altgeld's theories fed Darrow's conviction that criminal behavior is a result of social victimization.

In 1888 Darrow moved to Chicago. By joining various progressive social and political groups, including a Single Tax Club, and speaking publicly on a variety of social issues from a progressive position, he worked to gain public notice and foster his legal practice. He was appointed to a series of municipal positions culminating in his appointment as corporation counsel for the City of Chicago. Two years later, he became counsel for Chicago and North-Western Railway Company. Although strongly attracted to aspects of several different radical philosophies—George's redistribution of wealth, socialism, anarchism—until 1894, Darrow's legal practice had little about it that was radical.

In 1894, however, the Pullman Strike proved the catalyst of Darrow's active personal involvement in labor radicalism. The American Railway Union, headed by Eugene V. Debs, was conducting a bitter strike against the Pullman Palace Car Company and railroads using Pullman cars. When the railroads went to court to obtain an injunction against the strikers, federal troops were called in and violence erupted. Debs was indicted for criminal conspiracy and violating a federal injunction. Although Darrow had been appointed to the Strike Management Committee of Chicago and North-Western, he was deeply sympathetic to the strikers. He resigned from Chicago and North-Western and agreed to represent Debs. Although the criminal charge was dismissed, Debs was convicted of conspiracy.

Nonetheless, the case was an important turning point in the legal relations between management and labor. Darrow was one of the first lawyers to represent the interests of labor in its own terms, and to place labor radicalism in its broader social context in the courtroom. In this case he developed the argument he would use in many subsequent labor cases, that conspiracy charges were a device specially calculated to criminalize the thinking of the worker. Beginning with this case, Darrow would also argue that violence is justifiable to achieve political ends.

The Pullman case brought Darrow national recognition and a steady progression of labor and criminal cases. In 1898 Darrow won acquittal for

Thomas I. Kidd, president of the National Association of Woodworkers, accused of conspiracy in his union's strike against sash and door manufacturers in Oshkosh, Wisconsin. During 1903 hearings in front of the Coal Commission, Darrow represented the United Mine Workers in arbitration of their general strike against anthracite coal companies. The hearings awards represented a major victory for the union. In 1908, Darrow won acquittal of three officials of the Western Federation of Miners, including labor hero Big Bill Haywood, who were accused of the bombing murder of an ex-governor of Idaho.

In the midst of these cases, Darrow won election as an Independent to the Illinois legislature, and, six years after his divorce from his first wife, married Ruby Hamerstrom, to whom he remained married until his death.

In 1911, Darrow represented Joseph McNamara, secretary of the Structural Iron Workers Union, and his brother James, a member of the Typographical Union, charged with the bombing of the headquarters of the non-union *Los Angeles Times* during a general strike. A plea bargain and two subsequent indictments of Darrow for jury tampering damaged his reputation with labor supporters and the public alike. Although he was acquitted of the first bribery charge and the second was dismissed, Darrow retreated from cases of national scope for the next six years, limiting his practice to uncontroversial, mostly criminal cases after his return to Chicago.

In 1920, Darrow returned to the public stage with another sensational series of cases. This time he defended Benjamin Gitlow, Arthur Person, and several other members of the Communist Labor party accused of advocating the overthrow of the government by force. Darrow based his defenses on freedom of the press, speech, and assembly. Only Person was acquitted; but with these trials, Darrow regained his stature as a public radical.

In 1924 Darrow agreed to defend Nathan Leopold, Jr., and Richard Loeb, two wealthy young men who had murdered their acquaintance, fourteen-year-old Robert Franks, in an effort to commit the perfect crime. In the face of the brutal senselessness of the murder and the fact that both boys were the sons of millionaires, the public, and many of Darrow's friends as well, concluded that Darrow had sold out his convictions for personal profit. In fact, Darrow's position in this case was entirely consistent, both with his lifelong opposition to capital punishment and with his theories on the biological basis of mental illness and criminal conduct, which he had elaborated in *Crime, Its Cause and Treatment* two years earlier. Darrow pled Leopold and Loeb guilty and then offered the so-called irresistible-impulse defense, providing copious psychiatric evidence to demonstrate that mental illness had forced Leopold and Loeb to commit murder. He won a reduction in their sentences from the death penalty to life imprisonment, but at a cost of widespread public outrage.

A year later he undertook his most famous case, the defense of school-teacher John T. Scopes in Dayton, Tennessee, charged with violating the Tennessee Anti-Evolution Act. For some time, William Jennings Bryan had been leading a Fundamentalist crusade aimed at the public schools and universities against the teaching of any science that conflicted with the literal interpretation of Scripture. Darrow had sparred with Bryan on this subject in the editorial pages of the *Chicago Tribune* before Scopes was charged, and when he heard that Bryan had volunteered to head the prosecution of Scopes, he offered to lead the defense. The brief trial ended in the conviction of Scopes (overturned a year later by the Tennessee Supreme Court), but Darrow's defense had discredited Fundamentalist dogma as articulated by Bryan and prompted a new effort on the part of Fundamentalist leadership to rebuild intellectual credibility.

Two years later, Darrow was hired by the National Association for the Advancement of Colored People to defend eleven African Americans charged with murder: A white mob had attacked the home of Dr. Ossian Sweet, a black doctor who had moved into a white Detroit neighborhood, and one mob member had been shot. The trial of Dr. Sweet resulted in a hung jury, and he was never retried. His brother, Henry Sweet, was acquitted, and charges against the others were dropped.

After 1928, Darrow retired from the regular practice of law and for four years defended radical and unpopular causes on the lecture and debate circuit. He did take an occasional legal case that provided a forum for his most strongly held convictions, especially cases that involved obtaining pardons or reduced sentences for those facing the death penalty. In 1931 he initially agreed to defend the Scottsboro Boys, young blacks charged with raping a white woman, but withdrew in the face of what he believed to be the exploitative control of the case by the Communist party.

In 1932, he came out of retirement to defend Navy Lieutenant Thomas Massie who was accused, along with his wife's mother and two friends, of the Honolulu killing of a native Hawaiian charged with raping Massie's wife. The case triggered smoldering racial resentments in the Islands. Darrow's defense of Massie was widely criticized because the victim had been a poor, nonwhite worker and Massie and his wife both came from wealthy and socially prominent families. However, mainland Americans, who followed the case closely, generally sympathized with the rape victim and her husband. The conviction of the four defendants for manslaughter outraged the American public and resulted in congressional demands for a general investigation of the government of Hawaii. In response, the territorial governor commuted the sentences.

Darrow's final public controversy arose when Franklin Roosevelt appointed him to head an impartial review board charged with investigating small business complaints of price fixing and other injustices under the

National Recovery Act. The Darrow Board held four months of hearings and investigated three thousand complaints. Darrow submitted three reports to President Roosevelt. Darrow's recommendations for revising the NRA included eliminating price fixing, placing labor controversies in the hands of a special industrial-relations board, and giving the Federal Trade Commission responsibility for evaluating charges of monopolistic practices. In a personal appearance before the Senate Investigating Committee in March of 1935, Darrow summarized the board's findings. He outlined his conviction that the NRA materially increased the advantage of big business, to the detriment of small business. He made a plea for both a fair capitalism and a socialistic equal distribution of wealth. To many commentators, these positions seemed contradictory.

This was Darrow's last public appearance. He returned to Chicago, and shortly thereafter his health began to deteriorate. On March 13, 1938, at nearly eighty-one years of age, he died.

Clarence Darrow's political philosophy can be broadly defined as progressive, ranging from radical to reformist in its ideals and its proposed solutions to economic inequity and social injustice. Darrow supported those causes and programs he believed most surely increased rather than diminished individual liberty. At the same time, he sought solutions to the inequitable distribution of wealth and power under monopoly capitalism. At one time or another in his life he found socialism and anarchism appealing because they promised to fulfill one or another of these goals, but he was ultimately unable to formulate a consistent social philosophy and program. Darrow was not a particularly original thinker, and his personal philosophy encompassed ideas which often coexisted uncomfortably and embodied contradictions he never was able to resolve. Nonetheless, Darrow was a powerful and compelling voice for the concerns of the worker and for victims of social injustice of many kinds, and he fearlessly represented their interests.

Suggested Readings

Clarence Darrow, *The Story of My Life*. Originally published 1932. New York: Charles Scribner's Sons, 1960.

Alan Dawley, *Struggles for Justice: Social Responsibility and the Liberal State*. Cambridge: Harvard University Press, 1991.

Willard D. Hunsberger, *Clarence Darrow: A Bibliography*. Metuchen, N.J.: Scarecrow Press, 1981.

Arthur Weinberg, ed., *Attorney for the Damned*. New York: Simon and Schuster, 1957.

Arthur Weinberg and Lila Weinberg, *Clarence Darrow: A Sentimental Rebel*. New York: G. P. Putnam, 1980.

27

WILLIAM Z. FOSTER

James R. Barrett

William Z. Foster was the real article. "He personified the American proletariat as few radical leaders have ever done," Theodore Draper writes. Foster's life story, which encapsulates so much of the history of the American left, is in many ways a tragedy, conveying both the great potential of the radical working-class movement in the United States through the era of the Great Depression and its catastrophic defeat and disintegration in the postwar era. Foster stands above all as the historic symbol of American Communism. Understanding his grim commitment to this movement goes a long way toward explaining its rise and fall in the United States.

Born in Taunton, Massachusetts, in 1881, Foster was raised in the slums of Philadelphia, which he characterized as a "fine flower of capitalist civilization." He derived the two great influences of his early years, Irish republicanism and Catholicism, from his father, a Fenian stableman and street fighter, and his mother, a devout immigrant from the British textile town of Carlisle. His most enduring convictions, however, rose from the bitter resentment with which he faced the poverty engulfing his family and neighbors. Although he left school for work after the third grade, he read voraciously—history, natural and social science, and current events—and he acquired a love of learning that remained with him throughout life. Foster eventually taught himself to read in German and French, devoured the classic Marxist texts, and wrote dozens of books and pamphlets and hundreds of journal and newspaper articles.

During the early years of the twentieth century, Foster roamed North and South America, the Caribbean, Europe, and Africa, working as a laborer, streetcar motorman, and deep-water sailor before settling down as a railroad worker, first in the Pacific Northwest and later in Chicago. A keen observer of working-class attitudes and cultures, he developed a genius for organizing and leading diverse groups of workers in their struggles.

From his earliest days in the Socialist party, which he joined in 1901, Foster always identified with hard-core proletarian and revolutionary elements. His anarcho-syndicalist tendencies eventually lead him to join the Industrial Workers of the World (IWW) in the midst of the 1909 Spokane Free Speech Fight where he emerged as a leading figure. These natural sympathies took on greater intellectual coherence during Foster's travels in Europe from 1910 to 1911. From the French syndicalists he derived two fundamental concepts which continued to shape his theory and practice over the next generation—"boring from within" and the "militant minority." Rather than separate themselves from the American Federation of Labor (AFL) and establish dual unions, Foster argued, radicals must remain in the mainstream organizations with the mass of workers and win them over to a revolutionary program. This did not imply simply following the rank and file. On the contrary, the transformation of the unions required a self-conscious, well-organized militant minority to provide education and leadership. Foster devoted himself to developing and coordinating the work of these militants.

After failing to win the IWW over to such pure syndicalism, Foster established his own group, the Syndicalist League of North America (SLNA). The SLNA never attracted more than a couple of thousand members, but in the two years following its foundation in the fall of 1912, the organization sank deep roots in several Midwestern cities and created a network of talented radicals. Following its demise, Foster and the group of young activists around him focused their work on the Chicago Federation of Labor (CFL), which Foster characterized as "the most progressive labor council in the United States." Foster concluded that "the main revolutionary task in the [First World] war period was the building of trade unionism, the organization of the millions unorganized."

Working in their various trades, Foster and other syndicalists became CFL delegates, allied themselves with the federation's progressive president John Fitzpatrick, and soon turned to organizing the city's giant slaughtering and meatpacking industry. Here, in the summer of 1917, Foster became secretary of the Stockyards Labor Council, a committee of AFL unions representing the various trades as well as the industry's thousands of African-American and immigrant unskilled laborers. By the spring of 1918, the council had organized thousands of workers, secured federal intervention with the threat of a national strike, and won substantial improvements in wages and working conditions. The success brought Foster considerable acclaim, and in the summer of 1918 he set his sights on the nation's open-shop bastion—the steel industry.

Drawing on his experiences in packing and with the railroad systems federations, Foster convinced the AFL to establish the National Committee to Organize Iron and Steel Workers to coordinate the unionization of craft and unskilled production workers—another step toward the industrial unionism Foster and other radicals saw as the blueprint for success. Working with meager support from the AFL unions and against severe repression in the steel-mill towns, Foster and his organizers had swept about 100,000 steelworkers into the unions by the spring of 1919. That fall he lead the organization into the largest strike in the history of the United States. In the depression and political reaction of the postwar years, both the steelworkers' and packinghouse workers' organizations were destroyed in bitter strikes, but Foster had established a reputation as a brilliant organizer and strategist.

Foster's syndicalism continued to shape his ideas and behavior long after he joined the Workers (Communist) party in late 1921. Throughout the twenties he devoted his considerable energies and talents to individual work, which he viewed as the party's most promising path to developing the revolutionary potential of American workers. In late 1920, on the basis of his wartime experiences, Foster created the Trade Union Educational League (TUEL), a loose national network of trade union militants which constituted the only substantial opposition to conservative AFL leadership throughout the 1920s. As the league's national secretary, Foster directed the TUEL's work. While the TUEL was never formally integrated into the party, part of its importance lies in the fact that the league provided the Communists with their first significant influence within the trade union movement. In the early twenties Foster and league activists enjoyed considerable success with two key demands—for the amalgamation of craft unions and the establishment of a union-based labor party. The TUEL built its strongest bases where it was able to coordinate its work with indigenous rank-and-file movements—in coal mining, the garment industry, metalworking, and the building trades. By the mid-twenties, however, TUEL militants were increasingly isolated. While Foster and his group of Chicago-based trade union Communists fought to maintain

ties with mainstream labor progressives, another more theoretically sophisticated leadership faction demanded that the party confront such re-
formists and assert its own revolutionary line. At the same time, conservative labor leaders unleashed a vigorous attack against Foster and his
radicals, expelling militants and whole local unions. The party's factionalism and the AFL's widespread repression of rank-and-file dissent together
had the effect of dividing the trade union Communists from their progressive allies.

By late 1928, when the international Communist line called for the
establishment of separate revolutionary unions to compete with the main-
line organizations, the TUEL had already been reduced to what Foster
himself called an "underground organization." He bitterly fought the new
line, sensing the destruction it would cause to any lasting left-wing union
influence, but he eventually relented. He came close to expulsion before
yielding, a submission that clearly signaled a victory for party discipline
over common sense. Foster became national secretary for the new Trade
Union Unity League (TUUL), helping to establish separate Communist
unions in the coal, textile, garment, auto, and other industries and to
coordinate organizing of the unemployed in the early thirties. TUUL
activists led several important strikes between 1929 and the league's
dissolution in the mid-thirties. With the establishment of the Congress of
Industrial Organizations (CIO) in 1936, many TUUL activists went on
to careers in new industrial unions, and Foster frequently advised these
CIO-based Communist unionists throughout the late thirties and forties.

Foster's syndicalist background looms large for personal as well as
political reasons. In 1912, at the anarchist Home Colony on Puget Sound,
he met and later married Esther Abramovitz, a Russian immigrant garment
worker who remained with him to the end. Many of the militants with
whom Foster worked in the SLNA, the CFL, and the wartime organizing
campaigns also joined the Communist party, working with him throughout
his life.

While the TUUL's strategy of dual unionism troubled Foster, the party's
new ultrarevolutionary perspective otherwise suited both his own disposition and the situation of the early depression years rather well. With
characteristic zeal, Foster threw himself into a series of coal and textile
strikes and into organizing of the unemployed. Leading one of the nation's
first large unemployed demonstrations in New York City on March 6,
1930, he was arrested, and jailed for six months in an aged prison under
deplorable physical conditions. When he emerged at the age of fifty-one
in December 1930, instead of slowing down, Foster immersed himself
first in industrial organizing and then as the party's standard-bearer in
the 1932 presidential election. While traveling over 17,000 miles coast

to coast, Foster was beaten, jailed, and run out of town by armed groups of vigilantes. On September 12, 1932, he collapsed, suffering a major heart attack and a more general breakdown of his physical and perhaps also his emotional strength. It was a trauma from which he never fully recovered.

Foster's long convalescence of almost three years corresponded with the shift to the new Popular Front line and the ascendance of Earl Browder, Foster's protégé, to power in the party. As Foster had symbolized the revolutionary zeal of the early years, so Browder now embodied the new party—broad-based in its membership and appeal and reform-oriented in its politics, speaking as much to the progressive middle class as to America's workers. Physically and psychologically weakened from his ordeals, Foster was now also politically marginalized. Beginning in the late thirties, he devoted much of his time to writing—two autobiographical works, dozens of pamphlets, and columns for the *Daily Worker* newspaper on labor policy and politics and later on the conduct of the war.

Throughout the war, Foster represented the only significant left-wing opposition to Browder's planned evolution of the party in a social-democratic direction. His criticism grew sharper in early 1944 with Browder's formal dissolution of the Communist party in favor of a Communist Political Association and his argument that the postwar order would see peaceful coexistence not only between the United States and the Soviet Union but also between the working class and progressive elements in the capitalist community. For Foster this was genuine heresy, but he still maintained party discipline by never publicly criticizing Browder's theories or questioning his authority. Browder retained the loyalty of both the Soviet and American party leadership, and Foster's criticism at closed party meetings only further weakened his position, though he continued to be an important symbol of the party's proletarian membership.

Publication of the "Duclos Letter" in May 1945 brought a breathtaking reversal of fortunes. The criticisms of Browder's leadership and ideas and the vindication of Foster's more orthodox Marxism-Leninism by Jacques Duclos, a French party leader, assumed great significance because the letter clearly conveyed the Soviets' position. Certainly American Communists viewed it in this light. By the summer of 1945, Foster once again emerged as the party's leading figure—on the eve of its dramatic decline.

In the following decade, government repression and the party's own policies devastated the Communist movement. In the process of reasserting Communist orthodoxy, Foster led purges of "Browder revisionists" and "white chauvinists." Expulsions and a dissipation of membership followed. As U.S.—Soviet relations deteriorated in the late forties and early fifties, federal, state, and local authorities indicted, tried, and jailed virtually the entire Communist leadership. Foster himself was indicted in 1949 under the Smith Act along with the rest of the party's national board, though he was never formally tried because of ill health. Dozens of others, however, either entered prison or fled underground. The CIO purged many of its left-wing activists and organizations during the same period. By 1956 the party faced a new crisis, and Foster was once again at the center of events.

In February of that year the Soviet party formally acknowledged the extent of Stalin's crimes over the past two decades and in November Soviet tanks crushed a revolt of workers and reformers in Hungary. Reform elements within the American party took this opportunity to push for a truly democratic mass party of socialism based on American political and cultural traditions and independent of Soviet influence. But Foster successfully led a bitter opposition to their efforts. When the smoke cleared, the Communist party had been reduced to a few thousand members and cut off from its bases in the mainstream labor and progressive movements. The party's deterioration paralleled Foster's own physical collapse in the late fifties, ending the prospects for Communist political influence in the United States.

What does Foster's life represent in the broader context of the Communist party's history? First, he consistently combined a heavy emphasis on detailed trade union and industrial work with a fervent revolutionary commitment. From the early twentieth century on, and long after he assumed a leading position in the Communist party, he was most committed to and clearly at his best in "practical" industrial work—labor organizing, union politics, devising effective strike strategies, and advising militants on the ground in textile and steel-mill towns, in coal-company towns, and urban slums across the nation. Yet his hatred of the capitalist system usually meant that he found himself on the left wing, including virtually all of his years in the Communist party. His devotion to practical trade union work as the proper focus for radical organizing never led him to reformist politics, even during the heyday of the Popular Front when he was clearly at odds with the rest of the party leadership and particularly with Earl Browder.

William Z. Foster died on September 1, 1961, in a Moscow hospital, far from the industrial battlegrounds where he had earned his reputation. But his ashes were buried just outside Chicago at Waldheim Cemetery, beside those of dozens of other American labor radicals. This juxtaposition of Foster's deathbed and his final resting place suggests the two great influences in his life as well as the trajectory of his career. He was undeniably a product of industrial America and a genius of radical working-class organization. The origins of his radicalism and his remarkable talents surely lay in his vast experience as an industrial worker and practical organizer, but he was above all a loyal soldier of the international Communist movement. These loyalties sustained him throughout his life, but in the end, they were at odds. Both Foster and his Communist movement were born in the heart of the American working class, but their program and activities were fundamentally shaped by the influence of Soviet Communism. Foster and his party perished, isolated from American workers' daily lives and concerns.

Suggested Readings

Theodore Draper, *American Communism and Soviet Russia, the Formative Period*. New York: Viking, 1986.

William Z. Foster, *From Bryan to Stalin*. New York: International Publishers, 1937.

Fraser M. Ottanelli, *The Communist Party of the United States from the Depression to World War II*. New Brunswick, N.J.: Rutgers University Press, 1991.

Joseph R. Starobin, *American Communism in Crisis, 1943–1957*. Cambridge: Harvard University Press, 1972.

Arthur Zipser, *Working-Class Giant, the Life of William Z. Foster*. New York: International Publishers, 1981.

28

DOROTHY DAY

Nancy L. Roberts

—During the Jazz Age she worked as a young radical journalist in
New York, interviewing Leon Trotsky and hobnobbing with Eugene
O'Neill, Mike Gold, Max Eastman, and Malcolm Cowley.

—In 1933, now a devout Catholic convert, she cofounded the radical
Catholic Worker movement and paper advocating social justice and peace.

—At the age of seventy-five she was jailed for the seventh time, after
she took part in civil disobedience with Cesar Chavez and the United
Farm Workers in Fresno, California.

—Today she is being promoted for sainthood in the Catholic church.

Dorothy Day is one of the most interesting and significant figures in
twentieth-century American radicalism. Born in 1897 in Brooklyn
Heights, New York, she was the third of five children in a staid, middle-
class, marginally Episcopalian family.

Day's interest in social problems had already been awakened during
high school in Chicago (where she had moved with her family) when
she read Peter Kropotkin's radical alternative to the prevailing social
Darwinism. Reading Kropotkin's plan for an anarchism based on cooperation and common work "especially brought to my mind the plight of the

poor, of the workers," she wrote in her 1952 autobiography, *The Long Loneliness*. The social novels of Jack London and Upton Sinclair also influenced her. "Though my only experience of the destitute was in books," she wrote, "the very fact that the *The Jungle* was about Chicago where I lived, whose streets I walked, made me feel that from then on my life was to be linked to theirs, their interests were to be mine; I had received a call, a vocation, a direction to my life."

As a student at the University of Illinois in Urbana from 1914 to June 1916, Day joined the Socialist party, wrote for both the college and the town papers, and read more works that shaped her political, social, and ultimately, religious philosophy: those of Gorki, Chekhov, Tolstoy, Dostoyevsky, "Big Bill" Haywood, Eugene Debs, Elizabeth Gurley Flynn, Carlo Tresca, Mother Jones, and the Haymarket anarchists.

In 1916 she joined her family in New York City and began to look for a job on a newspaper. Her Republican newspaperman father disapproved of women in careers, particularly in journalism, and quickly contacted his city editor friends, telling them not to employ her. So Day approached Chester Wright, editor of the Socialist *Call*, and convinced him to hire her for five dollars a week. She moved to a tenement on the Lower East side and covered strikes, community demands for housing, health care, and schools. Not quite twenty, she interviewed Leon Trotsky and heard stirring speeches by radicals such as Elizabeth Gurley Flynn. Day recalled being "thrilled" by Flynn's "fire and vision" on behalf of Mesabi Iron Range strikers.

After World War I started, Day journeyed to Washington to protest the draft. Back in New York, she joined the staff of Max Eastman's irreverent *Masses,* the most exciting and lively radical magazine of the time. With much of the staff on vacation during the summer of 1917, Day single-handedly edited the August issue—the one that the government censored as subversive under the provisions of the Espionage Act. She next joined the staff of *The Liberator,* the successor to *The Masses,* edited by Eastman, his sister Crystal Eastman, and Floyd Dell. Day seemed cut out for the calling of radical writer like her contemporaries Mary Heaton Vorse, Josephine Herbst, and Meridel LeSueur. At that time writing, especially advocacy journalism, was one of the few public paths leftist movements approved for their women members.

As jazz and bathtub gin flowed freely, Day enjoyed fraternizing with New York's literary and social avant-garde. Her Greenwich Village companions included Mike Gold, Max Bodenheim, John Dos Passos, Malcolm and Peggy Baird Cowley, Caroline Gordon, Allen Tate, Kenneth Burke, and Hart Crane. The young journalist was an imposing presence: tall, with luminous blue eyes, and lovely high cheekbones that gave her a

Slavic appearance, though her ancestry was Scots-Irish. In the "Hell Hole," a popular Greenwich Village saloon, a drunken Eugene O'Neill often recited Francis Thompson's poem "The Hound of Heaven" to her. "Gene could recite all of it," Day wrote in *From Union Square to Rome* (1938), "and he used to sit there, looking dour and black, his head sunk on his chest." She was fascinated by "the idea of this pursuit by the Hound of Heaven [God]. The recurrence of it, the inevitableness of the outcome made me feel that sooner or later I would have to pause in the mad rush of living and remember my first beginning and my last end."

A card-carrying Wobbly, Day attended socialist and communist meetings, committed to the Old Left's brand of secular radicalism. After the out-of-wedlock birth of her only child, a daughter, in 1926, her spirituality, always a quiet if unacknowledged force in her life, was transformed. "No human creature could receive or contain so vast a flood of love and joy as I felt after the birth of my child," she recalled. "The final object of this love and gratitude was God." But why, of all religions, did she choose to join Roman Catholicism? her radical friends challenged. After all, as Day herself admitted, the Catholic church was "lined up with property, with the wealthy, with the state, with capitalism, with all the forces of reaction." Day became a Catholic because, she said, it was the church of the poor, the church of the masses.

For the next fifty-four years, until her death, she sought to combine the dedication to social justice and peace she had developed as a young American radical with a deep, traditional Catholic spirituality. This was a daunting task for any woman in the Catholic church in 1927, but particularly one who had belonged to leftist movements and who was a convert as well as a single parent with a child born outside of marriage. In 1932 when the editor of *Commonweal* sent Peter Maurin (1877–1949) to meet her, Day's course suddenly became clear. The eccentric French Catholic peasant intellectual gave her, as she put it, "a way of life and instruction." He had a three-point plan for radical social action based on Christian values. Maurin envisioned a lay, communitarian, anarchist (disavowing electoral politics) movement offering roundtable discussions, forums, and lectures for "clarification of thought," houses of hospitality in every urban parish to feed and shelter the poor and homeless, and farming communes which would break down "acquisitive" industrial society into more manageable, organic units where worker and scholar would live and learn in a community. Change in society must begin with individuals, so "personalism"—personal, individual action—to achieve social justice was paramount.

These ideas spring from the life and radical social teachings of Jesus as recorded in the Four Gospels of the New Testament. Other influential sources for Day and Maurin were the post–World War I group of Paris intellectuals known as "Christian personalists," especially Emmanuel Mounier and Jacques Maritain, and the Russian philosopher Nikolai Berdyaev. The ideas of English distributists such as Hilaire Belloc, G. K. Chesterton, and Eric Gill also influence Catholic Worker philosophy, as do the ideas of Dostoyevsky (especially as expressed in *The Brothers Karamazov*).

Without Dorothy Day, Peter Maurin would probably have spent the rest of his years lecturing to nonlistening audiences in Union Square. She became the practical "executive" who carried out his programs and added her own as well, ultimately becoming the real head of the Catholic Worker movement—the "Head Anarch," as Tom Cornell, a 1960s *Catholic Worker* editor, once affectionately called her.

In the early 1930s, more than twelve million Americans were out of work. Desperately seeking solutions to social problems they embraced the Catholic Worker movement and its House of Hospitality that Day and Maurin opened in the winter of 1933–34 on the Lower East Side. Some forty houses were open by 1940. Ultimately some 200 houses of hospitality were established—no one is sure exactly how many—across the country, concentrated in cities such as Boston, Washington, Cleveland, Chicago, Milwaukee, Seattle, Portland, and Los Angeles. More than a hundred exist today, including houses in Australia, Canada, Germany, Great Britain, the Netherlands, and Mexico. The farming communes have been fewer and less successful, more like rural houses of hospitality than the "agronomic universities" that Maurin envisioned.

At the outset the Frenchman had mentioned starting a newspaper to publicize his ideas, and Day quickly rose to the challenge. The *Catholic Worker* was distributed for a penny a copy at a Communist rally in Union Square on May Day, 1933. "It's time there was a Catholic paper printed for the unemployed," the paper announced. "Is it not possible to be radical and not atheist? Is it not possible to protest, to expose, to complain to point out abuses and demand reforms without desiring the overthrow of religion?" The *Catholic Worker* announced its aim "to popularize and make known the encyclicals of the Popes in regard to social justice and the program put forth by the Church for the 'reconstruction of the social order.' " The paper covered the day's issues: unemployment, labor conditions, strikes. By 1936 its circulation had reached 150,000.

During World War II, criticism of Day's work reached new heights on account of her paper's pacifist stance. Circulation plummeted to 50,500 and *Catholic Worker* salespeople were beaten in the streets. The paper was banned from some churches and several bishops forbade her from speaking to religious groups in their dioceses. Yet Day stood firm. When faced with such hostile scrutiny, she counseled her editors only to quote from unimpeachable sources: the papal encyclicals, the lives of the saints, and Gospel accounts of the life and teachings of Jesus. She never criticized Catholic teachings, only the church's failure to live up to them.

She made her Catholic Worker movement the single continuing voice for peace in the Catholic church from 1933 until 1980, always linking peace with social justice. Day often tied voluntary poverty directly to the Catholic Worker's nonviolence and pacifism. She believed that one of "the great modern arguments" for detachment from material possessions is the modern economy's dependence on war preparation industries.

To Dorothy Day, journalism was a form of activism in its own right, on a par with the public speaking she traveled by bus around the country to do. Continuing as editor and publisher until her death in 1980, she made her distinctive stamp evident on every page of the *Catholic Worker*. She recruited artists of the stature of Fritz Eichenberg and Adé Bethune and printed the work of an outstanding group of writers that included Lewis Mumford, Thomas Merton, J. F. Powers, Maria Montessori, Claude McKay, Catherine de Hueck Doherty, Danilo Dolci, and Daniel and Philip Berrigan. Michael Harrington's stint as a *Catholic Worker* editor in the early 1950s informed his book *The Other America* (1962), which helped inspire the antipoverty programs of Presidents Kennedy and Johnson. Day's own column became a favorite feature. In it she discussed everything from the soup line and her grandchildren to prayer and weighty spiritual and social issues. It was a riveting combination of the everyday and the ultimate and is still reprinted today in the *Catholic Worker,* which retains a circulation of about 100,000.

The power of Day's prose sprang from the strength and sincerity of her convictions. Like fellow radicals Henry David Thoreau and Eugene Debs, she allowed no separation between her beliefs and her actions; for nearly fifty years she lived in the rudest voluntary poverty at the Catholic Worker house in the slums of the Lower East Side, sharing her room with homeless women, taking her clothing from the common used-clothing bin. She portrayed the poor with dignity, solidarity, and eloquent insight. The appeals she wrote generated thousands of dollars to support the movement's activities, enough to keep it at least teetering financially on the edge of the red.

During the years 1955–1961, Day led Catholic Workers and others in several acts of civil disobedience to protest the state's war preparation activities. Given the prevailing Cold War climate of political repression and paranoia, these were courageous acts, ones that earned her three jail sentences by 1960. The first demonstration took place on June 15, 1955. With Catholic Workers and members of the War Resisters League and the Fellowship of

Reconciliation (including A. J. Muste), Day sat quietly on a bench in New York's City Hall Park and refused to participate in the civil defense air raid drill then taking place across the United States, Canada, and Mexico. Day explained in the *Catholic Worker* that the demonstration was also meant to be "an act of public penance for having been the first people in the world to drop the atom bomb, [and] to make the hydrogen bomb." She also stressed that "We are engaging only ourselves in this action, not the Church. We are acting as individual Catholics."

This last note may have been intended for the Catholic Chancery, which watched Day's activities over the years with a combination of consternation and admiration. Catholic leaders wanted their immigrant church to be accepted as part of the American mainstream, not discredited as a subversive force. And so Day's social criticism aroused their worst fears. Over the years she managed to deal with Catholic authorities diplomatically and ultimately effectively. Her willingness as a Catholic traditionalist to subject herself to the authority of the clergy was genuine. At the same time she was, as one of her associates once put it, "nobody's sweet little mother." Perhaps discerning that her status as a convert, former secular leftist, and single parent did not enhance her credibility with Catholic authorities, she often quoted "our founder Peter Maurin," the French immigrant and former Christian Brother who represented the prestige and respectability of European Catholicism. Scrupulously disavowing any official endorsement from the church, she kept the Catholic Worker a lay movement, realizing that laypeople could afford to make "mistakes" that clergy could not. At the same time she argued successfully with the church to retain the "Catholic" in *Catholic Worker,* which provided the likely unintended benefit of what historian Mel Piehl has called "protective coloration." Still, there was plenty of criticism, especially from conservative Catholic publications such as the *Brooklyn Tablet* and the *Wanderer.* Day was sometimes called "Moscow Mary" during the 1930s. In 1935 the *American Mercury* described Day as "a former Greenwich Village habituée and recent convert of the Church," an "unmistakable sign of the downfall of the Catholic Church in the United States."

By the end of the Vietnam War, the witness of her life allayed much of the hierarchy's concern. Notre Dame University named her the "Outstanding American Catholic" in 1972 and many considered her to be "First Lady of American Catholicism." In their 1983 pastoral letter, U.S. Catholic bishops indicated a historic shift in their teaching about war and peace when they wrote that pacifism is an acceptable moral and political choice for Catholics. Day was singled out along with Martin Luther King, Jr., as one who had provided "nonviolent witness" that had "had a profound impact upon the life of the church in the United States."

Father Daniel Berrigan describes the peace movement's debt to Dorothy Day:

> Without Dorothy, without that exemplary patience, courage, moral modesty, without this woman pounding at the locked door behind which the powerful mock the powerless with games of triage, without her, the resistance we offered would have been simply unthinkable. She urged our consciences off the beaten track; she made the impossible (in our case) probable, and then actual.

Many other contemporary Catholic peace activists—Jim Forest, Eileen Egan, Philip Berrigan, Robert Ellsberg, James W. Douglass, and Tom Cornell—acknowledge the power of Day's influence on them. But Day's impact extends beyond the peace movement. As historian David J. O'Brien has written, Dorothy Day profoundly influenced not only her church but several generations of Americans, challenging them to think differently about social issues. Whenever the roots of peace and social-justice activism are traced, Day's Catholic Worker movement surfaces. And Day's *Catholic Worker,* still being published at a penny a copy by her successors in New York, remains one of the most significant advocacy publications in U.S. history.

Dorothy Day would not like the current movement, spearheaded by a group of Chicago Claretians, to have the Vatican declare her a saint. She hated being placed on a pedestal, preferring to be considered an ordinary woman whose example could be followed by others. More than a dozen years after her death as Catholic Worker houses of hospitality flourish around the country and abroad and her ideas continue to change lives, her life does seem extraordinary.

Suggested Readings

Patrick G. Coy, ed., *A Revolution of the Heart: Essays on the Catholic Worker*. Philadelphia: Temple University Press, 1988.

Dorothy Day, *By Little and by Little: The Selected Writings of Dorothy Day,* ed. Robert Ellsberg. New York: Knopf, 1982.

James Forest, *Love Is the Measure: A Biography of Dorothy Day*. New York: Paulist Press, 1986.

William D. Miller, *Dorothy Day: A Biography*. San Francisco: Harper and Row, 1982.

Mel Piehl, *Breaking Bread: The Catholic Worker and the Origin of Catholic Radicalism in America*. Philadelphia: Temple University Press, 1982.

Nancy L. Roberts, *Dorothy Day and the "Catholic Worker."* Albany: State University of New York Press, 1984.

29

NORMAN THOMAS

Gary Dorrien

The image of Norman Thomas that prevails in most accounts of his time and career is that of an idealistic failure. It is an image that he endorsed. Norman Thomas became the national leader of the Socialist party in the United States shortly after the party was destroyed by the political ravages of the First World War and the opening round of this century's faction fights over communism. For nearly fifty years, he struggled to keep a dying socialist faith alive in the United States, while insisting that his innumerable campaigns for social justice, civil liberties, and world peace were doing little good. Thomas ran for the U.S. presidency six times on the Socialist party ticket. In his later years, when friends tried to console him with the fact that Franklin Roosevelt had carried out much of Thomas's political platform, Thomas invariably replied that Roosevelt carried it out "on a stretcher." This was Thomas's epitaph for American democratic socialism, which in his time was widely called "Norman Thomas Socialism."

Norman Thomas Socialism was, in part, a product of the Protestant Social Gospel movement. Born in 1884 in Marion, Ohio, Thomas was the son and grandson of conservative Presbyterian ministers. After graduating from Princeton in 1905, Thomas tested his own religious vocation as a street minister on Manhattan's Lower East Side and later served as a pastor in a tenement district church bordering Hell's Kitchen. Upon graduating from Union Theological Seminary in 1911—at the high tide of the American Social Gospel movement—Thomas was ordained to the Presbyterian ministry, though not without controversy. Like many of his Social Gospel classmates, Thomas was not a traditional believer in any sense excepting moral seriousness. He had little conception of the church beyond its capacity to serve as an agent of social transformation. When a caucus of conservative pastors protested his ordination, Thomas's father wrote to him that "these sensational rumors are exceedingly painful to me, who am conservative in my views." Shortly afterward, Thomas rejected a call from a wealthy Fifth Avenue church and chose to serve a poor, mixed-ethnic parish in East Harlem, where he pastored for seven years.

Thomas's radicalism deepened during this period. In 1916, he became a founding member and national cochair of the pacifist Fellowship of Reconciliation (FOR) and subsequently founded FOR's magazine, *World Tomorrow,* through which he protested against America's current preparations for war and proscription. His commitments to peace and to civil liberties led him during the same period to join Roger Baldwin in creating the National Civil Liberties Bureau of the American Union Against Militarism. This bureau, which Thomas kept in operation after Baldwin went to prison for refusing to register for the draft, was later renamed the American Civil Liberties Union.

Having entered the ministry primarily to raise the condition of the poor and to promote his progressive antiwar politics, Thomas was appalled when most of America's churches joined Woodrow Wilson's propaganda campaign to intervene in Europe. "How can we accept Christ as Lord and Master and deny his spirit by sharing responsibility for the unutterable horrors of war?" he pleaded. "Even in war the church ought to stand for a form of society transcending nationalism and national boundaries." Most of the churches were already banging the war drums when Wilson called America to war, however. The spectacle of a militarized Christendom drove Thomas to find an unlikely alternative vehicle for his idealism.

He was reluctant to join the Socialist party because he was repelled by its Marxist rhetoric and because he feared that socialism might rationalize new forms of state dictatorship. Thomas's moral sensibility, his uncompromising commitment to civil liberties, and his democratic spirit made him distrustful of any kind of Marxist or socialist movement that promoted violence, authoritarianism, or vanguardism. At the time, he was further chastened by the failure of the Socialist International to prevent its European working-class members from slaughtering each other in the name of nationalism. The war itself gave ample testimony to the failure of the socialist faith in Europe.

In the United States, however, the Socialist party bravely kept its antiwar faith in the face of severe government persecution. On the day after the United States entered the war, the party's national convention voted 140 to 36 to support Morris Hillquit's resolution condemning American intervention in Europe. "We brand the declaration of war by our government a crime against the nations of the world," the convention declared. Some of the party's most prominent English-language intellectuals resigned in order to support the war, and joined those condemning the party—a move extremely damaging to an organization compelled to justify its legal right to existence.

The Socialist party fought back spiritedly, however. By 1917–18, it won many local elections on an antiwar platform and mounted an extraordinary initiative through the People's Council of America for Peace and Democracy. It was this "peace" party that Thomas, particularly impressed by the courage of New York leader Hillquit, chose to join. Thomas proclaimed to his new comrades that he had "a profound fear of the undue exaltation of the State and a profound faith that the new world we desire must depend upon freedom and fellowship rather than upon any sort of coercion whatsoever."

Thomas had joined the Socialist party on the eve of its undoing, however. Debs was imprisoned for his speeches on the war, many of the important socialist newspapers were repressed, open meetings banned, elected legislators sometimes barred from state government, local leaders harassed, and foreign-born members threatened with deportation. Worse than all this, the appeal of Communists to form a new organization aligned with the Third International threw factions of the party against one another in a fury of internecine destruction. From an apex of more than 100,000 members in 1917–19, the Socialist party fell to a mere 12,000 by 1923. David Karsner later described the organization that remained as "a political ghost in the graveyard of current events seeking respectable burial."

This was the party that Thomas inherited. In the mid-1920s, the party's extinction was averted partly through Thomas's unrelenting speaking tours on its behalf. During the same period, Thomas organized and participated in dozens of other activist organizations. For the next forty years, Thomas gave hundreds of speeches each year to create or support movements for economic democracy, trade unionism, civil rights, gender rights, social equality, and world peace. His presidential campaigns, which began in 1928, became extensions of Thomas's ongoing campaigns against every form of discrimination, militarism, and oppression. In the early 1930s, he gave several thousand speeches across forty-four states and published

six books, including his massive account of the human ravages of capitalism, *Human Exploitation*. Thomas fought for civil liberties throughout
America throughout his career, most notably in the 1926 Passaic textile
strike, in the 1935 anti-Klan campaign in Tampa, and against the Hague
machine in Jersey City in 1938. He spoke repeatedly on behalf of the
Southern sharecroppers and later helped organize the Southern Tenant
Farmer's Union. In addition to the Socialist party, he was a leader or
director, at various times, of the Fellowship of Reconciliation, the American Civil Liberties Union, the League for Industrial Democracy, the
Workers Defense League, the Post War World Council, the Committee
for a Sane Nuclear Policy, and numerous other organizations.

Thomas's most significant electoral campaign was his 1932 presidential
bid, in which his party's platform called for agricultural relief, national
unemployment insurance, public works projects, a pension system, slum
clearance, a shortened work week, low-cost housing programs, a more
progressive income tax, and the nationalization of basic industries and
banks. Having regarded Franklin Roosevelt as little more than a wealthy
opportunist and failed governor, Thomas was surprised when Roosevelt
quickly enacted most of the Socialist party's platform. He strenuously
insisted throughout Roosevelt's presidency, however—sometimes in personal meetings with Roosevelt—that the only way to secure the New
Deal's gains toward greater equality and social justice would be to socialize
the major means of production.

In his powerful 1934 book, *The Choice before Us,* Thomas recalled
that when Roosevelt took office, the banking system had virtually collapsed and farmers were on the verge of rioting. Instead of socializing
the banking system, however, and thus directing credit toward production
for use, Roosevelt closed the banks, used public funds to patch the system,
"and gave it back to the bankers to see if they could ruin it again." That
is, Roosevelt used the power of the state to stabilize private ownership to
maximize private profit. Thomas reminded his readers that this economic
strategy had a name. It was the strategy of economic fascism. Thomas
quickly conceded that Roosevelt was not actually running a fascist government. He argued that, in fact, the chief safeguard against a fascist takeover
in America was precisely that Roosevelt was president. From his nationwide speaking tours, however, Thomas was well acquainted with and
greatly alarmed by the growth of fascist sentiment in the United States.
He was frightened by the parallels between America's racist, fascist-
oriented movements and similar movements in Germany and Japan. And
he was disturbed by the deep similarities between New Deal and fascist
economies. Thomas's books of this period repeatedly warned that American liberalism and democracy were imperiled by these trends. Democratic

socialism was, for him, the name of the system that extended and fulfilled the liberal democratic alternative to communism and fascism.

If the chief threat to American liberalism and democracy came from a convergence of fascist-type trends in American life, it followed, for Thomas, that a democratic socialist politics in America needed to make every effort to protect civil liberties, to fight corporate power, and to oppose American remilitarization. The latter task brought Thomas into conflict with Roosevelt's rearmament campaign in the late 1930s. Thomas believed that America's participation in another world war would seriously threaten American democracy. He was therefore willing to say nearly anything and to make alliance with nearly anyone to block Roosevelt from taking the United States into another war. These efforts became increasingly desperate in the late 1930s and early '40s. Thomas's hatred for war—"the monster I so utterly loathe"—drove him to make alliances with right-wing isolationists. By 1940, he was not above arguing that it was too late to stop Hitler from conquering Europe. Another war would surely destroy every social gain that he had struggled for. Thomas's worst fear for his country came to pass the following year. On the day after Japan attacked Pearl Harbor, he wrote to a friend, "I feel as if my world has pretty much come to an end, that what I have stood for has been defeated, and my own usefulness made small." Two days afterward, he announced in utter despair that he would support America's war.

Thomas refused to indulge his despair, however. He had promised in hundreds of speeches that if America did go to war, he would do everything in his power to prevent his prophecies from coming true. He would fight unceasingly to protect and extend American liberties and bring about a just world peace. Having seen his worst fear come to pass, Thomas responded to America's crisis, and his own, by redeeming his pledge to keep a vigil for freedom. He forcefully opposed the internment of Japanese "aliens" in concentration camps, arguing that Roosevelt's policy was plainly racist and outrageous. He repeatedly pleaded with Roosevelt to accept Jewish refugees into America, especially after reports about the Nazi extermination camps began to reach the United States. He condemned the media's wartime fascination with "Uncle Joe" Stalin and its absurdly idealized portraits of Soviet society. He denounced the obliteration bombing of German and Japanese cities, arguing that carpet bombing killed mostly civilians and sowed hatred in the minds of survivors. He opposed Roosevelt's insistence on unconditional German and Japanese surrenders and later appealed to President Truman to change Roosevelt's policy toward Japan. He warned that Roosevelt's insistence on an unconditional German surrender was laying the groundwork for Soviet control over Eastern and Central Europe. Thomas perceived that Roosevelt was preparing to abandon Eastern Europe to the Soviets; he therefore based his 1944 presidential campaign on his alternative peace plan. Thomas argued that the United States and England needed to create an international federation that would redraw Poland's borders and forcibly prevent Stalin from devouring Eastern Europe. The Yalta and Potsdam accords later confirmed his predictions concerning postwar Europe. Thomas vehemently denounced both agreements, claiming that Potsdam "represented a triumph of vengeance and stupidity" that "turned eastern and central Europe over to the communists."

Most of these were deeply unpopular positions in the United States during the war, which brought Thomas a heavy volume of hate mail. His most bitterly contested position, however, was his protest against Truman's atomic bombing of Hiroshima and Nagasaki. Thomas was horrified that his country incinerated a crowded city with no warning and then gratuitously destroyed another. He was ashamed that his country chose to slaughter 100,000 people as its first choice, without testing the alternatives of a conditional surrender or a demonstration bomb. Thomas and Truman later developed considerable respect for each other, and Truman sought Thomas's advice on numerous issues. Long before it became respectable to question Truman's use of atomic weapons, however, Thomas felt compelled to remind his American audiences of the unspeakable horror of Hiroshima and Nagasaki.

Thomas's major work, *A Socialist's Faith,* was written, with considerable difficulty, in the years following the war. The death of his wife, Violet, to whom he was deeply devoted, left him too depressed to complete the manuscript on time. When Thomas finally returned to the book in 1948, America's political climate had changed so much that he was forced to rewrite much of the text. During the war, he recalled, his warnings about the "essential evil of Communism" had been widely rejected by Americans eager to embrace their wartime Soviet ally. His militant anti-communism was derided not only by much of the liberal left, but also by America's mainstream media. In the years following the war, however, Thomas became alarmed at the rise of an equally dangerous and "rather hysterical anticommunism, which is being exploited by reactionaries."

He spent the rest of his life fighting both positions. Thomas's tour of the Soviet Union in 1937 had convinced him that Soviet communism was a mirror image of fascism. He was repulsed by the country's police state atmosphere and its perverted misuse of socialist rhetoric. In 1948, Henry Wallace's Progressive party campaign for the presidency represented the kind of pro-communist and anti-anticommunist leftism that Thomas despised. He therefore spent much of his own campaign attacking Wallace as an "apologist for the slave state of Russia, and preacher of peace by appeasement." For Thomas, nothing was more crucial to the future of democratic socialism than a clear-eyed socialist understanding of the brutality, mendacity and squalor of the communist experiment. His hatred for communism was fueled, in part, by his belief that the existence of Soviet totalitarianism was the chief obstacle to building a democratic socialist movement in the United States. For the same reason, he spent much of his career battling against conservatives and reactionaries who used "anticommunism" as a club to smash any form of progressive politics.

Thomas's conception of democratic socialism was conventional for his time and party. He prompted a "commanding heights" strategy in which public corporations would control society's basic industries, consumer cooperatives would control most retail outlets, and nonessential industries would remain under private control. Thomas was not an economic or political theorist, nor was he a strong party leader. He understood, as he wrote in *Socialism Re-examined,* that "socialism needs new answers," but he was not equipped to provide the new answers that his movement needed. His contribution to modern democratic socialism came chiefly not through his writings or his party leadership, but through his unsurpassed dedication, compassion, and eloquence, and through his insistent appeal to the vision of a good society. Near the end of his life, while taking part in demonstrations against America's war in Vietnam, Thomas was distressed by the character of much of the antiwar movement, which struck him as childishly vulgar and anti-American. His speech to the National Students Association in 1967 summarized his message to a younger generation: "I don't like the sight of young people burning the flag of my country, the country I love," he said. "If they want an appropriate symbol they should be washing the flag, not burning it."

He took small consolation from the accolades that admirers and even opponents heaped upon him throughout his later career. He was routinely described by the *New York Times* and other newspapers as the conscience of America. Martin Luther King remarked on several occasions that Thomas was the most courageous person he ever met. Thomas would have traded these tributes for greater success in making his country more equal, more cooperative, or less militaristic. His perception of himself as an idealistic failure revealed less about his accomplishments than about his seriousness in struggling for democratic socialism. For him, to behold his country's massive inequality, its pervasive racial injustice, and its foreign imperialism was to recognize that he had accomplished very little in his life. More than a decade after Thomas's death in 1968, however, Irving Howe offered a more appropriate measure of Thomas's legacy: "Even after he died Thomas remained, so to say, in my head, setting a standard of right action, pointing to the elusive path where the 'ethic of ultimate ends' and the 'ethic of responsibility' join. When I did something unworthy in politics, it was to his memory I had to answer; when I acquitted myself well, it was his approval I would most have wanted."

Suggested Readings

Harry Fleischman, *Norman Thomas: A Biography*. New York: W. W. Norton, 1964.

W. A. Swanberg, *Norman Thomas: The Last Idealist*. New York: Scribners, 1976.

Norman Thomas, *The Choice before Us: Mankind at the Crossroads*. New York: MacMillian, 1934.

————, *A Socialist's Faith*. New York: W. W. Norton, 1951.

————, *Socialism Re-examined*. New York: W. W. Norton, 1963.

30

LEWIS MUMFORD
Paul Buhle

Lewis Mumford's life and his prodigious literary output provide a handy parable on the limits and the lasting value of an eccentric, authentically American radical intellectual. Generally keeping his distance from the organized left, Mumford reached generations of readers who sensed something wrong but could not place it in political terms. Instead of an oppositional politics, he gave them a way to look at key elements of the modern order and the roots of these developments in a long and complex historical development.

Mumford's immensely popular histories of technology were, in fact, always more and less than they seemed. A hybrid cultural criticism, they remained the work of the master generalist who filled the gaps in his knowledge with shrewd but often imprecise generalizations. Yet by fighting the omnipresent and one-sided technological optimism of American culture, he provided insights into the approaching ecological catastrophe that few other critics from any point on the ideological spectrum could even admit as a possibility. He permitted no illusions about the devastating costs of reckless economic expansionism and its toxic military-industrial by-products. By the time of his death in 1989, his projections had been woefully vindicated but his visions of redemption remained uncertain.

At last, however, the political value of Lewis Mumford's ideas might be properly appreciated.

Mumford formed his intellectual identity as the sort of self-made thinker he would exemplify the rest of his life. Born in 1895 the illegitimate son of a prominent New Jersey, Jewish businessman's nephew and of the businessman's German-American household maid, Mumford could not even verify his father's identity until decades later. His mother and a German-born working-class grandfather raised him, and gave him a sense of his options in the flourishing public institutions of Progressive Era New York City.

The boy did well in public schools, read Emerson to gain self-reliance, and quickly learned to place his trust in the power of the mind. At fifteen, he engaged in the widespread amateur pastime of technological speculation, contributing his first publishable essay to a popular scientific magazine. Unable to afford Columbia University, he was also slightly tubercular and simply unwilling to keep a steady job. Instead, he lived at home and spent long hours at the New York Public Library and the Museum of Natural History, reading the classics and developing his own analogies between natural and human history.

In a different age, Mumford might have become an intellectual aristocrat drawn toward political conservatism by his feeling of superiority over the average minds around him. But the second decade of the new century offered the young New Yorker an avant-garde scene of unprecedented excitement. Taking classes irregularly at the New School, City College, and Columbia, he determinedly walked the streets of Manhattan neighborhoods observing the rapidly changing city, reading Walt Whitman for inspiration, and pondering better urban arrangements. He found himself especially attracted to Patrick Geddes, Scottish botanist, housing reformer, and early environmentalist. Never exactly a disciple, Mumford developed a Geddes-influenced "observational sociology" that interpreted community as the organic web between family, work, and geographic space within a properly organized social order.

He also fell among radicals and progressive liberals who shared the margins between academic and literary life. His first public address, given in 1917 at the anarchist Ferrer School on the subject of Prince Peter Kropotkin, was arranged by Irwin Granich (in a few years renamed "Mike Gold"), the future hard-boiled communist literary functionary. After a brief stint in the Navy—he enlisted but concluded later that the war had been a catastrophe for civilization—Mumford took a job at the *Dial* magazine with John Dewey, Thorstein Veblen, Helen Marot, and other sparkling literary figures. Beyond this circle, he made friends with Waldo Frank, Paul Rosenfeld, and Van Wyck Brooks, all participants in the precocious *Seven Arts* journal. Like Mumford, they sought to substitute in postwar America a voluntary community *culturalism* (what Mumford called "the belief in a system of common values, and the effort on the part of the community to work these values out in its daily life") for "its bastard offspring," the nationalism that invariably spawned war and brutality.

Such views had no vehicle to carry them forward. By the early 1920s, the most hopeful and democratic moments of the American left's challenge to capitalism had already come and gone with the repression of the Socialist party and the Industrial Workers of the World. True, the Russian Revolution excited many radicals. But the crew around the *Seven Arts* and the *Dial* had no taste for the Leninist program. American radicalism needed to reinvent itself, they believed, and they could make their own best contribution through sheer intellectual effort. Mumford, who held no university post until 1942 and thereafter taught only irregularly, also had to support a family on a writer's salary. He set himself to carry on the crusade through turning out popular books.

Mumford's first volume, *The Story of Utopias* (1923), succeeded brilliantly in establishing him as a popularist, and also in developing his chief theses. The alternative or antidote to American capitalism and Russian communism lay not (as many thought at the time) in the traditions of older European utopias that had placed their faith in elite planning and the powers of the state. Rather, it could be found in the life and culture of the old New England village. There, amid the small-town democracy and its functional architecture, the American "Eutopia" or realizable reality had already been foreseen by Emerson, Hawthorne, Thoreau, and their circle. And there, historically speaking, the battle had also been lost for a century. *Sticks and Stones: A Study of American Architecture and Civilization* (1924), often called the first inclusive architectural history of the United States, was cut from the same cloth as his earlier book, depicting a related promise and disappointment.

Like the tales of Nathaniel Hawthorne which he loved so, the intellectual apparatus of Mumford's early books could be described as the framing details of an allegory. That allegory had everything to do with America's claim to being the machine civilization par excellence, and the accompanying misconception that machinery applied to sufficient raw materials would resolve all the messy problems of the human condition. The possibilities of a humane technology had been wasted by the recklessness of the pioneer pushing West, he insisted, and by the merchant class building up a pseudoculture of American elites. On the one hand, the forces of barbarism advanced in real life, as the pioneer willfully abandoned European medieval culture in a vain attempt to escape history. On the other hand, the fictitious culture of gentility rendered the bourgeois aesthete a "pillager" of European *objets d'art* and the middle class a mere admirer of imitations. Only a renewal of the organic vision—technology suited to and reconciled with social needs—could hold out hope for a fundamental change of direction.

Elaborated in lucid essays and reviews (he contributed to many publications, but penned a prestigious *New Yorker* column, "Skylines," from the early 1930s), Mumford's view of architecture as result of tradition and social forces had great appeal. Ecoradicals had meanwhile pointed Mumford in the direction of a revitalized and radicalized regionalism. Benton MacKaye, a Socialist and the son of one of Henry David Thoreau's friends, first visualized for Mumford and his fellow members of the new Regional Planning Association of America a garden city alternative to the contemporary "realistic" planners' models of commercial megalopolis and accompanying agribusiness districts. Mumford strove to provide historical ballast to MacKaye's dreams, and to fill out the picture's details.

Technics and Civilization (1934) crystallized Mumford's reputation as technohistorian and guru-in-the-making. A popularly readable history of technology, it was at once sympathetic toward scientists and also critical of the ends toward which their discoveries had been put. He divided modernity into three major epochs: "eotechnic," from medieval life to the beginnings of the industrial revolution; "paleotechnic," the triumph of science, technology, and capitalism; and "neotechnic," the potential age ahead of organic experimentation and potential communal equality. Mumford may have been starry-eyed about the technological prospects, but he based his hopes firmly in an original interpretation of the early technological inklings and practical experiments, like timekeeping, which existed long before machines had taken over economic affairs. He sought to "out-Marx Marx," as he put it, by placing the real bourgeois revolution not with the rise of the bourgeoisie, but with the shift in *mentalité* from the organic to the mechanical.

Culture and the Cities (1938) was the capstone of Mumford's urban critique. Here, he retraced the last half-dozen centuries through details of city life, arguing that the city itself had once been and might again become not only a commodious living space but also the chief instrument of lifelong learning: "We must conceive of the city," as Mumford wrote later, "not primarily as a place of business or government but as an essential organ for expressing and actualizing a new personality."

Mumford's magisterial treatment of the medieval town completed and greatly popularized his banishment of "Dark Ages" myths. The nineteenth-century idea of Bad Old Days had been based upon misassessment of degraded remnants, and upon a presumptuous modern claim to superiority.

The open spaces, the public market sites and corridors that brought a healthful existence to the carefully defined lives of ordinary folk, had all passed with the chaos, greed, and organized brutality of rising industrialism and state power. The condensation of a growing populace—deprived of the best physical sites by the factories—had eventually placed even the honest builder in an untenable position. Filth and noise became a common possession of urban rich and poor, the suburb an early nonsolution to the problem of reintegrating life and work in some livable pattern.

Mumford waxed optimistic about the potential future city, as only a non-Marxist radical before the post–World War II period could. He envisioned a vast transformation almost at hand: new cities would be built when populations in the old ones exceeded about 50,000, and those new cities would become population centers of large garden districts. He also imagined that new sources of power and transport would bring an end to extractive mining and toxic fuels. He envisioned new mass dwellings, with space for everyone to live the good life, and with neat marketing centers connected by footpaths and bridges rather than highways. (He also imagined many other smaller but also wonderful details, such as the abolition of all public monuments celebrating dead heroes.) He made readers almost palpably feel the new society ahead.

No wonder he was asked to write the narrative for the documentary film *The City,* which became one of the most popular attractions at the 1939 World's Fair. A 1938 *Time* magazine put Mumford on the cover, gazing intensely from between two tree branches. "An extraordinary . . . new type of public figure," father of a new field of "bio-scholarship," unafraid to confront "the paranoia of the ruling class" or the "servility of the crowd," Mumford emerged as prophet of the architects and planners who had already begun to give new life to civilization.

Of course, Mumford's schemes demanded, as *Time* noted, the public ownership of land; fresh towns made possible by regional planning that would dwarf the scale (and the public tax bill) of the hotly contested Tennessee Valley Authority; and a vast internal rebuilding of the cities. Liberals and radicals chided him for his unwillingness to assess the entrenched opposition against any such plan. He blithely ignored them, perpetuating a sort of political dreamland that his highly educated devotees shared all too willingly.

Radical idealism of even this rather technocratic kind, given protective coloring by contemporary New Deal agencies, was soon destined for the scrap heap. President Truman replaced the surviving New Deal visionaries with pork-barrel politicians who made their own fortunes in accelerated government subsidies to largely harmful economic growth. By 1950, the various benefit programs underwriting urban flight—with the cities and racial minorities paying the price—had been fully hatched. The blossoming freeway, the suburb, and the intensified megalopolis devastated Mumford's fancies.

Under these circumstances, Mumford became a most individualistic Cold War dissident. Only a few years after throwing all his literary energy behind the antifascist effort (his only son, Geddes, died in combat in 1944), Mumford spoke out vividly on the catastrophe of the Nagasaki/ Hiroshima bombing. "Gentlemen, You Are Mad!" he wrote in a public manifesto, personally launching a campaign to halt atomic testing, eradicate atomic stocks, and submit U.S. handling of dangerous materials to a United Nations body. (A decade later, he added his name to the editorial supporters of the proto–New Left peace magazine, *Liberation*.) Relinquishing American atomic superiority was the furthest thing from the minds of the military chiefs and Truman, of course. In the growing military-economic-political attachment of elites to the mechanisms of the behemoth state, Mumford began to see confirmed the outline of the future that, in his pessimistic moments, he had long feared.

That observation reduced him, increasingly, to a prophet sounding jeremiads in the urban-industrial wasteland of Cold War culture. From here on, his books tend to repeat earlier themes, but now overlaid with a heavy moralistic tone and often with an uncharacteristic vagueness.

Yet he did not altogether lose his famous touch. His most original late work was a slim volume of archaeological and mythological speculation about the origins of society, *The Transformations of Man* (1956). Here, he best made his case—as noted anthropologists would later argue more precisely—that a common culture prompted Homo sapiens's social evolution. In short, "culture" was at no point a mere superstructure, but rather the structure itself, inscribed in the "symbolic language" that would become, in later decades, a favorite subject of postmodernists.

Repeatedly, according to Mumford's accounts, societies from ancient times onward had reached a dead end. Culture and social order endured because of infusions of new recruits from outside the system; and because of persistent, habitual survivals of wisdom and custom from the vanished "archaic society" that had existed before state and empire. The "axial" religions (Christianity, Judaism, Islam, etc.) had universalized aspirations for a transcendence of society's many limitations. But they failed to deliver. A new humanistic religion (although Mumford the atheist could not have called it that) would now be required for humanity to recover its organic self from the machine-mad age.

A less original but more publicly successful project occupied thousands of pages and most of Mumford's late productive years. The first volume in a new series, *The City in History* (1961), restating and refining Mumford's earlier views, won a National Book Award. Bellowing "Call Me Jonah!" at the awards banquet, he became the cantakerous Grand Old Man of American letters. He had indeed made some remarkable additions to his previous oeuvre. In particular, his assertion of a female-oriented prehistorical village life predated the similar feminist interpretations by a decade or two and buttressed his portrayal of the "trauma of civilization"—the origins of the power state, the military machine, and the organization of compulsory labor—as key to the modern dilemma.

The "machine" or "megamachine," avatar of evidently self-destructive twentieth-century life, had taken root here. Early communities, anxious about their survival and therefore eager to please the gods, sacrificed first their own inhabitants and then victims captured from other villages. The emerging cult of warfare conveniently diverted emerging social tensions away from the elites, and laid the basis for empire. Perhaps this had been inevitable, Mumford suggested, but only in the historical sense. Humanity could do better. Greece had escaped the cycle of power and destruction through nurturing the citizen as a rounded human being, and creating the polis as the expression of citizenship. This spirit could be returned to modern experience, if humanity took control of its destiny back from the megamachine and made the city's life the subject of conscious, democratic polity.

Mumford now argued more cautiously for the garden cities, in no small part because of his disappointment at the actual results of earlier experiments. He had added his voice to the defense of the city against the imperial road builder and architect of so-called urban renewal Robert Moses. As early as the forties, Mumford complained that highways had never solved a congestion problem, and later he predicted that urban space would finally become "a tomb of concrete roads and ramps covering the dead corpse of the city."

At his death—after several more, mostly autobiographical works—Mumford was still probing human purposefulness, seeking the origins of language as he lost his own ability to communicate by pen. "Resignation would be easier," he wrote privately, "if the world at large was in a more hopeful state." So he passed, never really finished. Mumford's prestigious ideas had, with one or two partial exceptions, no success in his lifetime of attempting to turn back the spread of urban ugliness he deplored, and no apparent impact in slowing the continued conversion of American society into the home base of a world empire whose sheer destructiveness the old man cursed until his last days. But in providing a framework for thinking about our crisis-ridden civilization, his books still can hardly be beat.

Suggested Readings

Casey Nelson Blake, *Beloved Community: The Cultural Criticism of Van Wyck Brooks, Waldo Frank, and Lewis Mumford*. Chapel Hill: University of North Carolina Press, 1990.

Thomas P. Hughes and Agatha C. Hughes, eds., *Lewis Mumford: Public Intellectual*. New York: Oxford University Press, 1990.

Donald Miller, *Lewis Mumford: A Life*. London: Weidenfeld and Nicolson, 1990.

Lewis Mumford, *Sketches from Life*. New York: Dial Press, 1982.

31

CLIFFORD ODETS

Norma Jenckes

You're suffering from the old American itch. You want to get there fast and you don't want to pay for the ride.

—Clifford Odets

Every once in a while an artist appears who articulates the aspirations, longings, hopes, and fears of an era. Clifford Odets scintillated across the dark sky of America's depression theater like a brilliant comet. Just as quickly as he gained ascendancy, he plummeted and left not a bright streak behind to mark his passage but a bitter scar of treachery. This is the popular image of Odets immortalized in the obituaries, gossip columns, and movie sections of daily newspapers. Clifford Odets in an unmatched series of plays in 1935 made artistic sense of the inchoate dreams of the American working class. He dared to rely on his experience of the quirky turns of Yiddish speech and character and brought alive, onstage for the first time, the rich, zesty language of the ethnic neighborhoods of New York City and Philadelphia. He even seemed for a short time to give hope to the Communist party, which had been searching for a proletarian writer. He took up the job that Walt Whitman began in American letters—to be an American Bard.

Handsome, charismatic, and vital, Odets impressed his contemporaries. Born July 18, 1906, in a brick row house of Philadelphia, Clifford Odets was the first child of what was to become an increasingly unhappy marriage. His mother, Pearl Geisinger, was a tubercular nineteen-year-old from Austria and his father, Louis Odets, a lusty, scrappy, twenty-year-old printer from Russia. Pearl suffered all her life from illness and was a constant depressive. As a young mother, she turned to her infant son to lavish her affection and attention on. She was impressed by his physical beauty and his platinum blond curls; his large blue eyes, which looked on the world with fresh curiosity, delighted her, and raised her hopes again. Pearl began reading voraciously and spent long hours teaching Clifford to spell when he was only two years old. Convinced that her son was special, she projected all her longings onto his future.

Rushing to meet his future, Clifford Odets was self-taught in many things. He dropped out of high school in the Bronx, where the family had moved when he was four. When he was seventeen he left school to begin a series of odd jobs. He continued to live with his family when they moved back to Philadelphia, this time to the more prosperous Oak Lane section of Northern Philadelphia. To his father's dismay, Clifford was attracted to the theater and found jobs with small companies in New York and Philadelphia and also worked on the radio. Between 1925 and 1927 he wrote two radio plays, *Dawn* and *At the Waterline.* He also began to play small acting parts, but there is little evidence that he was good at it. In two prestigious shows in which he secured parts, *R.U.R.* and *Marco Millions,* he had no speaking lines. In 1931, Odets joined the Group Theatre and played the Negro role of Uncle Reuben in the group's first production, *The House of Connelly.* In the second year, he landed the job as understudy to Luther Adler in John Howard Lawson's *Success Story.* Lawson became a role model and surrogate father figure to Odets. The older, communist playwright certainly influenced his decision to find the stuff of dramatic literature in the language and deeds of his own class and people.

When the plays came, they came in a flood of creativity. Nineteen thirty-five was the marvelous year for Odets. It began with a contest jointly sponsored by *New Theatre* and *New Masses.* Odets's *Waiting for Lefty* with its clarion curtain call for a "Strike" won the prize. In 1952 when testifying before the House Un-American Activities Committee (HUAC), Odets insisted that he never made more than a thousand dollars on the rights of the play. Yet it was performed in countless union halls and at strike rallies all over the United States. As Odets recalled, "It was . . . a kind of light machine-gun that you wheeled in to use whenever there was any kind of strike trouble."

The opening night audience on January 5, 1935, greeted it with tumultous applause. Witnesses such as Harold Clurman, Stanley Burnshaw, and members of the cast all agree that they felt they were at the beginning of a great, new movement in American theater. Clurman dubbed it "the birth cry of the thirties." Odets thrilled his audience with repeated references to labor struggles which would be fresh in their minds such as "the textile strike," "the San Francisco tie-up," and "the steel boys." However, the resonance of the play went deeper than its topical allusions. Odets chose a riveting dramatic premise that had been borrowed by many playwrights since. The situation of people waiting for someone who will make a great difference in their lives reappears in such plays as O'Neill's *The Iceman Cometh,* Beckett's *Waiting for Godot,* Gelber's *The Connection,* Pinter's *The Dumb Waiter,* August Wilson's *Joe Turner's Come and Gone,* and David Mercer's *After Hagerty.*

After the reception of *Waiting for Lefty,* Odets was able to have a play produced that he had written two years earlier, *Awake and Sing.* In fact, the Group had seen and produced one act of an earlier version, *I Got the Blues,* but found it too gloomy and the characters too unappealing. It took the success of *Lefty* to convince them to give the largely rewritten and renamed play a production. Rapidly placed into rehearsal, the played opened at the Belasco Theatre on February 19, 1935. The notices were acclamations, but more telling were the responses of the audiences when they at last saw reflected onstage the ethnic, neighborhood, and Jewish humor of their childhoods and their daily family lives. Walter Winchell counted fifteen curtain calls from an ecstatic public.

Many critics consider *Awake and Sing* to be Odets's best play. Discovering his unique voice, he scores with all the force of his stage dialogue, his poetry of the streets, and the vigor of Jewish family life. Besides establishing his command of snappy dialogue, Odets disclosed a message of vitalism which would haunt him for the rest of his life when Ralph complains to his mother that he doesn't "want life printed on dollar bills" and she urges him to "change the world if you don't like it."

Odets asserted a powerful life force against the weight of depression and entropy. His politics grew organically from the instinct that he must combat fiercely all the pressures which stifle growth and limit the development of human potential. This was Odets's natural and never-abandoned alignment with progressivism—his alliance with life against death. He hated poverty as only one who has experienced it can. He hated all the elements of elitism and exclusivism that discarded human beings when they were no longer able to produce a profit for owners and bosses. We can hear his voice rising out loud and clear even in the testimony that he gave to the HUAC when he insists, "if I were moved by certain situations of poverty this would be because my mother worked in a stocking factory in Philadelphia at the age of 11 and died a broken and an old woman at the age of 48, and when I wrote, sir, it was out of central, personal things. I did not learn my hatred of poverty, sir, out of communism." Nor did he have to learn his love of the peculiar and the down-and-out; it was bred in him. Odets wrote from what the literary establishment would define as the margins of American experience, but what his popularity and impact on the life of the thirties immediately forced into recognition as a central and dominant chord. Odets struck the true note in his first play, and he would continue to find ways to work changes on that same theme in the best of his later work.

The success of *Waiting for Lefty* inspired Odets to write a companion piece which could also be used for purposes of organizing by amateur groups. He claimed that he finished in four days the anti-Nazi play, *'Til the Day I Die,* that was paired with *Lefty* and ran for 136 performances on Broadway. The play was inspired by a short story, F. C. Weiskopf's *Those Who Are Stronger,* about the Nazi methods of torture and interrogation that lead a man to commit suicide rather than inform on his comrades. This play is not often revived, but might be interesting if produced in a double bill as it was originally intended. Together the two plays show Odets in the year that he was a member of the Communist Party willing to use his art to advance the cause of the party and dedicated to both the worker's struggle inside the labor movement and the international struggle against the rising tide of fascism.

In that same year yet another play of Odets was directed by Harold Clurman; *Paradise Lost* opened on December 9, 1935. Odets had begun the play before *Lefty,* and according to the playwright, it was his favorite play. The last speech of the play is an impassioned and optimistic statement of the future of the human race and it is enunciated by a man who is supposed to represent the American middle class, a man who is waking up. He proclaims, "Everywhere now men are rising from their sleep. Men, men are understanding the bitter black total of their lives." He concludes by insisting, "Oh, yes, I tell you the whole world is for men to possess. Heartbreak and terror are not the heritage of mankind! The world is beautiful. No fruit tree wears a lock and key. Men will sing at their work, men will love." This bears the true Odets stamp and is a prime statement of his Whitmanesque philosophy. Repeatedly, Odets bears witness to what he sees as the ignominy of the cash nexus. Probably that was his clearest and truest insight: he shrank from the reality that men and women had to sell themselves to secure the basic necessities of life. His spirit quailed at the idea, and in some naive fashion he never failed to be outraged by it. The ambition of *Paradise Lost* struck some critics as too grandiose, and there began in the press a kind of avid expectation that the young playwright would burn himself out very quickly.

After enduring some critical attacks especially from Joseph Wood

Krutch, Odets went to Hollywood for the first time. So the greatest single year of progressive drama in the history of the American stage ended with what was intended to be the temporary exile of the radical playwright. In that year Odets had also written two other pieces; one of them, entitled *I Can't Sleep,* for Morris Carnovsky, was a sort of extended monologue by a renegade worker who literally cannot face the music of "The Internationale" and is hiding from the sound of the May Day parade. Odets also finished a short piece called *Remember,* which was used to show the debilitating effect of public charity on the poor. In addition, in this busy year Odets had found time to lead a delegation to Cuba to investigate the treatment of artists and intellectuals by the right-wing government there. He got arrested and sent back to New York as part of an effort to draw public attention to the repressive conditions in Cuba.

One of the most quixotic moments in the same year was when Odets went with John Howard Lawson, another prominent Marxist playwright, to meet the visiting Italian writer Luigi Pirandello. They tried to talk Pirandello out of his support for Mussolini and to dissuade him from promoting Italian fascism and the war against Ethiopia, which was then under way. All of these literary, cultural, and political activities testify to the serious nature of Odets's commitment to the left agenda and his willingness to participate. By 1936 Odets had left the Communist party, but he never broke with his former associates and, as detailed in the HUAC report, he acted in cooperation with many United Front cultural organizations throughout the forties.

In the twenty-eight years before he died, Odets would carry on a love-hate relationship with Hollywood and the movies. He would earn and spend hundreds of thousands of dollars; he would fall in love with, marry, and divorce a glamorous movie star, Louise Rainer, and marry another, Bette Grayson. He would end up with his name on a total of seven films, although he worked on countless others as script doctor and adviser. One thing that all commentators seem to agree on is that Odets loved money; he loved the things that money could buy and he loved the freedom from anxiety that money guaranteed. What Odets hated about Hollywood was that it tempted him away from starting and staying with any serious work; and somehow, it made him feel like a trivial person. One of the myths of Odets's life is that he suffered a terrible writer's block when he was in Hollywood. The number and variety of the scripts he authored and improved does not uphold that myth. He wrote there, but he didn't write what he could respect.

In 1937 and 1938 two more outstanding plays came from his hand, *Golden Boy* and *Rocket to the Moon.* After those he never wrote anything that pleased him much, even though works like *The Country Girl* and

The Big Knife received respectful attention. In 1939 in the preface to *Six Plays,* he reminds us that "at the ripe age of thirty-three" he is writing what he thinks is only the first of many such prefaces to future collections. He apologizes a little for the immaturity of the work: "Let them stand, crudities and all, as a small parade of a young talent discovering and shaping itself." With the sad wisdom of hindsight, we read these words and know that this first great collection was his best and would not be surpassed by him. The failure to find that spark in himself again after 1940 surprised Odets and troubled him greatly. The recently published journal of 1940 gives us a day-to-day account of the way he spent his time, and we read there repeated avowals of his ambition and his fear of never realizing his potential.

The years that Odets spent in Hollywood were punctuated by sudden returns to New York to reclaim his soul by writing for the theater. The lure of salary, now in six figures annually, and the necessity to support his second wife and two children, Nora and Walt Whitman, would immediately lure him back to the studios. Working as a "troubleshooter," he would anonymously but lucratively patch and repair damaged screenplays. Some of his own scripts like those for *Sister Carrie* and a life of Gershwin never got made; others like *None but the Lonely Heart* (1944), *Deadline at Dawn* (1946), and *Humoresque* (1947) did. He unleashed invective at every opportunity against his environment, his employers, his work, and himself. In the *New York Times* of July 25, 1948, he complains, "I took my filthy salary every week and rolled an inner eye around an inner landscape." Odets was always enacting a complex interior drama of damnation and salvation. His unhappiness was palpable; the desire to complete something significant and genuine soured the daily writing of competent but empty movies. In *The Big Knife* (1948) one character reminds another that "half-idealism is peritonitis of the soul—America is full of it!" Odets experienced his own soul disease most vividly when he was in Hollywood which he equated with sin. The greatest sin to him was always the sin against his own talent.

In later years Odets would learn that his decision in 1952 to cooperate with the House Un-American Activities Committee and to name names was seen by some as his greatest sin. He was a cooperative witness, but the nature of his cooperation was very spotty. Again and again, he insisted on making his points to members of the committee about the abilities and good qualities of the Communists with whom he associated. At one point his exasperated questioner asks him, "Are all smart, quick people Communist Party members?" Odets also defends the constitutional right of the Communist Party to exist and suggests that if the committee wants to persecute people for being Communist they should first get a law passed making party membership illegal. However, he disappointed many friends and never recovered his political integrity.

Odets proved that it is possible to be a great radical American playwright—but not for long. Certainly, he participated in the sad charade of inquisitions that blots those years; Odets shared the tragedy of betrayal that all leftists felt when the hard-won battles of the thirties were replaced by the paranoia and corruption of the fifties. Odets's career must stand as both an inspiration and a cautionary tale. Whenever a playwright's words sing across the footlights and dissolve the distance between audience and actors, that writer owes a debt to Clifford Odets. In England playwrights like Arnold Wesker, David Storey and John Arden learned from him. The current eruption of *Angels in America* by Tony Kushner takes its inspiration from Odets's savage criticism of American power grabbing. With his primitive vitalism and his hatred of the profit motive, Odets could never be completely at home in the capitalist system. He imagined something larger for mankind—a life not printed on dollar bills.

Suggested Readings

Margaret Benman-Gibson, *Clifford Odets, American Playwright*. New York: Atheneum, 1982.

Harold Clurman, *The Fervent Years*. New York: Knopf, 1945.

Gabriel Miller, ed., *Critical Essays on Clifford Odets*. Boston: G. K. Hall and Co., 1991.

Clifford Odets, *The Time Is Ripe: The 1940 Journal of Clifford Odets*. New York: Grove Press, 1988.

Gerald Weales, *Odets the Playwright*. London: Methuen, 1985.

32

WOODY GUTHRIE

Craig A. Lockard

Woody Guthrie, the prototype of the politically engaged protest folk-singer, characteristically stated his self-defined mission in blunt terms: "Let me be known as the man who told you something you already know." Guthrie today is chiefly remembered through his songs, some of which have become national classics. Even schoolchildren learn his "This Land Is Your Land," "So Long, It's Been Good to Know You," "Roll On Columbia," "This Train Is Bound for Glory," and "Hard Traveling." Woody would undoubtedly be pleased that children still enjoy his compositions, although he would likely be distressed that the populist political sentiments that prompted them have for the most part been forgotten. Indeed, his songs document a wide variety of concerns: union organizing ("The Union Maid"), history ("1913 Massacre"), children ("Why Oh Why"), outlaws ("Pretty Boy Floyd"), society's underclass ("Tom Joad"), place ("Oklahoma Hills"), vagabonds ("Weary Hobo"), workingpeople ("Jackhammer John"), and socioeconomic inequalities ("The Philadelphia Lawyer"), among other topics. Most of his songs offer what Peter Welding described as "starkly powerful human documents that detail the plight of the oppressed, dispossessed, poverty and starvation-ridden, homeless, jobless, nameless, victimized and otherwise disenfranchised" common American.

His son, noted folksinger Arlo Guthrie, asserts that Woody "felt that he was born to write songs about all of his experiences and involvements with people and projects." Woody believed that a song could deal with any topic and hence his inspiration came from myriad sources: political developments, current news, the sights and songs around him in his endless travels "from the redwood forests to the Gulf Stream waters," topics from books and movies (such as Steinbeck's *Grapes of Wrath*). He never composed for the hit parade and disparaged Tin Pan Alley, contending that "it has been my hard luck many times to choose between what I thought was the truth, and a good paycheck, and that's why I go around so truthfully broke, I reckon." Guthrie songs reveal his strong innate sense of injustice; they speak simply and eloquently, often with a pungent, earthly sense of humor. He was a master of the narrative song, especially the talking blues idiom, and richly utilized old folk melodies. Woody wrote well over a thousand songs between 1936 and 1954, mostly about America and its peoples. As his friend Cisco Houston claimed, "when you hear them, you really hear America singing."

Guthrie chronicled the troubled 1930s and 1940s in his music. Over this period he rambled through nearly every state in the union, working and singing with union members, factory workers, millhands, farmers, loggers, coal miners, migrant workers, longshoremen, and cowboys, among others. Millard Lampell believes that "he was a rebel and a radical. He was for the outsider and the outcast, the working stiff and the one-mule farmer." Guthrie worked closely with black singers like Leadbelly. He strongly opposed bigotry based on race, ethnicity, or religion, and one of his most moving songs ("Deportee") condemns the exploitation of migrant Mexican workers. Reportedly he told the nurse issuing Arlo's birth certificate to identify their religion as either "all" or "none." Although not an intellectual in any conventional sense, the self-educated Guthrie was a voracious reader who closely followed news developments and wrote constantly in his ever-present notebooks. He was a man of many flaws, irresponsible and ornery, often drunk, who deserted his family many times for the lure of the road. His protégé Pete Seeger conceded that Woody "didn't always pay his bills, and he made life hard for his family and friends sometimes—always traveling, itching heels, ants in his pants—but Lord, Lord, he turned out song after song after song." Jerome Rodnitzky contends that Guthrie was an eminently complicated man, whose life was filled with contradictions. Hence, labeling him as a socialist, communist, radical, or even a folksinger is limiting and misses his universal appeal.

Woodrow Wilson Guthrie was born in 1912 in the farming and oil town of Okemah, Oklahoma. His father was a sometime real estate speculator, indeed a risk capitalist who embodied the spirit of the oil boom; he also played banjo and guitar. Hence Woody grew up with folk songs but also listened to country music, with the Carter Family a particular influence. But Woody's family history would be tragic. His sister died accidentally in a fire, his father failed in business and ultimately ended up a broken-spirited wreck, and his mother was committed to a mental institution. Woody's childhood family fortunes deteriorated rapidly from affluence to poverty, undoubtedly influencing his worldview. Left a virtual orphan by his teen years, he never finished high school and began traveling from his sometime base at an uncle's house in Pampa, Texas, seldom managing to hold a steady job. The area was badly hit by horrific dust storms, which inspired some of his most moving songs and determined struggles: "This old dust storm killed my baby but it can't kill me, Lord."

After his marriage to Mary Esta Jennings, he headed for California in 1935, working as a painter by day and a singer/songwriter by night, playing guitar and harmonica. He began chronicling the trials and tribulations of "Okies" and others in their migration westward to escape the ravages of the Dust Bowl and depression, including the harassment and filthy migrant camps they often faced in California. "Don't swap your old cow for a car," he cautioned would-be refugees, for the promised paradise in California masked a cruel reality "if you ain't got that do-re-mi." Woody consciously tailored his music to his perceptions of the world around him, viewing himself as a musical newspaper; he contended that he made up songs telling "what he thought was wrong and how to make it right, songs that said what everybody in the country was thinking."

Settling in Los Angeles he performed for a country music radio show but soon became obsessed with radical politics, singing for migrant workers and union gatherings. More and more he defined himself as a committed union militant and radical worker's minstrel, even producing a folksy column "Woody Sez" for the leftist West Coast paper *People's World* between 1939 and 1940. For a brief period in U.S. history, the Communist party was fashionable and relevant. When he moved to New York he contributed material to the *Daily Worker,* but never joined the party and avoided ideological debates, asserting "leftwing, rightwing, chicken wing—it's all the same to me." He also recorded extensively for Alan Lomax at the Library of Congress and was featured on radio shows in Los Angeles and New York. In 1940 Woody was commissioned to write songs for the Bonneville Power Administration, producing some of his most memorable work including "This Land," "The Grand Coulee Dam," and "Pastures of Plenty." Even here he addressed political themes: "Every

state in the union us migrants have been / We work in your fight, and
we'll fight till we win."

In 1941 he returned to New York, where he joined Seeger, Lee Hays,
and Millard Lampell in the Almanac Singers. They toured the country,
singing politically oriented music about union rights and promoting entrance into World War II (including Woody's famous song "The Sinking
of the Reuben James"). The Almanacs lived as a commune in Greenwich
Village. During these years he married his second wife, Marjorie
Greenblatt, and published his autobiography, *Bound for Glory,* a fascinating, turbulent, passionate, and characteristically unpolished document of
social history. Much later some of his other work would be published in
book form, including a collection of prose and poetry, *Born to Win* (1965),
and some essays and letters, *Pastures of Plenty* (1990). In 1943 Woody
joined the merchant marine, taking his music to Europe and North Africa
and surviving several torpedo attacks. After the war he started recording
for the new Folkways label, including an album of songs on the notorious
Sacco and Vanzetti case of 1927; indeed his recordings carried the company in the early years.

Woody came along just as the folk tradition was undergoing change.
The communication revolution (including radio and records) facilitated
wider distribution as well as introducing new styles and rhythms. The
proletarian and agrarian roots from which folk music sprang encouraged
a collective creative process that articulated the aspirations of ordinary
people. John Steinbeck believed that "the songs of the working people
have always been their sharpest statement, and the one statement that
cannot be destroyed . . . you cannot prevent singing." Earlier labor troubadours, most famously Joe Hill before World War I, had already established
a link between music and militancy. Spurred by the Great Depression,
during the 1930s folk music came to be used for partisan political purposes,
on union picket lines, or at rallies for the Loyalist cause in the Spanish
Civil War, all the while promoting underdog causes. Often words to
popular ballads were changed and politicized. Art became a weapon; as
Bertolt Brecht argued, "art is not a mirror that reflects society but a
hammer that forges it." Ultimately close association with the left both
helped and damaged the urban folk movement, liberating folk songs
from their insular origins but also isolating folksingers from the political
mainstream as they essentially "preached to the converted" militants. As
R. Serge Denisoff noted, folk music became a tool of class struggle, a
step toward transforming society while also linking the intellectual left
to a segment of the working-class population.

Guthrie soon entered this hothouse; indeed, Robbie Lieberman believes
he was the major influence on those linking radical politics with folk

music, with his recordings of Dust Bowl ballads played continually in left-wing schools and summer camps. Woody once described himself as "a folklore collector and a professional observer. I gather in, I sort, I weigh, the things that folks do, say, think, and sing. I go see, I drive and take a look. I'm a roller poet, and a mobile folklorist." He had seen firsthand the sufferings of ordinary people; his songs built on a strong sense of social justice and a somewhat naive populist patriotism. His guitar bore the inscription "this guitar kills fascists." Guthrie and Seeger together coined the phrase "hootenanny," named after the monthly fund-raising parties of left-wing clubs in Seattle. They began holding weekly "hoots" in Almanac House as a democratic art forum lubricated by music. New York attracted many radicalized folksingers and activists escaping harassment such as Aunt Molly Jackson and Leadbelly.

Although the Almanacs disbanded, they laid the basis for the development in the later 1940s of People's Songs as well as for participation by left-wing folksingers in Henry Wallace's progressive 1948 presidential campaign; Guthrie was deeply involved with both although some leftists considered him essentially an opportunist. People's Songs promoted militant unionism, civil rights, and U.S.-Soviet friendship through topical songs but crumbled in 1949 under congressional investigation and the opposition of unions appalled at cooperation with the Communist party. Leftist activity was increasingly circumscribed and even dangerous in the anticommunist hysteria of the late 1940s and early 1950s; union militancy had died and the prospective audience for politicized artists like Guthrie was severely reduced. Woody's creative energies and dedication began dissipating in 1949. Increasingly bohemian in his lifestyle, he divided his time between his base in Brooklyn and the road. Soon Woody fell victim to the inherited Huntington's disease that killed his mother and permanently entered the hospital in 1952. His depression about the "red-baiting" right-wing backlash may have lowered his resistance to, and hastened the progress of, this ultimately fatal, brain-destroying disease, from which he eventually died in 1967.

Perhaps a major reason so many Guthrie songs have endured is the innate optimism of his vision as he told about the social, political, and economic unrest of the times from his firsthand experience. His songs convey a positive attitude, as he wrote: "I hate a song that makes you think that you're not any good . . . just born to lose. Bound to lose. No good to nobody. . . . I am out to fight those kinds of songs to my very last breath of air and my last drop of blood. I am out to sing songs that will prove to you that this is your world . . . that make you take pride in yourself and your work." This was an optimistic, can-do spirit that was deeply American; people, his songs contended, can control their destiny through struggle and cooperation. Woody believed in positive action and militancy as the only possibility for change and was well aware of the power of songs: "I've sung them on picket lines, in union halls, in foc's'les, in river-bottom peach camps—everywhere—and I've never seen them fail. Folks sweat under the collar, throw their coats in the corner, stamp their feet, clap, and sing these songs. Our songs, our singing history."

Guthrie's influence would long outlive his career, with the resurgence of what became known as "Woody's Children." The Weavers, comprised of longtime friends and followers, put several of his songs on the hit parade in the early and mid-1950s. The link between activist progressive politics and folk music had a renaissance in the tumultuous 1960s, when a new group of folksingers would loudly proclaim their devotion to Woody's legacy. Many young folksingers, among them Bob Dylan, came to visit him in his final years as he became a source of inspiration and legend. Some of his protégés, including Dylan and Phil Ochs, recorded song tributes to their role model; others like Joan Baez, Judy Collins, and Peter, Paul, and Mary performed his songs or, like Dylan and Tom Paxton, created a Guthriesque style. In the 1970s and 1980s folk-protest singers and labor troubadours like Utah Phillips, Si Kahn, and Larry Long would maintain the Guthrie tradition; Long even began doing concerts and workshops on Guthrie in Okemah, whose business elite had long considered him a communist agitator. In the mid-1970s there was a warts-and-all movie about his life, *Bound for Glory,* with David Carradine playing Woody. Joe Klein's generally sympathetic biography appeared in 1980; it apparently helped politicize Bruce Springsteen's music. Woody became a fountainhead and wellspring, fathering a whole school of topical songwriters whose work addresses the inequities in society. Hence Judy Collins wrote that he "was an inspiration to all of us who knew his music and the very deep struggle that he went through in his life to remain always aware of his fellow human beings." And, Ochs asserted, the legacy of Woody "is the same as all the great poets of history: that of truth or the search for truth."

The Guthrie legend became as dramatic and significant as his actual life, considering that he was never famous during his career. Clearly he had a universal outlook; his songs offered a universal message in a universal language: "I tell you about everything in the world and on the world and above the world and about the world, as well as around the world and in the world and near the world." But his politics were highly partisan. Undoubtedly his radicalism has been amplified in the legend; he was somewhat naive politically and never the full-time revolutionary portrayed by many leftist admirers. Nonetheless, however much mythologized, his concerns and activities foreshadowed the social battleground of the 1960s and '70s. Ultimately, as this true people's poet and guerilla minstrel believed, "all you can write is what you see." Whatever the excesses of the myth, his greatest legacy is the magnificent body of songs he left to the world.

Suggested Readings

R. Serge Denisoff, *Great Day Coming: Folk Music and the American Left*. Urbana: University of Illinois Press, 1971.

John Greenway, *American Folksongs of Protest*. Philadelphia: University of Pennsylvania Press, 1953.

Wayne Hampton, *Guerrilla Minstrels: John Lennon, Joe Hill, Woody Guthrie, Bob Dylan*. Knoxville: University of Tennessee Press, 1986.

Joe Klein, *Woody Guthrie: A Life*. New York: Ballantine, 1980.

Robbie Lieberman, *"My Song Is My Weapon": People's Songs, American Communism, and the Politics of Culture, 1930–1950*. Urbana: University of Illinois Press, 1989.

Jerome Rodnitzky, *Minstrels of the Dawn: The Folk-Protest Singer as a Cultural Hero*. Chicago: Nelson-Hall, 1976.

33

RUTH FULTON BENEDICT

Mari Jo Buhle

The first anthropolgist to make the best-seller list, Ruth Fulton Benedict introduced hundreds of thousands of Americans to a sympathetic and comparative study of different cultures. Today, she might be regarded as a major forerunner of multiculturalism. In her own time, she was a militant antifascist and antiracist, denounced by conservatives and by Cold War liberals for communistic, anti-American leanings.

In an era when the labor movement and the Communist party won the sympathy if not actual participation of most American radicals, Ruth Benedict avoided outright organizational entanglements. She devoted herself to scholarly and academic life, teaching and managing the anthroplogy department of Columbia University, and reserving her sabbaticals for fieldwork. Her influence spread far beyond the classroom, as she made her case for "enlightened change," with Americans educated to appreciate the immense diversity of cultures in the range of human societies.

Benedict's role as a "public intellectual" can be appreciated today, perhaps, better than ever before. Well positioned to help overturn the evolutionary paradigm that assigned Western civilization supremacy of a global cultural hierarchy, she forcefully made her argument in popular books, essays, and lectures. She fleshed it out by providing information and analysis of unfamiliar settings, boldly suggesting that Americans reconsider their own practices and prejudices.

Ruth Benedict's biographers have commonly concluded that their subject's empathy for "difference" stemmed from lessons learned during her own childhood. Born in New York City in 1887 to Bertrice Shattuck Fulton, a Vassar graduate, and Frederick Fulton, a promising homeopathic physician who died less than two years after his daughter's birth, Ruth Fulton grew up in a family atypical for Anglo-Saxon Protestants. Her mother supported the small household of Ruth and her sister Margery in genteel poverty, first resuming a career in teaching and then in 1898 taking an administrative job in the Buffalo Public Library. Benedict remembered this period of her early adolescence as especially traumatic. She lost her childhood friends in moving to Buffalo, fell into a deep depression, and felt yet more distant from an emotionally reclusive mother. Part of this estrangement stemmed from Bertrice Fulton's inability to address openly the consequences of her daughter's impaired hearing, treating the young girl as obstinate rather than outside the orbit of the family's conversation.

Ruth Fulton rediscovered friendship and developed a taste for intellectual pursuits after she entered Vassar College on a scholarship in 1905. Following her graduation in 1909, she traveled to Europe and then worked for a spell as a teacher in Pasadena, California. Eager to leave behind a job she did not like, Ruth Fulton married Stanley Rossiter Benedict, a biochemist, in 1914. She relished foremost the leisure ensured by her husband's financial support and eagerly devoted herself, not to housekeeping, but to intellectual pursuits.

Benedict's earliest endeavors reveal her desire to apply her talents at research and writing to educate the public and to bring readers into the feminist camp. While the movement for woman suffrage rushed toward its peak in effective mass mobilization, Benedict planned a series of biographies of notable women intellectuals. She completed a manuscript on the early British feminist Mary Wollstonecraft, describing her as a woman who "made no apologies for her brain." Studies of Margaret Fuller and Olive Schreiner remained undone, the very idea extinguished when Houghton Mifflin declined to publish her first submission. The ratification of the suffrage amendment and the bitter disillusionments of World War I also quelled the young writer's optimistic ardor for feminism per se. Benedict entered the 1920s determined to carry out the difficult tasks required to create "the new democracy of peace that is to come."

A pair of prominent radical scholars and social critics encouraged Benedict to develop her scholarly talents. In 1919 she began to take courses at the New School for Social Research, mainly, as she put it, "to have something really to do." There she met anthropologists Alexander Goldenweiser—who studied with equal interest Marxism and the rising discipline of psychology—and Elsie Clews Parsons, one of the first women to practice professionally as an anthropologist. The two teachers agreed that their precocious student should pursue graduate work at Columbia University where their own mentor, Franz Boas, directed the Department of Anthropology.

Under Boas's tutelage, Benedict grew into the role this mentor conscientiously carved out for his students, "world improver." Nurturing perhaps the most productive generation of American anthropologists ever, Boas, along with his students, transformed the discipline. They undermined biological explanations for differences among groups of people, and they successfully substituted an antiracist, cultural perspective. Equally important, the evolutionary racialism which had prevailed since the ascendancy of Darwin and Spencer fell away as Boas and his colleagues made the comparative study of cultures a major vehicle for promoting the principles of relativism. As modernists, these anthropologists not only accepted but celebrated diversity as a source of human creativity. By examining the world's multitudinous cultures, Boas believed, Americans might gain an understanding of the weaknesses in their own patterns and practices and then act concertedly to change them. He once wrote that his "whole outlook upon social life is determined by the question: how can we recognize the shackles that tradition had laid upon us? For when we recognize them, we are also able to break them."

Benedict readily embraced these relativistic notions and refashioned them into a clarion call for toleration. "Modern civilization, from this point of view," she explained, "becomes not a necessary pinnacle of human achievement but an entry in a long series of possible adjustments." In her major, best-selling work, *Patterns of Culture* (1934), she compared three sharply contrasting cultures—Pueblos of New Mexico, Dobuans of Melanesia, and Kwakiutl of the U.S. Northwest—in both sociological and psychological terms. Each society presented a distinctive "configuration" of cultural traits and values, grounded not in human biology but in its unique history and environment. "Culture," she insisted, "is not a biologically transmitted complex." In noticeably different ways and for different purposes, the Pueblos, Dobuans, and Kwakiutl each made use of "a certain segment" of what Benedict termed "the great arc" of possible human behavior.

"These portraits of a near-socialistic, a jealously possessive, and highly competitive society," respectively, one recent biographer has noted, "told a powerful lesson to a 1930s America facing the Great Depression." Like many of her contemporaries, Benedict watched with dread the rise of

European fascist movements and feared similar tendencies in her own country. Like Margaret Mead, a former student and intimate friend, Benedict applied to her own society the lessons drawn from ethnographic fieldwork, searching out the processes by which American culture failed to accommodate "extremes" of personalities or groups labeled "deviant." Armed with such knowledge, she believed, Americans could change their existing social arrangements to provide greater room for nonconformity, thus producing fewer individuals who succumbed to "neurosis" or suffered persecution.

Benedict, Mead, and their contemporaries expressed particular concern about aspects of American society that they deemed "repressive." As early as the 1920s, anthropologists discovered in the Pacific islands peoples who suffered few of the sexual dysfunctions and prejudices routinely noted among Americans in the early twentieth century. Mead's research among the adolescents of Samoa and children of New Guinea indicated, for instance, an easier and less jarring transition to adult sexual norms than in heavily inhibited contemporary American society.

Both Benedict and Mead questioned the American medical practice of defining homosexuality at worst as a pathology, at best as aberrant. In the early 1930s, Benedict raised the examples of ancient Greece where homosexuality was viewed as a "major means to the good life," and of the institution of berdache, common among Dakota tribal societies, wherein some men honorably occupied roles usually filled by women. Although Benedict took pains to obscure her own sexual orientation—after her marriage dissolved during the 1920s, she lived the remainder of her life in the company of women—she nevertheless insisted that the singular issue was self-esteem.

By the mid-1930s, questions of race and racial prejudice predominated. The rise of Nazism in Germany provoked Benedict to lend her prestige to the list of signatures of various open letters and ad hoc committees, and she collaborated with her mentor and colleague Franz Boas to protest fascism in Europe and to preserve civil liberties in the United States. In 1936 she joined the Progressive Education Association's Commission on Intercultural Education, which aimed to counter racism and anti-Semitism by promoting the virtues of cultural diversity. The next year, as the Spanish Civil War deepened, Benedict signed the Open Letter on Culture and Democracy in Spain and also supported the Columbia University Faculty Committee for Aid to the Spanish People.

These activities prepared Benedict to join the University Federation for Democracy and Intellectual Freedom, which formed in December 1937 and became in 1939 the American Committee for Democracy and Intellectual Freedom. "Now more than ever," she wrote, "in view of the fascist threat to world peace and culture, it is imperative that we join in defense of democracy." She also served on the executive committees of the National Council for Pan-American Democracy and the Council Against Intolerance in America. Benedict likewise joined the Descendants of the American Revolution, a left-leaning organization founded in opposition to the ultra-conservative Daughters of the American Revolution (DAR) and its Anglo-Saxon pretensions.

All these political involvements flowed from Benedict's antipathy toward intolerance, an issue that became yet more compelling with the approach of World War II. At Boas's behest, she spent her sabbatical year in 1939–40 writing a book on the subject specifically for general readers. Although Benedict herself had not directly researched race questions, she used existing scholarship to craft an argument disputing the existence of "pure" races and the entire idea of racial traits. The second half of *Race: Science and Politics* (1940) took up questions of racism, which she called simply "a pretentious way of saying that 'I belong to the Best People. . . . I belong to the Elect.' "

With the publication of *Race,* Benedict decided to make her research more readily accessible to the public and policymakers alike. Working with Mildred Ellis, a secondary-school teacher, she transposed the basic arguments in *Race* into a curriculum entitled *Race and Cultural Relations: America's Answer to the Myth of a Master Race* that focused on prejudices against African Americans, Jews, and Asian Americans. In 1943 Benedict joined other Columbia professors to produce *The Races of Mankind,* a ten-cent Public Affairs Pamphlet that compared the world emerging from war to "one neighborhood" comprising "peoples of all races of the earth." Stressing cultural over biological determinants, the authors emphasized above all the imperative to appreciate "differences" and to resist interpreting them as "inferiorities."

Designed for use by the army in training recruits, *Races of Mankind* created a furor. Andrew J. May, who chaired the House Military Affairs Committee, vehemently rejected its observation that whites from Kentucky, his home state, had routinely scored lower on intelligence tests than Northern blacks. Although May managed to prohibit distribution of the pamphlet in the army, *Races of Mankind* sold nearly one million copies over the next decade, was translated into German, French, and Japanese for overseas distribution, was refashioned into a comic book entitled "There Are No Master Races," and was even made into an animated film sponsored by the United Auto Workers of America.

During World War II, Benedict devoted her scholarly energies to studying the cultural and political accommodations necessary for peace and she placed great hope in plans for the United Nations. With funds from the

Office of Naval Research and the participation of Columbia University's Research in Contemporary Culture, Benedict and other scholars studied cultural patterns in China, Thailand, Czechoslovakia, France, Poland, Russia, and Germany, among other countries. She hoped that anthropologists could supply enough information on different cultures to create the basic conditions for international cooperation.

Benedict feared correctly, however, that Americans would refuse even to contemplate seriously an expansive notion of democracy that respected and preserved cultural differences rather than promoted assimilation. In "Recognition of Cultural Diversities in the Postwar World," published in 1943, Benedict described democratic practices in other parts of the world that resembled scarcely at all the system of government in the United States. The prospect for world peace nevertheless rested, she believed, on the ability of great powers to respect such variations.

Benedict took for the topic of her second major book an extraordinarily sensitive matter for most wartime Americans: Japanese culture. Following the bombing of Pearl Harbor and the subsequent internment of Japanese Americans living on the West Coast, racism against "Orientals" flourished. A steady flow of wartime propaganda—government publications, Hollywood movies, cartoons—against the enemy "Japs" revived the "yellow peril" imagery from the late nineteenth century and added a host of new racist twists. Within a month of Japan's surrender in 1945, Benedict began work on *The Chrysanthemum and the Sword: Patterns in Japanese Culture* to push back the tide of ethnocentrism and to provide policymakers within the U.S. government a more dispassionate view of their former enemies. She aimed, simply, to allow Americas to see the Japanese as "human." Benedict did not play down differences between Japanese and American cultures. To the contrary, she constructed her analysis as a complex series of comparisons, emphasizing the disparities between the two peoples while simultaneously affirming the moral legitimacy of each. She warned that U.S. Occupational Government in Japan could not impose democracy "by fiat."

Ruth Benedict died following a heart attack in 1948, just two years after the publication of *The Chrysanthemum and the Sword*. Smeared as a communist fellow traveler for her antifascist involvements, Benedict abjured all ideologies as enforcers of conformity. She acted foremost to advocate acceptance of difference, marking the way toward a multicultural curriculum decades after her death.

Although Benedict achieved a wide popular audience for her writings, her critics treated her relativistic ideas with skepticism, an attitude sharpened by Cold War assertions of American cultural superiority in the decade after her death. *The Chrysanthemum and the Sword* (which, like

Patterns of Culture, had become a best-seller) prompted the retort that Benedict had not conducted field research in Japan. World War II had of course prevented all travel to Axis nations, but following Japan's surrender, Benedict still could not get to Japan. "All my male friends went," she wrote, "but the American army and the American government insisted that the Japanese would all rape me." Her radical efforts to build toleration were stymied, as so often, by the assumptions and attitudes that she worked her entire life to quash.

Suggested Readings

Margaret M. Caffrey, *Ruth Benedict: Stranger in This Land.* Austin: University of Texas Press, 1989.

Margaret Mead, *An Anthropologist at Work: Writings of Ruth Benedict.* Boston: Houghton Mifflin, 1959.

Judith Modell, *Ruth Benedict: Patterns of a Life.* Philadelphia: University of Pennsylvania Press, 1983.

34

CARLOS BULOSAN

E. San Juan, Jr.

At the peak of McCarthyism in the fifties, Carlos Bulosan was a black-listed writer (perhaps the only Filipino writer on the FBI hit list) scheduled for deportation as a dangerous subversive, together with Chris Mensalvas and Ernesto Mangaong, leaders of the International Longshoreman's and Warehouseman's Union (ILWU), Local 37, based in Seattle, Washington. But how could the government deport this writer commissioned by President Franklin Roosevelt to write an essay celebrating his "four freedoms," a manifesto exhibited at the Federal Building in San Francisco in 1943?

By that time, Bulosan, the author of best-sellers like *The Laughter of My Father* (1944, translated in over a dozen languages) and *America Is in the Heart* (1946), was cited in *Who's Who in America, Current Biography,* and other directories of international celebrities. His praise of populist democracy, "Freedom from Want" (*Saturday Evening Post,* March 6, 1943), fulfilled the strategic aim of artists capturing terrain in the dominant ideological mode of production. It succeeded in infiltrating a singular message that escaped the censors: "But we are not really free unless we use what we produce. So long as the fruit of our labor is denied us, so long will want manifest itself in a world of slaves."

Obscure and penniless, Bulosan died on September 11, 1956, at the height of the Cold War. He was a victim less of neurosis and despair (as critic Dolores Feria alleged) than of cumulative suffering from years of privations and persecutions since his arrival in the United States in 1931. By that time, over 100,000 Filipino workers had been recruited from the hinterland of the United States' only Asian colony, the Philippines, to work in the plantations of Hawaii, the Alaskan canneries, and the farmlands of the West Coast. The depression inflicted on Filipinos severe unemployment, intense labor exploitation, and racist vigilante violence. In 1928 and 1930, Filipinos were attacked by racist vigilantes in Yakima Valley, Washington; Watsonville, California, and other towns. On top of this, in 1935, when emigration from the Philippine Commonwealth was limited to fifty persons, Filipinos were threatened with deportation. Since the 1898 annexation of the islands up to 1946, Filipinos in the United States (called "Pinoys") inhabited a limbo of indeterminacy: neither citizens, aliens, nor wards, they were "nationals" without a sovereign country. On the eve of Pearl Harbor, Bulosan summed up his years of experience as labor organizer and nomadic exile: "Yes, I feel like a criminal running away from a crime I did not commit. And the crime is that I am a Filipino in America." Although it gestures toward a popular-front politics against global fascism, his ethnobiography written in the middle of the war, *America Is in the Heart,* is a testimony to those years of struggle and resistance to imperial racism and violence. It is essentially a critique of the paradigm of ethnic/immigrant success celebrated by mainstream apologists of assimilation into late capitalist polity.

In his *America,* Bulosan returns to what Amilcar Cabral calls "the source" to recover a submerged tradition of indigenous revolutionary culture rooted in over three hundred years of anticolonial insurgency against Spain and the United States. He recalls the 1931 peasant uprising against semifeudal landlords and compradors, native agents of the U.S. colonial state, and before that the 1896–98 insurrection against Spain. One leader of the 1931 Tayug revolt, Pedro Calosa, was in fact a veteran of the 1924 strike of Filipino workers in the Hawaiian plantations.

It seems a fortuitous coincidence that Calosa lived in the same province of Pangasinan where Bulosan was born on November 2, 1911. Bulosan's adolescent years were shaped by the survival craft of a large poor peasant family barely subsisting on a small plot of land. In his letters collected in *The Sound of Falling Light* (1960) as well as in *The Laughter of My Father,* Bulosan describes the earthly, sometimes cunning but always carnivalesque spirit of his father trying to outwit landlords, merchant-usurers, and petty bureaucrats in providing for his extended family. But most of all, Bulosan celebrates the exuberant resourcefulness of his mother—that "dynamic little peasant woman" who sold salted fish in the public market of Binalonan and nurtured Bulosan's open, adventurous spirit. Her image is sublimated in the samaritanic woman characters in *America Is in the Heart* and by transference refigured in the loyal and brave companions of Bulosan who may be read to represent the "other" eclipsed visage of a racist, alienating America.

Bulosan depicted the resistance culture of the plebeians among whom he grew up in *The Laughter of My Father*. In response to the philistine dismissal of these folkloric vignettes and fables as a commercialization of exotic humor and mere local color, Bulosan himself emphasized the allegorical thrust of his imagination:

> My politico-economic ideas are embodied in all my writings. . . .
> *The Laughter* is not humor; it is satire; it is indictment against an economic system that stifled the growth of the primitive, making him decadent overnight without passing through the various stages of growth and decay. The hidden bitterness in this book is so pronounced in another series of short stories, that the publishers refrained from publishing it for the time being.

These latter stories, attacking the predatory excesses of elite property owners and the horror of primitive accumulation in a Third-World peripheral formation, are now available in *The Philippines Is in the Heart* (1978).

The native's return thus began with his departure for the United States. Bulosan's apprenticeship as an organic intellectual of the masses (in Gramsci's sense) started with the trials of his family to overcome colonial and feudal tyranny. After Bulosan followed his two brothers, Aurelio and Dionisio, to California in order to escape the hopeless poverty of his village perpetuated by U.S. reinforcement of iniquitous property relations, his life on the West Coast, where he worked in restaurants and performed odd jobs in the early thirties, exposed him to the vicissitudes of itinerant workers and initial union organizing. His friendship with Chris Mensalvas of the United Cannery, Agricultural, Packing and Allied Workers of America (UCAPAWA) led to his stint as editor of *The New Tide* in 1934; this bimonthly workers' magazine brought him into contact with progressive writers like Richard Wright, William Carlos Williams, William Saroyan, and Sanora Babb (she and her sister Dorothy, as well as Josephine Patrick, should be credited for sustaining Bulosan in body and soul for two decades). Later, Harriet Monroe, editor of *Poetry*, "discovered" Bulosan and inaugurated his inchoate reputation as an "American" writer.

But unlike his compatriot Jose Garcia Villa, Bulosan was never really accepted by the U.S. literati. Despite a short-lived fame, he was suspect, a fringe or marginal author from the "boondocks" (from the Tagalog term for mountain, "bundok"). His radicalization began with an act of "popular memory" triggered by the circumstances of colonial uprooting and subsequent oppression in the metropolis. U.S. literary historians now take account of Asians like Maxine Hong Kingston and Bharati Mukherjee, but not Villa or Bulosan.

From 1936 to 1938, Bulosan was confined at the Los Angeles General Hospital for tuberculosis and kidney problems. It was his reading of Pablo Neruda, Dreiser, Farrell, Nazim Nikmet, Steinbeck, Gorky, Marx, Whitman, Agnes Smedley, Lillian Hellman, Nicolas Guillen, Edgar Snow, among others, and periodicals like *New Masses, New Republic,* and *Nation,* that (Bulosan confessed) "opened all my world of intellectual possibilities—and a grand dream of bettering society for the working man." Even while in the hospital, he began writing the stories satirizing feudal despotism and patriarchal authority collected in *The Laughter of My Father* and the poems that make up the volumes *Chorus for America* (1942), *Letter from America* (1942), and *The Voice of Bataan* (1943), most of which were broadcast overseas by the Office of War Information. Before the crisis of global capitalism ended, Bulosan had already plotted out his project of remapping the U.S. cultural landscape: "I want to interpret the soul of the Filipinos in this country. What really compelled me to write was to try to understand this country, to find a place in it not only for myself but my people." "Self" here equals the collective agency of all colonized subjects. Such a place in the U.S. cultural canon and public consciousness has yet to be claimed and staked out by people of color following in his wake.

Yet Bulosan should not be categorized simply as another "ethnic" author in a putative multicultural shopping mall. The proletarianization of his sensibility surpassed the imperatives of nativism, the nostalgic return to a mythical past, or the chauvinist pride of postmodern borderland critics. While Bulosan continued his role as "tribune" of multiethnic workers (including Euro-Americans) in writing for newspapers like *New Masses, Commonwealth Times* (founded by Mensalvas and Bulosan in 1936), the *Saturday Review of Literature,* and others, his conscientization shifted to a global horizon with the rise of fascism in Europe and Japan. Several poems like "Portraits with Cities Falling," "Who Saw the Terror," and "To Laura in Madrid," expressed Bulosan's commitment to the socialists and anarchists defending the Spanish Republic against Franco's hordes. It was easy for Bulosan to make the connection between the reactionary authoritarianism of the Falangists who had the support of Filipino landlords/compradors and the thugs of U.S. corporate agribusiness assisted by the state's ideological apparatus (police, courts, prison). His version of the united-front strategy explains the somewhat melodramatic and sentimental paean to Whitmanian democracy, as well as his deployment of the utopian metaphor of "America" as a classless and racism-free society, which pervades the texts of this period.

When Japan occupied the Philippines in 1942–44, Bulosan's attention and sympathy focused on the popular resistance to another invader—a more brutal repeat of the Spanish and American conquests—which then became the germinal site for the theme of "national liberation" in his letters and particularly his novel *The Cry and the Dedication* (published as *The Power of the People,* 1977). The latter was inspired by his friendship with imprisoned vernacular poet Amado V. Hernandez and by the Huk rebel Luis Taruc's autobiography, *Born of the People* (1953). About the time when Bulosan was composing his narrative of Huk guerillas reconstructing their nation's history and establishing linkage with U.S. partisans, he expressed his lifelong agenda in an autobiographical sketch in *Twentieth Century Authors:*

> The question is—what impelled me to write? The answer is—my grand dream of equality among men and freedom for all. To give a literate voice to the voiceless one hundred thousand Filipinos in the United States, Hawaii and Alaska. Above all and ultimately, to translate the desires and aspirations of the whole Filipino people in the Philippines and abroad in terms relevant to contemporary history. Yes, I have taken unto myself this sole responsibility.

Given his dialogue with both victims and masters, Bulosan may be the first "postcolonial" writer in the postwar United States because he envisioned an inscription of the negative or dialectical power of the "Third-World" subaltern in the archive of Western knowledge, questioning and undermining it but also rewriting it from what Frantz Fanon and Aimé Césaire call a "liberationist" perspective.

In his fiction and poetry, Bulosan reinvented the conjuncture of class, gender, race, and ethnicity that underpins the epochal antagonism between capitalism and various socialist experiments around the world. In retrospect the Cold War offered an occasion for Bulosan to transcend the nationalist program (the Filipino community was then conceived as an "internal colony" like the black ghetto and the Latino barrio) with a view toward a socialist transformation of the empire. In the process, the boundary erected by U. S. hegemony between the Southeast Asian writer-exile and his peasant/ethnic heritage proved illusory when Bulosan encountered racist exclusion and bourgeois exploitation in the heartland of capital. Stories like "The Story of a Letter," "Be American," and particularly, "As Long as the Grass Shall Grow" (the title was inspired by Bulosan's enthusiasm for *Black Elk Speaks*) dramatized the truth that Filipinos suffered not only class disadvantage and gender discrimination (antimiscegenation laws condemned them to a bachelorhood constantly preyed upon by gamblers and hustlers) but also national oppression. In this the Filipinos shared a predicament similar to that of workers of other races and nationalities. In his letters and in essays like "My Education," "I Am Not a Laughing Man," and "Labor and Capital," and in *The Power of the People*, Bulosan argued that the Filipino nationality cannot exercise its right of self-determination as long as the Philippines was a dependent colony of a power that claimed to be "democratic" but in practice fostered racial and class discrimination. Overthrowing capitalism meant breaking its stranglehold on "Third World" peoples in the colonies (one such colony is contemporary Puerto Rico), the source of superprofits and of cheap labor and natural resources.

In 1965 the Filipino workers on the grape farms, led by Bulosan's contemporaries Larry Itliong and Philip Vera Cruz, began the historic strike that evolved into the founding of the United Farm Workers of America. It was the culmination of pioneering work initiated in the early thirties by Bulosan and his associates in the Congress of Industrial Organizations (CIO), some of whom were members of the U.S. Communist party. Such groundbreaking action vindicated the aspiration of these dispossessed and disinherited Malayan "natives" for equality and justice. They allied themselves with Native Americans, African Americans, and Chicanos—all of them drawing from a grass-roots memory of centuries of resistance to oppression, a heroic narrative of "soul-making."

More than two million Filipinos today constitute the largest segment of the Asian American population in the United States, yet their creative force for social renewal is still repressed and unacknowledged. Bulosan endeavored to articulate its presence in his chronicles of multiracial conflicts and individual quests for happiness, insisting however on the fundamental primacy of labor or cooperative praxis as the guarantee of liberation for all humans across class, race, and gender lines. In an earlier testament of his socialist convictions, he stated: "Writing was not sufficient. . . . I drew inspiration from my active participation in the worker's movement. The most decisive move that the writer could make was to take his stand with the workers." A few years before he died, Bulosan reiterated this belief and guiding principle in his editorial to the 1952 ILWU *Yearbook* where he underscored the Filipino activists' devotion to "the collective interest and welfare of the whole people."

Because of his broadly socialist orientation, Bulosan may be the first consciously multicultural writer in the U.S. landscape whose roots in anticolonial protests and antifascist campaigns defy assimilation or co-optation into the hegemonic liberal canon. As long as the Philippines remains a U.S. neocolony and the Filipinos an oppressed nationality here, Bulosan's texts remain necessary as instruments for exploring the articulation of the Filipino identity and its complex, often ambiguous maneuvers of self-affirmation, within the political economy of U.S. imperial domination. It remains exemplary for other people of color claiming their right to be recognized as makers of U.S. history. What Mark Twain at the turn of the century saw as the ordeal and crucible of the American republic in subjugating the Filipinos who up to now persist in their refusal to be enslaved, as Bulosan's lifework attests to—this arena of struggle, I submit, may prove decisive in charting the possibilities and fate of the radical democratic transformation of U.S. society in the twenty-first century.

Suggested Readings

Carlos Bulosan, *If You Want to Know What We Are: A Carlos Bulosan Reader*. Albuquerque, N.M.: West End Press, 1983.

———, *The Philippines Is in the Heart*. Quezon City: New Day Press, 1978.

———, *The Power of the People*. Manila: National Book Store, 1986.

———, *The Sound of Falling Light,* ed. D. Feria. Quezon City: University of the Philippines Press, 1960.

E. San Juan, Jr., *Carlos Bulosan and the Imagination of the Class Struggle*. Quezon City: University of the Philippines Press, 1972.

———, *Bulosan: An Introduction with Selections*. Manila: National Book Store, 1983.

35

A. J. MUSTE

Staughton Lynd

Abraham Johannes (or as he always called himself, A. J.) Muste was the prophetic spokesperson of the peace movement in the United States from the mid-1930s until his death in 1967. He walked his talk: a famous photograph showed A. J., then aged seventy-four, climbing the fence of the Mead Missile Base in Omaha, Nebraska, in 1959 to protest United States missile policy. As a former labor movement organizer and Marxist, A. J. was also concerned to transform the whole of society. He believed in revolutionary nonviolence, and has been called a forerunner of Liberation Theology.

A. J. Muste was born in Zierikzee, the Netherlands, in 1885. His father worked as a coachman. In 1891 the family emigrated to Grand Rapids, Michigan. Arriving in the hard times of the early 1890s, A. J.'s father was lucky to get a job as a teamster at a local furniture factory. He made six dollars a week for a sixty-hour week.

A. J. was educated, first at a parochial school of the Dutch Reformed Church, and after a year or two in public school. When A. J. was in the eighth grade, he entered an essay contest sponsored by the Grand Rapids Trades and Labor Council on "Child Labor." The prize was $15 worth of books and publication of the prize essay in the souvenir book issued by the Council on Labor Day. A. J. won, and used his prize money to buy Emerson's essays and other books.

From an early age A. J. was expected to become a minister. At Hope College he met Anna Huizenga, daughter of a Dutch Reformed minister in Iowa. A. J. attended a Dutch Reformed seminary in New Jersey. During the summer of 1908 he served as a supply preacher at a church on Second Avenue and Seventh Street in New York City's Lower East Side. It was his first encounter with city slums, and what he called "a very different poverty from that of furniture-factory workers or even that of the poor farmers of the Middle West." A. J. graduated in 1909, married Anna, and became minister of a Dutch Reformed church in Washington Heights.

In 1914 A. J. informed his congregation that he could no longer accept the literal inspiration of Scripture or the whole corpus of Calvinist dogma. He resigned, and early in 1915 was installed as minister of a Congregational Church in Newtonville, near Boston.

Less than three years later A. J. resigned from the Newtonville church, too. He had come to be a pacifist, and after the United States entered the war and young men from the congregation had begun to be killed, he and his parishioners agreed that he must leave. As would be true of so many other leavings, A. J.'s departure from the Newtonville church was without recriminations on either side. Church officers declared their "honor, respect and love" for Reverend Muste. A. J. was offered three months of leave, and then a fourth, to make a new beginning.

What brought A. J. Muste to pacifism? Neither he nor his biographers are quite sure. He writes in his autobiographical sketches that "in all the study of Scriptures through which I had been led in that citadel of orthodoxy, New Brunswick, and in the hotbed of heresy which was Union [Theological Seminary] I had never been given an inkling that there might be such a thing as a pacifist interpretation of the gospel."

A. J. recalls that he had to face whether he could reconcile passages like 1 Corinthians 13 ("Though I speak with the tongues of men and of angels, and have not charity, I am become as sounding brass") with participation in war. He also says that he was influenced by Quakerism.

> As far as reading is concerned, what undoubtedly influenced me most, during the critical months of inner wrestling, to conclude that I could not "bend" the Sermon on the Mount and the whole concept of the Cross and suffering love to accommodate participation in war, was the serious reading of the Christian mystics. Among the important books on some of these mystics were those by Rufus M. Jones, a

leading Quaker. Thus I came to know about Quakers of past and present, Quaker meetings, the Quaker "peace testimony." It was the first time that these things suggested anything to me other than the man on the Quaker Oats box.

Although he would later renew his clerical credentials within the mainstream of Protestant Christianity, writes biographer Jo Ann Robinson, "the Society of Friends remained Muste's real spiritual home for the rest of his life."

After they were obliged to leave Newtonville the Mustes were taken in by the Providence, Rhode Island, Friends meeting. A. J. and Anna, together with their infant daughter Nancy, were given a home and some expense money in exchange for his teaching a Bible course at the nearby Friends school, helping to form adult discussion groups, and maintaining a reading room in the basement of the old Meeting House. All the progressive and radical magazines and pamphlets of the day were available in that reading room, A. J. later wrote. "On Saturday evenings throughout the war, the various unorthodox, persecuted individuals in the city gathered to talk and, metaphorically, hold hands."

As the war wound down in the fall of 1918, the Mustes moved to a house "adjacent to Back Bay, but on the wrong side of the New Haven Railroad tracks" rented by the Boston affiliate of the Fellowship of Reconciliation. The house became the headquarters of a group that called itself "the Comradeship." The core of the group was A. J.; Harold Roetzel, another minister who had lost his pulpit during the war; and Cedric Long, whose pacifism had prevented him from obtaining a church appointment.

A. J. recalls that in the winter of 1918–19 he and Roetzel got up at five o'clock in the morning and "bundled ourselves in our overcoats while we read the New Testament—especially the Sermon on the Mount—together." "Strikes were not in our thoughts at all," he adds.

However, early in 1919 an impending textile strike at nearby Lawrence gave the Comradeship a chance to put its faith into practice. A. J. and his friends visited Lawrence, thinking to help with strike relief. They were invited to the meetings of an incipient strike committee. Those present, Muste writes, were "some middle-aged Belgian, Polish and Italian weavers" who had been involved in the great 1912 strike in Lawrence led by the IWW; a radical-minded English carpenter "whose command of English made him the chairman"; and a number of young men who had been teenagers in 1912. The workers were devoted, honest, and courageous, but had "almost no contacts outside the mills and their respective language groups" and "no experience or training in organization techniques or publicity." No other leadership was in sight. At the end of the first week of the strike, A. J. was asked to become executive secretary of the strike committee.

Sixteen dramatic weeks later, the second Lawrence textile strike ended in victory. The ex-minister from out of town had led 15 to 30,000 strikers of twenty or more nationalities in successful (but nonviolent) class struggle.

At the end of the Lawrence strike A. J. was thirty-four years old. He had earned great credibility with two dissimilar networks of persons: radical pacifists, including members and supporters of the Comradeship; and trade unionists interested in industrial unionism and fundamental social change.

Both groups were essential to A. J.'s next major venture, Brookwood Labor College. Brookwood was located on a forty-two-acre estate north of New York City, near Katonah. The property belonged to Helen and William Fincke. They were members of the Fellowship of Reconciliation and William Fincke, like A. J. and Harold Roetzel, had been forced to give up his pulpit during the war on account of his pacifism. Leading progressive intellectuals, including Jane Addams, John Commons, Herbert Croly, Stuart Chase, and Freda Kirchwey, endorsed an initial fund drive.

The trade unionists who gathered in 1921 for the meeting that decided to set up the school included James Maurer, president of the Pennsylvania Federation of Labor; Franca Cohn, educational director of the International Ladies Garment Workers Union; Abraham Lefkowitz, a leader of the American Federation of Teachers, then in its infancy; and A. J. himself, who after the Lawrence strike was employed for two years as general secretary of the independent Amalgamated Textile Workers of America. Some, like Maurer, were active in the Socialist party.

Brookwood opened its doors to its first class in September 1921. There were about twenty students, ranging in age from their late teens to early forties. According to A. J., they were textile workers, garment workers, machinists, a cooper, and a couple of coal miners from Ohio. After the first year or two, the building trades and railroad workers were also represented in the student body. The students presumably had some financial support from sponsoring unions. All were obliged to give up whatever jobs they had in order to come to the school.

Brookwood Labor College, directed by A. J., flourished from 1921 to 1933. Many of the noncommunist organizers of the 1930s came from Brookwood. The school was a place where, on the one hand, the expression of all sorts of views was encouraged, but where also, education was understood to be intended to be practical and to change the world. The curriculum ranged from instruction in basic English (many students had not gone beyond eighth grade) to world history, taught by A. J. Nationally recognized academics such as labor historian David Saposs taught at Brookwood, part- or full-time. The members of the school community were expected to do manual work toward its upkeep.

The American Federation of Labor regarded Brookwood with suspicion from the beginning, and in 1928 condemned it outright, instructing member unions to withhold financial support and students. Brookwood responded by organizing a series of conferences and entities with the purpose of creating an organizing center, separate from both the American Federation of Labor and the Communist party. The coming of the depression caused A. J., among others, to put less and less emphasis on the school, and more and more emphasis on the school's "extension work," organizing away from campus. A difference of opinion as to the school's direction caused A. J. to resign in 1933.

From 1933 to 1936 A. J. was a full-time organizer and agitator. Influenced by Marxism, he briefly gave up his religious orientation and his pacifism. In 1932 he declined to sign a statement in support of the Gandhian independence struggle in India. "Nonviolence may be important, but I do not want to discredit the left-wing elements in India that believe in violence," he said on this occasion.

These years are the least researched of A. J.'s life. It is clear that he was present during the Auto-Lite strike in Toledo in 1934 and the sit-down strike in Akron in 1936, but the full picture of his involvement, personally and through coworkers, is presently unknown. In a remarkable 1935 essay entitled "Trade Unions and the Revolution," A. J. sketched a process whereby the general strike of all workers in a community (as in Toledo) leads to a situation in which

> the strike organization would have had to give orders to, interfere with, in greater or less degree, replace, the mayor, the police, the health authorities, the public utilities commission, etc. To the extent that it did so, it would have foreshadowed and approximated a Soviet, a workers' council.

"Thus the Central Labor Union . . . becomes the Soviet of a given city," he wrote.

In aid of this strategy A. J. formed or joined a series of explicitly Marxist organizations: the American Workers Party, the Workers' Party of the United States (after a merger with the Trotskyists), and the Socialist party (after the merged Musteites and Trotskyists entered the Socialist party).

Early in 1936, friends gathered a fund to make it possible for an exhausted A. J. and Anna Muste to vacation in Europe. A. J. went first to Norway for weeklong conversations with Trotsky himself, then to a meeting in France with leaders of the Trotskyists' Fourth International.

Shortly thereafter he (or he and his wife) stepped into the church of St. Sulpice in Paris. Here he experienced a reconversion to Christianity and to pacifism that did not change during the remainder of his life.

From 1936 until his death in 1967 A. J. Muste was the leading spokesperson for opposition to war, the nuclear arms race, and institutionalized violence in all forms, in the United States. He was employed from 1937 to 1940 as minister of the Labor Temple in New York City, and thereafter worked for the Fellowship of Reconciliation (FOR) from which he also received a small pension after his so-called retirement.

Personally wounded by his experience with the faction fighting of the Marxist left, A. J. was an indefatigable reconciler of radical persons and radical ideas. During the 1950s he created a so-called American Forum in which communists and noncommunists might exchange experiences. At the same time he helped to found *Liberation* magazine, through which he, Dave Dellinger, Bayard Rustin, Sid Lens, Paul Goodman, and later, Barbara Deming and I, sought to find words for a "new left" approach to social change. I vividly recall the early editorial meetings of *Liberation*. A. J., Dave, and Bayard, together with David McReynolds, the magazine's executive secretary, sat around a table. Acolytes like myself sat in a second circle next to the wall. Although manuscripts were discussed, it seemed that the major topic was always the demonstration that A. J. or Bayard had just returned from, what had been learned from it, and to what next steps it pointed.

Racial equality was a consistent concern, and the historical record is clear about A. J.'s impact. As executive secretary of FOR, A. J. encouraged James Farmer, Bayard Rustin, and George Houser to create the Congress of Racial Equality in the 1940s. Later, Martin Luther King and James Lawson were among those whose lives changed after hearing A. J. lecture. Dr. King has written: "I would say unequivocally that the current emphasis on nonviolent direct action in the race relations field is due more to A. J. than to anyone else in the country."

Opposition to war was A. J.'s burning main preoccupation in the years after World War II. When the Committee for Nonviolent Action (CNVA) was formed in 1957, A. J. served as chairperson and was arrested in many of its actions. It was largely through his diplomacy that a group of San Francisco-to-Moscow peace walkers were able to enter, and to demonstrate in, Poland and the Soviet Union. He refused to pay war taxes, and was one of the principal participants in a campaign in the late

1950s to refuse to take shelter during "civil defense" drills in New York City.

With the escalation of the Vietnam War in the early 1960s, A. J. became the perennial chairperson of coalitions against the war. Thus, after Students for a Democratic Society (SDS) declined to coordinate the burgeoning antiwar movement, A. J. and coworkers like Dave Dellinger took up this role, first through the Fifth Avenue Peace Parade Committee in New York City and then through the national Mobilization Committee to End the War in Vietnam.

A. J. never ceased to engage in direct action. In May 1966, in company with Barbara Deming and Bradford Lyttle, A. J. traveled to South Vietnam to make contact with Vietnamese dissenters. The group was deported for demonstrating against the war in the streets of Saigon. In December 1966, A. J. visited North Vietnam in the company of Martin Niemoller and other church figures. En route, in Paris, he told a reporter that he wished "to convey the spirit of peace to the stricken people of Vietnam." He added, "If it is the last thing in my life that I am able to do, I shall be content." He returned to the United States after the grueling journey late in January 1967. Two weeks later he was dead.

Suggested Readings

Nat Hentoff, *Peace Agitator: The Story of A. J. Muste.* New York: Macmillan, 1963.

A. J. Muste, *The Essays of A. J. Muste,* ed. Nat Hentoff. Indianapolis: Bobbs-Merrill, 1967.

Jo Ann Ooiman Robinson, *Abraham Went Out: A Biography of A. J. Muste.* Philadelphia: Temple University Press, 1981.

36

VITO MARCANTONIO

Gerald Meyer

Vito Marcantonio defied the truism of American politics that in the United States a radical politician has only two possible fates—defeat or co-optation. Marcantonio was the most electorally successful radical politician in modern American history: between 1934 and 1950 he served seven terms in Congress. And from his first term, when he proposed "reopening and operating . . . shut-down factories by and for the benefit of the unemployed . . . producing for use instead of profit," until his last, when he cast the only vote against the Korean War, his commitment to radical politics never wavered. Unfortunately, to date, the remarkable story of this memorable man remains little known.

Marc was born on December 10, 1902, in a tenement in the heart of Italian Harlem, a community located between Third Avenue and the East River in East Harlem that consisted of seemingly endless rows of tenements [built for the immigrant poor before housing codes required that some space be left for air and light and that apartments contain bathrooms]. It was also the largest Italian community in the United States, housing in 1930 eighty thousand Italian Americans, especially the poorest Southern Italian immigrants, congregating and replicating their ways of life in what has been called the most Italian of America's Little Italy's. When

Marcantonio died in 1954, he lived only four blocks away. His friends continued to be his boyhood pals, including those who had joined the Mafia. He explained: "I was born and raised in that district and I know everybody in that district, good, bad, doctors, lawyers, Indians, thieves, honest people, everybody." He had his face shaved every morning in the barbershop across the street from his home, bought his newspaper from the corner newsstand, and although he did not attend Sunday mass he marched in the annual procession of the *festa* of Our Lady of Mount Carmel. His entire life and career were inextricably connected with this remarkable community.

Marc was one of only two boys who graduated from his elementary school to go on to high school, and the other dropped out. His elementary-school principal praised his "tenacity of purpose, his initiative, his courage, and his innate leadership." Italian Harlem had no high school so Marc traveled across town to attend De Witt Clinton High School. He was only able to continue his studies by hiding his books in a nearby candy store before reaching his block so he could escape the taunt "little professor" from the other neighborhood boys.

He might never have graduated had he not met Leonard Covello, who having taken a position as a French teacher on a short-term basis, became obsessed with how few Italian school children attended the school and how poorly they were doing. Marcantonio immediately became engaged in Covello's stratagems for supporting the Italian-American students. He enrolled in Covello's first Italian-language class and he became an officer in Il Circulo Italiano, a student club dedicated to working in the Italian community. Covello, who remained childless, and Marcantonio, whose father died while he was in high school, became lifelong collaborators. Ultimately, they lived in adjacent brownstones on Italian Harlem's *corso,* East 116th Street. Covello continued to provide keen understanding of the community's mind and Marcantonio helped ensure the building of a grand edifice to house Benjamin Franklin High School, an academic high school in Italian Harlem's center.

Soon after graduating, Marcantonio enrolled in New York University Law School. However, he devoted his greatest energies to preparing immigrants for citizenship under Covello's direction at La Casa del Popolo, a settlement house that met the needs of the Italian community while respecting its culture. At the same time he worked on the staff and helped organize rent strikes at another settlement house, Harlem House.

There in 1925 he and the chief social worker, Miriam Sanders, married despite disparities of age, height, and background—she was eleven years older, four inches taller, and hailed from a New England family which could trace ancestors back to the *Mayflower*. Marcantonio always re-

What became widely known as the "Marcantonio Anti–Poll Tax Bill" passed the House a number of times but was successfully filibustered by the Southern Democrats and their Republican allies. In 1945, Marcantonio was able to thwart these same forces when they imperiled the appropriation for the Fair Employment Practices Commission, by utilizing his almost unrivaled knowledge of parliamentary procedure to threaten the blocking of funding for agencies vital to the war effort. For once, the *Nation* exalted, the "agile Southern parliamentarians were beaten at their own game." In the postwar era, Marcantonio attached what he called "the all-Harlem Rider" on innumerable appropriations bills. Stating that "this issue of white supremacy has to be fought out," his amendment demanded that no government funds be paid to any firm or individual which discriminated against its employers on the basis of race, nationality, or religion. In this way, he repeatedly placed civil rights at the heart of the House deliberations. In 1951, along with Paul Robeson he presented the United Nations with a petition charging the United States with the crime of genocide against the Negro people.

What made Marcantonio utterly unique among all other congressmen was his insistence that the Communist party was an "American political party operating in what it considers to be the best interests of the American working class and people." When the party or individuals associated with it came under attack, no one more ardently or effectively came to their defense. Moreover on most—though certainly not all—issues Marcantonio powerfully advocated for those positions most closely associated with the party. For example, he carried out a root-and-branch attack against the Cold War foreign policies of the Truman Administration. The Marshall Plan, he furthermore insisted "is being used by Wall Street to extend their monopoly control all over Europe."

Marcantonio's connection with the Communist movement released a firestorm of opposition. The press campaign intended to discredit Marcantonio, in its scope and the extent of its vilification, has perhaps been unequaled in the entire history of New York City politics. For example, in 1950 the *Daily Mirror* published fifty-eight articles attacking Marcantonio. In 1944 his district was gerrymandered to include Yorkville, an area south of East Harlem whose major ethnic groups—German Americans and Irish Americans—expressed hostility to left politics. The Wilson-Pakula Act of 1947 prevented him from entering the major-party primaries, thereby necessitating his running solely on the American Labor party (ALP) line at a time when it was almost universally identified as Communist controlled. And ultimately in 1950, he was defeated by the "gang up," a coalition candidate of the Democratic, Republican, and Liberal parties.

Marcantonio was able to overcome this opposition in large part because his Italian-American, Puerto Rican, and African-American constituents viewed him as an articulate tribune of the people advocating for those who had been left out of the American Dream. Perhaps more pertinently because he lived among them, shared their lives, and personally tended to their problems, he achieved a legendary, even saintly, status. Many recalled his reaching into his pockets to help those facing eviction or in need of school clothing for their children. When I queried an old time resident if anyone in Italian Harlem opposed Marcantonio, she asked: "Didn't people oppose Christ when he walked the earth?" A Puerto Rican woman who wrote Marcantonio requesting "a small turkey for my children" stated: "You are the bread of the poor people."

The people's devotion to Marcantonio was concretized, however, by the work of the Vito Marcantonio Political Association, a unique political beast which combined the structure of a big-city political machine with left-wing ideological content. The association provided for the delivery of services to Marcantonio's constituents with an efficiency and on a scale unrivaled anywhere else in the city, indeed perhaps in the entire United States. Simultaneously, it maximized voter participation. Into this structure poured the creative abilities, the organizational skills, the people power, and the finances of the left. The reelection of Marcantonio was the explicit election priority of the Communist party; its members and the organizations that it led devoted themselves to this goal.

Marcantonio's electoral successes also required the complex configuration of New York City's political party structure of that time. As for so many of their Italian-American constituents, the Republican party provided La Guardia and Marcantonio with a refuge from the machine politics of the Irish-American-dominated Democratic party.

In 1936, however, a more appropriate political home appeared. With Franklin Delano Roosevelt's approval, the American Labor party was founded by the leaders of New York City's needle trade unions to provide an electoral line that would enable some of the hundreds of thousands of New York City's Socialist party voters to comfortably vote for Roosevelt. Marcantonio immediately enrolled in the ALP and assumed leadership of its Communist party–oriented left wing. In 1941 he became the chair of the crucial New York County organization and from 1948 until 1953 he officially served as state chair. The ALP was the most important and the longest lived of the state progressive parties, averaging between 1936 and 1950 approximately fourteen percent of New York City's vote. The ALP also pioneered in advancing the political representation of minorities: it was responsible for the election in 1937 of Oscar García Rivera for state assembly—the first Puerto Rican to hold high public office in the

United States—and in 1941 provided a line for Adam Clayton Powell's election contest for city councilperson.

The ALP provided Marcantonio with enormous political leverage. The ALP willingly traded endorsements with the major parties in exchange for their endorsement or, when that was impossible, for their soft-pedaling their opposition to Marcantonio. But, his unyielding advocacy of the left's agenda finally caused the Republican and then the Democratic party to refuse to treat with him and ultimately with the ALP. However, in East Harlem, the ALP endorsements for state assembly and state senatorial seats effectively quelled any opposition from the local leaders of the major parties. This caused one commentator to astutely remark: "Marcantonio's organization cuts through all political lines, sometimes on the surface, often-times undercover by 'arrangements' known only to the very inner circles of the Republican and Democratic party organizations."

Thus Marcantonio brazenly maneuvered within the complex web of New York City's politics. He had won his first election by 655 votes. In 1936, despite the more than five thousand votes he garnered on the Communist party–sponsored All People's Party line (that year the ALP only ran a line on the ballot for Roosevelt and Herbert Lehman for governor), he was narrowly defeated. After he joined the ALP, he continued to contest the major-party primaries, winning one of the major-party primaries in 1938, 1940, and 1946, and both the Democratic and Republican party primaries in 1942 and 1944. Finally, when the Wilson-Pakula Act forced him to run solely under the designation of the ALP, Marcantonio bested his Democratic and Republican opponents. Only the "gang up" could allow Marcantonio's relatively poor showing in Yorkville to overcome the undying loyalty of his East Harlem bastions.

Most of Marcantonio's associates are convinced the events after his defeat in 1950 hastened his death. His advocacy for the Puerto Rican cause gave rise to a myth, widely repeated by his electoral opponents and published in the New York City press, that he had brought the Puerto Ricans to New York and put them on relief so that he could politically exploit them. In Richard Nixon's successful 1950 senatorial election, his major campaign tactic against his opponent, Congresswoman Helen Gahagan Douglas, was the distribution of over one-half million copies of a leaflet printed on bright pink paper purporting to prove that she and "the notorious party-liner Congressman Vito Marcantonio had voted the same way 354 times." While acting as coattorney for the Communist party before the Security Activities Control Board, he meanwhile engaged in increasingly acrimonious disputes with the party over the fate of the ALP. Convinced that a full-fledged fascist state was imminent, the Communist party began to withdraw its forces from all overtly left-wing organizations, including the ALP. Marcantonio led a group outside the party which insisted that the United States was experiencing a period of political repression not qualitatively different from the Alien Sedition Act or the Palmer Raid periods, and that the left should stand firm and salvage what was possible until political conditions improved. In 1953, the withdrawal of the party's support caused Marcantonio to resign as state chair of the ALP.

On August 9, 1954, while returning from the printer with the proofs for petitions for his candidacy for Congress on the Good Neighbor Party—on the east side of Broadway at Warren Street with City Hall in the background—Marcantonio fell dead. Although he had a metal crucifix and a St. Frances Xavier Cabrini religious medal on his person and he had always identified himself as a Catholic, Cardinal Francis Spellman denied him a Catholic burial. Later the Catholic Worker movement sang a requiem Mass for Marcantonio, and Dorothy Day's eulogy averred that: "The thing that we will remember Vito Marcantonio for was, in the words of the Psalmist, 'he understood concerning the needy and the poor.' "

Italian Harlem, a community where unity was strongly expressed in death rites, responded by organizing the largest funeral in its history. Leonard Covello, his barber, W. E. B. DuBois, whom he had successfully defended against the charge of being an agent of a foreign government, Puerto Rican independence leaders, Communists, and local politicians acted as pallbearers. Paul Robeson distributed a press release which called Marcantonio the "Thaddeus Stevens of the first half of the twentieth century." Over twenty thousand persons passed his bier and his ninety-seven-vehicle cortege, which included fifteen flower cars, passed a community where black-draped signs read "We Mourn Our Loss." In Woodlawn Cemetery, fifty feet from La Guardia's burial place, an impressive tombstone reads: "Vito Marcantonio: Defender of Human Rights."

Aside from Public School 50 located in El Barrio, which was named for him, no other memorial to date has been raised in memory of this politician who when he died had an estate worth less than $10,000, and who in 1950 when faced with almost inevitable defeat could rise to his feet and declare to the House of Representatives: "I have stood by the fundamental principles which I have always advocated, I have not trimmed. I have not retreated, I do not apologize, and I am not compromising."

Suggested Readings

John Salvatore LaGumina, *Vito Marcantonio: The People's Politician*. Dubuque, Iowa: Kendall/ Hunt, 1969.

Gerald Meyer, *Vito Marcantonio: Radical Politician: 1902–1954*. Albany: SUNY Press, 1989.

Felix Ojeda Reyes, *Vito Marcantonio y Puerto Rico: por los trabajadores y por la nación*. Rio Piedras, P.R.: Ediciones Huracán, 1978.

Annette Rubinstein, ed., *I Vote My Conscience: Debates, Speeches, and Writings of Vito Marcantonio*. New York: Vito Marcantonio Memorial, 1956.

Alan Schaffer, *Vito Marcantonio: Radical in Congress*. Syracuse, N.Y.: Syracuse University Press, 1966.

37

PAUL ROBESON

Lamont H. Yeakey

The origins of Paul Robeson's radicalism are to be found, first, in his family background and upbringing amid Jim Crow America. The youngest of six children born to Maria Louis Bustill and William Drew Robeson, Paul inherited from both sides of his family significant legacies of African-American pride and achievement. His mother, a member of the prominent Bustill family of Philadelphia, could trace her lineage to the colonial era and Cyrus Bustill, who had baked bread for George Washington and his starving troops at Valley Forge. The Bustills had later founded the Free African Society, maintained agents in the underground railroad, and provided ministers, teachers, and artisans to the Northern free black community. Less is known about Paul's father's family, but William was born a slave in North Carolina, escaped North, joined the Union Army, and fought to overthrow slavery. During Reconstruction he aided the destitute and attained a divinity degree at Lincoln University. He pastored a small, poor Presbyterian church in Princeton, New Jersey, and, after Maria's death, relocated the family in Somerville.

Born in 1898, Paul was raised by his father from the age of six, in a society where racism had reached an apex. Popular images distorted and denigrated black people, as they were victimized and economically exploited, politically disenfranchised, savagely lynched, and socially excluded from the mainstream. Reverend Robeson provided what his son later called a "home in that rock," nurturing in him values of discipline, service, pride, and self-respect. Paul did family chores, worked with his father in church activities, sang in the choir, and heard many stories about slavery and African-American life. He also excelled in primary and secondary school, earning a scholarship to Rutgers University at seventeen years of age.

Robeson's college career is legendary. Until 1915, only two African Americans had been admitted to Rutgers (Princeton barred blacks entirely), and he was the only one attending between 1915 and 1919. Striving for perfection, he earned grades among the highest in his class, was admitted to honor societies and wrote a senior thesis, "The Fourteenth Amendment: The Sleeping Giant of the American Constitution," which presaged the argument of the Supreme Court's *Brown v. Board of Education* decision in 1954. A master of elocution contests as well, he won first prize in his class four consecutive years. Meanwhile, the magnetically handsome six-footer excelled in football, track and field, basketball, and baseball, winning twelve major letters. Walter Camp called him the "greatest defensive back ever to trod the gridiron," and he was elected to the all-American team twice, the first player so honored in any sport at Rutgers.

Fellow students had been mean and nasty to Robeson when he entered Rutgers. By his graduation, however, he had been elected to the student council, and he delivered the official class commencement oration. He won recognition for Rutgers, stimulated intercollegiate athletics, and encouraged better relations between black and white students nationally. Proving himself superior to the vast majority of white undergraduates athletically and academically, he single-handedly demonstrated the absurdity of the popular belief in black inferiority.

Robeson entered Columbia University's law school in 1920. A year later he met and married Eslanda. Goode Cordozo, a graduate chemistry student; they had one child, Paul, Jr., in 1927. As Paul's desire to practice law waned, his interest in the theater grew. By the time of his graduation in 1923, he had already begun a stage career.

First appearing in a benefit play for the Harlem YMCA, he caught the eye of the Provincetown Players, Greenwich Village's premier group. They offered him leading parts in two unusual race-theme dramas by Eugene O'Neill, *All God's Chillun Got Wings* and *The Emperor Jones,* both produced in 1924. He made theater history in the former, when a leading black man unprecedently played opposite a white woman (and kissed her!). In *The Emperor Jones,* he simply dominated the stage, striking down a white guard in one scene (film-version frames depicting this action were expunged from copies shown in various parts of the country). Immediately acclaimed and condemned—their staging threatened by the Ku Klux Klan—these performances presented a new and different type of artistic production. Indeed, with the exception of Charles Gilpin, Robeson was the earliest black man in modern times to play serious roles on the American stage.

Numerous other productions followed, including *Porgy* (1927), *Show Boat* (1928), *Stevedore* (1935), and *John Henry* (1939). Robeson toured Europe in the late 1920s and lived there through much of the 1930s, perfecting his talents and drawing huge, enthusiastic audiences. His performance of *Othello* at London's Savoy Theatre in 1930 received twenty curtain calls at the opening performance. His New York performances as Othello (1943–44), still hold the record for the longest run of any Shakespearean play on Broadway.

Robeson made, by contrast, relatively few motion pictures, only eleven features and five documentaries. He felt particularly satisfied with *Proud Valley* (1939), which dealt with the harsh realities of Welsh coal miners, and with his narration for *Native Land* (1942), which depicted the life of black and white farmers and industrial laborers who worked together to overcome adversity during the Great Depression. He objected, however, to characteristically demeaning and stereotypical roles and to film editing which, in his view, badly misrepresented his efforts. "That made me think things out. It made me more conscious politically," he suggested later. He abandoned films and returned his attention to the stage where he could determine his own image in every performance.

Early in his career he augmented his acting by singing spirituals, launching an illustrious musical career that brought him to the heights of commercial celebrity. Soon, he broadened his repertoire to include the music of other nationalities, including Chinese children's songs, ballads of Mexican peasants, folk songs of various European workers, and African chants and lullabies, to mention a few. A typical concert of traditional melodies, classic, popular, and folk music might include Beethoven's "All Men Are Brothers" (from the Ninth Symphony), African-American spirituals such as "Climbing Jacob's Ladder" and "Sometimes I Feel Like a Motherless Child," Jewish songs like "Zog Nit Keynmol" (song of the Warsaw Ghetto uprising) or "Kaddish" (a Hassidic ballad), Irish tunes, and American labor ballads. Jerome Kern's "Ol' Man River" became his signature tune, employed to conclude every concert. In 1939, for the CBS radio show "Pursuit of Happiness," Robeson sang John Latouche and Earl Robinson's "Ballad for Americans." This song, with lyrics identifying the various ethnic groups comprising the population of the United States, was so popular that (according to *Time* magazine) his recording sold more copies during World War II than Kate Smith's "God Bless America."

As Robeson became extremely successful in the theater and on concert stage, he devoted himself more and more openly to the plight of African Americans. He believed that his music and acting would help convince whites that "we are moved by the same emotions, have the same beliefs, the same longings—that we are all humans together." He simultaneously embarked on a campaign to educate black people about the virtues of their own heritage, arguing that African history was as important as any other in the world. Meeting Africans from many walks of life, he studied their histories and cultures, insisting that black people everywhere, but especially in Africa, had a unique and valuable contribution to make in humanizing the world through their philosophy and art. He saw himself essentially as an African: "In my music, my plays, my films I want to carry always this central ideal," he insisted, "to be African. Multitudes of men have died for less worthy ideas; it is even more eminently worth living for."

Robeson's commitment to Africans and African Americans propelled him to sympathize with other oppressed people: "Only those who have lived in a state of inequality will understand what I mean—workers, European Jews, women . . . those who have felt their status, their race or their sex a bar to a complete share in all the world has to offer." He devised his own sense of cultural pluralism, learning more than two dozen languages. He believed that art could be the vehicle to unite humankind against the common enemies of poverty, exploitation, bigotry, political violence, and war.

At the invitation of Sergei Eisenstein, the great Russian filmmaker, Robeson made the first of several trips to the Soviet Union in 1934. He was also one of the few American entertainers to sing in the Spanish trenches to support the Loyalist troops. He called for "immediate action" to save European Jews even if it meant "heavy sacrifice and death." Robeson also supported the Committee to Aid China, condemned Japanese imperialism, gave concerts, and even made a special album of Chinese songs recorded in the language to generate funds for relief. A foremost spokesperson against European colonialism, he raised money to fight the Italian invasion of Ethiopia, led a campaign for African independence, and became chairman of the Council on African Affairs, which he helped establish (at first called the International Committee on Africa) in 1937.

During the 1930s and '40s perhaps no other U.S. figure—save the American presidents—became so well known around the world. His concerts during World War II, including some of the largest military and civilian audiences ever assembled during wartime, were all-out triumphs.

Naively expecting this to be the "final war," he believed that its conclusion would "attain a speedy freedom and equality for all peoples." He was soon disappointed.

In the immediate postwar years, four issues brought Paul Robeson into fierce conflict with the U.S. government: Robeson's campaign for civil rights; his opposition to colonialism; his peace advocacy during the Cold War; and his defense of civil liberties. He jeopardized fame, fortune (earnings in excess of $100,000 per year), and a brilliant career to devote himself full-time to these crucial matters. The nature of his confrontation with the government is instructive for understanding the extraordinary character of this American radical.

On civil rights, he insisted that racial barriers had to be removed and dismantled. Second-class citizenship could no longer be tolerated. He demanded that President Truman put an end to Southern lynchings and to segregation everywhere, insisting, "What difference is there between the Master Race idea of Hitler and the White Supremacy Creed of [Southern Senator James O.] Eastland?" He led a delegation of over thirty organizations which asked the president to institute a civil rights program immediately. The resulting report, "To Secure These Rights," dramatically admitted just what Robeson had been charging, that African Americans remained second-class citizens in virtually every aspect of American life. The pressure compelled a reluctant Truman to send a ten-point civil rights bill to Congress (the first of its type since Reconstruction) and to move to desegregate the military. Long before the movements of the 1950s urged mass, nonviolent direct action to achieve what Congress would or could not, Robeson urged such action.

On colonialism, Robeson became more determined than ever to work for the independence of African, Asian, and Caribbean peoples. He wrote on behalf of Philippine freedom from American domination, and his was the most prominent voice against continued colonial rule in Africa, insisting that President Roosevelt's intentions and not Winston Churchill's be decisive. He chided the United Nations Assembly for inaction while helping launch the anti-apartheid movement for South Africa, as he worked with such future African leaders as Kwame Nkrumah and Jomo Kenyatta. He dubbed Ho Chi Minh the "Toussaint L'Ouverture of Indo China," ridiculed the United States for sending arms to French imperialists, urged Indian independence, and applauded the Chinese revolutionary victory.

If Robeson's previous support for national liberation escaped official criticism, his campaign now ran against the tide of the Cold War. Although not a member of the Communist party, he refused to condemn Communism or to name Communists he had known. Instead, he drew the dangerous conclusion that civil rights, anticolonialism, and the cessation of exploding East-West conflict were interrelated; and the failure of the United States to fight for these causes was the fault of America's rulers. He spoke at union halls, churches, public parks, from the concert stage, in private clubs and homes, and on college campuses. He saw the arms race and possible atomic war as a threat to all life, including that of the planet itself. The destruction of Hiroshima and Nagasaki struck him as a clear warning. His record "La Petite Fille est morte" became a major public memorial to the children who died in these explosions.

Robeson's public role in peace conferences and similar activities cost him dearly. As the distinguished economist Robert S. Browne suggested later, "For a black man even to harbor such independent ideas was heresy; to utter them was treason." The State Department, the FBI, and the tabloid press conducted a campaign unprecedented in its viciousness toward an American entertainer. For his address at the April 1949 Paris Conference, he was branded an "un-American communist sympathizer." Robeson answered his critics without hesitation. When he was called before government committees to testify regarding his loyalty to the United States and Congressman Gordon Scherer of Ohio asked why the artist did not move to Russia, Robeson retorted "because my father was a slave, and my people died to build this country. . . . I am going to stay here and have a part just like you." But the authorities had their way: Robeson's name was rapidly stricken from the canon of the American arts, his enormous public reputation defamed and then removed entirely from sight.

Actual violence erupted when Robeson journeyed to Peekskill, New York, in August, 1949, to give his annual open-air concert. A mob of "vigilantes and hoodlums," unhindered by legal authorities and incited by the local Junior Chamber of Commerce, rioted with brass knuckles, billy clubs, and rocks, burning books and seriously injuring thirteen people. A large indignation meeting in Harlem answered this outrage with protest, and a second concert of 20,000, defended by trade unionists, went on peacefully—but was followed by a worse riot, with vigilantes injuring 140 and destroying hundreds of automobiles. New York Governor Dewey denied victims a hearing, blaming "Communist groups" for the violence, and a civil suit by Robeson and twenty-six other plaintiffs was dismissed in federal court. Many self-avowed liberals, in *Commentary* magazine and elsewhere, abandoned civil liberties and African-American concerns to blame Robeson and to defend the rioters against criticism.

Blacklisting and intimidation meanwhile cost Robeson his theatrical and concert career. When he sought to travel abroad to audiences still eager to hear him, the State Department revoked his passport "solely" (as the department's brief explained) "because of his recognized status as spokesman for large sections of Negro Americans [and] . . . in view of his frank admission that he has been for years active politically in behalf of independence of the colonial people in Africa." Fearlessly, he refused to capitulate to official terrorism, saying to 30,000 Canadians and Americans who heard him sing at the Peace Arch Park:

> Some of the finest people in the world are under pressure today, facing jail, facing hostile courts, for the simple fact that they are struggling for peace—struggling for a decent America where all of us who have helped build that land can live in decency and in good will. As for myself, as I said last year, I am the same Paul that you have known throughout all these years—the same Paul—but time has made it so that everyone—I included—must fight harder today to preserve the basic liberties guaranteed to us Americans by our constitution.

The government sought to create an anti-Robeson consensus in the African-American community. In a kind of litmus test for loyalty, officials called on black leaders to condemn Robeson, and some did cower before the intimidation. Many continued to admire him but safely, in secret, as Robeson assailed Cold War policies, charging at the National Labor Conference for Negro Rights in 1950 that "our nation has become the first enemy of freedom and the chief tyrant of the mid-century world."

Exiled in his own country, Robeson continued to speak out and fight back through the pages of numerous periodicals. Foremost among these was *Freedom,* a 1950s newspaper which listed Robeson as its publisher. Based in Harlem, it had many other notable writers that included John Killens, Lorraine Hansberry, Shirley Graham, Ruby Dee, John Henrik Clarke, and above all W. E. B. Du Bois, who had similarly refused to cave in to Cold War pressure. *Freedom's* successor, *Freedomways* (1961–85), a quarterly journal, published Margaret T. G. Burroughs, Ossie Davis, Harry Belafonte, Ron Dellums, James Baldwin, Jesse Jackson, and Robeson's dear friend, C. L. R. James, among many others. *Freedomways* stood as a tribute to Robeson's life and accomplishments.

Tragically, as the blacklist finally lifted, Robeson was all but exhausted from chronic health problems and recurrent depression. His passport reinstated in 1958, Robeson published an autobiography, *Here I Stand,* and launched a concert and speaking tour across Europe and Australia. Curious and sympathetic crowds gathered everywhere, recalling his earlier days of artistic triumph. A few years later, however, he retired permanently from the stage and other public activities and remained in seclusion until his death in 1976.

During his lifetime, Robeson won Nigeria's Africa Freedom Award; India's Nehru designated a national day in his honor; the American Academy of Arts and Sciences proferred him the Gold Medal for Best Diction, and the Donaldson Award was given to him for the finest acting performance—to name only a few of the honors heaped upon him. He clearly presaged and helped to make possible the achievements of Martin Luther King, Jr., Malcolm X, and Jesse Jackson, as well as the work of countless black artists. Victor Navasky, editor of the *Nation,* accurately reflected that if most American whites "either dismissed him as a Communist dupe or regarded him with regret as a tragic figure . . . for many blacks, he was the sun around which all else revolved."

Sidney Lens once defined the radical as an activist who demonstrates several characteristics, among which are opposition to privilege, advocating equality between "those who have too much and those who have too little," and working "to replace hate with love, division with unity, war with peace." Few individuals in any age exemplified this definition better than Paul Robeson. The United States and the world we know today (for all that is deficient and all that holds promise) is an immeasurably better place because of this American radical.

Suggested Readings

Martin B. Duberman, *Paul Robeson*. New York: Knopf, 1988.

Philip S. Foner, ed., *Paul Robeson Speaks: Writings, Speeches, Interviews, 1918–1974*. New York: Brunner/Mazel, 1978.

Freedomways, the editors, *Paul Robeson: The Great Forerunner*. New York: Dodd, Mead, and Co., 1985.

Paul Robeson, *Here I Stand*. Originally published 1958. Boston: Beacon Books, 1988.

Sterling Stuckey, "On Being African: Paul Robeson and the Ends of Nationalist Theory and Practice," in S. Stuckey, *Slave Culture, Nationalist Theory and the Foundations of Black America*. New York: Oxford University Press, 1987.

Charles H. Wright, *Robeson: Labor's Forgotten Champion*. Detroit: Balamp Publishing Co., 1975.

38

ELLA JOSEPHINE BAKER

Barbara Ransby

Ella Josephine Baker was born in Norfolk, Virginia, in the winter of 1903. She died in Harlem, New York, on her eighty-third birthday, December 13, 1986. While she is best known for her extensive involvement in the civil rights movement of the 1950s and '60s, her career as a political activist, organizer, and consummate coalition builder extends as far back as the 1930s. She helped to organize black cooperative campaigns in Harlem during the depression, worked as a grass-roots organizer and national leader of the NAACP in the 1940s, and served as the first interim director of the Southern Christian Leadership Conference in the 1950s. She was a colleague, and critic, of Dr. Martin Luther King, Jr., and was one of the founders and chief sources of inspiration for the Student Nonviolent Coordinating Committee, which was founded in 1960. A survey of Ella Baker's protracted political career chronicles a rich legacy of black radical ideology and grass-roots struggles spanning more than a half century. In her extensive political work she also facilitated links between activist communities which transcended the boundaries of race, class, region, and generation. In addition to being an important historical and political bridge, Ella Baker also offered the activists with whom she worked, a radical philosophy and strategy for social change which promised empowerment, not for a handful of national leaders, but an entire class of dispossessed people. She was an egalitarian in her personal as well as her political work, and one who saw personal transformation as an essential component of a larger effort to transform the economic and political structures of the society. A strong advocate of grass-roots group-centered leadership models, she was confident that those at the very bottom of the social and economic hierarchy had the ability and the incentive to enact fundamental social change. Baker's views did not fit neatly into any of the orthodoxies of the left, rather, she borrowed from different left traditions, many of them rooted in the African-American community, to forge her own unique revolutionary praxis.

Ella Baker came from a lower-middle-class North Carolina family. Her father, Blake Baker, had a job as a waiter on a Chesapeake steamship, which was a stable and well-paying job in those days. Her mother, Georgianna Ross Baker, was an educated and deeply religious woman who worked briefly as a teacher before her marriage, after which she devoted most of her time to Baptist missionary work and to tutoring young Ella and her two siblings, Maggie and Blake Curtis. Ella Baker often credited her family and childhood community with shaping her nascent political outlook. She was taught early on that, while her family was better off materially than some of their neighbors, this privilege carried with it, not the assumption of superiority, but the special responsibility of helping those less fortunate. Ella Baker's most vivid childhood memories were of the strong ethos of self-help and mutual cooperation which permeated her entire community. Cooperative farming practices built a strong sense of interdependency and group solidarity. In times of crisis, Ella Baker recalls her family pooling their modest resources with others to stave off hardship. Her grandfather mortgaged the family farm at least twice to buy food to feed other families in the county during hard times. The community of Littleton and adjacent Elams were bound together in a network of reciprocal obligations.

Ella Baker's mother, and her maternal grandfather, Mitchell Ross, were probably the two most important figures in her early development. Ross was an independent and hardworking farmer who was proud of the fact that, some twenty years after emancipation, he had saved up enough money to purchase a portion of the North Carolina land he had once lived on as a slave. A minister and recognized community leader, Ross was an ardent proponent of equal rights and black suffrage. He was a proud and defiant black man and young Ella admired him greatly. She also admired her mother, Georgianna, for her strength of character and unwavering commitment to principle. Ella Baker often went with her mother to meetings of the women's missionary association and observed firsthand a group of strong, capable, and confident black women, making decisions, running meetings, and conducting business. These female role models undoubtedly influenced Ella's sense of confidence in herself as a woman, and her sense of her potential as a leader. It was also Ella Baker's mother who gave her a sense of the value of education, the power of the spoken word, and the art of persuasion. Georgianna Baker tutored her children at home, coached them in public speaking, and as Ella recalled, insisted on perfection. As a result, Ella Baker was an eloquent orator and a formidable debater. Overall, there was a great sense of pride and a clear sense of history among Ella Baker's relatives. All of Ella's grandparents had been slaves and their experiences, passed on to Ella and her siblings, became a part of her own repertoire of stories which connected her in a very personal way to the legacy of slavery and to more than a century of black resistance. This upbringing, rooted in a tradition of racial pride, resistance to oppression, and a deep sense of community cooperation, formed the core of her strong social conscience.

In 1918, as World War I raged in Europe, Ella Baker left her hometown and went away to Shaw boarding school in Raleigh, North Carolina, the high school academy of Shaw University. Her parents felt this was the best option open to them for Ella's education and her future. Founded in the mid-nineteenth century by the American Baptist Home Mission Society, Shaw, like most Negro colleges at that time, was a conservative institution, run by paternalistic Northern white benefactors. The curriculum was "classical," in contrast to the basic vocational training offered at many other Negro schools of that era. Shaw students studied literature, philosophy, foreign languages, and mathematics. Ella Baker excelled academically at Shaw, graduating as valedictorian of her college class of 1927. She also worked in the chemistry lab part-time and served briefly as the associate editor of the school newspaper. At the same time, however, her tenure there was punctuated by a series of conflicts with the school's socially conservative administration. She led or participated in several protests against school regulations pertaining to student conduct and was called into the dean's office on more than one occasion. At this juncture, however, she was a rebel, pushing against the confines of authority, but not yet a radical, committed to fundamental social change.

After her graduation from Shaw University, Ella Baker contemplated moving to Chicago to pursue graduate studies at the University of Chicago, but settled in New York instead. She had relatives there who helped her to get settled and gave her an initial place to stay. One of Ella Baker's first jobs was at a restaurant in Greenwich Village across from New York University. She often enjoyed strolling in Washington Square Park across from the school during her breaks. It was there that she met a young

Russian immigrant, struck up a conversation, and first learned about communism. This was the beginning of a long and enduring association with the left. During her early years in New York, Ella Baker immersed herself in political discussions and debates that were going on throughout the city. The human devastation caused by the depression, and the growing radical political culture in New York City in the 1930s had a tremendous impact on her evolving political consciousness. She traveled all over the city attending meetings, rallies, forums, and discussions. This period proved to be a turning point in her life. It was during her first few years in Harlem that Ella Baker began to define the radical perspective that would inform her political activity for the rest of her life.

In the winter of 1930 Ella Baker joined with the iconoclastic writer George Schuyler and others to form the Young Negroes Cooperative League (YNCL) and became the group's first national director in 1931. The league, whose expressed purpose was to gain economic power through consumer cooperation, was headquartered in New York City and was made up of nearly two dozen affiliate councils scattered throughout the country. Affiliates were organized into buying clubs, cooperative grocery stores, and cooperative distribution networks. On a practical level, the hope was that the YNCL would serve as a survival mechanism for African Americans by urging them to consolidate their meager resources and use their power as consumers more economically. On another level, the founders of YNCL were harsh critics of capitalism and saw their modest efforts as a step in the direction of a more egalitarian alternative, although the particular characteristics of that alternative remained ill-defined. The league was also a decentralized organization which emphasized the inclusion of women, the importance of grass-roots involvement, and rank-and-file decision making. In many respects the YNCL's organizational philosophy foreshadowed a very similar youth organization with which Baker was closely affiliated some thirty years later, the Student Nonviolent Coordinating Committee. The YNCL survived for several years but financial hardship took its toll on the group and it eventually faded out of existence.

It was during the mid-1930s that Ella Baker secured a job with the Worker's Education Project of the Works Progress Administration where she initially worked as a teacher and later coordinated the project's consumer education program in Harlem. This position allowed her to continue the work she had begun in the YNCL. She organized workshops, lectures, and exhibits in storefronts, churches, and hospitals to educate the Harlem community about cooperative buying strategies. The WPA also afforded Ella Baker the opportunity to meet and interact with an array of progressive and radical young activists; among them, socialists, anarchists, and communists. It was also during this time that Ella Baker became loosely associated with the Lovestonites, socialist followers of Jay Lovestone, who ran the New Workers School where lectures and debates about radical politics were held. While there is no evidence that Baker joined the Lovestonites or any other socialist organization, the intellectual and political debate created by such groups appealed to her greatly. Ella Baker also honed her writing skills during this period publishing articles in such forums as the *National News, Crisis,* and the *West Indian News.*

Although Ella Baker never considered herself a feminist or women's rights advocate per se, her political praxis promoted the empowerment of women and placed women's concerns at the center of her political agenda. During the 1930s, she supported and worked with various women's groups such as the Women's Day Workers and Industrial League, a union for domestic workers; the Harlem Housewives Cooperative; and the Harlem YWCA. Baker also refused to be relegated to a separate "woman's sphere" either personally or politically. She often participated, without reservation, in meetings where she was the only woman present, and many of her closest political allies over the years were men. Similarly, in her personal life Ella refused to comply with prevailing social norms about women's place or women's behavior. When she married her long-time friend, T. J. Roberts in the 1930s, the marriage was anything but conventional, which typified Baker's rebellious spirit. First of all, Baker never assumed her husband's name, an unusual act of independence in those days. And even though she was married for over a decade, she never framed her identity as a woman around that of her husband, and seemingly never allowed domestic obligations to interfere with her principal passion, which was politics.

In 1938, upon the suggestion of a friend, Ella Baker applied for a position with the major civil rights organization of the day, the National Association for the Advancement of Colored People (NAACP). In 1940 she was hired as a field secretary and later succeeded William Pickens as national director of branches in 1943. As an NAACP organizer, Ella Baker traveled several months out of the year visiting local chapters and drumming up membership for the organization. Throughout her relationship with the NAACP she fought to democratize the organization and to move it away from legalism as a primary strategy for combatting discrimination. She was a staunch advocate of the kind of campaigns and strategies which she felt could involve and engage the masses of the NAACP's membership and link struggles for racial equality with other campaigns for social justice. She was specifically interested in enhancing the decision-making ability and leadership skills of local members. Toward this end, she conducted a number of leadership training sessions throughout the South, one of which was attended by Rosa Parks, who would later inspire the landmark Montgomery bus boycott and be heralded as the "mother of the modern civil rights movement."

Through her work with the NAACP Ella Baker established a vast network of contacts in grass-roots African-American communities throughout the South. It was this network of relationships and contacts that formed the foundation for much of the civil rights activity of the 1950s and '60s. For example, when Baker conducted outreach for SCLC's Crusade for Citizenship in 1957, and when SNCC volunteers engaged in voter registration and desegregation campaigns in the early 1960s, her web of contacts in the South proved to be an indispensable resource.

Ella Baker remained on the staff of the NAACP until 1946, when, fed up with the top-down bureaucratic structure of the organization and its legalistic strategy for social change, she resigned as director of branches. Another factor which influenced her resignation was the added responsibility she assumed when she took custody of her nine-year-old niece Jackie. Although Baker resigned her paid position as director of branches she continued to work with the NAACP in a volunteer capacity as the president of the New York branch, the first woman to hold that post. In that role Baker was a leader of school reform campaigns which demanded the desegregation of New York City schools and greater parent involvement in decision making. She headed a coalition called Parents Against Discrimination in Education which held numerous forums and rallies throughout the city and eventually met with the mayor of the city to express their concerns in 1957. It was also during the 1950s that Ella Baker became associated with the Liberal party and ran unsuccessfully as a party candidate for New York City Council in 1951. During the late 1950s she also spoke out against McCarthyism and the growing anticommunist sentiments in the nation. She herself was a target of government surveillance for many years because of her left-wing political affiliations.

By the mid-1950s rumblings of a resurgent black freedom movement were being heard throughout the South and Ella Baker had her ear to the ground. In the wake of the historic Montgomery bus boycott of 1955–56, which catapulted Martin Luther King, Jr., to fame, Baker and two of her political colleagues in New York City, Bayard Rustin and Stanley Levison, talked extensively about how the boycott could be used to ignite a mass-based political movement against racism in the South. Out of these discussions the Northern-based civil rights group In Friendship was formed in New York City in January of 1956. Ella Baker served as executive secretary to the coalition and was a catalyst for bringing together the broad array of groups that united under the In Friendship banner. In Friendship raised funds to support the Montgomery Improvement Association and other activists who were victims of reprisals and counterattacks as a result of their civil rights activity in the South.

By 1957 Levison and Rustin had become close advisers to Martin Luther King, Jr., and persuaded him to allow Ella Baker to come to Atlanta and head up the Crusade for Citizenship, a voter rights campaign being launched by the newly founded Southern Christian Leadership Conference. SCLC had been formed in 1957 as a regional coalition in order to sustain and build upon the momentum of the successful Montgomery bus boycott. In this new organizational context Baker again took up the fight she had waged within the NAACP some ten years earlier—the fight to decentralize decision making and to create accessible channels through which local grass-roots people, many of them women, poor people, and youth, could give greater leadership to the movement. In the NAACP Ella Baker had come up against the formidable power of the association's chief executive, Walter White. In the SCLC she had to contest the almost unquestioned authority of Dr. King. While Ella Baker respected Dr. King, she felt that the increasing reliance on his public persona and charisma to mobilize people was dangerously channeling the movement's energies in the wrong direction. Ella Baker's message was simply that "strong people don't need strong leaders."

Baker's relationship with SCLC was fraught with tensions and contradictions from the beginning. She recognized that many of SCLC's leaders, mostly male ministers, had been reluctant to accept her leadership within the organization. She was strong, experienced, outspoken, and she was a woman. Fifty-four years old and a veteran organizer when she came to SCLC, Baker often felt the treatment she received was disrespectful and demeaning. She felt the leadership style of the organization and the ministers' reluctance to embrace campaigns that would ignite and sustain a new wave of mass activism limited how far the organization could go. After serving temporarily as SCLC's interim executive director, Ella was not invited to stay on. At around the same time, however, new developments in the Southern civil rights movement caught Ella Baker's attention.

When the student desegregation sit-in movement erupted in Greensboro, North Carolina, in February, 1960, Ella Baker began immediately to invest her energies into what would prove to be the cutting edge of the black freedom movement. Just as she had sought to extend the gains of the Montgomery boycott through her work with the SCLC, Baker once again strove to maximize the momentum of this new upsurge in mass direct action. Lunch counter sit-ins then sprang up across the South in an explosion of protest. Anticipating that the activity would either fizzle out or be co-opted by more moderate black leaders, Baker moved quickly to create a launching pad for a new independent youth organization which would be militant in its tactics and egalitarian in its structure. While still on staff at SCLC, Baker convened a conference of sit-in leaders in April 1960 at her alma mater, Shaw College in Raleigh, North Carolina. This gathering led to the formation of the Student Nonviolent Coordinating Committee (SNCC). SNCC leaders quickly became important catalysts for the upsurge of civil rights activity that occurred in the early 1960s. They helped to coordinate and participated in the historic freedom rides to desegregate interstate transportation in 1961. And in 1964 SNCC leader, and Ella Baker protégé, Bob Moses, coordinated the Freedom Summer campaign to expand black voter participation in the Deep South. During both campaigns young civil rights workers were jailed and beaten, and several even lost their lives. Finally in 1964 SNCC helped to launch the Mississippi Freedom Democratic Party, an organization which championed the plight of disenfranchised black sharecroppers and workers, and challenged the liberal leadership of the Democratic party to take a firmer stand against racism. These campaigns and initiatives elevated SNCC to national prominence, and Ella Baker played an important behind-the-scenes role in all three efforts.

In its founding principles, SNCC embraced the basic convictions Ella Baker had fought for for most of her adult life. It was a homecoming. She served as an adult adviser, role model, and intellectual mentor to many of the young SNCC leaders throughout most of the life of the organization. Former SNCC executive secretary Jim Forman once described the role of Ella Baker in SNCC as follows: "Throughout the decade of the sixties, many people helped to ignite or were touched by the creative fire of SNCC without appreciating the generating force of Ella Jo Baker." After leaving SCLC, Ella Baker took jobs with the YWCA and later with the Southern Conference Education Fund as a way of remaining in the South and remaining close to the Southern-based movement. As movement activity waned in the South by the mid to late 1960s and the battlefields of confrontation shifted northward, Ella Baker returned to New York City where she spoke out against the Vietnam War, lent her support to the Puerto Rican independence movement, and worked on behalf of African independence struggles.

Suggested Readings

Ella Baker, "Developing Community Leadership—An Interview," in Gerda Lerner, ed., *Black Women in White America*. New York: Random House, 1970.

Ellen Cantarow and Susan Gushee O'Malley, "Ella Baker: Organizing for Civil Rights," in *Moving the Mountain: Women Working for Social Change*. New York: Feminist Press, 1980.

Fundi: The Story of Ella Baker, a film by Joanne Grant. Franklin Lakes, N.J.: New Day Films, 1981.

Joanne Grant, "Mississippi Politics—A Day in the Life of Ella Baker," in Toni Cade, ed., *The Black Woman*. New York: New American Library, 1970.

Charles Payne, "Ella Baker and Models of Social Change." *Signs: Journal of Women in Culture and Society,* vol. 14, 1989.

39

I. F. STONE

Eric Alterman

I. F. Stone is one of those lucky people who all but attended their own funeral. Like Tom Sawyer and Huck Finn ("He warn't bad so to say," cried Aunt Polly, "only mischeevous"), Stone, on the occasion of his eightieth birthday and the publication of his final book, *The Trial of Socrates* (1987), was treated to the kind of mass media respect and veneration that is almost always reserved for the comfortably deceased. The very establishment press organs that had shunned his reporting, ignored his scoops, and branded his views dangerously radical at best, procommunist at worst, joined in the celebration of what one article at the time called "Izzymania." When Stone's heart gave out eighteen months later, the entire process was repeated, with the lengthy respectful obituaries, op-ed page tributes, and two standing-room-only memorial services attended by the biggest names in the business.

That Izzy Stone led one of the more fruitful and eventful lives of twentieth-century American journalism is beyond argument. Born in Philadelphia on Christmas Eve, 1907, Stone was a first-generation child of Russian-Jewish immigrants. He began his sixty-seven-year journalism career at age fourteen when he published his own newspaper called the *Progress*. In the three issues published before his parents forced him to close down production fearing neglect of his schoolwork, Stone thundered against William Randolph Hearst's yellow-peril offensive and William Jennings Bryan's religious fundamentalism, while calling, unabashedly, for forgiveness of all war debts and the speedy approval of Woodrow Wilson's plans for the League of Nations.

Graduating forty-ninth in a high-school class of fifty-two, Stone attended the University of Pennsylvania, which was obliged to accept male applicants from Philadelphia, but did not fare much better in college than he had in high school. Ignoring his studies once more, he ended up working ten-hour shifts for the *Philadelphia Inquirer* copy desk during his junior year. Earning the small fortune of forty dollars a week, Stone gave up on his formal education and began working as a journalist full-time.

Hired by the liberal newspaper magnate J. David Stern to write for the *Philadelphia Record,* Stone soon made a name for himself, at age twenty four, writing pro–New Deal editorials in the *Record;* radical, though not-quite-ready-to-abandon-Roosevelt broadsides in the *Nation* and the *New Republic;* and scathing socialist political tracts in V. F. Calverton's *Modern Monthly* (where he shielded himself under the self-revealing nom de plume Abelard Stone). For the next twenty years, Stone moved through a succession of liberal newspapers, writing from New York, Washington, Paris, and Palestine, impressing both progressive journalists and left-wing intellectuals, while straddling the line between the two callings. Fiercely independent and stubborn-minded, Stone was frequently quarreling with his editors, quitting one job or another over some issue of political principle, but always landing on his feet, frequently combining two or three simultaneous jobs in order to remain true to his political vision while still earning a decent living for his family.

Stone's remarkable ability to apply both historical perspective and a self-conscious moral and ethical framework to his journalism gave his work a quality that not only distinguished it from that of his contemporaries, but served to lift it into the rank of contemporary history. A quick reading of Stone's collected work, published in six volumes by Little, Brown, and Company under the series title *A Non-Conformist History of Our Times* demonstrates time and again an ability to mine current events for larger historical trends and unforeseen problems that is matched, perhaps, only by Walter Lippmann among Stone's contemporaries.

This is particularly true of Stone's writings about the Middle East, any of which read like prophecy today. In the fall of 1945, the *Nation* sent Stone to Palestine. He entered the country from Egypt, where he found unrelieved misery, poverty, and a "whole horde of self-serving phonies," along with "Egyptian officials [who] seem to treat their own people with

an arrogance and contempt beyond that of the worst foreign imperialist."
In Palestine, however, Stone found that Arabs were "better dressed,
healthier looking by far, than the Arabs in Egypt whose usual dress is a
dirty, old-fashioned, single piece garment which is almost an exact replica
of the nightshirt grandpa in America used to wear."

More significant by far than his views on Arab fashion wear, however,
was Stone's enraptured description of the achievements of Jewish Palestine. "In the desert, on the barren mountains," he wrote,

> in the once malarial marshes of the Emeck [sic], the Jews have done
> and are doing what seemed to reasonable men the impossible. Nowhere
> in the world have human beings surpassed what the Jewish colonists
> have accomplished in Palestine and the consciousness of achievement,
> the sense of things growing, the exhilarating atmosphere of a great
> common effort infuses the daily life of the Yishuv. I came away
> feeling that no obstacles, no setbacks, nothing but perhaps a Third
> World War and atomic bombs in the Middle East, could stop this
> people.

Yet despite his intense feelings of admiration and human fellowship for
the Jews, Stone found himself pained by their unwillingness to treat the
Palestinian Arabs with the same kind of decency and respect that they
were demanding from the British.

A year later, Stone was invited by the Palmach to be the first American
journalist to accompany Jewish concentration camp survivors on an illegal
sea voyage to Palestine. Stone's reportage made no pretenses toward
objectivity. His book-long report, *Underground to Palestine,* is dedicated
to "those anonymous heroes the Shelikhim of the Haganah." He wrote
"not as a newspaperman merely in search of a good story but as a kinsman,
fulfilling a moral obligation to my brothers." Nevertheless, despite his
overwhelming feelings of sympathy and kinship for the Palestinian pioneers, Stone could not paper over his disagreements with the Zionist
mainstream, despite the inducement of a $25,000 advertising campaign
(in 1948 dollars!) offered by Zionist partisans if only he would remove
the sentence in which he called for a binational state. Stone refused,
thereby dooming the book's chances for bestsellerdom.

Stone's unwillingness to temper his disappointment over Israel's continued mistreatment of its Arabs, and later, those in the occupied territories,
made him a pariah in the American Jewish community, where devotion
to Israel had all but replaced the Talmud and Torah as the primary organ
of Jewishness. Though loathe to admit it publicly, this deeply wounded
him. He called himself a "proud Jewish atheist" and never lost his devotion
to the cause of the kind of Israel he could support wholeheartedly.

Stone felt compelled to address himself to uncomfortable truths that American liberals, particularly Jewish-American liberals, were unready to face. Yet this marginalization was reproduced virtually across the board. As a columnist and reporter for *PM,* Stone occupied a place in a left-wing culture that simply shriveled up under the pressures of Cold War conformism. When the *Daily Compass,* a fragile successor to the faded glories of *PM* folded in 1952, Stone found no press organ willing to sponsor his brand of left-wing reporting. The result was the creation of *I. F. Stone's Weekly,* which, staffed by the tireless Esther Stone and a series of happily exploited young assistants, lasted for nineteen years until 1971, when Stone's doctors forced him to give it up. Stone then joined the *New York Review of Books* as a contributing editor.

During the course of the newsletter, Stone shunned leaks, interviews, and press briefings with high officials, and relied instead upon a scouring of the public record for clues to stories that the mainstream press was either too lazy or cowed to discover on its own. In one instance, in 1953, comprising what Stone called his "best scoop," Izzy single-handedly disproved the Eisenhower administration's contention that it honestly desired to end the nuclear arms race, but was stymied by an inability to verify Soviet compliance. The story, which provides a textbook illustration of Stone's method, occurred in late 1957 after the president announced he would sign a comprehensive weapons test-ban accord if only it could be properly verified. The Russians agreed to allow the United States to place seismic listening posts at 1,000 kilometer intervals inside the Soviet Union. Ike seemed sincere, but his experts convinced him that underground tests were impossible to monitor. The issue, therefore, was considered closed.

On September 19 the United States conducted its first underground nuclear test. The *New York Times* reported the following day that "the experiment seemed to have conformed with predictions of AEC [Atomic Energy Commission] scientists that the explosion would not be detectable more than a few hundred miles away." But the paper also carried wire reports noting that the shock of the test had been recorded in Rome and Toronto. Stone noticed the inconsistency, but he had neither the resources nor the contacts to cable Rome or Toronto to inquire about it. He filed the clipping away in his basement.

Seven months later, the AEC released its own report on the test and noted that the maximum distance at which earth waves were recorded from the test was at the seismological station in Los Angeles, about 250 miles away. If this were true, then clearly Moscow's verification offer would have been inadequate. A thousand kilometers is over 600 miles. Stone read the report, remembered the clippings downstairs, and got to work. He called the AEC, to ask how its report squared with detections in Rome and Toronto. The scientists said they'd get back to him. Not one to wait around for a phone call, Stone then called on the scientists at the Coast and Geodetic Survey at the Commerce Department, who, according to Stone's recollection, hadn't seen a reporter since "Noah hit Mount Ararat." There he discovered that the Nevada explosion had been recorded by nineteen separate listening posts, including Fairbanks, Alaska, over 2,300 miles from the original site.

Seconds after Stone got home, he got a call from the press officer at the AEC. The official told him, "Izzy, we heard you were sniffing around at Coast and Geodetic. It's too late for us to get Nevada on the Teletype, but we'll call you tomorrow. Maybe there's a mistake." A few days later, the AEC issued a "note to editors" asking that the last two sentences of its March 6 previous press release be deleted and a sentence admitted that "semismological stations of the U.S. Coast and Geodetic Survey as far away as College, Alaska, about 2,320 miles from the shot mesa recorded the earth waves." No explanations were offered. That was it. The next day's papers contained no mention of the correction. I. F. Stone, working alone from the clippings in his basement and the phone in his den, revealed the truth about the experiment to 10,000 *Weekly* subscribers in the March 10, 17, and 24 issues.

In the days and months that followed, the true purpose of the discrepancies was revealed by a series of statements by U.S. officials. The acting AEC chair told a congressional hearing on March 6 that the test ban was a bad idea because "if you stop testing them, you are stuck with . . . the present arsenal and that is just about it." The chair of the Joint Chiefs of Staff at the time, General Nathan Twining, explained to *U.S. News and World Report* that "only by continuous testing can the versatility of our nuclear weapons be increased." The next month, Eisenhower went on record in favor of more tests and a crucial window of opportunity for a complete test ban was nailed shut. Had the mainstream media picked up on Stone's lead, assuming Eisenhower's sincerity, the arms race might have ended many decades and billions of dollars earlier. But save for the 10,000 subscribers, nobody was paying attention.

So what about Stone made it so easy for the political system to ignore even his unopinionated reporting? In a word, or rather two, it was the Cold War. Anticommunism was the passport to "responsible" discussion in mainstream American politics. Izzy never applied for one. In fact, he went out of his way to make certain he was ineligible.

Throughout the 1930s and 1940s, Stone maintained an ambiguous relationship with the U.S. Communist party, never joining himself, but clearly allying himself with its aims and many of its partisans. Stone defined himself as a man of the left in the widest sense, and in a nation where the forces of reaction were so powerful, it was extremely difficult for him to conceive of having any adversaries save conservatives and reactionaries. When, in August 1935, Georgi Dimotroff, secretary-general of the Comintern called for "a people's anti-Fascist front," Stone, like the editors of the *Nation* and the *New Republic,* signed up not only with his pen but also with his heart. His commitment to the idea of a popular front against fascism, coupled with his romantic belief in the liberatory possibilities of socialism, was so powerful that it clouded his view of the Soviet Union for the next two decades.

Seven months before Dimotroff's announcement, in December 1934, during the Kirov murder and the execution of sixty-six of his alleged coconspirators, Stone proved tremendously clear-eyed about Stalin's Machiavellian machinations, comparing the Soviets to the Nazis in their thugishness. But the Popular Front left a mark on Stone that took him more than twenty years to shake. While he did not accept the 1936 purge trials at face value, as did the editors of the *Nation* and the *New Republic,* neither could he bring himself to condemn them outright. His mind at war with his heart, Stone wrote an editorial in the *New York Post* tellingly titled "?????????." In it he seemed ready to excuse the purges, noting that "Revolutions do not take place according to Emily Post." Stone was even willing to consider the possibility that, "perhaps, as Stalin contends, a vast counterrevolutionary conspiracy has been uncovered. We don't know."

Stone began to back off from his "fellow traveling" following the Hitler-Stalin pact, but he still tended to give the Soviets an enormous benefit of the doubt. Once the United States entered the war, he began defending the Soviet Union, going so far at one point as to tell American progressives to "keep their shirts on" over the arrest of sixteen Polish underground partisans who were thrown into Soviet prison. Not until Nikita Khrushchev made his "secret" speech regarding the crimes of Joseph Stalin was Stone able to see the Soviet Union without the rose-colored blinders he had donned at the dawn of the popular front. Like so many on the left, Stone's romanticism about socialism also allowed him to fool himself about Castro's Cuba, which he defended long after it had become evident that the revolution had gone awry.

Stone's problem, aside from an engaging naiveté that led him to try to see the best in any underdog, was his misapprehension during much of the Cold War that the United States was on its way to fascism. During the height of the McCarthy scare, Stone considered moving his family abroad, simply to escape what he believed to be the nation's stifling political atmosphere. One can sympathize with his feelings. Here he was—one of the most accomplished journalists of his generation—and he was unable to find a job doing honest reporting because the "free and independent" American press had no place for anyone of even mildly radical views. Stone lived and worked in a profession—an allegedly "liberal" one at that—whose official headquarters, the National Press Club, refused to serve him lunch because he brought a judge to dine with him who happened to be a black man. Although he always went to great lengths not to allow his isolation to embitter him, it nevertheless must have taken a massive psychic toll on so ambitious and gregarious a man.

Yes, he was a "socialist" and he believed in "the revolution." But more important, Stone was an uncompromising democrat, in a time and place where such a commitment could brand one as dangerous and irresponsible. But what strikes one about Stone, finally, are not his politics, but his gentle nature and good humor. As he explained once to a fellow reporter, "When Socialism comes I'll fight for the right to spit in the nearest bureaucrat's eye. [But] I own a house in Washington and I won't want proletarians trampling petunias on their way downtown to overthrow the government by force and violence."

Suggested Readings

Robert C. Cottrell, *IZZY: A Biography of I. F. Stone*. New Brunswick, N.J.: Rutgers University Press, 1992.

Andrew Patner, *I. F. Stone: A Portrait*. New York: Pantheon, 1988.

I. F. Stone, *A Non-Conformist History of Our Times*. Boston: Little, Brown, and Co., 1988. Six volumes.

40

WILLIAM APPLEMAN WILLIAMS

Edward Rice-Maximin

The Cold War, with its enormous financial, human, and planetary costs, had no victors, recently observed George Frost Kennan, once a chief architect of the "containment" of the Soviet Union. If William Appleman Williams had lived to read this acknowledgment, he surely would have recognized the conclusions that he himself had reached over four decades earlier. Arguably the most influential and controversial American historian since Charles Austin Beard, Williams had at least sounded the warning.

In launching a wave of New Left or "revisionist" history, Williams successfully helped to reshape the way many scholars and activists looked not only at foreign relations but also at the deeper assumptions underlying the American empire. Rarely an activist, scarcely an organizer, and never the formal member of any radical group, Williams was a "socialist of the heart" (in C. Wright Mills's words) who always believed that ordinary Americans had it in themselves to put an end to the empire and establish genuine social communities. His actual influence, however, remained intellectual and scholarly; he had little impact on nonacademics, much less on policy changes in Washington.

Born in 1921, Williams grew up in rural Atlantic, Iowa. When his father, an Army Air Corps pilot, was killed during flight exercises in 1929, his hard-pressed mother, Mildrede, enrolled in a teacher's training school, leaving young Bill largely to the care of his grandparents. He was always proud of being part of an extended family of "people who had community values at the center of their lives." He won a basketball scholarship to Kemper Military Academy in 1939 and worked summers as a YMCA camp counselor, an experience that gave him "a real feel for the excitement of teaching."

Williams received a congressional appointment to the U.S. Naval Academy two years later. Bored and restless at first, he "almost flunked out," but he was always extremely proud of his Annapolis experience, of having associated with so many "high-powered" and "first-rate" people, and of having been taken "very damn seriously." Upon being commissioned in 1944, he served as an executive officer on landing craft for fifteen months in the Pacific, suffering serious back injuries that would always plague him. Sent at the end of the war to Corpus Christi to train as a naval flyer, he engaged in civil rights activities with the local NAACP, a few Quakers, and some Communists (for whom he had "enormous respect"). The FBI harassed him, his landlord evicted him, and the local police worked him over.

For the first time Williams consciously became a radical, questioning his deeply held beliefs in "this great American democracy." Although the Navy tried to transfer him to Bikini to participate in mock amphibious landings following atomic blasts, he was "in such bad shape physically" that he had to spend thirteen months in naval hospitals, giving him plenty of time to mull over the nature and purposes of American society. At length he resolved to study history to "make some sense out of what the hell was going on."

Williams received a medical discharge in 1947, and applied to the University of Wisconsin where a unique group of Beardian historians held forth against the scholarly drift toward a Cold War liberal apologia for the dark side of the American past. Although admitted on probation because of his mediocre scholastic record at Annapolis, Williams "went for it like a fish to water." Among an unusually dynamic group of students were other returning veterans who shared "the same hopped-up concern to figure out what the hell had been going on during the war."

His major professor, Fred Harvey Harrington, encouraged a broad study of American foreign relations that examined a variety of influences, particularly economic ones, behind government policies. Accordingly Williams focused his doctoral dissertation on Raymond Robins, a Midwestern Progressive Republican and social reformer who had headed the American Red Cross mission to Russia during the Revolution and later campaigned vigorously for United States recognition of the Soviet Union. Williams's initial interest in Russia had less to do with ideology or politics than a curiosity about the "fascinating society" that had done the most to win the World War. Perhaps Americans could actually *learn* something from the Russians. He also spent five months during 1948 studying social-ist economics at Leeds University in England, where he first thrilled to visions of decentralized socialism provided by British Marxists and several members of a dynamic Labour government.

Having received his Ph.D. in 1950, Williams took a couple of temporary jobs, including one at Ohio State where he became friends with Harvey Goldberg, another Wisconsin radical and a Marxist. Together they edited *American Radicals,* a collection of biographies (1957), to which Williams contributed an article on Beard. He had already published his first book, *American-Russian Relations, 1781–1947* (1952) that showed the United States perpetually on the offensive, determinedly seeking an "open door" for influence and wrongfully shunning potential Russian cooperation against German and Japanese expansionism. He sharply criticized "con-tainment" and advocated accommodating the U.S.S.R.'s legitimate con-cerns.

In 1956 appeared *The Shaping of American Diplomacy,* a massive two-volume collection of readings, documents, and introductory essays that informed a whole generation of students eager to learn about how various interest groups and power brokers influenced foreign policy decisions. Meanwhile, Williams made national contacts on the left, writing occasion-ally for *Science and Society, Monthly Review,* and the *Nation,* and joining the advisory board of the pacifist and early New Left magazine *Liberation.*

After several years at the University of Oregon, where McCarthyism had made his life miserable, Williams moved back to Wisconsin in 1957 to achieve national renown and train several dozen graduate students, many of whom continued the revisionist onslaught. A few, including Walter LaFeber, Thomas McCormick, and Lloyd Gardner, became lead-ing foreign relations historians. The Madison students found Williams's personal charisma and commitment to socialism "mind-blowing," while his fascinating lectures revealed "a world-class intellectual thinking on his feet." Some of them launched, in 1959, *Studies on the Left,* the first of the scholarly New Left publications in the United States, with deep impact on the student movements of the 1960s, particularly Students for a Democratic Society (SDS). Williams contributed a couple of masterful essays on how the United States had tried to crush the Bolshevik Revolu-tion from its very inception.

Williams's most famous work, *The Tragedy of American Diplomacy,* appeared in 1959. Open-door imperialism, far from being an aberration, he argued, was at the heart of the American experience. Without constant economic expansion, most Americans believed their democracy and prosperity could not survive. Increasingly, marketplace capitalism had become central to American politics, culture, and society. Such a worldview had brought the United States into ever-increasing conflicts with peoples who wanted to reorder their lives in different fashions. By pursuing freedom through imperialism, moreover, Americans had vitiated their own values and ideals.

"Brilliant but perverse" typified a "favorable" review of *Tragedy*. Many historians tried to ignore it, and some even forbade their students to read it, but the disturbance rustled through the profession. Arthur M. Schlesinger, Jr., an archetypal liberal "consensus" historian, who always defended the U.S. record in the Cold War, privately told historical association officials that Williams was "pro-Communist." Former New Dealer Adolphe Berle, however, admired how the book undermined the "containment" theses, and sought to tempt Williams to work under Kennedy on Latin American affairs. Ironically, he would have joined Schlesinger, who, only a few years later, found himself deliberately deceiving Congress over the U.S. role in the Bay of Pigs invasion. Williams wisely decided not to trust the Kennedys. Instead, he produced *The United States, Cuba, and Castro* (1962), showing how, when New Deal–style corporatism collided with Third World revolutionary socialism, the world had come to the brink of nuclear catastrophe.

Tragedy had nevertheless so upset Washington policymakers that the House Committee on Un-American Activities tried to subpoena Williams's next manuscript, *The Contours of American History*. Williams did not have the legal funds to fight the case, but refused to surrender the manuscript (seizing it would have required a Supreme Court order). Although the IRS harassed him for several years, Williams at least kept his job, thanks to Wisconsin's free-thought tradition and President Harrington's staunch support.

Contours secured William's reputation as a major scholar of the entire spectrum of the American experience. Unlike *Tragedy*, which had in many ways expanded on lines already set out by Beard and Frederick Jackson Turner's "Frontier Thesis," *Contours* (1961) was an original, far-ranging interpretation of how certain leading weltanschauungen or worldviews (mercantilist, *laissez-nous-faire,* and corporatist) had informed and distorted the national experience. Williams conducted an especially scintillating critique of how the Founding Fathers (especially Jefferson) had hedged fragile democracy with expansionism, and how the framework of a commonwealth had broken down into dog-eat-dog individualism under Jackson Democracy (thus turning on its head Schle-

singer's sentimentalization of that furiously expansionist period). Ironically, Williams admired certain enlightened conservatives, such as Herbert
Hoover (traditionally anathema to the left), who had seen through to the
roots of the American dilemma, more than such corporatist liberals as
Woodrow Wilson or Franklin Delano Roosevelt, who had assiduously
avoided coming to grips with it. Even though Harvard's Oscar Handlin
dismissed the book as "an elaborate hoax," *Contours* caught on heavily
with younger scholars, including many outside the field of history.

Despite his inveterate Americocentrism, and deliberately distancing
himself from much of the Old Left, Williams, in Madison, maintained
a lively interest in Marx, sharing it particularly with such colleagues as
Goldberg and George Mosse (both Europeanists), and the sociologist
Hans Gerth (formerly of the Frankfurt School). The result was his 1963
volume *The Great Evasion: An Essay on the Contemporary Relevance
of Karl Marx and on the Wisdom of Admitting the Heretic into the Dialogue
about America's Future*. As Marx himself might have predicted, American
expansionism had neither avoided social conflict nor alleviated economic
misery.

Williams was increasingly at odds with the New Left, for its failure
to read Marx or to engage in dialogue with the general public. Although
he had participated in a number of "teach-ins" about the Vietnam War
and was viewed as a "guru" by many radical students, Williams felt the
New Left was too inclined toward campus confrontations and youth culture. Partly for this reason (and because of the overwhelming work in
directing graduate studies), he abandoned Madison for Oregon State University in 1968 to live by the ocean in a diversified community of "ordinary" Americans.

Here he produced his last major work based on extensive archival
research, *The Roots of the Modern American Empire* (1969), which argued
that agrarian interests were keener to seek international markets and colonial possessions at the end of the nineteenth century than East Coast
industrialists or bankers. Paradoxically, while traditional historians
praised him for his scholarship, partisans of the Populists were outraged.
Williams also irritated radical historians by having demonstrated a certain
"consensus" in American social history, though, unlike such liberal historians as Schlesinger, he did not find that consensus benevolent.

From his Oregon outpost, Williams remained as prolific as ever. *Some
Presidents: Wilson to Nixon* (1972), revealed his wry sardonic wit at
its best. *America Confronts a Revolutionary World, 1776–1976* (1976),
written for the bicentennial, argued that the United States had subverted
its original commitment to self-determination to become a counterrevolutionary power. *Americans in a Changing World* (1978), ostensibly a

"textbook," was actually a series of original and incisive essays on a number of social and political topics, including African Americans and women, that he had previously slighted. *Empire as a Way of Life: An Essay on the Causes and Character of America's Present Predicament Along with a Few Thoughts about an Alternative* (1980) called upon Americans to confront their past, limit and improve the empire, or dismantle it and create genuine communities. Finally, *America in Vietnam* (1985), coedited with McCormick, LaFeber, and Gardner, was a superb collection of essays and documents, primarily for college courses. By the late 1980s, however, Williams, worn out by all the battles fought, was in increasingly poor health. He died of cancer in 1990.

When William Appleman Williams had begun writing, the historical profession had been dominated by liberal "consensus" historians who dismissed conflict in American history, considered diplomatic history essentially "an exchange of notes among clerks," and held an idealistic view of America's role in world affairs. Williams greatly disturbed such people. The social conflicts of the sixties and the trauma of the Vietnam War, moreover, made him immensely popular with a younger generation of students and scholars. By 1980, he, and the "revisionist" historians he had inspired, had so thoroughly transformed the study of American foreign relations that the Organization of American Historians elected him its president, a signal triumph over the Cold War liberals.

Today, although "pure revisionism" has passed, most mainstream diplomatic historians, usually calling themselves "postrevisionists," now accept Williams's principal premises: that America *is* an empire, the United States *did* bear a heavy responsibility for the Cold War, and economic factors *are* important, even if these historians tend to bury such considerations amid a myriad of other issues. Other scholars, sometimes labeled "neorevisionists," have built more directly on Williams. Some stress "corporatism" to explain the commitment of liberals to business and warfare. Others examine "world-systems" to provide a transnational view of world imperialism. Whatever they call themselves, or however they may deny it, the work of a large number of American historians testifies, at least implicitly, to Williams's seminal and pervasive influence. It seems that, as long as the empire continues, so will the basic insights of William Appleman Williams.

Suggested Readings

Henry W. Berger, ed., *A William Appleman Williams Reader*. Chicago: Ivan Dee, 1992.

Paul Buhle and Edward Rice-Maximin, *Learning from History: William Appleman Williams and the Challenge of Empire*. Minneapolis: University of Minnesota Press, 1995.

Peter Novick, *That Noble Dream: The "Objectivity Question" and the American Historical Profession*. New York: Cambridge University Press, 1988.

William G. Robbins, "William Appleman Williams: Doing History Is Best of All. No Regrets," in Lloyd C. Gardner, ed., *Redefining the Past: Essays in Diplomatic History in Honor of William Appleman Williams*. Corvallis: Oregon State University Press, 1986.

Mike Wallace, "Interview with William Appleman Williams," in MARHO: Radical Historians Organization ed., *Visions of History*. New York: Pantheon, 1983.

4I

RACHEL CARSON

Vera Norwood

Most Americans know Rachel Carson as the author of *Silent Spring,* the 1962 book which became a rallying point for the environmental movements of the 1960s and '70s. *Silent Spring* posed a radical critique of the country's dependence on chemical pesticides. The book issued a militant call to laypeople to question the power scientific and industrial groups held in the application of these environmentally hazardous chemicals to agricultural land, suburban green spaces, national parks, and forest preserves. But Rachel Carson, the woman who raised national concerns about such issues, has not been portrayed as a radical.

Why would the book seem more radical than its author? A radical often is perceived as someone whose revolutionary actions place her on the boundaries of her culture. A radical violates social conventions. Initially, her voice may reach a small audience of like-minded individuals; she might publish in alternative newspapers and small presses. Even if she achieves a national reputation in mass culture, as Carson did with *Silent Spring,* she still conveys a message at odds with key aspects of that culture.

Rachel Carson does not appear to be a revolutionary individual largely because her personal militancy was masked at the moment *Silent Spring*

was published by a gendered smear campaign waged by chemical companies and some men in the scientific establishment. These forces sought
to discredit her book by casting its author as marginal in a more pedestrian
sense than that implied by the social rebel. The scientific and industrial
establishment imaged Carson as a middle-class female bound by the
stereotypical roles assigned women in the late 1950s, with no credentials
and no right to engage in the public arena debates *Silent Spring* engendered.

For example, in 1962, John Leonard, science editor for *Time* magazine,
wrote a scathing review of *Silent Spring,* accusing its author of being
"hysterically overemphatic." In his 1963 critique of the book for the
Archives of Internal Medicine, Dr. William B. Bean appealed to his
professional audience's domestic experience to justify his contempt for
Carson's work: "*Silent Spring,* which I read word for word with some
trauma, kept reminding me of trying to win an argument with a woman.
It cannot be done." Such comments called on stereotypical images of
women as more emotional than men to discredit Carson and, by extension,
her book.

Attempts to counter Carson's work by casting aspersions on her gender
were based on a key narrative of the period: women could involve themselves in public life only under the condition that they did so with deference
to the male professional and governing establishment. Women's identification with the private spheres of home and family seemed to buttress
such bounding of their public life. Home was cast as a female-organized
space representing emotional intimacy, and as a conservative place separate from and protected by the rapidly developing scientific and industrial
world of post–World War II America. A woman responsible for the home
appeared unable to mount revolutionary critiques of public arenas.

Ironically, Carson's training as a female and her own experience as a
family member in fact positioned her to attack the powerful interests of
the burgeoning pesticide industry. With the publication of *Silent Spring,*
Carson brought values learned from her mother and identified as women's
particular concern to bear on what she saw as troubling trends in environmental policy-making. Her application of an ethic derived from female
culture to critique the public arenas controlled by a professional male
establishment posed a radical assault on mainstream culture. Carson also
encouraged and acted in concert with other women as they militantly
used citizen forums and the legal process to halt the use of pesticides.

From her earliest years, Rachel Carson was poised for conflict with
many values identified with the rising professional class of scientifically
trained resource managers and agricultural agents who tended to view
nature as a commodity. Born on May 27, 1907, she grew up just outside

Springdale, Pennsylvania. Like many middle-class, educated women of her day, her mother, Maria Carson, viewed nature study as central to her domestic responsibility to educate her children. Maria and Rachel toured the family grounds and the neighborhood learning local birds and plants. Rachel never married and, by the time she was thirty, had become the sole support of her mother and two orphaned nieces. The family lived in Carson's homes in Maryland and Maine, continuing their nature walks in local neighborhoods and green spaces. Rachel Carson credited her mother with giving her an intellectual interest in nature and with instilling in her respect and concern for all forms of life on earth.

Throughout her life, then, many of Carson's most intense experiences of nature were connected to home. In college she pursued courses in English (to fulfill her passion to write) and biology (to fulfill her interest in nature). In 1932 she received an M.A. in Zoology from Johns Hopkins University. Her studies introduced her to the new science of ecology whose practitioners imaged the earth as an interconnected household. The idea that all of nature could be seen as a web of interdependent relationships like those existing in any family perfectly matched her feeling for nature as an integral part of her home life and domestic round.

Although she worked in the 1930s and '40s as a writer and editor for the U.S. Fish and Wildlife Service, by the 1950s she had found personal fulfillment (and national and international fame) in her enormously popular books depicting plants and animals living in their own homeplaces along the coasts and in the oceans. *Under the Sea-Wind* (1941), *The Sea around Us* (1951), and *The Edge of the Sea* (1955) taught Americans to approach nature with "a sense of wonder" and to respect the integrity of the web of life. While earning Carson widespread fame in a public arena, these books also recapitulated the role her mother had played in teaching Rachel and her siblings about the natural world. Carson's reputation at the time was that of a woman who had found a gender-appropriate career niche in her "sensitive" nature studies.

Carson's fame established her as a spokesperson for nature, but her implicit critique of attempts by the scientific-industrial complex to manipulate and control nature was not widely recognized. Further, few understood that in making a popular connection between middle-class 1950s domesticity and the natural web of life ecologists dubbed earth's household, Carson had given her female audience a powerful argument for taking their concerns for the safety of their own homes, and their expansive feeling of responsibility for the homes of other animals, into public arenas controlled by professional men.

Rachel Carson had been alarmed at the environmental dangers posed by pesticides like DDT as early as 1945, but had focused her own attempt to preserve the birds and wildflowers of America in her evocative descriptions of nature's beauties. Her decision to take a more radical approach to protecting nature was engendered in 1958 by a letter from her friend Olga Owens Huckins who was in despair over an aerial pesticide spraying campaign that destroyed the birds in the small wildlife sanctuary she had created in her suburban yard. Huckins asked Carson for ideas about how to stop the spraying of DDT. Spurred on by this letter, and by similar concerns among many of her correspondents, Carson began to work on *Silent Spring*.

Carson addressed *Silent Spring* to the ordinary citizen. She aimed to educate laypeople about the destructive effects of chemical pesticides and to pinpoint those human agents responsible for disseminating these environmental hazards. Carson posed two radical critiques of basic ideologies of the time. First, interconnections between human homes and nature as home, so celebrated in the household metaphors of Carson's earlier books, took on new urgency as the unity of all life became a nightmare in *Silent Spring*. Dangerous chemical pesticides—chlorinated hydrocarbons like DDT and organic phosphates like malathion—now pervaded the environment: "They have been found in fish in remote lakes, in earthworms burrowing in the soil, in the egg of birds—and in man himself. For these chemicals are now stored in the bodies of the vast majority of human beings, regardless of age. They occur in the mother's milk, and probably in the tissues of the unborn child." As Carson described the webs of contamination resulting from reliance on chemicals, home offered no haven from the world.

Second, *Silent Spring* documents how, rather than protecting home as a sanctuary from such devastation, scientists developed the instruments of death which industry and government then applied. Entomologists narrowly focused their research on helping create chemicals destined for futile eradication campaigns against single insect species. Government agents sprayed chemical pesticides over flower beds and bird baths and failed to adequately regulate residues in heads of lettuce and gallons of milk. Agencies mounted pest eradication campaigns that invaded the private spaces of home, killing domestic pets and wildlife, harming children, and poisoning gardens. Advertisements prompted individual consumers to buy chemicals for waging similar battles against their crabgrass and household crickets. In imagery encouraging families to view such products as harmless, industry took little responsibility for the user's safety.

In framing her critique, Carson publicly questioned the methods and goals of a powerful elite composed mostly of professional men. She attacked the predominant ideology that cast home as a space separate from the public decision-making arenas of science, government, and industry. By focusing on the threats to suburban homes pesticides like DDT posed, she made a specific call to women to step into the public arena and take their rights as citizens with a voice in decision-making processes seriously. Each of these assertions launched a radical assault on mainstream values in American culture of the time.

Carson was not an eccentric lady birdwatcher who stumbled unknowingly into public terrain in which she had no place. Rather, she was a widely known, influential writer who used fame and her connections to stimulate the changes she called for in *Silent Spring*. In fact, well before she began writing *Silent Spring*, Carson used her prestige to encourage women into active participation in public decisions about the future of the earth. During the 1950s, national women's clubs and organizations like the American Association of University Women and the National Council of Women gave her awards for her sea books and invited her to speak at their meetings. In an April 21, 1954 talk before the national gathering of Theta Sigma Phi, the women journalists' fraternity, Carson encouraged these influential press women—whose roles as "housewives and mothers" she felt gave them extra cause for concern—to turn their attention to the environmental dangers posed by our "perilously artificial world."

After *Silent Spring* appeared, Carson collaborated with a widespread network of women to rouse citizen outrage at the reliance on chemical pesticides. Her friends and colleagues in various women's clubs and organizations worked to get *Silent Spring*'s findings placed on political action agendas. Carson also enjoyed an excellent network among professional women in publishing. People like Agnes Meyer, owner of the *Washington Post*, made sure that Carson received a forum in their newspapers. As she researched *Silent Spring*, Carson developed correspondents among local women in Audubon clubs and garden societies who were concerned about the impact of pesticides on birds and wildflowers. Carson and such women advised each other on lawsuits against local pesticide spraying campaigns and shared strategies for countering agricultural extension agents touting new chemicals.

Carson and many of her colleagues were aware that they most often confronted forms of masculine institutional power. One of the most radical aspects of Carson's environmental warning was that it threatened to disrupt the social contract that placed women at home and men at the helm. A representative example of the problem surfaced in 1963 when the Virginia Deptartment of Agriculture planned an aerial spray campaign in the Norfolk area to destroy the white-fringed beetle. A contingent of fifteen women and one man, representing local garden clubs, appeared before the all-male officers of the city council to protest the planned spraying. During the meeting, passages of *Silent Spring* were read aloud. National and local newspapers made note of women's key role in the public outcry. In a January 16, 1963, letter to the editor of the *Virginia Pilot,*, one woman laid out the nature of the conflict when she argued that government agents had cast themselves in "father knows best" roles: " 'Papa' does not always know best. In this instance it seems that 'papa' is taking an arbitrary stand, and we, the people are just supposed to take it, and count the dead animals and birds." Such public awareness of the gendered nature of the conflict suggests that John Leonard's characterization of Rachel Carson as "hysterical" in his *Time* magazine review was a conscious attempt to drive the rising tide of militant female environmentalists back inside their homes.

Rachel Carson died on April 14, 1964, but not before she had seen her concerns validated by President John F. Kennedy's Science Advisory Committee and by a Senate committee on environmental hazards. Carson and her colleagues helped push the country into an era of environmental protection heralded by bans and strict controls on chemical pesticides, increased funding for biological forms of insect control, legislation aimed at improving air and water quality, and the establishment of the Environmental Protection Agency. Following on the 1960s middle-class, suburban outrage at the pollution of their homes, other disenfranchised citizens have stepped in to question the toxic environments created by government and industry. In 1978, Lois Gibbs, a high school–educated housewife living at Love Canal in Niagara Falls, New York, took on the scientific community to prove that her family and neighbors were suffering from health problems caused by a nearby hazardous waste dump. Gibbs is one among a network of women nationwide, many living in poor or minority communities most at risk from toxic wastes, who are taking political action to force cleanup of poisoned homes and neighborhoods.

In 1962 Rachel Carson challenged women to confront the fact that their homes and neighborhoods were threatened by a professional elite whose methods showed little consideration for the safety of their children or the protection of plants and animals they held dear. *Silent Spring,* the vehicle she used to alert her generation to threats facing the environment remains the most visible expression of her own alienated stance from many mainstream values of her society. Behind the book, however, lived a radical woman who devoted her life to challenging her country's environmental decision makers and who helped other women find the strength to make their own militant cases against policies and products that continue to threaten the earth—the only home humans will ever inhabit.

Suggested Readings

Paul Brooks, *The House of Life: Rachel Carson at Work*. Boston: Houghton Mifflin, 1972.

Rachel Carson, *Silent Spring*. Boston: Houghton Mifflin, 1962.

Thomas Dunlap, *DDT: Scientists, Citizens, and Public Policy*. Princeton, N.J.: Princeton University Press, 1981.

Vera Norwood, *Made from This Earth: American Women and Nature*. Chapel Hill: University of North Carolina Press, 1993.

42

MALCOLM X

Michael Eric Dyson

Malcolm X, one of the most complex and enigmatic African-American leaders ever, was born Malcolm Little on May 19, 1925, in Omaha, Nebraska. Since his death in 1965, Malcolm's life has increasingly acquired mythic stature. Along with Martin Luther King, Jr., Malcolm is a member of the pantheon of twentieth-century black saints. Unlike King, however, Malcolm's heroic rise was both aided and complicated by his championing of black nationalism and his advocacy of black self-defense against white racist violence.

Malcolm's ideas of black nationalism were shaped virtually from the womb by the example of his parents, Earl and Louise Little, both members of Marcus Garvey's United Negro Improvement Association (UNIA). As president of the Omaha branch of the UNIA, Earl Little, who was also an itinerant Baptist preacher, vigorously proclaimed the Garveyite doctrine of racial self-help and black unity, often with Malcolm at his side. Louise Little served as reporter of the Omaha UNIA. A native of Grenada, Louise was a deeply spiritual woman who presided over her brood of eight children even as she endured the abuse of her husband, and together they heaped domestic violence on their children.

According to X, his family was driven from Omaha by the Ku Klux

Klan while he was still an infant, forcing them to seek safer habitation in Lansing, the capital city of Michigan eighty miles northwest of Detroit. Their respite was only temporary, however, as the Little family house was burned down by a white hate group, the Black Legionnaires, during Malcolm's early childhood in 1929. This experience of racial violence, which Malcolm termed his "earliest vivid memory," deeply influenced his unsparing denunciation of white racism during his public career as a black nationalist leader.

When he was only six, Malcolm's father died after he was crushed under a streetcar. It is unclear whether Earl died at the hands of Black Legionnaires, as Malcolm reports in his autobiography, or, as recent scholarship has suggested, whether his death was accidental. In either case, his loss bore fateful consequences for the Little family, as Louise Little was faced with raising eight children alone during the depression. She eventually suffered a mental breakdown, and her children were dispersed to several foster homes.

Malcolm's life after his family's breakup went from bleak to desperate, as he was shuttled between several foster homes. Malcolm stole food to survive and began developing hustling habits that he later perfected in Boston, where he went to live with his half sister Ella after dropping out of school in Lansing upon completing the eighth grade. Before leaving school, Malcolm had become seventh-grade class president at Mason Junior High School. But a devastating rebuff from a teacher—who discouraged Malcolm in his desire to become an attorney by claiming that it was an unrealistic goal for "niggers"—finally sealed Malcolm's early fate as an academic failure.

It was in Boston that Malcolm encountered for the first time the black bourgeoisie with its social pretensions and exaggerated rituals of cultural self-affirmation, leading him to conclude later that the black middle class was largely ineffective in achieving authentic black liberation. It was also in Boston's Roxbury and New York's Harlem that Malcolm was introduced to the street life of the Northern urban poor and working class, gaining crucial insight about the cultural styles, social sufferings, and personal aspirations of everyday black people. Malcolm's hustling repertoire ranged from drug dealing and numbers running to burglary, the latter activity landing him in a penitentiary for a six to ten-year sentence. Malcolm's prison period—lasting from 1946 to 1952—marked the first of several extraordinary transformations he underwent as he searched for the truth about himself and his relation to black consciousness, black freedom and unity, and black religion.

While in prison, Malcolm read widely and argued passionately about a broad scope of subjects, from biblical theology to Western philosophy, voraciously absorbing the work of authors as diverse as Louis S. B. Leakey and Friedrich Nietzsche. Malcolm read so much during this period that his eyesight became strained, and he began wearing his trademark glasses. It was during his prison stay that Malcolm experienced his first religious conversion, slowly evolving from a slick street hustler and con artist to a sophisticated self-taught devotee of Elijah Muhammad and the Nation of Islam, the black nationalist religious group that Muhammad headed. X was drawn to the Nation of Islam because of the character of its black-nationalist practices and beliefs: its peculiar gift for rehabilitating black male prisoners; its strong emphasis on black pride, history, culture, and unity; and its unblinking assertion that white men were devils, a belief that led Muhammad and his followers to advocate black separation from white society.

Within a year of his release from prison on parole in 1952, Malcolm became a minister with the Nation of Islam, journeying to its Chicago headquarters to meet face to face with the man whose theological doctrines of white evil and black racial superiority had given Malcolm new life. Through a herculean work ethic and spartan self-discipline—key features of the black puritanism that characterized the Nation's moral orientation— Malcolm worked his way in short order from assistant minister of Detroit's Temple Number One to national spokesman for Elijah Muhammad and the Nation of Islam. In his role as the mouthpiece of the Nation of Islam, Malcolm brought unprecedented visibility to a religious group that many critics had either ignored or dismissed as fundamentalist fringe fanatics. Under X's leadership, the Nation grew from several hundred to 10,000 members by the early 1960s. The Nation under Malcolm also produced forty temples throughout America and purchased thirty radio stations.

During the late 1950s and early '60s, enormous changes were rapidly occurring within American society in regard to race. The momentous *Brown v. Board of Education* Supreme Court decision, delivered in 1954, struck down the "separate but equal" law that had enforced racially segregated public education since 1896. And in 1955, the historic bus boycott in Montgomery, Alabama—sparked by seamstress Rosa Parks's refusal to surrender her seat to a white passenger as mandated by a legally sanctioned segregated public transportation system—brought its leader, Martin Luther King, Jr., to national prominence. King's fusion of black Christian civic piety and traditions of American public morality and strong democracy unleashed an irresistible force on American politics that fundamentally altered the social conditions of millions of blacks, especially the black middle classes in the South.

On the other hand, the civil rights movement barely affected the circumstances of poor Southern rural blacks. Neither did it greatly enhance the plight of poor Northern urban blacks whose economic status and social standing were severely handicapped by forces of deindustrialization, the rise of automated technology that displaced human wage earners, the severe decline in manufacturing and in retail and wholesale trade, and escalating patterns of black unemployment. These social and economic trends, coupled with the growing spiritual despair that, beginning in the early 1950s gripped Rust Belt cities like New York, Chicago, Philadelphia, Detroit, Cleveland, Indianapolis, and Baltimore, did not initially occupy the social agenda of the Southern-based civil rights movement.

Malcolm's ministry, however, as was true of the Nation of Islam in general, was directed toward the socially dispossessed, the morally compromised, and economically desperate members of the black proletariat and ghetto poor who were unaided by the civil rights movement. The Nation of Islam recruited many of its members among the prison populations largely forgotten by traditional Christianity (black and white). The Nation also proselytized among the hustlers, drug dealers, pimps, prostitutes, and thieves whose lives, they believed, were ethically impoverished by the forces of white racist neglect of their most fundamental needs: the need for self-respect, the need for social dignity, the need to understand their royal black history, and the need to worship and serve a black God. All of these were provided in the black-nationalist worldview of the Nation of Islam.

Malcolm's public ministry of proselytizing for the Nation of Islam depended heavily upon drawing contrasts between what he and other Nation members viewed as the corruption of black culture by white Christianity (best symbolized in Martin Luther King, Jr., and segments of the civil rights movement), and the redemptive messages of racial salvation proffered by Elijah Muhammad. Malcolm relentlessly preached the virtues of black self-determination and self-defense even as he denounced the brainwashing of black people by Christian preachers like King who espoused passive strategies of resistance in the face of white racist violence.

Where King advocated redemptive suffering for blacks through their own bloodshed, Malcolm promulgated "reciprocal bleeding" for blacks and whites. As King preached the virtues of Christian love, Malcolm articulated black anger with unmitigated passion. While King urged nonviolent civil disobedience, Malcolm promoted the liberation of blacks by whatever means were necessary, including (though not exclusively, as some have argued) the possibility of armed self-defense. While King dreamed, Malcolm saw nightmares.

It was Malcolm's unique ability to narrate the prospects of black resistance at the edge of racial apocalypse that made him both exciting and threatening. Malcolm spoke out loud what many blacks secretly felt about racist white people and practices, but were afraid to publicly acknowledge. Malcolm boldly specified in lucid rhetoric the hurts, agonies, and frustrations of black people chafing from an enforced racial silence about the considerable cultural costs of white racism.

Unfortunately, as was the case with most of his black-nationalist compatriots and civil rights advocates, Malcolm cast black liberation in terms of masculine self-realization. Malcolm's zealous trumpeting of the social costs of black male cultural emasculation went hand in hand with his often aggressive, occasionally vicious put-downs of black women. It is this aspect, especially, of Malcolm's public ministry that has been adopted by contemporary black juvenile culture, as well as by its cultural creators, notably rappers and filmmakers. Though X near the end of his life would renounce his sometimes vitriolic denunciations of black women, his contemporary followers have not often followed suit.

But as the civil rights movement expanded its influence, Malcolm and the Nation came under increasing criticism for the latter's deeply apolitical stance. Officially, the Nation of Islam was forbidden by Elijah Muhammad to become involved in acts of civil disobedience or social protest, ironically containing the forces of anger and rage that Malcolm's fiery rhetoric helped unleash. This ideological constraint stifled Malcolm's natural inclination to action, and increasingly caused him great discomfort as he sought to explain publicly the glaring disparity between the Nation's aggressive rhetoric and its refusal to become politically engaged.

Malcolm's growing dissatisfaction with the Nation's apolitical posture only deepened his suspicions about its leadership role in aiding blacks to achieve real liberation. Malcolm was also aware of the internal corruption of the Nation—unprincipled financial practices among top officials reaping personal benefit at the expense of the rank and file and extramarital affairs involving leader Elijah Muhammad. Moreover, there is evidence that Malcolm had privately forsaken his belief in the whites-are-devils doctrine years before his widely discussed public rejection of the doctrine after his 1964 split from the Nation of Islam, his embrace of orthodox Islamic belief, and his religious pilgrimage to Mecca.

The official cause of Malcolm's departure from the Nation of Islam was Elijah Muhammad's public reprimand of Malcolm for his famous comment that President John F. Kennedy's assassination merely represented the "chickens coming home to roost." Malcolm was saying that the violence America had committed in other parts of the world was returning to haunt this nation. Muhammad quickly forbade Malcolm from speaking publicly, initially for ninety days, motivated as much by jealousy of Malcolm's enormous popularity among blacks beyond the Nation of

Islam as by his desire to punish Malcolm for a comment that would bring the Nation undesired negative attention from an already racially paranoid government.

In March of 1964, Malcolm left the Nation of Islam after it became apparent that he could not mend his relationship with his estranged mentor. He formed two organizations, one religious (Muslim Mosque, Inc.) and the other political (Organization of Afro-American Unity, or OAAU). The OAAU was modeled after the Organization of African Unity, and reflected Malcolm's belief that broad social engagement provided blacks their best chance for ending racism. Before establishing the OAAU, however, Malcolm fulfilled a long-standing dream of journeying to the Muslim holy city, making a hajj to Mecca. While there, Malcolm wrote a series of letters to his followers detailing his stunning change of heart about race relations, declaring that his humane treatment by white Muslims, and his perception of the universality of Islamic religious truth, had forced him to reject his former narrow beliefs about whites. Malcolm's change of heart did not blind him, though, to the persistence of American racism and the need to oppose its broad variety of expressions with aggressive social resistance.

After his departure from the Nation of Islam, Malcolm traveled extensively, making trips to the Middle East and Africa among other places. Malcolm's travels broadened his political perspective considerably, a fact reflected in his new appreciation of socialist movements (though he didn't embrace socialism) and a new international note in his public discourse as he emphasized the link between Afro-American liberation and movements for freedom throughout the world, especially in African nations. Malcolm didn't live long enough to fulfill the promise of his new directions. On February 21, 1965, two months shy of his fortieth birthday, Malcolm X was gunned down by Nation of Islam loyalists as he prepared to speak to a meeting of the OAAU. Fortunately, Malcolm had recently completed his autobiography with the help of Alex Haley. That work, *The Autobiography of Malcolm X,* stands as a classic of black letters and American autobiography.

Malcolm only lived fifty weeks after his break with the Nation of Islam, initiating his last and perhaps most meaningful transformation of all: from revolutionary black nationalist to human rights advocate. While Malcolm never gave up on black unity or self-determination—and neither did he surrender his acerbic wit on behalf of the voiceless millions of poor blacks who could never speak their pain before the world—he did expand his field of vision to include poor, dispossessed people of color from around the world, people whose plight resulted from class inequality and economic oppression as much as from racial domination. Had he lived, we can only hope that vexing contemporary problems from sex to gender might have exercised his considerable skill at giving voice to fears and resentments that most people can only speak in private.

During the last year of his life, Malcolm's social criticism and political engagement reflected a will to spontaneity, while his analysis was an improvisatory and fluid affair that drew from his rapidly evolving quest for the best means available for real black liberation, but a black liberation connected to the realization of human rights for all suffering peoples. In the end, Malcolm's moral pragmatism and experimental social criticism linked him more nearly to the heart of African-American culture and American radical practices than it might have otherwise appeared during his controversial career. Malcolm's complexity resists neat categories of analysis and rigid conclusions about his meaning.

It is this Malcolm—the Malcolm who spoke with uncompromising ardor about the poor, black, and dispossessed, and who named racism when and where he found it—that appealed to me as a young black male coming to maturity during the 1960s and '70s in the ghetto of Detroit. I took pleasure in his early moniker "Detroit Red," feeling that our common geography joined us in a project to reclaim the dignity of black identity from the chaotic dissemblances and self-deceptions induced by racist oppression. As I have matured, journeying from factory worker to Ivy League professor, it is the Malcolm who valued truth over habit who has appealed most to me, his ability to be self-critical and to change his direction, an unfailing sign of integrity and courage. But these two Malcolms need not be in ultimate, fatal conflict, need not be fractured by the choice between seeking an empowering racial identity and linking ourselves to the truth no matter what it looks like, regardless of color, class, gender, sex, or age. They are both legitimate quests, and Malcolm's career and memory is an enabling agent for both pursuits. His complexity is our gift.

Suggested Readings

Peter Goldman, *The Death of Malcolm X:* Urbana: University of Illinois Press, 1979.

James H. Cone, *Martin & Malcolm & America: A Dream or a Nightmare*. Maryknoll, N.Y.: Orbis Books, 1991.

Eugene Victor Wolfenstein, *The Victims of Democracy: Malcolm X and the Black Revolution*. London: Free Association Books, 1989.

Malcolm X and Alex Haley, *The Autobiography of Malcolm X*. New York: Grove Press, 1964.

43

MARTIN LUTHER KING, JR.

James H. Cone

No one made a greater impact upon the struggle for racial justice in America than Martin Luther King, Jr. Before King, America was a contented segregated society—de jure in the South and de facto in the North. The idea of racial equality and freedom was a marginal issue in American life, seldom mentioned by government officials and other public figures, and largely confined to the legal work of the NAACP and the academic writings of a few scholars. Martin King changed all that. Through his civil rights activity, public speeches, and writings, he placed the problem of race at the center of American life and forced this nation to acknowledge racism as its greatest moral dilemma.

Martin Luther King, Jr., was born into a prominent middle-class family in Atlanta, Georgia, January 15, 1929. His father, Martin Luther King, Sr., was the pastor of Ebenezer Baptist Church and also active in the NAACP. At home and at church, "M.L.," as the younger Martin was called during childhood, acquired ethical and religious values that influenced him to become a minister and to devote his life to the struggle for justice.

After Martin King's graduation from Morehouse College, he went to Crozer Theological Seminary (Chester, Pennsylvania) and later to Boston

University where he received a Ph.D. degree in systematic theology. King's education played an important role in shaping his views about race and justice in the United States. At Morehouse, the problem of racial injustice in the social, economic, and political life of America was frequently discussed in his classes. He was a sociology major. Benjamin E. Mays (Morehouse's president) and George Kelsey (a professor of religion) showed King that the ministry could be socially relevant and intellectually respectable.

At Crozer and Boston University King was introduced to theological and philosophical ideas about God, social justice, and the worth of human personality that reinforced what he had learned from his parents and heard in the sermons, prayers, and songs of black churches. With an intellectual foundation for his religious convictions, King began his pastoral ministry at Dexter Avenue Baptist Church in Montgomery, Alabama, in September 1954—about three months after the celebrated Supreme Court decision outlawing segregation in public schools.

Martin King did not go to Montgomery with the intention of starting a national civil rights movement. His social consciousness was defined primarily by the NAACP, an organization he greatly admired, and he influenced Dexter to become its largest contributor in Montgomery. He was also active in human relations organizations that brought a few black and white middle-class professionals together to talk about how to improve race relations. There was nothing in King's graduate school essays or his sermons at Dexter and other black churches that suggested that he was interested in organizing a mass movement or that he would become America's most influential radical in the African-American struggle for racial justice.

Martin King was a reluctant radical. He did not start the Montgomery bus boycott that made him into an internationally known leader. The boycott was started by a group of professional black women (Women's Political Council) when they decided that the arrest of Rosa Parks (December 1, 1955), for defiance of the bus-seating law, should not go unchallenged. They organized a protest and asked King and other ministers in the city to join them. Initially, King was reluctant to become involved and asked for time to think about it. The preparations for a full-scale boycott of the city buses moved so fast that King was surprised when he was chosen as the leader. He did not decline the choice (as he had done earlier when asked to be the president of the NAACP) because he believed that the *call* came from God who was acting through the people, empowering them to protest.

With only twenty minutes to prepare the most important speech of his life, King stood before an overflowing crowd of five-thousand blacks and told them that "we are not wrong in what we are doing." Both the God of the Bible and the Constitution of the United States gave people "the right to protest for right." Through an appeal to the biblical idea of justice and the American democratic tradition of freedom, King urged the masses of blacks to "stick together" and have "the moral courage to stand up for their rights." They did. For 381 days fifty thousand blacks, under King's courageous leadership, "walked the streets of Montgomery with dignity rather than ride the buses in humiliation." They "substituted tired feet for tired souls" and thereby created a "New Negro," one who was ready to die for freedom.

The Montgomery bus boycott initiated the involvement of the masses in the struggle for racial justice. It was followed by the sit-ins (1960), the freedom rides (1961), and many other organized demonstrations for freedom throughout the South. The social disruption that the civil rights movement created forced the great majority of white people to reevaluate the meaning of America for its citizens of African descent. Although there were many courageous and intelligent activists in the civil rights movement, Martin King was its most influential leader and philosopher.

Martin King developed a philosophy and a method of social change (nonviolent direct action) that was effective in destroying legal segregation and blatant klanlike activity throughout the South. It also transformed the social and political relations of blacks and whites throughout the nation. Infusing Mahatma Gandhi's method of nonviolence with the spirituality of the black churches, King, in his sermons and writings, urged blacks to nonviolently disobey laws that transgressed their dignity as human beings. He challenged whites to join blacks in the struggle for justice, because we are all "caught in an inescapable network of mutuality, tied in a single garment of destiny." King challenged politicians to recognize that America cannot claim to be the leader of the free world and also remain a segregated nation. "If democracy is to live," he said, "segregation must die."

After the Montgomery bus boycott, King's most successful campaigns were the Birmingham demonstrations (1963) and the Selma March (1965). Both events created so much social disruption that the leaders of the federal government were pressured into enacting the Civil Rights Act (1964) and Voting Rights Bill (1965). King's most memorable speech was his great "I Have a Dream" address at the March on Washington (August 28, 1963) where he electrified the nation with the hope that America could become a just society, an integrated community without racial animosity or religious prejudice. It was his greatest moment in the eyes of most who loved and adored him. *Time* magazine chose him as "Man of the Year" and called him " 'the unchallenged voice of the Negro people—and the disquieting conscience of the whites." King also received the Nobel Prize in 1964, thereby making him not just a black or an American leader but a world spokesperson for justice and peace.

However, the most radical phase of Martin King's work began after the Selma March. He thought initially that the widespread support for the voting rights of blacks meant that his work as a civil rights leader was almost over. But he was grossly mistaken. His most difficult battles for justice were still ahead of him. The Los Angeles riots (August 11, 1965), which happened only five days after President Johnson signed the Voting Rights Bill, revealed despair among blacks such as King had not seen in the South. When he took the movement to Chicago to fight against de facto segregation in housing, education, and employment, he soon realized that the racism which created economic exploitation in the Northern cities was much more entrenched and detrimental to the humanity of blacks than the racism that created legal segregation in the South. The liberal Northern whites in government, churches, and labor who supported the civil rights movement in the South often opposed it in the North. Getting rid of legal segregation did not cost America much. But to rid the nation of economic poverty would cost plenty—$100 billion was King's estimate.

With an escalating war in Vietnam, President Johnson and the Congress were not interested in paying the cost to eliminate domestic poverty. King knew, therefore, that his linking together war, poverty, and racism would not gain friends among whites and blacks in government, churches, the civil rights movement, and even among his own staff and board in the Southern Christian Leadership Conference. Many of his friends pleaded with him to stick with civil rights and to stop talking about the war, because the civil rights and peace movements were distinct and separate. But King vehemently disagreed, saying that the "two problems are inextricably bound together," because "you can't have peace without justice and justice without peace."

King's greatest hour as an antiwar activist was his "Beyond Vietnam" speech at Riverside Church in New York City, April 4, 1967. Before a capacity crowd, he called the war immoral and unjust and then proceeded to indict America as "the greatest purveyor of violence in the world today." He spoke as a "child of God and brother to the suffering people in Vietnam," whose land, home, and culture were being destroyed. "Somehow this madness must cease," he proclaimed. "We must stop now."

On April 15 King spoke at a United Nations rally to end the war and called America's involvement in Vietnam an attempt to "perpetuate white colonialism." He urged President Johnson to "stop the bombing" and "save American lives and Vietnamese lives." In almost every sermon and address, King called upon Americans to protest "one of history's most cruel and senseless wars."

President Johnson and his supporters were greatly troubled by King's decision to join the voices of protest against the Vietnam War in the peace movement. Once the most beloved of all civil rights activists, who could get audiences with the president and other government officials, King came to be regarded as an arrogant Negro preacher who spoke out on foreign policy issues in which he had no expertise whatsoever. Media editorials criticized him severely for making the "serious tactical mistake" of fusing the civil rights and peace movements. Prominent civil rights leaders disassociated themselves from him and ignored his demand that they "take a forthright stand on the rightness or wrongness of the war."

Martin King's spirituality sustained his radicalism in the midst of much controversy. He really believed that "all reality hinges on moral foundations." Hostile criticism did not persuade him to keep quiet or to soften his views about the war. His perspective was not defined by what was politically expedient or financially beneficial for SCLC. Rather, King's radicalism was defined by his faith, his deep conviction that "the universe was on the side of right." "When you stand up for justice," he said, "you never fail."

King's faith gave him hope, as friends rejected him and the government turned his dream of a just and peaceful world into a nightmare of violence. Instead of making him passive, King's belief in "cosmic companionship" empowered him for radical action. He moved toward a socialist path, condemning capitalism and advocating the need for a radical restructuring of the whole of American society.

During his later years, King became especially disappointed with liberal whites. He called them "unconscious racists," because their response to the riots in the cities showed that they were "more concerned about order than they were about justice." King began to move toward an acceptance of Black Power and even advocated "temporary segregation" as the only way to achieve genuine integration. Of course, King was no separatist in the sense advocated by Malcolm X. But since tokenism was the only kind of integration that whites were implementing, King became concerned that blacks would be integrated out of the little power that they had. He became so militant that a *New York Times* reporter told him that he sounded like a nonviolent Malcolm X.

Although King rejected any public association with Malcolm X, he realized that their views were converging and, through mutual friends, made private initiatives to meet with Malcolm. Malcolm was killed on February 21, 1965, the Sunday before the meeting they had scheduled for the following Tuesday.

Approximately three years after Malcolm's death and exactly one year after his "Beyond Vietnam" speech, Martin King was assassinated in Memphis, Tennessee, on April 4, 1968. At the time, he was organizing a march for sanitation workers on strike for better pay and job conditions. He was also preparing for the Poor People's Campaign in Washington, D.C. Both events highlighted his fight against racism and poverty. In King's second March to Washington, unlike the first in 1963, he did not have the support of the president and Congress. He was planning a militant civil disobedience that was designated to pressure Congress into enacting legislation that would guarantee employment or, for anyone unable to work, a decent income.

On January 20, 1986, eighteen years after his assassination, the Congress and President Reagan established King's birthday as a legal public holiday—making him the only American to hold such an honor. This honor is both an acknowledgment of King's great moral power and an attempt to co-opt his radicalism. Through his powerful oratory and militant, nonviolent civil rights activity, King inspired blacks and pricked the conscience of whites, and thereby enabled both, along with other Americans, to join together in a common struggle for justice. A coalition of conscience among people of all races and faiths came together under King's leadership and transformed the meaning of America—from a nation of *white* people to a nation of *all* the people. That was no small achievement!

The meaning of Martin King is not defined primarily by the civil rights laws that he pressured the government to enact. King's radicalism was derived from the moral power he embodied in his life and message—transcending race, religion, culture, and nationality. He was America's moral conscience. When Martin King spoke, America and the world listened, even though they did not always obey his call to end racism, poverty, and war.

King's moral power has inspired people struggling for justice around the world. "When the Berlin Wall came down, they were singing 'We Shall Overcome,'" Andrew Young correctly commented. "When the Polish shipyards workers went on strike, they were singing 'We shall Overcome.' When the students went to Tiananmen Square, they wrote 'We Shall Overcome' on their T-shirts. It is clear that the legacy . . . [of] Martin Luther King . . . was universal."

Because King inspired people to fight for justice, he also frightened government leaders. J. Edgar Hoover, the FBI director, called him "the most dangerous Negro in America." Most government officials, including President Johnson, agreed and thereby had made King the most reviled person in America at the time of his assassination. But despite the moral blindness of yesterday's politicians, few people today could deny that Martin Luther King, Jr., black preacher of nonviolence and love, was America's most effective radical and most courageous prophet.

Suggested Readings

Taylor Branch, *Parting the Waters: America in the King Years, 1954–1963*. New York: Simon and Schuster, 1988.

James H. Cone, *Martin & Malcolm & America: A Dream or a Nightmare*. Maryknoll, N.Y.: Orbis Books, 1991.

David G. Garrow, *Bearing the Cross: Martin Luther King, Jr., and the Southern Christian Leadership Conference*. New York: William Morrow, 1986.

44

MICHAEL HARRINGTON

Robert A. Gorman

Edward Michael Harrington was born in St. Louis on February 24, 1928. He grew up in a warm, loving family and a pleasant middle-class Irish-Catholic neighborhood. His father was a patent attorney who had fought in France during World War I, and his mother was a teacher. After attending parochial school in St. Louis, Harrington received the B.A. in 1947 from Holy Cross College, dropped out of Yale Law School a year later, and transferred to the University of Chicago to study English literature, where he earned a Master's Degree.

In college, Harrington challenged his family's New Dealism by flirting briefly with Taft Republicanism. After leaving Yale, however, he became a poet and a self-styled radical for whom capitalism was not so much cruel and exploitative as crass and vulgar. Then one rainy day in 1949, Harrington entered a dilapidated house near the Mississippi River

> which stank of stopped-up toilets, dead rats, and human misery. It was a terrible shock to my privileged, middle-class nostrils. I had come there as a temporary and opportunistic social worker trying to save up enough money to go to New York and be a poet and a Bohemian. An hour or so later, riding the Grand Avenue streetcar,

> it dawned on me that I should spend the rest of my life putting an
> end to that house and all that it symbolized.

Lanky and freckled, with a boyish grin and broomstraw hair, Harrington arrived in Greenwich Village in late 1949, where he wrote poetry in the day and passed the beer-filled evenings with bohemian literati at the White Horse Tavern, the San Remo Cafe, and the Cedar Tavern. The glamour of Village life in the early 1950s was irresistible, but Harrington was haunted by that St. Louis slum. He spent two years at Dorothy Day's Catholic Worker on Chrystie Street, enlisted in the army and was honorably discharged as a Conscientious Objector and finally decided, in 1952, to enter the political arena.

An aspiring poet and a profoundly spiritual Catholic atheist, Harrington wasn't cut out to be a communist minion. He also admired pragmatists like Walter Reuther and Norman Thomas, and was intrigued by the Trotskyist Max Shachtman. He decided to join the Socialist party's youth branch as well as the little-known Youth Socialist League, an organization of about 200 students and young workers that was fraternally linked with Shachtman's Independent Socialist League until 1954, when they were formally merged. Here, Harrington debated doctrinal questions with Bayard Rustin, Dave Dellinger, Norman Thomas, Paul Goodman, Dwight Macdonald, and A.J. Muste. They pulled the young Harrington into socialism's turbulent orbit.

In September 1958, YSL-ISL members, led by Harrington and Shachtman, entered the Socialist party as a bloc. The SP was America's largest noncommunist socialist party. Its political potential, and the chance to work with Thomas and Shachtman, inspired democratic socialism's heir apparent. Harrington became the editor of the SP's official journal, *New America,* and in 1968 was selected as national cochair.

Harrington's formidable personal skills—he was intelligent, articulate, hardworking, and a sensational orator—fueled a meteoric rise to power among socialists. But he hadn't discovered a singular voice, or even considered whether social democracy could ever be as popular in America as it was in Europe. In 1962, Harrington's life and legacy were dramatically transformed by two unexpected events.

First, *The Other America—Poverty in the United States* became Harrington's one and only gigantic commercial success. Harrington was always embarrassed by its remarkable performance because the text, which evoked poverty's "look, its smell, its often twisted spirit, with just a few rudimentary references to the underlying trends," never mentions the word socialism. *The Other America* was nonetheless a book for the times. Liberal intellectuals, sickened by the 1950s' bland euphoria, used it to catalyze public aid programs. Tired of eating goldfish and piling into Volkswagens, but still unable to locate Vietnam on a map, students stumbled on a cause worth fighting for. The book is said to have inspired President Kennedy to initiate reforms that became the War on Poverty. Harrington was then thirty-four years old and without much money. The royalties and subsequent lecture fees exceeded his wildest dreams.

Second, Harrington was invited to attend a meeting of young radicals in Port Huron, Michigan, to draft a platform for the fledgling movement known as the New Left. The activist Tom Hayden, a leader of the Students for a Democratic Society, had written in 1961 that his generation trusted only three people over thirty: C. Wright Mills, Norman Thomas, and Michael Harrington. Harrington thus assumed that the Port Huron Conference, under Hayden's leadership, would meld the New Left and the Socialist party into a potent force. Hayden looked forward to receiving from the left's old guard financial and political support for his movement. Instead, the meeting quickly deteriorated into bitter name-calling and suspicion.

Hayden and the New Left wanted to forget the past and junk socialism's tired formulas. They believed that radicalism had to reflect the real experiences of people in advanced industrial societies like America. Labor leaders and New Deal liberals—Hayden called them "an undifferentiated mass of old fogies and sell-outs"—had grown rich and sluggish. Activist students had replaced workers as the vanguard of progressive change. They had learned, moreover, that the "evils" of communism were caused by capitalist mistrust and provocation. Hayden thought the debates among the old left groups had become irrelevant. New Leftists also saw the escalating conflict in Vietnam as an internal struggle, the nature of which was unaffected by communist support for the freedom-fighting rebels. They demanded that America immediately withdraw its troops.

Harrington was steadfastly prounion and anticommunist, against endorsing the call for unconditional withdrawal from Vietnam, and outraged that youngsters were altering the course of American socialism without his approval. Neither side would give, although Harrington did his best to intimidate and obstruct his adversaries. He finally backed off, and a negotiated settlement was approved by both sides, after Norman Thomas and others who were embarrassed by the gutter fighting objected. Socialism's civil war had ended, but the wounds never entirely healed.

Harrington earned the dubious honor of emerging from Port Huron as the biggest loser. Psychologically, he was devastated. He had spent over a decade cultivating an image and a constituency, and in one foolish evening managed to destroy both. In the eyes of rebellious young people he irrationally had joined the enemy. His self-image was shattered. Professionally, Harrington was now a man without turf. Stereotyped as a strident anticommunist, anticapitalist, and anti–New Leftist, Harrington found himself simply ignored altogether by scholars. To date, no significant books on Harrington have been published, and surprisingly few serious articles. And politically, Harrington was left hanging all alone. Communists would have nothing to do with him. New Leftists never fully accepted his apology, and questioned his slow about-face on Vietnam and his tolerance of Cold War hawks. Harrington's mushy stance on Vietnam transformed liberal discomfort into outright hostility. The electoral center and right were alternately enchanted by Harrington's independence, and dismayed by his radicalism. For as long as he remained marginalized, the articulate, celebrated leftist was occasionally hired as a media commentator. It harmlessly reaffirmed corporate America's democratic credentials, and probably boosted ratings as well.

After Port Huron, Harrington was a lonely figure on the political landscape, alienated from every major progressive constituency. A new generation of radicals had arisen, and Harrington had silently plunged into middle age. The whiz kid of American socialism was no longer a kid. His aura of invincibility had also evaporated in the furnace of taunts and insults that heated the chilly Michigan evenings. Almost overnight, Harrington became a rejected, isolated, aging maverick socialist. With unanticipated riches tossed in, the wonder is not that, in 1965, he crashed and spent four years in psychoanalysis, but that he was able to recapture most of his old reputation as America's leading socialist.

In 1962, Harrington thought like a traditional Old Left socialist. Every social problem was reduced to class conflict between workers and capitalists. New Leftists realized that economism couldn't explain life in the 1960s, or mobilize a vanguard. With their incomes rising, American workers simply didn't think in terms of class, even though capitalism exploited them. Bereft of critical ideas, however, New Leftists ended up discarding the socialist baby with the Old Left bathwater. Harrington's painful apology to Hayden enabled him to rethink socialist politics and theory. His new socialism didn't reduce life to economics. Nor, like New Leftism, did it bet the barn that quirky emotions could be turned into social activism.

Part of the problem, Harrington decided, was that American socialists were lousy politicians. Why didn't they invite the Democratic party's left wing, which stood to gain more than lose in socialism, into a progressive alliance with blue-collar workers? During the 1960s, he tried to pry open the hawkish, union-dominated Socialist party to include liberal and radical members of the middle class—the so-called new politics constituency. Clearly isolated in his own party, upset by vicious internecine haggling, and disillusioned with Vietnam, Harrington resigned as cochair in October 1972, two months before leading 250 of his followers out of the SP to found, in February 1973, the Democratic Socialist Organizing Committee. Shachtman's winning faction renamed the party Social Democrats, USA, and turned it into perhaps the most right-wing socialist party in the world.

Harrington used DSOC to lobby Democratic party officials, defeat unfriendly Democrats, and extend New Deal reforms. He wanted to attract liberals, minorities, and feminists, whose economic interests were shared by blue-collar workers, and nudge their Democratic party to the left. DSOC recruited more than 4,000 members by 1980, but the predominantly economic nature of its program alienated many young, nontraditional leftists concerned with cultural empowerment. Harrington set his sights on those New Leftists who, in 1972, had formed the New American Movement to succeed SDS. In 1983, DSOC and NAM were merged into the Democratic Socialists of America, which became the largest democratic socialist organization since the Socialist party of 1936. The DSA agenda combined DSOC's realignment tactic with NAM's more urgent struggle for cultural change. Harrington became DSA's first chair, and retained this post—which he later shared with Barbara Ehrenreich— for the remainder of his life.

The indefatigable Harrington worked hard for civil rights, promoted unions, advised federal antipoverty officials, wrote for the *New York Herald Tribune,* was appointed to the faculty of Queens College in New York City, and became a hot item on the lecture circuit. Harrington was also active in the Socialist International, where in 1983 he penned the first draft of a new declaration of socialist principles, which was adopted some years later.

Harrington, in short, dragged socialists from their faded texts into everyday life. But he always kept one foot in politics and one in theory. He was a prodigious writer, whose output—seventeen books and hundreds of articles—ferried socialist theory from the *Manifesto* onto mainstreet.

When we eat delicious fresh-baked bread, we taste the final product, not flour, water, yeast, and olive oil, even though each ingredient is special. Life, Harrington wrote, also was a rich blending of ingredients. Economics was important, even fundamental, because it governed how we eat, drink, and find shelter. It was, however, part of an irreducible whole. Base and superstructure were organically linked.

Socialism, then, didn't merely redistribute wealth or nationalize factories. It was a lifestyle rather than an economic doctrine, and it let common people decide what the future would be like. Harrington thus urged American socialists to unionize workers and decentralize investment decisions. His long-term strategy was to have workers share, and then gradually take over, factory decision making. Economic resources could then create jobs for everyone instead of profits for the few. Harrington nonetheless had the courage of his democratic convictions. Enlightened private firms, he conceded, were more progressive than unresponsive, inefficient public ones. Harrington also suggested that socialists cobble progressive electoral majorities inside the Democratic party. Capital now ran the state, but popular forces could win valuable practical victories that would ripple through society, floating "normalcy" leftward.

Socialists have traditionally been preoccupied with economics or politics. This one-dimensional package didn't sell. People were often too busy with practical activities and cultural interests to notice or care. Meanwhile public life in America had disintegrated into isolated, self-absorbed groups. Americans needed a new sense of purpose in their everyday affairs that sanctioned a beloved heritage and also helped them live better. Harrington challenged socialists to embrace public culture, once contemptuously called the superstructure, and gently open democracy's floodgates. He designed a new socialist morality to reach into America's heartland and touch its republican pulse. Harrington's socialism resembled those "little republics" that Jefferson once said guaranteed liberty. It was part of the nation's ethical conscience: that nonelitist, democratic mentality Harrington called a "particularly American spirit." He wanted socialists to reclaim this republican sentiment, which sadly had been kidnapped and abused by Reaganites.

Socialists also needed to empower disenfranchised people. For one thing, collectively they represented more than half the nation's population. For another, groups based on gender, race, religion, sexual preference, or ethnicity often emotionally sustained their members to such an extent that other political organizations no longer could take their place. Harrington always knew that cultural emancipation is almost meaningless if people are poor. Socialist economics was thus in every oppressed group's interest. In his last books he warned socialists to stand up for progressive interests as well as establish a common denominator of economic need. Democratic socialism, he had learned, actually promoted cultural diversity.

New Leftists understood that initial groups may be founded on noneconomic identities like race or sex. However, they neglected universal processes that were fettering production. Old Leftists magnified the big picture without emotionally touching workers who didn't always understand or even care about economic classes. Harrington spoke to both traditions in a voice neither fully understood. He realized that socialism can succeed only as part of a large strategy that empowers all people economically and politically, defends progressive special interests, and challenges everyday capitalist values without trashing them. Harrington befriended, educated, trained, and inspired many young people who then established distinguished careers in politics, communications, academia, and labor organizing. Some of his ideas will surely seep into the crevices that have fissured the postcommunist left. Socialists then might begin taking part in public debate on the nation's future.

"America is different," politicians insist, "socialism can never work here." Perhaps they are mistaken. Once they also said that the Soviet empire would last forever. Harrington was a socialist who proudly spoke American. He plugged into the nation's democratic traditions, turning public culture into a vehicle for change, a place where socialism becomes real. He read *Das Kapital,* but he believed in America's Constitution, in Paine and Jefferson and Whitman, and in every citizen who ever struggled for democracy. Socialism fulfilled the American dream. By glorifying selfishness and inequality, capitalism was un-American.

When Harrington died of cancer on July 31, 1989, he left his wife, Stephanie, his sons, Alexander Gervis and Edward Michael 3d, his many friends and associates, and a legacy that keeps pace with America's swelling problems.

Suggested Readings

Michael Harrington, *Fragments of a Century.* New York: Saturday Review Press/E.P. Dutton, 1973.

———, *The Long-Distance Runner.* New York: Henry Holt, 1988.

———, *The Other America.* New York: Macmillian, 1962.

———, *Socialism Past and Future.* New York: Little, Brown, and Co., 1989.

Robert A. Gorman, *Speaking American—Michael Harrington and Public Culture.* Minneapolis: University of Minnesota Press, 1994.

45

ABBIE HOFFMAN
Marty Jezer

Abbie Hoffman's life brings into focus the turbulent and contradictory strains of 1960s radicalism: its attempt at fusing culture and politics and its ambivalence regarding such crucial tactical issues as violence vs. nonviolence, direct action vs. electoral politics, and reform vs. revolution. Hoffman's radicalism was rooted in the American experience. His activism encompassed, and often exacerbated, a dilemma that has always plagued the American left. How to reconcile the artistic, liberational, and transcendental agenda of a bohemian-influenced left (with its romantic call to youth of all ages) with the less spectacular, even dull, coalition-building priorities of the programmatic left (with its more mundane, workaday, reformist agenda)? Abbie Hoffman's experience as an organizer reminds us that both perspectives must be cultivated, but that there is no easy way to end or nullify the dilemma.

Abbie Hoffman was born Abbott Howard Hoffman in Worcester, Massachusetts, on November 30, 1936. His grandparents emigrated to the United States from Russia around the turn of the century. He was the eldest of three children born to Florence (née) Schanberg, a housewife, and John Hoffman, a conservative Republican and civic booster who founded the Worcester Medical Supply Company.

Growing up in Worcester's upwardly mobile Jewish community, Hoffman drew his identity from America's secular culture, cultivating an image of himself as a rebel, hanging out with street toughs, gambling, and hustling pool. He nourished this persona—as a street-smart outlaw-rebel—throughout his life, but it represented only one side of his personality, for he was also a bookish intellectual, a jock, and an enthusiastic salesman, first for his father's wholesale medical supply business, and later for social change and revolution.

At Brandeis University (1955–59) and as a graduate student at Berkeley (1959–60), Hoffman's sense of himself as a rebel took a more serious turn. He admired the beat writers, African-American music, and the hip comedian Lenny Bruce. But the sense of alienation that defined student bohemianism in the 1950s didn't interest him. He was drawn to the disaffected beats, he would later say, because they "talked American, saw poetry in the American experience, supermarkets and baseball."

His psychology professor at Brandeis, Abraham Maslow, was his intellectual mentor. A founder of humanist psychology, Maslow taught that rebelling against an oppressive situation was psychologically healthier than social conformity. His theories about self-actualization and human potential, and his belief that love, altruism, and creativity were basic human drives, provided Hoffman with an intellectual rationale for his own rebel identity. "Maslovian theory laid a solid foundation for launching the optimism of the sixties," Hoffman wrote in his autobiography. "Existential, altruistic, and up-beat, his teachings became my personal code."

Returning to Worcester without completing his Master's Degree, Hoffman worked as a staff psychologist at Worcester State Hospital and helped organize the first civil rights and peace demonstrations in the Worcester area. In 1962 he was an organizer in the independent U.S. Senate campaign of H. Stuart Hughes—one of the first major left-wing electoral efforts since the 1948 defeat of the Progressive party. Running as a critic of American foreign policy, Hughes got just 2.4% of the vote.

In 1964 Hoffman was a leader of a group of young white and black activists who took over the Worcester chapter of the NAACP and, against the policies of the national office, transformed the local into confrontational, direct-action organization. But his major civil rights involvement was with Friends of SNCC, the Northern support group of the Student Nonviolent Coordinating Committee. In 1965 he was hired by the Mississippi Poor People's Corporation to establish retail outlets in the Northeast for its cooperatively produced craft products. Throughout this period, Hoffman worked as a salesman for a pharmaceutical company, using the company car and company time to do civil rights work. Fired from his selling job in 1966, Hoffman joined the Senate campaign of Thomas

Boyleston Adams, who got 7.7% of the vote as an antiwar candidate in the 1966 Massachusetts Democratic primary.

In the autumn of 1966, Hoffman moved to New York to establish Liberty House, a retail outlet for the Poor People's Corporation. During this period, SNCC abandoned its integrationist goals and purged the organization of its white members. Hoffman responded by publicly criticizing SNCC's Black Power advocates for building their movement by guilt-tripping whites. Movements are built by positive thoughts, Hoffman wrote. "I believe that when one actualizes his [sic] inner potential, he is rewarded. He feels better, he enjoys life, he is, in every sense of the word, FREE."

The hippie counterculture was then emerging in the bohemian ghetto on the Lower East Side where Hoffman lived. Older than the hippies, and a veteran of the civil rights movement, Hoffman at first disparaged the young dropouts for their deficient work ethic and their lack of a political vision. But as he himself began to experiment with psychedelic drugs, Hoffman began to see in the emerging counterculture the seeds of a social revolution. Rather than continue to oppose the nationalist direction of the civil rights movement, Hoffman turned his energy to organizing the hippies on the Lower East Side and drawing them into the movement against the Vietnam War.

Although his heated rhetoric often blurred the distinction, Hoffman insisted that the hippie counterculture was just one component of what he envisioned as a broader antiwar movement. Just as he opposed the politics of black nationalism, he opposed the cultural nationalism of countercultural leaders who advocated that young people drop out of society, disengage from the existing political process, and build their own new and separate revolutionary society.

The antiwar movement was still a marginal enterprise in 1967. Hoffman came into it with a critique of its organizing tactics that, while new at the time, was shared by others in the bohemian community. Young people would best be attracted to radical politics by a positive and joyful vision of the future rather than by what Hoffman considered the movement's negative emphasis on moral outrage, self-sacrifice, and the politics of guilt. Refusing to enter the debate about the efficacy of nonviolent tactics, Hoffman argued that communicating with the public was all that counted and that the highly disciplined Gandhian nonviolence advocated by many pacifists in the antiwar movement grated against the spontaneous, enthusiastic, and individualistic attributes of the American social character.

Understanding that visual imagery, especially if televised, communicates ideas more effectively than the printed word, Hoffman sought to transform street demonstrations into political theater. (As media critic

Doug Ireland observed in the *Village Voice,* "Long before Roger Ailes, he [Hoffman] understood that whoever dominated the nightly news held the key to the country's soul.")

One of Hoffman's first theatrical events was to organize a contingent of hippies to join a prowar "Support Our Boys" parade in New York City. His idea was, first, to show that the peace movement was patriotic and that "supporting our boys" could mean keeping them out of the war. But also he wanted to create an image of hippies as political activists who, like civil rights activists, were willing to put their bodies on the line for what they believed. As Hoffman anticipated, photos of prowar marchers beating up the "Flower Brigade" dominated the evening news. In his best-known piece of political theater, Hoffman led a group of hippies to the visitors gallery of the New York Stock Exchange and threw dollars bills down to the trading floor. The sight of stockbrokers greedily crawling on the floor to pick up the money was the image of capitalist greed that Hoffman wanted to reveal.

In 1968, Hoffman and a group of activists on the Lower East Side, including Jerry Rubin, founded the Youth International Party, "Yippie" for short. The Yippies did not exist as a real organization. The idea behind it was to attract the media's attention in order to publicize plans for an antiwar demonstration at the 1968 Democratic National Convention in Chicago in August 1968. Hoffman wanted to a promote a "Festival of Life" to contrast peaceful countercultural values with the prowar views of President Lyndon Johnson's wing of the Democratic party. But he was not averse to provoking the authorities, believing, with Rubin, that young people would be radicalized under political repression.

In the months leading up to the Chicago convention, American society began to fracture. Excited by escalations of the Vietnam War, the assassinations of Martin Luther King and Robert Kennedy, urban riots, and the evidenced enthusiasm of young whites for the hippie lifestyle, Hoffman concluded that the country was entering into a revolutionary situation. The plan for Chicago, which had originated for Hoffman as a tactic for bringing youth into the antiwar movement, was now transformed into a strategy for revolutionizing society with hippie baby boomers (and black militants) serving as the vanguard.

Chicago's Mayor Richard J. Daley was determined to prevent antiwar demonstrations at the Chicago convention. By refusing to negotiate honestly with the Yippie leaders and cracking down violently on all peace demonstrators, Daley succeeded in frightening activists away from Chicago. Hoffman had spoken of a hundred thousand young people "dancing" in the streets of Chicago, but less than 10,000 actually showed up there, and many of these were police and military undercover agents. The

Chicago police could easily have contained the outnumbered demonstrators but, instead, began to attack them violently. Hoffman initially played a calming role in what federal government investigators would later call a "police riot," attempting to lead young demonstrators out of physical danger. But after being taken by police, beaten, and then released without charge, he reappeared in a manic, combative mood and tried, on the last day of the convention, to wrest control of a protest march away from movement marshals and lead it through police lines into the black ghetto where he apparently hoped to touch off a full-scale rebellion. Writing of this incident immediately after it happened, Hoffman boasted of his own revolutionary fervor and bitterly assailed what he considered the cowardice of the peace movement's marshals. In his autobiography, written ten years after the incident, Hoffman apparently had second thoughts and didn't mention the incident.

The violence of the Chicago police temporarily united the radical antiwar movement with the peace wing of the Democratic party. But the libertine conduct of the Yippie demonstrators offended the cultural sensibilities of many Americans, including opponents of the war. Bolstered by what was interpreted as a victory in the streets of Chicago, Hoffman (and others in the antiwar movement) rejected an alliance with the antiwar liberals and pursued a more revolutionary course, openly siding with the Vietnamese Communists and trying to polarize the nation along generational and cultural lines. It was during this period that Hoffman's politics took an uncharacteristically churlish and anti-American turn. He and his allies in the radical wing of the antiwar movement turned their backs on a liberal-left alliance exactly at the point when such a coalition was possible, and fed the fires of right-wing backlash.

After Chicago, Hoffman and other antiwar leaders were victims of ongoing police harassment. Subpoenaed by HUAC to testify about communist influence in the antiwar movement, Hoffman appeared wearing an American-flag shirt and disrupted the hearings by doing Yo Yo tricks and ridiculing committee proceedings. Hoffman (and Jerry Rubin, his comrade in these antics) so undermined the authority of HUAC that it was never taken seriously again.

In 1969 Hoffman and seven other leading radicals were indicted for conspiring to commit violence during the Chicago demonstrations. Certain that they could not get a fair trial in the courtroom of Federal Judge Julius Hoffman, the "Chicago Seven," under Abbie Hoffman's urging, sought to transform the trial into a showcase for hip culture and antiwar politics, often protesting the judge's rulings with ridicule and defiance. (In one incident, Hoffman and Rubin appeared in court in judicial robes. To show their disgust for Judge Hoffman's authority they ripped them off and began to stomp on them.) Hoffman and four other defendants were found guilty on all counts and sentenced to five years in prison. For his courtroom behavior, Hoffman was sentenced an additional eight months for twenty four counts of contempt of court. Both the conviction and contempt citations were overturned on appeal.

The conspiracy trial made Hoffman a popular speaker on college campuses. Onstage (as well as off) he was a funny, electric performance artist (even before there was such a thing as performance art). Like all good entertainers, he had the ability to make carefully thought-out *shticks* seem spontaneously out of control. But the delight he took in his media fame violated the egalitarianism of the radical movement and he was criticized for his egotism. Realizing that a revolution was not pending and the war was not ending, Hoffman rethought his position regarding coalition politics. In 1972, he again led demonstrations at the Democratic National Convention. This time, however, the Yippies supported the antiwar candidacy of Senator George McGovern and served as a counterweight to more radical elements who wanted to embarrass the Democrats and recreate the polarizing conditions of the Chicago convention.

Criticized and isolated by other radicals, Hoffman withdrew from activism. In the summer of 1973 he was arrested for selling cocaine to New York undercover police. Faced with a ten-year sentence and wanting to reestablish his radical credentials, Hoffman went underground. There he suffered several mental depressions and in 1980 was diagnosed as suffering from bipolar disorder, sometimes known as manic depression.

While underground and using the pseudonym Barry Freed, Hoffman settled in the Thousand Islands of New York. In 1978 he learned that the U.S. Army Corps of Engineers was planning to dredge the St. Lawrence River and open it up to winter navigation. Believing that the plan would upset the ecological balance of the region, Hoffman/Freed organized Save the River, a grass-roots organization that led to a successful fight to block the proposal. During his Yippie days Hoffman had used cultural issues to polarize society. Now he sought to find common ground, "breaking bread," as he put it, with the diverse members of the local community, including conservative workingpeople and wealthy Republicans. Hoffman's success brought kudos from opponents of the dredging plan. New York Senator Daniel Patrick Moynihan, speaking against the project during a visit to the Thousand Islands, commended Hoffman/ Freed for his organizing abilities and said, "Now I know where the sixties have gone. Everyone owes Barry Freed a debt of gratitude for his organizing ability."

Determined to take public credit for Freed's success and, in addition, publicize his autobiography, *Soon to be a Major Motion Picture*, Hoffman surrendered to authorities. After serving six months in jail, he resumed his career as a campus speaker and serving as a consultant helping local communities fight environmental battles.

His most successful organizing effort was in Bucks County, Pennsylvania, where he led a last-ditch effort to stop construction of the Point Pleasant Power Station on the Delaware River. Hoffman entered the fray two weeks before construction was to begin. Noting the area's proximity to the site where George Washington crossed the Delaware, Hoffman appropriated popular patriotic symbols and transformed an environmental struggle into a patriotic rally. Occupying the construction site (which he decked out in red, white, and blue banners and called "Valley Forge II"), Hoffman's effort to "capture the flag" generated enough local support to stop construction of the plant.

The excitement of this struggle touched off a manic episode that crested into a deep depression and, in May 1984, Hoffman attempted suicide. Recovering, he settled in Bucks County and continued to fight construction of the pumping station. (Despite a referendum victory and a defeat of propump elected officials, construction was started in 1987 as a result of a court order.) In the summer of 1988 Hoffman was in an auto accident that plunged him into another long-lasting mental depression, and on April 12, 1989, he committed suicide at his home in Solebury Township, Pennsylvania.

In his last years, Hoffman worked hard at teaching young people how to be effective political organizers. Though considered by many a castoff from the 1960s, Hoffman had learned from his earlier mistakes. When not debilitated by unpredictable mood swings, he was a source of sensible political wisdom. "Isms are was*isms,* " he often said. You keep your eye on the prize and do what works.

> There's no conflict between working inside and outside the system; keep a foot in both. . . . Activism during the 1960s encompassed electoral politics, lobbying, door-to-door canvassing, teach-ins, forums, as well as demonstrations, guerrilla theater, civil disobedience, and militant resistance. Demonstrations in the street create movement within the political system; movement in political institutions creates opportunities to organize in the street.

Ever positive in outlook, despite his own psychological troubles, Hoffman remained optimistic about people's capacity for change. Rebellion runs deep in the American psyche, Hoffman believed. A spirit of equality, tolerance, and justice was there to be tapped if only American radicals would believe in their own political heritage. Democracy is not an abstract ideal, it's something you *do*. "All you need is a little nerve and a willing-ness to be considered an embarrassment." Hoffman wrote. "Then you just keep pushing."

Suggested Readings

David Dellinger et al., *The Conspiracy Trial*, ed. Judy Clavir and John Spitzer. Indianapolis: Bobbs-Merrill, 1970.

David Farber, *Chicago '68*. Chicago: University of Chicago Press, 1988.

Abbie Hoffman, *The Best of Abbie Hoffman*. New York: Four Walls Eight Windows, 1990.

————, *Soon to be a Major Motion Picture*. New York: Putnam, 1980.

Marty Jezer, *Abbie Hoffman: American Rebel*. New Brunswick, N.J.: Rutgers University Press, 1992.

46

AUDRE LORDE

Lisa Duggan

This was how Audre Lorde lived: She took her
frailties and misfortunes, her strengths and passions,
and forged them into sometimes searing, sometimes
startling, always stirring verse. Her words pranced
with cadence, full of their own rythyms, all punctuated
with resolve and spirit. With words spun into light,
she could weep like Billie Holiday, chuckle like Dizzy
Gillespie or bark bad like John Coltrane.

—*Renée Graham*

Audre Lorde (1934–1992) identified herself on her calling card as Poet.
But her poetry was produced and read through the lens of her political
commitments, expressed in her essays and her activism, in her journals
and her letters, as well as in her poetry. Those commitments developed
early, from bitter experience transposed into anger and insight.

In 1947 Audre Lorde wrote her first angry letter denouncing an injustice.
She was thirteen years old, and had taken a summer trip to Washington,
D.C., with her parents and two older sisters. Her mother had packed two
roasted chickens and other treats for the train trip; she didn't tell her
daughters that they couldn't eat in the dining car because they were black.
While touring the city, her father pointed out the Lincoln Memorial as
the place where opera singer Marian Anderson had performed after the
Daughters of the American Revolution refused to allow her to sing in
their auditorium because of her race.

Late one afternoon during this trip to the seat of American democracy,
the Lorde family stopped in for refreshments at a Breyer's ice cream and
soda fountain. Sitting lined up at the counter they faced a waitress who
told them, embarrassed, "I kin give you to take out, but you can't eat
here. Sorry." Though no one else in her family protested, Audre composed

her outraged letter and addressed it to the president of the United States. Her father told her she could type it out on his office typewriter.

Audre Lorde made her second trip to Washington, D.C. in 1953, this time with the primary intention of picketing the White House to protest the scheduled execution of Julius and Ethel Rosenberg. Along with fellow members of the Committee to Free the Rosenbergs she marched, sang, and handed in petitions of mercy. One week after this trip President Eisenhower signed into law an executive decree ending racial discrimination in public accommodations in the capital city. One week later still, the Rosenbergs were electrocuted.

Lorde made more trips to Washington, D.C. to protest other injustices. In 1983 she made a controversial appearance at the March on Washington for Jobs, Peace, and Freedom. March organizers had originally barred any openly gay or lesbian speaker from addressing the crowd, but intensive lobbying by the National Coalition of Black Lesbians and Gays and a sit-in at the offices of D.C. delegate Walter Fauntroy (leading to four arrests) forced a reversal of this decision. By now an internationally known black lesbian feminist poet, essayist, and activist, Audre Lorde was chosen to speak on behalf of lesbians and gay men to the 100,000 or so marchers assembled. She told them:

> We marched in 1963 with Dr. Martin Luther King, and dared to dream that freedom would include us. And today we march again, lesbians and gay men and our children, standing in our own names together with all our struggling sisters and brothers here and around the world.

Audre Lorde's odysseys of protest and dreams of freedom began in New York City's Harlem neighborhood, where she was born to a Grenadian mother and a Barbadian father in 1934. According to her autobiographical "biomythography" *Zami: A New Spelling of My Name* (1982), her childhood there was hellish. Her parents, recent immigrants to the U.S. mainland, worked as a laborer and chambermaid in a New York hotel. Though struggling, they did well enough during the depression and war years to send their daughters to Catholic schools, first in Harlem then in Washington Heights. Audre, the youngest of three daughters, had a difficult time both at home and in those carefully chosen schools. She was legally blind until thick glasses clarified her world; she didn't speak in sentences until she was four years old. She was often humiliated, punished, or beaten for "bad" behavior by her proud, stern, exacting mother and by the nuns who had been instructed to spank her whenever necessary. She felt excluded by her sisters, and found her father distant and sometimes "scary."

By the time both the depression and the war ended, things had begun to improve somewhat for Audre. Her father enjoyed some success in real estate, and she entered Hunter High School where she found friends among the young bohemian students who called themselves "The Branded." She began to write poetry. But her battles with her mother only escalated, motivating her to leave home at the age of seventeen.

Her early years on her own were economically and emotionally precarious. She worked as a nurse's aid, a factory worker (and union member), and at clerical jobs. When she was unemployed she pawned her typewriter and sold her blood. She had a brief, disappointing affair with a young white man, became pregnant, and had an illegal abortion. But she also began to build both a political and social life for herself in the Village. She joined the Labor Youth League and the Harlem Writers Guild. She opened her apartment to a circle of young women who hung out in the "gay girls" bars and read *The Ladder,* published by the Daughters of Bilitis. She had her first love affairs with other women—some exhilerating, some tragic. She traveled to Mexico on her savings, where she read the NAACP's *The Crisis,* learned about the Supreme Court's decision in *Brown v. Board of Education,* and felt hopeful. She went to City College and Columbia University School of Library Science. She wrote poetry.

Lorde drew on many tensions, conflicts, and contradictions in her life, from this early period and later, to develop a powerful critique of the limited vision of various movements for political and social change. Her commitments to leftist organizations and projects in the 1950s and '60s, driven by her opposition to economic inequality and racial injustice, were tarnished by fears of denunciation for homosexuality. In *Zami* she explains:

> I could imagine these comrades, Black and white, among whom color and racial differences could be openly examined and talked about, nonetheless one day asking me accusingly, "Are you or have you ever been a member of a homosexual relationship?" For them, being gay was "bourgeois and reactionary," a reason for suspicion and shunning. Besides, it made you "more susceptible to the FBI."

These fears were not imaginary. In 1955 her roommate moved out after being denounced by a "higher-up in progressive circles" for associating with Lorde.

Her social life among the Village "gay girls" was no refuge from such difficulties. Though a small number of black women in her circles were

accepted in many ways and Lorde's own interracial relationships flourished, there was often unacknowledged racial tension and hostility, or
willful ignorance about the differing situations of black and white women.
Bar bouncers repeatedly carded Lorde; friends and acquaintances made
offensive jokes about her "tan."

During the 1960s and '70s, Lorde's active participation in the civil
rights and black liberation movements, and in feminist and gay and lesbian
projects for social change, led her to expand her critical view of the limits
of organizing around any single axis of oppression. She aggressively
critiqued the sexism of various black liberation spokesman and organizations, and the unacknowledged racism among even the most radical of
white feminists. In a 1979 letter to Mary Daly (widely circulated and
later published) criticizing her book *Gyn/Ecology*, Lorde wrote:

> To imply . . . that all women suffer the same oppression simply
> because we are women, is to lose sight of the many varied tools of
> patriarchy. It is to ignore how those tools are used by women without
> awareness against each other. . . .
> The oppression of women knows no ethnic or racial boundaries,
> true, but that does not mean it is identical within those boundaries.

It was as a poet and essayist that Lorde was best known, however.
She published seventeen books of poetry, essays, and autobiography
before her death in 1992. This literary output was in no way disconnected
from her activist and personal life; Lorde repeatedly emphasized the
importance of making meaningful connections among the political and
material world, her emotional and social passions, and her cultural productions. Two of her most widely quoted essays developed these connections
explicitly. In "Poetry Is Not a Luxury" she wrote that "poetry is not only
dream and vision; it is the skeleton architecture of our lives. It lays the
foundations for a future of change, a bridge across our fears of what has
never been before." In "The Uses of the Erotic" she argued:

> When we begin to live from within outward, in touch with the power
> of the erotic within ourselves and allowing that power to inform and
> illuminate our actions upon the world around us, then we begin to be
> responsible to ourselves in the deepest sense. For as we recognize
> our deepest feelings, we begin to give up, of necessity, being satisfied
> with suffering and self-negation, and with the numbness which so
> often seems like their only alternative in our society. Acts against
> oppression become integral with self, motivated and empowered from
> within.

During the 1980s, Lorde's political and cultural influence grew. Along with many other women of color writing during this decade, she expanded her critique of the limits of various movements of social change into a powerful vision of the creative force of human differences. In 1981, she cofounded Kitchen Table, Women of Color Press in New York. Kitchen Table became a major force in circulating the writings of women of color in the United States, especially through their 1983 republication of the groundbreaking 1981 anthology *This Bridge Called My Back: Writings of Radical Women of Color,* edited by Cherrie Moraga and Gloria Anzaldua. Included in this anthology was Lorde's 1979 speech at the Second Sex Conference in New York, "The Master's Tools Will Never Dismantle the Master's House," in which she argued:

> Advocating the mere tolerance of difference between women is the grossest reformism. It is a total denial of the creative function of difference in our lives. For difference must be not merely tolerated, but seen as a fund of necessary polarities between which our creativity can spark like a dialectic. . . .
>
> As women, we have been taught to either ignore our differences or to view them as causes for separation and suspicion rather than as forces for change. Without community, there is no liberation, only the most vulnerable and temporary armistice between an individual and her oppression. But community does not mean a shedding of our differences, nor the pathetic pretense that these differences do not exist.

Lorde's analysis of the workings of difference in constructing political identities and communities was developed further during the 1980s and ultimately constituted her central contribution to feminist, race, and class theory during that decade. In her essay "Age, Race, Class, and Sex: Women Redefining Difference" she argued for the existence of a "mythical norm" that nearly everyone defines as "not me." She explained:

> In america, this norm is usually defined as white, thin, male, young, heterosexual, christian, and financially secure. It is with this mythical norm that the trappings of power reside within this society. Those of us who stand outside that power often identify one way in which we are different, and we assume that to be the primary cause of all oppression, forgetting other distortions around difference, some of which we ourselves may be practising.

This developing analysis was taken up politically and theoretically by writers and activists working to displace the kind of identity politics common in the United States—a politics which seemed able to address only one form of difference, one kind of injustice, at a time. One particular passage of Lorde's, from *Zami*, has been so widely quoted in such writing that it has become emblematic, a kind of signifier for the effort to forge political alliances and communities that can transcend the limits of identity politics:

> Each of us had our own needs and pursuits, and many different alliances. Self-preservation warned some of us that we could not afford to settle for one easy definition, one narrow individuation of self. At the Bag, at Hunter College, uptown in Harlem, at the library, there was a piece of the real me bound in each place, and growing.
>
> *It was a while before we came to realize that our place was the very house of difference rather than the security of any one particular difference* (emphasis added).

Audre Lorde was employed at Hunter College in New York City as a professor of English during much of the productive decade of the 1980s. During this time she also helped found the organizations Sisterhood in Support of Sisters in South Africa (SISA) and the National Coalition of Black Lesbians and Gays. In addition, she battled the breast cancer which had been diagnosed in 1978. This battle increasingly consumed both her personal-emotional and her intellectual-critical attention. In 1980 she published *The Cancer Journals* in order to examine the larger political context for her personal struggle with disease. In a 1988 essay, "A Burst of Light: Living with Cancer," Lorde wrote: "The struggle with cancer now informs all my days, but it is only another face of that continuing battle for self-determination and survival that Black women fight daily, often in triumph." At the end of the decade, Lorde moved to the island of St. Croix in the Virgin Islands with her partner Gloria Joseph. Her cancer metastasized and appeared in her liver; in November 1992 she died, survived by Ms. Joseph, two children (by her marriage in the 1960s to Edwin Rollins), and four sisters.

Though her work was most widely known, read, and praised by feminist and African-American political activists and writers, Lorde was also recognized by mainstream cultural institutions. In 1973 she was nominated for the National Book Award for her book of poetry *From a Land Where Other People Live*: in 1983 she received the American Book Award for her essays collected in *A Burst of Light*. In 1991 she received the Walt Whitman Citation of Merit for New York, making her the state's poet laureate, and was described by Governor Mario Cuomo as "a voice of eloquent courage and unflinching honesty."

Suggested Readings

Sagri Dhairyam,"'Artifacts for Survival': Remapping the Contours of Poetry with Audre Lorde." *Feminist Studies,* vol. 18, 1992.

Mari Evans, ed., *Black Women Writers (1950–1980): A Critical Evaluation.* Garden City, N.Y.: Anchor-Doubleday, 1984.

Audre Lorde, *A Burst of Light.* Ithaca, N.Y.: Firebrand Press, 1988.

———, *Zami: A New Spelling of My Name.* Watertown, Mass.: Persephone Press, 1982.

Cherrie Moraga and Gloria Anzaldua, eds., *This Bridge Called My Back: Writings by Radical Women of Color.* Latham, N.Y.: Kitchen Table Press, 1983.

Cheryl Wall, ed., *Changing Our Own Words: Essays on Criticism, Theory, and Writing by Black Women.* New Brunswick, N.J.: Rutgers University Press, 1989.

AFTERWORD

A generation of writing has revealed the manifold ways in which American life has been determined by inequalities and conflicts of class, race, ethnicity, and gender. The magnitude and significance of this work compels the reconsideration of American history and the revaluation of the role of the American radical tradition within it. Our chapters render no singular version of America's past, but the lives and campaigns presented here do speak to the rearticulation of our national experience.

The narrative of America emergent in these pages is the struggle for liberty, equality, and democracy. It is a narrative insisting that we recognize and appreciate the crucial role of the radical tradition as the prophetic memory of American experience—the tragic, the ironic, the progressive—and of the persistent and original possibilities to be found there. As these biographical portraits begin to account, in every generation men and women of diverse upbringings and identifications have stood to challenge oppression and exploitation and to reassert the fundamental proposition that "We, the People," shall rule. However varied their respective concerns and aspirations, America's radical activists, writers, and artists have conducted a long and continuing struggle to expand both the "we" in "We, the People," and the democratic process through which "the people" can genuinely govern.

Yet this project has been motivated by more than historiographical interests and imperatives. Responding to larger events and developments, it is intended as a contribution to the renewal of American historical memory, consciousness, and imagination. We hope that reflection on the experience and agency of America's radical tradition of revolutionaries, rebels, and reformers will strengthen awareness that the making of an ever more free, equal, and democratic polity and society is possible.

For too long we have been subject to political and cultural campaigns seeking to reverse the changes wrought in the 1960s by movements for the civil rights of racial and ethnic minorities, the social rights of the poor, the equal rights of women, the civil rights of gays and lesbians, and the cessation of imperial wars, along with those instigated by the less celebrated but no less significant insurgency of workingpeople demanding changes in industrial organization and practices. All of these movements are recognizable as reassertions of the finest traditions of American politics and history. And yet, in the course of the 1970s the powers that be mobilized in opposition to the reforms and advances accomplished and, also, to preempt the threat of a possibly broader popular movement promising even more radical-democratic changes. With significant encouragement and material support from the corporate elite, a "New Right" coalition of conservatives, neoconservatives, and right-wing single-interest groups formed whose ascendance to political power was realized in the presidential elections of the 1980s.

A prominent feature of the New Right's attacks and of their efforts to mobilize support has been the use and abuse of history. This has entailed advancing renditions of the past, and attempting to impose conceptions of historical study and thought at all levels of schooling, which look not toward making critical contributions to the further development of liberty, equality, and democracy but, rather, to serving the interests of the powerful and supporting, at best, the status quo.

Subordinating the past and making historical education a servant to power are, of course, perennial goals of governing classes and elites. And in the face of both political crisis and critical historiography they become even more urgent activities. Most important is the suppression or marginalization of historical movements and visions which suggest that ordinary men and women can change the world and have done so in the past. Far more effective to exercise power and authority with a narrative of history representing the contemporary order of things as the way they must be and ought to be or, at least, the best they can be, than with one which compels reflection, hope, and, possibly, even action by recalling the justice and progress achieved by individual and collective human agency.

We saw such ambitions in the late 1950s when Americans were assured by politicians and intellectuals that the fundamental divisions and conflicts of industrial-capitalist society had been resolved or were resolvable through appropriate management and administration. In fact, it was claimed that the progress of American political life had led to the "end of ideology." Although the protests and struggles of the sixties showed otherwise, we recently have been hearing such proclamations again.

The New Right has endeavored to promote a narrative of American and world history which audaciously, but unoriginally, declares that we are witness to the final act of universal historical development, that the United States as "heir to Western Civilization" has attained the highest possible forms of liberty, equality, and democracy and, thus, we have arrived at the "end of history"! In this scenario, the best we can hope for is that which we have already achieved; the most we can aspire to is the extension of that which we have already accomplished. The story they tell, and would teach in our schools, not only neglects both the paradoxical formation and the underside of Western and American experience, it eschews our rich traditions of dissent and struggle from below.

Given the nation's foundations in revolution and the recurring role of radicalism in its development, the radical tradition cannot be completely suppressed and denied. Nevertheless, the New Right's "histories" portray it in the most conservative and least challenging of manners. They relegate to the past not only the lives of America's radicals but, also, their critical arguments and visions.

A conservative governing consensus has not been established, but there can be no ignoring the consequences of conservative government. Its policies have produced confusion, disarray, and hardship. We have suffered a long decade of greed in which the rich were made richer and workingpeople and the poor poorer. Along with growing inequalities of class, antagonisms of race and gender were exacerbated and for most Americans life became less secure than before as both urban and rural communities were allowed to deteriorate and political and cultural freedoms were undermined by governmental and extragovernmental initiatives.

In one significant respect conservatism may have triumphed. The struggles against racism, sexism, and corporate power which had once been perceived as so threatening persist. But, besieged by the forces of the New Right, these movements are enervated and fragmented. New movements have emerged—for reproductive rights, AIDS awareness and treatment, the protection of the environment, the defense of the family farm, and the treaty rights of American Indian communities—but there is no solidarity and no shared vision. At the same time, the political center of American politics appears to have shifted even further in a conservative direction and critical voices have been moderated. Indeed, across the political spectrum commentators and critics complain of the decline of public debate and discourse and the withered state of American politics and civil society. Expressing a widespread concern and anxiety, Philip Mattera has observed: "These days there is not much collective dreaming in America." Imperative is the revitalization of American radicalism.

We are not so naive or romantic as to believe that the historical redemption of the American radical tradition alone will necessarily inspire the reinvigoration of the prophetic memory of American democracy. For a start, the record we have begun to recount is a mixed one and it needs to be examined carefully. Nevertheless, contrary to the desires of those who are so eager to proclaim the present order eternal, we remain hopeful. Within the continuing contradictions of American life we recognize real possibilities and, again, however evident the tragedies and the ironies, the legacy of American radicalism clearly testifies that campaigns for justice can succeed and struggles for liberty, equality, and democracy can prevail: independence was won, workingmen were enfranchised, slavery was abolished, women gained the right to vote, unions were organized, African Americans and other minorities were guaranteed their civil and voting rights, and corporations were subjected to public regulation. Harvey Goldberg's words in *American Radicals* more than thirty-five years ago, on the eve of the tumultuous sixties, remain apropos:

> For very compelling reasons, the study of American radicals should be essential homework for this generation: because their record can give heart and stomach to Americans who are watching democracy weaken under the weight of conformism; and because their insights and errors, their accomplishments and failures can cast light, even many years later, on the problems of the present.

ADDITIONAL SUGGESTED READINGS

American Social History Project, *Who Built America? Working People and the Nation's Economy, Politics, Culture, and Society*. 2 vols. New York: Pantheon, 1989 and 1992.

Mari Jo Buhle, Paul Buhle, and Dan Georgakas, eds., *Encyclopedia of the American Left*. New York: Garland Publishing, 1990.

Paul Buhle and Alan Dawley, eds., *Working for Democracy: American Workers from the Revolution to the Present*. Urbana: University of Illinois Press, 1985.

Paul Buhle, *Marxism in the United States*. Rev ed. London: Verso, 1991.

Margaret Cruikshank, *The Gay and Lesbian Liberation Movement*. New York: Routledge, 1992.

Martin Duberman, Martha Vicinus, and George Chauncey, Jr., eds., *Hidden from History: Reclaiming the Gay and Lesbian Past*. New York: New American Library, 1989.

Sara M. Evans, *Born for Liberty: A History of Women in America*. New York: Free Press, 1989.

Eric Foner, ed., *The New American History*. Philadelphia: Temple University Press, 1990.

Philip S. Foner, ed., *We, the Other People: Alternative Declarations of Independence by Labor Groups, Farmers, Woman's Rights Advocates, Socialists, and Blacks*. Urbana: University of Illinois Press, 1976.

Harvey Goldberg, ed., *American Radicals: Some Problems and Personalities*. New York: Monthly Review Press, 1957.

Russell L. Hanson, *The Democratic Imagination in America: Conversations with Our Past*. Princeton, N.J.: Princeton University Press, 1985.

Vincent Harding, *There Is a River: The Black Struggle for Freedom in America*. New York: Random House, 1981.

Leo Huberman, *We, the People: The Drama of America*. Illustrated by Thomas Hart Benton. Originally published 1932. New York: Monthly Review Press, 1960.

Harvey J. Kaye, *The Powers of the Past: Reflections on the Crisis and the Promise of History*. Minneapolis: University of Minnesota Press, 1991.

Staughton Lynd, *Intellectual Origins of American Radicalism*. Originally published 1968. Cambridge: Harvard University Press, 1982.

Charles A. Madison, *Critics and Crusaders: A Century of American Protest*. New York: Henry Holt and Co., 1947.

J. Carroll Moody and Alice Kessler-Harris, eds., *Perspectives on American Labor History*. DeKalb: Northern Illinois University Press, 1990.

Alfred P. Young, ed., *Dissent: Explorations in the History of American Radicalism*. DeKalb: Northern Illinois University Press, 1968.

Howard Zinn, *A People's History of the United States*. New York: Harper and Row, 1980.

HISTORICAL GLOSSARY

American Civil Liberties Union (ACLU). Formed in 1920 by Clarence Darrow, Helen Keller, John Dewey, Norman Thomas, and other opponents of government repression of dissidents during World War I, the ACLU has defended the civil liberties (especially free speech) of unpopular—often radical—persons or groups in a nonpartisan fashion ever since.

American Federation of Labor (AFL). Formed in 1886 out of the Federation of Trades and Labor Unions, the AFL has represented mostly the skilled (and overwhelmingly white, male) section of the workforce. Socially conservative and politically Democratic for the most part, it has, however, included many radical unionists and a few left-leaning unions. Since its merger with the Congress of Industrial Organizations in 1955, it has continued to set the cautious, bureaucratic tone for the combined forces of labor.

Anarchism. The theory or advocacy of a society with no "State" (coercive government) to interfere with individual liberty, anarchism has influenced a variety of radical intellectuals and artists and certain sectors of immigrant workingpeople in America. Especially popular in the late nineteenth century and among voluntary cooperative communities or movements, anarchism has continued to touch radicals in educational experiments, and (by the 1960s) in a variety of causes, including peace, feminism, and environmentalism.

Communism. Originally a synonym for "socialism," a society with property held in common, communism became attached with communal or utopian movements in the nineteenth century and was discarded for several generations. In the twentieth century, the followers of V. I. Lenin adopted "communism" to mean the final stage of human equality, and "communist" to mean the leading parties which would guide humanity through social revolutions and transitional postrevolutioary society, or "socialism." By the end of the twentieth century, "communism" had come to signify those state-run regimes discredited by their oppressive actions.

Communist Manifesto. The famous document composed by a young Karl Marx and Friedrich Engels in response to the European workers' uprisings of 1848, the *Communist Manifesto* proclaimed that the rule of capitalism was about to be ended by an international working-class revolution. Taken as a popular polemic and declaration of intent, the *Communist Manifesto* was translated into hundreds of languages and circulated around the world, becoming one of the all-time favorite documents of radicalism.

Congress of American Women (CAW). Formed in 1946, the CAW was the U.S. branch of the Women's International Democratic Alliance, a worldwide movement of more than eighty million women in forty-one countries. In its short life, the CAW stressed a postwar program of women's equality, assistance to children, and peace for all. It expired from pressures of the U.S. government on its members.

Congress of Industrial Organizations (CIO). Formed in 1935 within the American Federation of Labor as the Committee for Industrial Organization, the CIO broke with its parent organization the following year to launch a mass drive to organize the unorganized, officially becoming the Congress of Industrial Organizations in 1938. Representing mostly unskilled workers in mass-production industries, its affiliated bodies were largely headed by radicals until the Cold War, and it encompassed nearly all minorities and women assembled into unions without, however, representing them significantly in its leadership.

Council on African Affairs (CAA). Founded as the International Committee on Africa in 1937 by leading radical African Americans, the CAA sought to promote the liberation of colonialized African nations through educating in the United States and lobbying the American government. Widely influential in the black community through the middle 1940s, the CAA was charged in 1953 with failing to register as a foreign agent, due to its connections with the African National Congress. It dissolved shortly thereafter.

Cultural radicalism. A term generally meant to signify the ideas and works of various kinds of the radical or avant-grade intelligentsia. Especially important in Greenwich Village around the time of World War One, it returned to central importance during the 1960s.

Engels, Friedrich. Collaborator with Karl Marx, Engels was the son of a British factory owner. He contributed many important works to the classical body of Marxist history and theory, including *The Condition of the Working Class in England* and *Anti-Düring*. Late in his life (he died in 1892), he tried unsuccessfully to provide guidance to socialists in the United States.

Espionage Act. Enacted by Congress in 1917, the Espionage Act provided the principal legal justification for arrest of many different kinds of radicals, including those agitating against U.S. involvement in world war and those "guilty" merely of advocating unionization or remaining loyal to the Socialist party or to the Industrial Workers of the World.

Fellowship of Reconciliation. Formed in 1918 by antiwar Christian Socialists, the Fellowship of Reconciliation offered an institutional framework during the 1920s and

'30s for leading pacifists, including Norman Thomas and A. J. Muste. In later decades, it actively promoted nonviolence in the civil rights movement, opposed the development of atomic and nuclear weapons, and protested the U.S. role in Vietnam.

Fourth International. Inspired by Russian revolutionary Leon Trotsky, the Fourth International formed in 1938 with the intent of succeeding the "Third International," or "Comintern" of world Communist parties, directed from Moscow. (Marx and trade unionists had founded the First International during the 1860s, and European socialists had organized a Second International during the 1890s.) Forming its strongest affiliated party in the United States, it remained an international network of small, fraternally allied organizations.

Free soil. "Free soil" is the belief in settled territory or states in which the institution of slavery is not permitted; it was advocated from the 1830s through the 1850s by "free soilers" who wanted more "free states" created in the West to offset the power of the "slave states" in the South.

Free thought. A concept of untrammeled discussion, mainly to allow antireligious or nonreligious thinkers (many of them political radicals) to challenge the power of religious institutions. Important mainly in Europe, free thought had a significant influence in many ethnic communities of the United States—German, Jewish, Italian, Slavic, and others— where a particular religious body exercised great influence.

Greenwich Village. New York's neighborhood roughly east of Union Square and south of Fourteenth Street, where bohemians and the intelligentsia have located their favorite living and public performance space, from the early years of the century to the present. The "Village" has been known especially for its gender radicalism and its artistic performance.

House Un-American Activities Committee (HUAC) or House Committee on Un-American Affairs. Formed in 1946 from the earlier Dies Committee (so-called for its leader, Congressman Martin Dies), "HUAC" conducted many public hearings ostensibly to uncover Communist subversion, but actually to persecute individual radicals and to weaken the progressive forces of unionism and civil rights. In 1969, already much weakened, HUAC changed its name to the House Committee on Internal Security and in 1975, it was abolished.

Knights of Labor. The most important social movement of U.S. labor of the nineteenth century, the Knights (founded in 1869) mobilized more than a half-million workers in the mid-1880s, including thousands of African Americans and women. It declined rapidly thereafter. But the Knights remained a model, in some ways, of labor as a democratic social force rather than a mere interest group.

Labor Youth League (LYL). Formed in 1949 as a Communist-linked youth organization and successor to the once powerful Young Communist League, the LYL had its main influence among intellectuals on a handful of U.S. campuses engaged in local reform, especially civil rights, and in reappraising the Soviet Union. The LYL dissolved in 1957 as most of its branches turned against the legacy of Joseph Stalin, but some of its members went on to great intellectual prominence in the New Left.

League for Industrial Democracy (LID). Formed in 1921 as successor to the socialist-leaning Intercollegiate Socialist Society, the LID was intended to encourage discussion on campuses and promote research on socialistic subjects. Through its affiliate, the Student League for Industrial Democracy (SLID), it intermittently played an important campus role from the 1930s to the 1950s. Nearly defunct, it was renamed in 1962 the Students for a Democratic Society, soon to become the most important student radical group of the century.

Liberation Theology. A theological persuasion and social movement popular during the 1970s and '80s, treating socialism (or cooperative society) as the proper outcome of Christian commitment. Deeply influential in Latin America and powerful to a lesser degree in Africa, Asia, and Europe, it provided inspiration to U.S. movements created to support Latin revolutions. Liberation Theology was beaten back everywhere, during the 1980s, by papal forces under the guidance of conservative Cardinal Joseph Ratzinger.

Marx, Karl. Founder of "scientific socialism," the notion that capitalism's decline is inevitable, and the rise of the proletariat or working class to leadership of society the most likely outcome. Marx's analysis has inspired socialists, communists, and even anarchists and social zionists over generations of American radicalism. His death in 1883 brought many public memorial meetings in the United States and great sorrow.

McCarthyism. The doctrines and practices of repression, so named for Wisconsin Republican senator Joseph McCarthy, who from the late 1940s to the early 1950s pursued a theme of Communist subversion through endless congressional hearings. He frequently charged that the armed forces or even the White House were under "red" guidance, thereby undercutting his own considerable influence.

Mexican Revolution. A successful popular uprising in 1910 that overthrew the existing government. The Mexican Revolution established (by the Constitution of 1917) the right of Mexicans to "nationalize" (or expropriate) landed estates and American-owned businesses and aroused the widespread sympathy of Mexican Americans. Continuing Mexican events prompted the United States to invade Mexican territory in 1914 and again in 1916, prompting many American radicals to protest.

Modernism. A style of art often applied to an era of social and intellectual history, modernism is contrasted with Victorianism, the late nineteenth-century culture with fixed social or aesthetic rules and a sexual double standard. By contrast, Modernism, at its apex in the 1910s through 1940s, is said to be artistically fluid or experimental, and related to the emancipation of women (and of minorities). It has been succeeded by "Postmodernism," a concept yet more uncertain in precise definitions.

Moscow Trials. The name given Joseph Stalin's purge of the "Old Bolsheviks" (leading members of the Bolshevik party that seized power in 1917) in 1935–39, marked by false confessions of guilt and by executions of leading revolutionaries. The Moscow Trials divided U.S. radicals around the question of loyalty to Soviet Communism.

National Association for the Advancement of Colored People (NAACP). Founded in 1909–10 (and succeeding the Niagara movement), the NAACP has at most times been a movement of African-American elites seeking ordered and peaceful if sweeping change in racial relations. For decades known best as the publisher of the monthly magazine *The Crisis* (edited by W.E.B. Du Bois) and occasionally quite radical, the NAACP became by the 1950s a cautious movement guiding a legal strategy to end segregation.

New Left. The name given the post-1960 radicals to set them off from the Marxist-oriented "Old Left" of Communists and Socialists. Comprising such organizations as the Students for a Democratic Society (SDS) and Student Nonviolent Coordinating Committee (SNCC), the New Left had a more anarchistic, decentralized method of operation, and a goal of diminished state authority rather than more state control over society and the economy (sought by the "Old Left").

Pan-Africanism. A general term meaning the community of spirit for all the peoples of the African diaspora, from Africa and Europe to Latin America, the Caribbean and the United States. Most Pan-African movements have been headquartered outside America, but many outstanding Pan-African leaders (such as W. E. B. Du Bois, Marcus Garvey, and C. L. R. James) have resided and worked in the United States.

Popular Front. In response to the rise of fascism in Europe, various Communist parties proposed a "front" with socialists and others against common enemies, a position formally adopted by the Comintern in 1935. The Popular Front in the United States garnered Communist support for Franklin Roosevelt and the New Deal, eclipsed in 1939, but was restored to prominence (under the changed title of "United Front") after the German invasion of the Soviet Union in 1941.

Populism, or People's Party. Names given the agrarian movement of the 1870s to the 1890s, which sought to create large-scale cooperative institutions and which, as a political force, aspired to overthrow the bank and railroad owners' undue power over society (including farmers). Collapsing after 1896, Populism was resurrected as a term in the 1970s and '80s, but mostly as a regional term of Midwestern or Western lawmakers, without significant radical intent.

Red Scare. A term associated with the intense publicity of "Communist danger" accompanying the suppression of radicals during and shortly after World War I. The "danger," as described by authorities and the commercial press, seemingly legitimated vigilante violence and state or federal persecution, and especially the Palmer Raids on radical organizations during 1919–20. "Red Scare" was later a synonym for the McCarthyism of the late 1940s and early 1950s, and specifically the role of press and government officials creating a false sense of crisis.

Rosenberg Execution. In 1953, accused "atom bomb" spies Julius and Ethel Rosenberg were repeatedly denied appeals and executed, amid international protests and the Rosenbergs' insistence of their innocence. Many observers felt that the executions were not only an injustice in themselves, but mainly a warning to Jews and to radicals of all kinds not to oppose the Cold War actions of the government. Their conviction and execution successfully intimidated many dissenters.

Sacco-Vanzetti Case. In 1920, a shoemaker and a fishpeddler, both immigrant Italian radicals, were arrested for a robbery and fatal shooting in South Braintree, Massachusetts. Although evidence was hazy at best, Massachusetts authorities chose the pair as "dangerous" anarchists and aliens whose trial would send a warning to radicals. They were executed in 1927 despite wide international protests and a remarkable defense campaign led by U.S. intellectuals. The Italian-American left, in particular, never recovered from this blow while many other immigrants were terrified by government actions.

Scottsboro Boys. Nine young black men arrested for purportedly raping a young white girl on a train in Alabama in 1931 and convicted without council or significant evidence, the Scottsboro Boys became a cause célèbre of black activists, white liberals, and radicals during the 1930s. Defended by the NAACP and ardently supported by Communists, the Scottsboro defendants won partial vindication (four were released in 1937 but only in 1950 were the last of them released) through the courts. But the active defense of them both won wide African-American sympathy for Communist causes, and prompted militant tactics for civil rights activity decades later.

Single-Tax. The economic proposal of reformer and prominent author Henry George in the early 1880s, the single tax on land was intended to end land speculation (then widespread in the United States) and open up economic development for ordinary people, bringing a more egalitarian society.

Socialism. The term most associated with the society destined to arrive after capitalism, before the Civil War socialism meant any kind of planned, cooperative order; afterward it suggested a society governed by a body elected mainly from the working classes. Only in the twentieth century, and with the examples of European social democracies and the Soviet Union's state dictatorship, did socialism signify mainly the state ownership of the means of production and distribution, and the prospect of a society of widespread coercion.

Society of Friends, or Quakers. The most peace-minded of major Christian sects, with roots in the religious "Reformation" of the 1600s, the Quakers sought to eliminate the institutional barriers between God and the human conscience. Leading Quakers founded Pennsylvania as a relatively tolerant society for its time with unusual prerogatives for women. Pennsylvania Quakers themselves became wealthy classes, manufacturers, and even slave traders. Still, through the nineteenth and twentieth centuries, the Friends contained a disproportionate share of radicals, especially those for women's rights and against slavery, racism, and war.

Southern Christian Leadership Conference (SCLC). Founded in the wake of the Montgomery, Alabama, Bus Boycott of 1955–56, the SCLC provided an organizational forum for Martin Luther King, Jr., and other younger leaders to supersede traditional black leadership and launch the massive civil rights direct action against segregation in the later 1950s and early 1960s.

Stalin, Joseph. Pen name for Iosif Vissarionovich Dzhugashvili, who succeeded V. I. Lenin in leadership of the Soviet Union and made himself a foremost Communist dictator. Leading figure in the Soviet triumph over fascism in the 1940s, a ruthless enemy of individuals and whole populations he regarded as potentially disloyal, he was discredited after his 1953 death by his successor, Nikita Khrushchev, at the Soviet Twentieth Congress in 1956.

Student Nonviolent Coordinating Committee (SNCC). Founded shortly after the lunch-counter sit-ins in Greensboro, North Carolina, SNCC grew rapidly into the foremost radical civil rights group of the 1960s. Representing a younger generation restless at the black ministerial leadership of the Southern Christian Leadership Conference (SCLC), SNCC adopted a tone of "black nationalism," demanding that whites leave the organization. SNCC leaders Stokely Carmichael and H. Rap Brown served as major public orators in the late 1960s. Merging with the Black Panther Party in 1969, SNCC disappeared due to severe government repression and internal divisions.

Temperance. A historic and sometimes highly influential movement from the 1830s to the 1910s, advocating the moderate consumption of intoxicating liquids, or their outright prohibition. "Temperance" grew as a "cause" in the later nineteenth century largely as a women's effort to control male behavior and was often closely associated with the woman suffrage movement. Sections of the labor and agrarian movements, however, embraced temperance as well. Its formal goal achieved in the Nineteenth Amendment banning the sale and distribution of spirits in 1919, the temperance movement all but disappeared.

Trotskyism. A political movement formed around the leadership and ideas of Leon Trotsky, dating to his expulsion from Russia in the late 1920s, Trotskyism rose to its maximum political and economic influence during the 1940s. "Trotskyists" sought to restore working class-influence in the Soviet Union and to set international socialism on a revolutionary course. Through various notable writers and critics, most of them former Trotskyists, the movement continued to exert an influence on American intellectual life into the 1960s and '70s. See also Fourth International.

United Front. Another name given the Popular Front "against fascism." See Popular Front.

Universal Negro Improvement Association (UNIA). Founded in 1914 in Kingston, Jamaica, by Marcus Garvey and Amy Ashwood for various modest reform aims, the UNIA took on a more radical character and significant influence in Harlem during 1917–18. Existing purportedly to repatriate African Americans (also Afro-Caribbeans) voluntarily to Africa, it also served as a vehicle for a variety of racial demands including equality or the establishment of a "black nation" within the United States. The UNIA faded rapidly as an organized force in the 1920s, but its legacy of black nationalism has remained alive in the African-American community.

Utopianism. The ancient theory of a perfect society, utopianism has been used mainly since the early nineteenth century to describe individual colonies established to show the rest of society how a nonviolent, cooperative order might successfully operate.

Workers Defense Union (WDU). Name given to the first unified organization (representing various unions and radical political groups) created to defend workingpeople and others falsely accused of crimes by various governmental bodies. The WDU, founded in 1915, defended mainly strikers and strike leaders. It was succeeded in the 1920s by the International Labor Defense (under Communist influence), the Workers Defense League (under Socialist influence), and by the less labor-oriented ACLU. See American Civil Liberties Union.

CONTRIBUTORS

Eric Alterman, senior fellow of the World Policy Institute at the New School for Social Research, is a columnist for *Mother Jones* and the author of *Sound and Fury: The Washington Punditocracy and the Collapse of American Politics* (1992).

Michael W. Apple is John Bascom Professor of Education at the University of Wisconsin-Madison. A former president of a teachers union, he is the author of many books, including *Education and Power* (1985), *Teachers and Texts* (1988), *The Politics of the Textbook* (1991), and *Official Knowledge: Democratic Education in a Conservative Age* (1993).

James R. Barrett teaches American labor and social history at the University of Illinois at Urbana-Champaign. He is the author of *Work and Community in the Jungle: Chicago's Packinghouse Workers, 1894–1922* (1987) and coauthor of *Steve Nelson, American Radical* (1981). He is currently completing work on a biography of William Z. Foster.

Rosalyn Baxandall is Professor of American Studies at the State University of New York at Old Westbury. She is the author of *Words on Fire, the Life and Writing of Elizabeth Gurley Flynn* (1987), the coeditor of *America's Working Women, an Anthology of Women's Work. 1620–1970* (1976), and coauthor of *The Rise and Fall of the Suburban Dream, 1945–2000* (1993).

Mari Jo Buhle teaches in History and American Civilization at Brown University. A MacArthur Prize Fellow, she is the author of *Women and American Socialism. 1870–*

1920 (1980) and *Women and the American Left: A Guide to Sources* (1983), and coeditor of *Encyclopedia of the American Left* (1990).

Paul Buhle is Director of the Oral History of the American Left at Tamiment Library, New York University. He is the author, editor, or coeditor of eighteen books, including *Marxism in the USA* (1987), *C. L. R. James: The Artist as Revolutionary* (1989), and *Encyclopedia of the American Left* (1990). With Edward Rice-Maximin, he is currently coauthoring a biography of William Appleman Williams.

James H. Cone is the Charles A. Briggs Distinguished Professor of Systematic Theology at Union Theological Seminary and author of many books, including *Black Theology and Black Power* (1969), *A Black Theology of Liberation* (1970), and *Martin & Malcolm & America* (1991).

Robert D'Attilio has written on Italian-American radicalism, the Sacco-Vanzetti Case, and the photographer Tina Modotti. He is also the cotranslator of Luigi Galleani's "The End of Anarchism?" He lives in the Boston area.

Gary Dorrien is Associate Professor of Religion, Dean of Stetson Chapel, and Chair of the Humanities at Kalamazoo College. He is author of *Reconstructing the Common Good* (1992) and *The Neoconservative Mind: Politics, Culture, and the War of Ideology* (1993), and his forthcoming book, *The Commonwealth of Freedom*, will explore developments in the theory and practice of economic democracy.

Gregory Evans Dowd teaches history at the University of Notre Dame and is the author of "The French King Wakes Up in Detroit: Pontiac's War in Rumor and History," in *Ethnohistory* (1990), and *A Spirited Resistance: The North American Indian Struggle for Unity, 1745–1815* (1992).

Ellen Carol DuBois is Professor of History at the University of California-Los Angeles. The author of several books on the nineteenth-century woman suffrage movement in the United States and the coeditor of *Unequal Sisters: A Multicultural Reader in U.S. Women's History* (1990), she is currently working on a biography of second-generation suffragist Harriot Stanton Blatch.

Lisa Duggan teaches in the Department of American Civilization at Brown University. Her essays on sexual politics and history have appeared in a variety of periodicals and anthologies. She is currently completing a book on the construction of lesbian subjectivity at the turn of the century.

Michael Eric Dyson teaches Afro-American Studies and American Civilization at Brown University and is the author of *Reflecting Black: African-American Cultural Criticism* (1993).

Eric Foner is the DeWitt Clinton Professor of History at Columbia University and President of the Organization of American Historians for 1993–94. His many books include *Free Soil, Free Labor, Free Men* (1979), *Tom Paine and Revolutionary America* (1976), *Nothing but Freedom: Emancipation and Its Legacy* (1983), and *Reconstruction, 1863–1877* (1988).

Elizabeth Francis is a Ph.D. candidate in American Civilization at Brown University. Her dissertation is titled "Feminism and Modernism: Gender and Cultural Politics in America, 1910–1940."

Dan Georgakas teaches labor studies at Queens College and the Van Arsdale School of Labor Studies-Empire State College. He is coeditor of *Solidarity Forever: An Oral History of the IWW* (1985), *Encyclopedia of the American Left* (1990), and *The Immigrant Left* (1994). He is an editor of *Cinéaste* film quarterly and of a book series in labor studies.

Paula Giddings, a Guggenheim and National Humanities Center Fellow in 1993, is currently writing a biography of Ida B. Wells.

Lori D. Ginzberg is Associate Professor of History and Women's Studies at Pennsylvania State University. She is the author of *Women and the Work of Benevolence: Morality, Politics, and Class in the Nineteenth-Century United States* (1990), the cowinner in 1991 of the National Historical Society Book Prize in American History. A city kid, she lives in Philadelphia and commutes to State College.

Juan Gomez-Quiñones is Professor of History at the University of California-Los Angeles. The author of numerous works on Mexican and Chicano political, cultural, and labor history, he was a founding editor of *Aztlan, International Journal of Chicano Studies Research*. Also, he remains active in civic affairs and community organizing efforts in the Los Angeles area.

Robert A. Gorman is the Liberal Arts Distinguished Professor of the Humanities at the University of Tennessee. He has written six books on modern socialism and related topics. His latest work is *Speaking American—Michael Harrington and Public Culture* (1994).

Elliott J. Gorn teaches History and American Studies at Miami University. Author of *The Manly Art* (1986), and with Warren Goldstein, *A Brief History of American Sports* (1993), and a coeditor of *The Encyclopedia of American Social History* (1993) and, with Harvey Kaye, the series *American Intellectuals and Public Culture*, he is currently working on a biography of Mother Jones.

Thomas C. Holt, Professor of American and African-American History at the University of Chicago, has a long-standing professional interest in issues of race, especially the experiences of peoples in the African diaspora. His most recent book is *The Problem of Freedom: Race, Labor, and Politics in Jamaica and Britain, 1832–1938* (1992), and he is currently working on a biography of W. E. B. Du Bois.

Joseph Jablonski is a longtime unionist who has written many articles on labor topics, radical culture, and the history of religious communism in America. He has contributed to the *Haymarket Scrapbook* and *Industrial Worker*, as well as well as *Cultural Correspondence, Arsenal,* and *Free Spirits*.

Norma Jenckes teaches dramatic literature and playwriting at the University of Cincinnati. She is the editor of the journal *American Drama* and she has published articles on Bernard Shaw, John Howard Lawson, Clifford Odets, and Eugene O'Neill.

Marty Jezer has been an activist in peace and justice movements since the early 1960s. He is the author of *Abbie Hoffman: American Rebel* (1992), *The Dark Ages: Life in the U.S., 1940–1960* (1982), and the biography *Rachel Carson* (1988). He lives in Vermont and is writer-researcher with the Working Group on Electoral Democracy.

Harvey J. Kaye is the Ben and Joyce Rosenberg Professor of Social Change and Development and Director of the Center for History and Social Change at the University of Wisconsin-Green Bay. The author of *The British Marxist Historians* (1985), *The Powers of the Past* (1991), and *The Education of Desire* (1992), he is currently working on a project titled "Democracy, the prophetic memory."

Craig A. Lockard is Professor of History and Social Change and Development at the University of Wisconsin-Green Bay. He has published numerous works on Southeast Asian, especially Malaysian, history and politics, comparative and world history, and folk music and social change. He is presently writing a comparative study of popular music and politics in the Third World.

Staughton Lynd is a historian and a lawyer. Among his writings is *Intellectual Origins of American Radicalism* (1968). He worked with A. J. Muste during the years 1957 to 1967 on the editorial board of *Liberation* magazine and in the movement against the Vietnam War. He presently lives in Youngstown, Ohio, where he is employed as a Legal Services attorney.

Robert K. Martin is Professor of English and Chair of the department at the Université de Montréal. He is the author of *The Homosexual Tradition in American Poetry* (1979), and *Hero, Captain, and Stranger: Male Friendship, Social Critique, and Literary Form in the Sea Novels of Herman Melville* (1986), as well as editor of *The Continuing Presence of Walt Whitman* (1992).

Waldo E. Martin, Jr., is Professor of History at the University of California-Berkeley. The author of *The Mind of Frederick Douglass* (1984) and numerous articles on African-American history and culture, he is presently working on a book entitled *"A Change Is Gonna Come:" Black Cultural Politics and the 1960s*.

Joanne Pope Melish is a doctoral candidate in American Studies at Brown University. Her dissertation explores the emancipation of New England slaves as a process of racial formation.

Gerald Meyer is Coordinator of Social Science at Hostos College, City University of New York and author of *Vito Marcantonio: American Radical* (1989).

Greg Mitchell is the author of *The Campaign of the Century: Upton Sinclair's Race for Governor of California and the Birth of Media Politics* (1992), winner of the 1993 Goldsmith Prize from Harvard University. Formerly the editor-in-chief of *Nuclear Times*, he is presently writing a book on the 1950 contest for the U.S. Senate in California between Richard Nixon and Helen Gahagan Douglas and editing a cultural history of the 1970s.

Scott Molloy is an assistant professor of Industrial Relations at the Labor Research Center, University of Rhode Island.

R. David Myers, Director of the Library at the State Historical Society of Wisconsin, has organized an annual series of conferences on American workers and the labor movement held in Madison, Wisconsin. He has published and lectured about Robert La Follette and the Wisconsin Idea and written a variety of essays on the American New Left.

Vera Norwood is an associate professor of American Studies at the University of New Mexico, where she teaches courses in environmental studies and gender studies. She is the author of *Made from this Earth: American Women and Nature* (1993). Writing and research always seem to interfere with her gardening, so her next project is on gardens in everyday life—perhaps beginning with her own.

Nell Irvin Painter, Edwards Professor of American History at Princeton University, is the author of three books in United States and Southern history. She is currently completing a biography of Sojourner Truth as a Fellow of the National Endowment for the Humanities.

Daphne Patai, Professor of Women's Studies and of Spanish and Portuguese at the University of Massachusetts at Amherst, is the author of *The Orwell Mystique: A Study in Male Ideology* (1984) and *Brazilian Women Speak: Contemporary Life Stories* (1988). Also, she has edited *Looking Backward, 1988–1888: Essays on Edward Bellamy* (1988), and coedited *Rediscovering Forgotten Radicals: British Women Writers, 1889–1939* (1993).

Barbara Ransby, a longtime activist in African-American and women's rights issues, teaches History at De Paul University. Currently completing her Ph.D. in African-American History at the University of Michigan, she is a member of the editorial board of the journal, *Race and Class,* and the author of a variety of articles in African-American and women studies.

Edward Rice-Maximin teaches history at various colleges and universities in the Philadelphia area. He is the author of *Accommodation and Resistance: The French Left, Indochina, and the Cold War, 1944–1954* (1986), and is currently working with Paul Buhle on the book *Learning from History: William Appleman Williams and the Challenge of Empire.*

Nancy L. Roberts is an associate professor in the School of Journalism and Mass Communication, University of Minnesota, and the author of *Dorothy Day and the "Catholic Worker"* (1984) and *American Peace Writers, Editors, and Periodicals: A Dictionary* (1991).

Franklin Rosemont, editor of *Arsenal/Surrealist Subversion* and coeditor of *The Haymarket Scrapbook,* has also edited and introduced works by surrealist André Breton, dancer Isadora Duncan, libertarian socialist Mary Marcy, IWW humorist T-Bone Slim, and utopian Edward Bellamy.

Robert A. Rosenstone, Professor of History at the California Institute of Technology, is author of *Crusade of the Left: The Lincoln Battalion in the Spanish Civil War* (1969) and *Mirror in the Shrine: American Encounters in Meiji Japan* (1988). His best-known work, *Romantic Revolutionary: A Biography of John Reed* (1975), has appeared in five European-language editions.

E. San Juan, Jr., teaches English and Comparative Literature at the University of Connecticut, Storrs. In 1993 he was Fellow at the Institute for the Humanities, University of Edinburgh. The author of *Carlos Bulosan and the Imagination of the Class Struggle* (1972), he has more recently published *Writing and National Liberation* (1991), *Racial Formations/Critical Transformations* (1992), and *Reading the West/Writing the East* (1992).

Dorothy Sterling has been writing about black and women's history for forty years. Her books include *Freedom Train: The Story of Harriet Tubman, Lucretia Mott: Gentle Warrior, Captain of the Planter: The Story of Robert Smalls, Black Foremothers, We are Your Sisters: Black Women of the Nineteenth Century*, and, most recently, *Ahead of Her Time: Abby Kelley and the Politics of Antislavery* (1991).

Kenneth Teitelbaum teaches in the School of Education and Human Development at the State University of New York at Binghamton. He has written extensively on education and the labor process and is the author of *Schooling for "Good Rebels" : Socialist Education for Children in the United States, 1990–1920* (1993).

Alice Wexler is the author of *Emma Goldman in America* (1984) and *Emma Goldman in Exile* (1989). Her essay "Emma Goldman and the Anxiety of Biography" appeared in *The Challenge of Feminist Biography* (1993). She is currently researching the social and cultural history of Huntington's disease.

Lamont H. Yeakey teaches American and African-American history at California State University in Los Angeles. He is presently completing work on three book projects, *We Shall Overcome: The Montgomery Bus Boycott, 1955–56, and the Origins of the Civil Rights Movement; Third World Images in Film: Power, Ideology, and Race Relations in the Media;* and *Paul Robeson: Twentieth-Century Renaissance Man.*